Getting the Most Out of
The Master Genealogist

Getting
the
Most
Out of

The Master
Genealogist

Compiled and Edited by
Lee H. Hoffman

GATEWAY PRESS, INC.
Baltimore, MD   2003

The information herein is believed by the authors to be accurate as of the time this book was printed. There may be differences between the program in use by the reader and that represented by this book. Any statement herein by the authors is not an indication that any change may or should be made to the program by Wholly Genes, Inc. Neither Wholly Genes, Inc. nor the authors shall be held responsible for mistakes found herein.

The Master Genealogist, Family Tree SuperTools, GenBridge, Visual Chartform and Chartform Delivery are trademarks of Wholly Genes, Inc.

Windows®, WindowsME®, and Windows XP® are all registered trademarks of Microsoft Corp.

Windows 98™, and Windows 2000™, are trademarks of Microsoft Corp.

Please direct all correspondence and inquiries to:
Lee H. Hoffman
410 Nevada Ave.
Mt. Sterling, KY 40353-1036

Library of Congress Control Number 2003103799
ISBN 0-9721567-0-4

Published for the editor by
Gateway Press, Inc.
1001 N. Calvert Street
Baltimore, MD 21202-3897

Printed in the United States of America

Contents

List of Illustrations

Chapter 1 – Introduction

By Lee H. Hoffman

The Master Genealogist™ (TMG) has long been known as an excellent computer program for genealogists. Touted as a program for the well-experienced researcher as well as the less-experienced researcher, TMG is very flexible and adaptable to the user's way of working.

However, some TMG users feel that the wealth of features and its power is such that they fear that they will take a long time learning to use it. Many requests have been made for a book like this to help users learn more of the features of TMG. With the release of version five of TMG, the editor and the authors agreed that now was the time to answer those requests. Thus we have written this book so that others can enjoy more of the capability and power of The Master Genealogist™. So we hope this book will help all users to take advantage of the many features of The Master Genealogist™ and through it achieve the reader's family history research goals.

The Intended Reader

This book is intended for those who have purchased version five of The Master Genealogist™. It might be called a supplement to the user documentation that comes with TMG v5.x. It is also intended that the reader have some basic knowledge of computers and of TMG. Having a basic knowledge of computers would include knowing how to start programs, finding files on the computers, and other rather basic information. Having a basic familiarity with TMG means knowing what the various main displays look like and generally how to move from one view or menu option to another without having to study a lot.

The Master Genealogist™ is, in most cases, a rather intuitive program and easy to learn. However, due to its great flexibility and power, it is also somewhat complex. But being complex does not mean it is complicated. On the contrary, most users can comfortably use TMG within a few hours of installing the program. Their use may not be at the expert level immediately, but they can achieve most of what they want fairly easily. Their continued use

of the program then will allow them to use more and more of the features of the program.

Thus it might be said that this book is intended for the intermediate user. But the word, intermediate, is used loosely. Some readers will be very familiar with computers, other programs, and have just installed The Master Genealogist™. These might be considered intermediate users. On the other hand, there will be some that have just started using computers and are just barely comfortable with starting and stopping programs and finding files on the computer. If these have installed TMG, and have moved from screen to screen, entered some data in various fields, and worked through the User Guide that is furnished with TMG, then they can also be said to be intermediate users.

Thus we wrote this book for almost any user of The Master Genealogist™ hoping that every TMG user will be able to profit from it. It should be noted that while this book is written to cover the entire program, some features may be changed or function in a slightly different way than we describe here. This is due to a later upgrade changing that feature or function. In most cases, the changes will be minor and easily understood. In rare cases where the change is not easily understood, we suggest that you look to the online Help in TMG for further information or ask for an explanation on one of the Internet forums.

Layout of the book

Each chapter in this book is almost completely separate from any other chapter. If the reader desires, they may read a chapter near the end without missing a great deal from not having yet read an earlier chapter. However, we have hopefully arranged the chapters in a progressive order so that if the reader starts at the beginning, the information in one chapter will be reinforced in the next or later chapters. Different authors well versed in The Master Genealogist™ have written chapters about subjects with which they felt most comfortable. All have had a lot of experience with the program and are recognized as experts on the program.

Conventions used

The book is written with the following conventions.

1. All screen labels, Help topics, and references to features specific to TMG are capitalized.

2. Keys are enclosed within angles, <>, e.g., <F4> or <Ctrl>+<F3>.

3. Buttons are enclosed with square brackets, [ ], e.g., [Close].

4. Menu items are **Bold**.

5. Project and data set names are all-capped. E.g., SAMPLE.

6. A greater than angle, >, is used between menu levels to show the connection of one menu option to the next, e.g., File > Data Set Manager.

7. *Italics* and **bold** are used for emphasis, and, of course, for references to book titles.

Suggestions for Learning to Use the Program

There are many ideas one can use to learn to use The Master Genealogist™. Perhaps the best learning plan is for the user to play with the program for a few hours after it is installed. This play might be just trying out things, looking at different menu options, or just seeing what is in the program.

Another method the user might employ and one that we recommend is a little more structured approach. That method is to use the SAMPLE project to become familiar with navigation within the program. Following this, you would *play* with the SAMPLE project by adding, changing people and data to it. The steps below can be used to give you a quick introduction to the main parts of the program and some initial ways to navigate from one part of the program to another. Use these steps to investigate the different parts of the program trying different things. The remaining chapters here will

address the details of each of these. But for now, just play with TMG and have some fun.

1. Getting Around
Note the **Main Menu** at the top of the screen. Clicking on each menu selection will give you a drop-down sub-menu. Some sub-menus will have a small right-arrow at the right of a menu entry indicating a further sub-menu. Almost everything that you can do in TMG may be chosen or selected from one of these menus. Depending on what you are doing, the **Main Menu** may alter slightly and there will be different menus or sub-menus. Also some menu selections will be grayed out, as they are not available in the current context.

In addition to the **Main Menu**, there are a number of Toolbars composed of icons allowing you to select a function directly instead of choosing a menu option or series of menu options. The display of Toolbars may be customized to your preferred display. Also you may design your own Toolbar.

The main part of the TMG screen will contain from one to seven windows. These windows may be turned on or off as desired using the Windows menu. Arrangements of the windows may be saved via the Manage Layouts option on the **View > Layouts** menu.

Usually you will use the Details window most to enter or display data. You will enter people usually from the Tree View or Family View. Adding, changing or deleting specific information for a person will usually be done from the Person View.

Most other windows in the Layout will be related to the person displayed in the Details window. The Project Explorer may or may not be connected to the other windows depending on your choice.

As indicated above, the Details window allows you to choose different displays or views by clicking on tabs. In some of the other windows, you may choose different actions by clicking on buttons. While looking at the Person View of the Details window, double-click on one or more of the tags (events) there to see the Tag

Entry Screen. Explore the Tag Entry screen to see where data may be entered in it.

2. Finding Persons

The Project Explorer window can be used to find people. It can be filtered to reduce the number of people displayed to just those desired.

The Picklist is another method of finding persons. You would access it by clicking on the binoculars icon on the Toolbar.

3. Entering New Persons

A new person is usually entered from the Add a Person window. Initial access to this window is usually done via the Add menu or by clicking on the stick figure icon in the Toolbar.

Most persons are added in relation to some previously entered person. Occasionally a new person added to the data set is unrelated to any other person presently in the data set. This is, of course, the case for a new data set in which no one has been entered.

While looking at the Person View of the Details window, click on the Add menu and choose to add a tag (Add > Add Tag). Select a tag from the Tag Type List to display its Tag Entry screen.

4. Citing Sources

When you add information about a person, you will want to support that data by telling where the information was and could be found. Known as "citing a source", this means that you will describe the source document from which you obtained the data. You may add a new Source by accessing the Master Source List from the Tools menu.

Many of your Sources will be books and similar documents that can be easily found. Other Sources will be harder to find and you will need to record where you found them. In those cases, you will enter a Repository in the Master Repository List accessed from the Tools menu or by clicking the Add new repository button [+] on the Attachments tab of the Source Definition screen.

When you attach a Source to entered data, you are creating a Source Citation. This means that you connect the information to the Source (and through it to a possible Repository). In addition you may record other information as Citation Details such as volume, part, section, page, frame, or other detail of the Source that tells exactly where the information was obtained.

5. Other features

Another feature in TMG is called Exhibits. Exhibits are various kinds of files such as image, video, text, or audio files. These may be attached to various records in the data set for a number of purposes. The Exhibit Log may be accessed via the Tools menu or by clicking on the camera icon from various places in the program – the Toolbar or in different windows.

Timelines are databases of events based on dates. These are usually historical in nature such as when the different censuses were taken in the U.S., or the reign of different British monarchs, or when counties or parishes were formed. Timelines can then be displayed showing what was happening during the life of a person.

Once you feel more comfortable moving around in TMG, start adding or changing data in the SAMPLE project. Because this added or changed information is only used to help you learn how TMG works, you can use any data that you wish. The SAMPLE project can be helpful in continued learning of the program, but most users will feel that they can learn more by using their own data.

Probably the best way to learn by using your own data is to create a practice project (*See Chapter 2, Project Management*) and then start entering yourself, adding your children, your parents, and your grandparents. Some may go on and add their great grandparents (*See Chapter 5, Customizing the Data*). The idea is that you would only enter the basic information at first on any one individual so that you will quickly have enough persons entered to cover from two to four generations. Then you may add more information to any individual trying out the different features and functions of the program.

This writer has a practice project that he has used for many years. It originally started with about a dozen people and has slowly grown to about three dozen or so persons - some real and some imaginary. While the practice project should be your data to allow familiarity, it doesn't have to be accurate data. For example, I wanted to try something in my main project. Since I was unsure how it might look on-screen or in reports, I wanted to try it different ways. So I used the practice project to try it. In doing so, I had to use a different person in my practice project because the actual person in my real project was from a different family. This didn't matter, as my intent was to learn how best a certain feature function worked. So I found where a similar family connection might be made and entered the data there. That entry is still in my practice project along with many other similarly slightly inaccurate entries. I don't worry about this, as nothing in the practice project will ever be published.

Following the creation and entry of the practice project data, try generating and printing some simple reports to see how they look with your own data (*See Chapter 9, Controlling Narrative Reports*). TMG has three Preview reports available from a Toolbar that you may use to quickly see how your data appears in print. The Preview reports are displayed on screen although you may select to print that report.

After you have viewed these reports, you may want to add or edit various data to your practice project and print the same or other reports to see the difference those entries have made. Remember that most reports have a number of different options so that you may select to produce the report in the form that you prefer (*See Chapter 10, Customizing Reports*).

Now that you have become more familiar with TMG and its basic operation, you will want to start working with your real data. If you are coming from another genealogy program, you will probably want to import your data from that program either directly using GenBridge™ technology or via GEDCOM (Genealogical Data Communications) (*See Chapter 3, Importing Data*). Alternatively, you may be just starting out or wish to start your data entry from the beginning. There is no wrong way to

start the next step here. The choice is yours. As you will learn, The Master Genealogist™ is very flexible and will allow itself to be adapted to your way of doing things unlike many other genealogy database programs that force you to adapt to their requirements. The entire design goal of TMG according to Wholly Genes is that the integrity of your data be protected and that the program helps you in your research. So we hope you enjoy this book and TMG. Happy researching!

Suggested Data Entry Conventions

Whether you convert your data from another program or immediately start entering your data in The Master Genealogist™, it is suggested that you create a standard set of data entry conventions to use. This will help you ensure that you are consistent during entry of your data. When you enter data in a consistent manner, it is easier to search for something later, to filter your data for specific information (*See Chapter 11, Filtering and Sorting*), to prevent a lot of editing in narrative reports (*See Chapter 6, Sentence Structures, Chapter 9, Controlling Narrative Reports, and Chapter 10, Customizing Reports*), and to make your data set appear cleaner and neater.

Below are standard considerations that others and I use. While occasionally data might be entered differently than in accordance with the rules set forth below, we try to follow these conventions as closely as possible for consistency. Remember that these are our standards with some suggested choices with some variations due to each of our preferences.

You may have differing ideas of what you want. Type these standards into your word processor, and adjust them as you think best. You will note that some of these rules conflict with other rules. In such cases, you will need to choose the rule you prefer and disregard the conflicting ones.

One thing that should be emphasized here is that whatever you decide as a set of data entry standards should consider the accurate entry of the data you find in your research and balance that with the ease of searching and analyzing of that data. Often there will be a conflict in what you see in the source record and what you believe it should be. Many will just enter the data as shown in the source even though it may make searching and analyzing somewhat more difficult. However, others will enter what might be called a standard spelling or name and note the difference in an appropriate text field. Either method will be a compromise to something. But if you select one and follow it faithfully, then you should have no problems. When you define your set of conventions, keep in mind the objective of your research. If you have more than one data set or project, you may want to create a set of conventions for each. Thus each set of standards can help you toward a different goal for each data set or project.

Names

- Enter ALL names in full, if known and select the one you think best for the Primary name.
- Enter names in mixed case, and capitalize only the usual letters.
- Do not capitalize letters that are usually lowercase (i.e., de Silva).
- If a surname or given name is not known, leave the field(s) blank. Later, you may find the appropriate name and can add it then. In the meantime, TMG has a default substitute "(--?--)"[which you may change] to print in reports when a Given name or Surname is left blank. For more information, see *Chapter 9, Controlling Narrative Reports* and *Chapter 10, Customizing Reports.*
- When a woman has prior marriage(s) and only her married name is known (i.e., Mrs. Jane Doe), enter her GivenName (Jane), leaving her Surname field blank. Then enter her earlier husband in his own record using her married surname (i.e., Doe) adding any other information known about him.
- Accept the prompt to create a married Name Tag. Leave the default of only the Surname (i.e., do not add Prefix, Given Name, or Suffix unless the change would be different from the norm. This presumes you have set the Preferences (*See Chapter 4, Customizing the Program*) to automatically create the married name tag.
- Enter a name variation tag showing the person's desired name at any time, if different from the Primary Name. Leave this Surname field blank if it is the same as the Subject (Primary) Name. Again TMG will infer the Primary Surname for use with the Picklist.
- Review ALL Name Tags for consistency when changing the Primary Tag. When the Primary Surname is altered, this will also change how non-Primary names without a Surname is displayed on the Picklist. Also a change in the Primary GivenName will change the Picklist entry of blank non-Primary GivenNames. Thus any change in the Primary name should cause you to review all non-Primary name tags to see if they are affected by the change.
- *See Chapter 5, Customizing the Data* for information about Name Styles.

Dates

- Select the "dd Mmm yyyy" date format in the System Configuration. If a date is known to be "old style" (*see Chapter 4, Customizing the Program*), enter it in that format. If your preferred date format is different, select the one that best suits your needs.
- Do NOT convert any date for entry in the Date field, i.e., enter "2nd Sunday after Trinity in 1709" in the Date field, acknowledge, and ignore the irregular date notice.
- Do convert dates as necessary for the Sort Date field, i.e., enter "9 Jun 1709" for "2nd Sunday after Trinity of 1709".

Places

- Make all entries in mixed case using the usual capitalization.
- Leave unknown or unused fields blank.
- All place entries should be entered as shown in the source document that names the place. However, for consistency, ease of searching and other reasons, you may wish to "standardize" on a single spelling or language entry for any one place. If you do this, you should definitely note the actual source document entry in either the Tag Memo field, the Citation Detail or some other place in your data set.

- Enter common abbreviations rather than full spelling (e.g., St. Louis, Mt. Sterling).
- Do not abbreviate name modifiers (e.g., county, parish). Spell them in full. Enter name modifiers if they are used with that name only. For example, enter County Durham, but only enter Cornwall, both being counties in England.
- For independent cities (e.g., Richmond, Virginia or St. Louis, Missouri), place an entry like"-Independent City" as the County name (the hyphen indicates it is excluded data and will not print). But if the city is not independent, enter the county name (e.g., Jacksonville, Florida is in Duval County).
- Some will prefer entering a place name as it appears in a geographic database such as those accessible on the Internet via the Web menu of TMG.
- It is preferable to enter a location name as it was known at the time of the event. That is, enter it as given in your source. For example, Mt. Sterling, Kentucky is now in Montgomery County, Kentucky, but was in Clark County, Kentucky. Before that, it was in Bourbon County, Kentucky, and before that it was in Fayette County, Kentucky; and before that, in Fayette County, Virginia; and before that in Kentucky County, Virginia. This kind of situation should be noted in the introduction to all generated reports for places that are noted very often. A place like this that is only noted a very few times might include a notation like: Mt. Sterling, Clark County (now Montgomery County), Kentucky. Note that this may cause later readers to have difficulty finding a place that no longer exists under that name unless you do note such changes. So you should ensure that some notation is made as to where that place was located and what it might be named currently.
- Make all entries in the English equivalent form for consistency in searching and filtering but paying attention to how the source reads. If needed, note the difference in the Memo field or Citation Detail or otherwise note the difference. Also some users are heavily into data from another country using a different language. In that case, decide by country how to enter the place entries. For example, if entering German data, enter the German place names and similarly for Norway, France, etc.
- Abbreviations in place names (except as noted above) should be avoided. These change periodically and are often sources of confusion. This is especially true when read by someone from a distant place. For example, the current postal abbreviation for Kentucky is KY, an older abbreviation was Kent, and I have often seen someone abbreviate it as KT. Kent could be mistaken for a non-abbreviation (it is a county in England), and who knows what someone might make out of KT. As for the current KY, it might be changed by the post office in later years and thus there would be another source of confusion.
- U.S. locations:
  - <u>Detail</u>: Enter the church, cemetery, hospital, etc. as needed.
  - <u>City</u>: Enter the full name of the city or town.
  - <u>County</u>: Enter the name of the county (parish for Louisiana and other places). A full U.S. county/parish name includes the modifier "County" ("Parish" if Louisiana) as part of the name to distinguish it from a city/town name. Enter the County name with an Exclusion Marker if the City has been entered and is found on most maps. For non-U.S. areas larger than the City, but smaller than the next larger area within a country give the complete name. Some users may prefer to abbreviate the modifier, i.e., "Co" or "Par".
  - <u>State</u>: Enter the full name of the state.
  - <u>Country</u>: For the United States, enter "-USA" unless pre-Revolutionary data. If a smaller (geographically-speaking) pre-Revolutionary geographic name is known, enter it otherwise use

"America" (some users might wish to use "British Colony")

- Non-U.S. locations:
    - Develop a convention based on the culture being reported. This will differ from country to country and may also depend on the time period involved. This should take into consideration the inclusion or exclusion of a name modifier based on the local custom. For example, a few English counties include the word "County" as part of the county name, some include "shire" as part of the name, and some have no modifier. You should follow the custom of the local culture.
    - Detail: Enter the church, cemetery, hospital, etc. name as needed.
    - City: Enter the full name of the city or town.
    - County: Enter the name of the county, shire or other division that is larger that the city or town and smaller that the state, province or comparable place.
    - State: Enter the province, state, or comparable name.
    - Country: Enter the usual English version of the country name of that time. Again if you are heavily into different countries and languages, use the language of your choice.
- *See Chapter 5, Customizing the Data* for information about Place Styles.

Surety Values

Assign Surety Values based on the following value definitions:

- **-** = Information known to be incorrect.
- **0** = Estimates and guesses with little or no support.
- **1** = Data from a source which is known to be less than reliable.
- **2** = Data from a respected document/source (a secondary source).
- **3** = Primary source data.

A primary source may contain secondary source data (e.g., birth data on a death certificate). In such cases (at least so far as the secondary source data is concerned), the source should be considered to be a secondary source while remaining a primary source for primary data.

Tags

The Tag and Witness Sentences will determine to some extent how you enter some data. In most cases, it is rather straightforward. In other cases, you may want to consider how you enter data and may wish to change the Sentences to more closely fit your needs.

Census

- Enter the head of household as Principal #1.
- Enter all other household members as witnesses.
- Non-family members may be included as desired. These non-family members may and often do wind up part of the family in later years.
- Leave Principal #2 blank.
- Note: Those interested in other ways to enter census data should visit Terry Reigel's TMG web site or Lee Hoffman's TMG Tips web site for links to TMG-related sites containing other methods. (For URLs, see below)
- Study the census records as they apply to your situation. They differ from country to country and from census to census. Select a method that works best for you.

Residence

- Enter spouse as Principal #2.
- Enter other family members as Witnesses.

Marriage and Divorce

- Enter males as Principal #1.
- Enter females as Principal #2.

Use the reverse if desired. Either will allow simpler report filters. You may wish to periodically use John Cardinal's TMG Utility program (see below) to ensure that this convention is maintained for consistency. Knowing that males are always Principal #1 and females are Principal #2 will make it easier to design filters for use within the program or for reports (*See Chapter 11, Filtering and Sorting*).

Flags

- Living - Set to N for one born before 1900, married before 1920, or died. The year is up to you and may be earlier or later. This is related to the Assumed maximum lifespan in the Preferences (*See Chapter 4, Customizing the Program*).
- Birthorder - Set ONLY if known AND if birth dates are not known. The Primary Birth date controls the order in which children are listed in some narrative reports. If this Flag is set, it will override the Primary Birth date as to sequencing children in those reports. Thus some will set this Flag when a Birth date is not known and the setting may alter the proper sequence of the children in a family.
- Multibirth - Set if known.
- Adopted - Set to Y or N only if known otherwise leave as "?".
- Some users do not use one or more of these flags, and thus set them to Inactive.
- You may have added certain Custom flags. Add them to this list as needed.

Gold and Silver Editions

While most users will have the Gold Edition (the full program), there are many that will have the Silver Edition. The Silver Edition of The Master Genealogist™ does not have some of the features of the Gold Edition. The features that the Gold and Silver Editions have are shown in a comparison table on the Wholly Genes, Inc. web site (see URL information below).

Generally the features in the Gold Edition that are not in the Silver Edition are:

- The ability to generate reports in the native format of many word processors.
- The ability to create many wall and fan charts (Silver can produce a top-down descendancy chart).
- The ability to create HTML output for web pages.

Because the Silver Edition does not allow output to be sent to word processors (only plain text and Rich Text Format are available), there are a number of other features that also are not available. Those other features are: no indexes of people, places, and marriages, no table of contents, no Footnotes/endnotes and Bibliography output to a file, no images integrated in some reports.

Therefore, users of the Silver Edition should keep in mind the features that are not available as they read this book. Users of the Gold Edition will have no need to be concerned in that all features are discussed.

Family Tree SuperTools™

While this book is intended for users of The Master Genealogist™, users of the Family Tree SuperTools™ (FTST) program can learn a lot about it here. FTST has been called a "read-only" or "demo" version of The Master Genealogist™ Version 5. That is, you may import your data into FTST using the same features and functions that are available in TMG. While you may see and manipulate your data in FTST (much like in TMG), you will not be able to add, change, or delete that data. A few charting reports in FTST are the same as those in TMG although TMG has much greater report generating capability. So if you have FTST and have some questions, it is likely that you can find the answer here. Just remember that there are no functions to alter your data in FTST. If you have imported data into FTST from another program and wish to change some of that data, go to your other program, and make the changes there. Now go to the Data Set Manager of FTST (*See Chapter 2, Project Management*) and select to Refresh the data set. This will update the FTST Project with the original (now changed) database reflecting the changes that you just made. The alternative is to upgrade to TMG and import the FTST Project into a full TMG Project allowing you to take full advantage of the power of TMG.

Places to find help on the Internet

While the intent of the book is to help you become more comfortable with TMG and thereby enjoy using it, there will always be things that we didn't discuss. Also there will be situations that one reader has that are unique and would not be covered here.

Of course, most of these unique situations aren't really that rare; they just aren't the everyday kind that most genealogists experience. In addition to these reasons, a user may wish to take advantage of the flexibility of TMG and do something most users don't do. But, in many cases, a user would like to discuss the idea with another (preferably more experienced) user. There are a number of places on the Internet where TMG (and FTST) users can find answers to specific questions. Some of the more important web sites and discussion forums or mailing lists are identified below. There are many others - particularly web sites hosted by or for local users groups. Check with your local user group or use your favorite search engine to help find them.

Web Sites:

Wholly Genes Software
http://www.whollygenes.com
This site has pages telling about TMG and FTST, an online store, and other information of interest to users including user groups throughout the world.

Lee Hoffman's TMG Tips
http://www.tmgtips.com
This site contains information about TMG, articles and tutorials about TMG, links to other sites, and examples of various features and functions in TMG.

John Cardinal's TMG Companion Programs
http://freepages.genealogy.rootsweb.com/~johncardinal/TMG/
John's utility programs for use with TMG are available here.

Allen Mellen's TMG Resource Page
http://www.geocities.com/Heartland/Hills/2909/tmg.html
Allen has some helps for TMG users.

Terry Reigel's TMG Tips
http://reigelridge.com/tmg
Terry has many articles on using TMG posted here.

Discussion Forums and Mailing Lists

TMG-L

This is a mailing list (similar to newsgroup) to which a user may subscribe (for free) to receive messages containing questions, answers, and discussions relating to TMG. When a subscriber posts a message to the list, a copy is sent to each subscriber. Thus each subscriber will receive each individual message posted to the list. RootsWeb.com hosts this mailing list. To subscribe, send an e-mail message to:

TMG-L-request@rootsweb.com

with the text of the message containing only the word "subscribe" (no quotes). Be sure to turn off any signature lines.

TMG-D

This is the same as above except many individual messages are gathered into a single message or digest and sent to this group of subscribers. This reduces the number of separate messages a subscriber will receive each day. To subscribe, send an e-mail message to:

TMG-D-request@rootsweb.com

with the text of the message containing only the word "subscribe" (no quotes). Be sure to turn off any signature lines.

FTST-L

This is a mailing list similar to TMG-L (see above) but designed for questions, answers, and discussions relating to FTST. To subscribe, send an e-mail message to:

FTST-L-request@rootsweb.com

with the text of the message containing only the word "subscribe" (no quotes). Be sure to turn off any signature lines.

FTST-D

This is the same as above except many individual messages are gathered into a single message or digest and sent to this group of subscribers. This reduces the number of separate messages a subscriber will receive each day. To subscribe, send an e-mail message to:

FTST-D-request@rootsweb.com

with the text of the message containing only the word "subscribe" (no quotes). Be sure to turn off any signature lines.

TMG Forum

Another discussion list, this one is available only through the World Wide Web and your browser. Genealogy.com hosts this forum. Posting of messages must be made via your Internet browser although you may elect to have replies posted to you in e-mail form. The URL for this site is:

http://genforum.genealogy.com/tmg/.

TMG Newsletter

Wholly Genes operates a subscription mailing list for distribution of their free periodic newsletter. This is a mail-only list that does not accept messages sent to it. You may subscribe via your Internet web browser set to the web site at:

http://www.whollygenes.com/newsletter/subscribe.j sp

or by visiting the Wholly Genes web site and selecting to jump to the Newsletter option.

Acknowledgments

Many people have contributed to this book and the editor and authors would like to express their appreciation to them. First and foremost, we would like to thank Wholly Genes, Inc. and its president, Bob Velke. It might be obvious that this book would not have been written without them, but it was at their suggestion that the book came into being. Another staff member at Wholly Genes, Inc., Lissa Soergel, also gave us a lot of help. Any computer program of this size has a development team and a beta testing team. While the development team may be employees of Wholly Genes and the beta testers are volunteers, both have contributed in many ways to this book for which we are grateful. Also Ms. Ann Hughes and Ms. Kate Boyer of Gateway Press have been of great assistance.

Richard Brogger wishes to acknowledge the help Jill Miller gave while reading and making suggestions for his chapter. Robin Lamacraft would like to acknowledge the assistance of Bryan Wetton and Judy Philip in the VCF chapters.

We would also like to thank our families for their patience and assistance. In addition, many family members have helped proofread various parts of the book. Some of them did not know the program at all and indicated places where the text was unclear. We gratefully acknowledge their assistance.

The Master Genealogist™, GenBridge™, Visual Chartform™, Family Tree SuperTools™, and Wholly Genes are trademarks of Wholly Genes, Inc.

Chapter 2 – Project Management

By Jeffry L. Clenard

General Overview

The Master Genealogist™ (TMG) v5.x introduces a number of advanced features designed to ease the chore of managing family history data, and enhance collaboration with fellow researchers. Among its many innovations is a new approach to storing data – in data sets that are contained within a project. A TMG data set is a collection of ancestor and/or descendant data and related events, sources, repositories, research tasks and exhibits. A "project" in TMG may contain one or more independent data sets that are separated from each other by a "firewall" that protects data in one data set from data in other data sets. So your data can be "commingled" with that of other researchers' without the fear of contaminating your own.

In addition, multiple projects, or multiple views of the same project, can be open concurrently and navigated independently from one another. In a network environment, researchers can even share simultaneous access to the same project(s). The network need not be a local area network (LAN), but can in fact extend to a wide area network (WAN) as some ingenious TMG v5.x users have already discovered.

Its developer, Wholly Genes characterizes TMG as "the complete family history project manager." It is difficult, at best, to separate the thousands of available features into groups that are, or are not, part of project management, for it is the sum of *all* of TMG's features that contribute to its whole. But, for the sake of this chapter, project management includes discussions about:

- Data Sets and Projects
- Multiple Data Sets
- Multiple Monitors
- Multi-User
- Project Management Functions
- Preserving Your Data

Data Sets and Projects

As noted above, a TMG v5.x data set is a collection of ancestor and/or descendant data and related events, sources, repositories, research tasks and exhibits. In this respect it is analogous to what other genealogy applications refer to as a "family file" or "database." Like many of these other applications, individuals in a TMG data set can:

- Be linked to many events whether they are standard or custom.
- Be linked to several exhibits or research tasks.
- Be linked to other individuals by a parent/child relationship, or by marriage.
- Be linked to the same set of sources.
- Be included in reports, charts, and forms with each other.
- Have access to the same set of standard or customized tags and source types.

But, the similarities end at that point. For example, individuals in a TMG data set can also appear as Witnesses in each other's event tags. Also the limitations above are removed in TMG. So users are not restricted to the number of events, exhibits, relationships, sources or repositories associated with any subject in a TMG project.

In addition, if one takes a system administrator view of other genealogy applications, a data set or "family file" or "database" is actually a collection of several files, perhaps several dozen files if you include both data files and index files. This collection of files pertains to a single collection of individuals, families, etc. and is the familiar file structure for previous versions of TMG (v4.x and earlier). Any data that is commingled with this collection of files is by design commingled with all data in the files.

TMG v5.x extends an innovative approach for storing data that was first introduced in its sister product, Family Tree SuperTools™. A TMG v5.x data set is stored in a container called a Project. In the TMG v5.x world, it is a Project, not a data set, which is a collection of many files. So from a system administrator point of view, it is a TMG v5.x Project that is analogous to the "family file" or "database" of other genealogy applications. The key difference being the ingenious design that allows for multiple TMG v5.x data sets to be stored as "independent logical files" in a single collection of TMG files. Thus, TMG v5.x allows multiple collections of independent data (people, families, etc.) to reside within a single collection of files called a Project.

Good File Storage Practices

Storing Projects

If you retained the default value set during TMG installation, the data files for your projects will be stored in the Projects folder C:\Program Files\The Master Genealogist\Projects\. The Projects folder can be changed, if desired. From the Main Menu bar select **File > Preferences > Program Options, General** and update the 'Default Project Path' field. *While it is not mandatory to store each project within its own sub-folder, it is prudent.* A good place to locate the sub-folders for each project is under the **Default Project Path** defined in Preferences. Each project sub-folder will then be visible on the **Open Project File** dialog screen that opens when you select **File > Open Project** from the Main Menu bar.

Storing Exhibits

More and more users of genealogy software are taking advantage of the relative low cost of digital cameras, high-resolution scanners and color printers to incorporate images of family members, primary source documents and/or historical locations with their family history. With the release of TMG v5.x Wholly Genes, Inc. introduced a number of significant enhancements to integrate multimedia with your projects. *(See Chapter 12, Multimedia and Exhibits for a complete discussion of these advanced new features.)*

Before taking full advantage of these new features it is wise to step back and plan how to best use them for your own computing environment. Most multimedia files can be stored either internally, as data within a TMG project, or externally in their native file format(s). In both cases these files are known as TMG exhibits. When stored as external exhibits the user should take the following into consideration.

- No two external exhibits linked to your project (or projects if the exhibit is used in multiple projects) should have the same filename *over all folders* that hold exhibits.
- Any multimedia file linked to a TMG project should have a unique filename. In other words, if you have an image file linked to a TMG project, you should not have another copy of that image or a different image using that same filename *within all folders* that hold exhibits.
- The exhibits for a single project should be stored in a single folder, or in a folder tree based on a single folder. A single folder will work for a great percentage of the user population who have one project. Once the user's experience grows, he or she will see the advantage of a more elaborate exhibit filing system based on a tree of folders. Persons who have both a laptop and a desktop computer will quickly discover that they should try to maintain the same exhibit paths on both machines.

  The default exhibit folder path is: C:\Program Files\The Master Genealogist\ Pics\.

- Users who are in the practice of linking Exhibits that are stored on removable media such as diskette, CD-ROM or memory stick must insert the media into the appropriate drive prior to each TMG Backup and Restore process. It also helps to re-label the CD-ROM drive to a fixed letter like Z: to avoid problems of drive letters changing when another storage device (e.g., compact flash reader, etc.) is added to the computer.
- Users are encouraged to develop a naming convention for their external exhibits, both for purposes of organization and to adhere to the points made in the first two bullets of this section.

Common questions

Can I have a data set without a project?

  No, TMG v5.x data sets require the existence of a Project in which they reside.

Should I maintain a single Project or multiple Projects?

The answer to this question depends upon your own personal needs and approach to research. For many users, a single Project will suffice, perhaps with multiple data sets contained within it. Others may decide to use a subset, or copy, of their "master" project in a separate project as a "sandbox" to test new ideas without the fear of accidentally damaging the master. Users who are engaged in both personal and family association work may decide to use separate Projects. Professional genealogists may consider creating a separate Project for each client.

Can I open more than one Project at a time?

Yes, additional instances of TMG can be started from either the desktop, or from inside of TMG by selecting **File > Open Project.** When asked if you would like to close the current project select [No]. You can also display more than one view of the same Project concurrently simply by opening it again.

Can I open a specific Project directly from a desktop icon?

Yes, simply create a new shortcut for each Project that you would like to start from the desktop. Here are the steps:

Right-click on the desktop.

Enter the folder location of tmg.exe surrounded by quotes followed by the location of the target Project file also surrounded by quotes. The following example shows how to create a shortcut for the Sample Project based on the default installation folders:

"C:\Program Files\The Master Genealogist\ tmg.EXE" "C:\Program Files\The Master Genealogist\sample\sample__.PJC"

Can I open a specific Custom Layout directly from a desktop icon?

No. The last used layout is stored in the APP.INI file, and there is only one instance of this file on each computer. Use the Layout Manager to change to a different layout after launching TMG.

Can I copy data between data sets?

Yes, as long as both data sets are enabled and reside in the same Project. You can copy either an individual, or a group of people based on those selected on the Project Explorer or in the current Focus Group.

Can I copy data between Projects?

No. Data to be copied must reside in the same Project. If the data is in different Projects you must first merge the two Projects together.

Multiple Data Sets

If you maintain more than one data set within a project, each data set is completely independent of the other(s). This characteristic allows multi-data set projects to be used in a number of different ways. For example:

- For *collaboration* between researchers
- To use subsets of your master data for *special reporting* purposes
- For *training* purposes
- To *split* your main data set along family lines

Collaboration

TMG's multiple data set feature provides a convenient, yet secure, framework to view data from a fellow researcher in relationship to your own data without actually merging it together. This is accomplished by using the Project Explorer (PE) to view a list of people contained in all of the data sets. The PE utilizes a Windows Explorer-like interface that becomes a viewable and navigable descendant chart simply by clicking the plus sign (+) next to a person who has one or more lines of descent. The PE can be linked to other windows so they are automatically refreshed as you navigate through it. It can be sorted in a number of different ways – by surname, given name, data set, and person ID number among others. The PE can also be filtered by a number of criteria defined by the user to speed navigation and provide new insights into the data.

Special Report Data Sets

It is often advantageous to extract a subset of your master data into another data set in order to generate a special report (see *Chapter 10, Customizing Reports, List of People)* This special report data set may be temporary, or it may be semi-permanent. Consider creating a separate "Special Reports" project just for these data sets.

Import each special report data set into the "Special Reports" project as they are defined and extracted from your master data set. Make sure to save each data set with a memorable name and the date of import.

Training

There is nothing quite like leaning while using your own data. The challenge is to protect your data while you are learning. This challenge is easily overcome by using multiple data sets. Consider a project that contains two data sets – your master data set and a second "training" data set that contains a subset of the master. Use the Data Set Manager to disable the "training" data set until it is needed.

The next time you want to learn about new and/or advanced TMG features, but do not want to "play" with your master data, use the Data Set Manager to disable your master data set and enable the "training" data set for your training.

Split Family Lines

Some researchers find it beneficial to maintain a single data set that contains information about all of their family lines. Other researchers find it more beneficial to maintain two or more data sets that are split along family lines. Both approaches work, but which one is "best" is purely subjective, and based upon the characteristics of the research, the amount and type of information gleaned from it and stored electronically, and the capabilities of the computer being used.

In many cases, an advantage to maintaining a single data set in a project translates as a disadvantage to maintaining multiple data sets and vice-versa. Advantages to maintaining a single data set that contains information about all family lines include:

- Reporting – Reports that depend upon links between people (e.g., all ancestor and descendant reports, charts and forms) all subjects are in the same data set.
- Navigation – All people are accessible from the same data set.

Advantages to maintaining multiple data sets that are split along family lines include:

- Navigation – All people are accessible from all enabled data sets via the Project Explorer.

- The number of individuals listed on the Project Explorer can be reduced, perhaps significantly, by disabling one or more data sets, rather than by creating a complex filter.
- Provides the safest method of viewing data from fellow researchers alongside your data without the possibility of contaminating your own data.
- Better results can sometimes be achieved by creating a subset of your master data as a separate data set prior to running some reports.

Disadvantages to maintaining multiple data sets include:

- Reporting – Some duplication of data will be required since there are no links between people in different data sets. A person may be stored as a child in a parent/child relationship in one data set, and stored as a parent in another.
- Reporting – Since there are no links between people in different data sets, several reports that depend upon these links (e.g., Ahnentafel, Ancestor Box Chart, Descendant Indented Narrative, Descendant Indented Chart, Fan Chart, Hourglass Box Chart, Journal and Pedigree) will not include people from data sets that are not in focus at report run-time.
- If consistency of customized tag types and source types is desired across data sets, they will need to be managed individually for each data set.
- Common sources and repositories are duplicated.

Multiple Monitors

Many users are taking advantage of the low cost of computer displays by adding a second monitor to their system. These multi-monitor users experience increased flexibility with software applications by having more of them open and visible at any point in time. TMG's highly configurable screen layout capabilities lend themselves quite well to this environment.

Multi-User

Almost anything that can be done with TMG v5.x in a single user environment can be done in a multi-user environment as well. But, there are some caveats. For example, multiple users can edit different records simultaneously, but only one user can edit a given record at a single point in time. Additional users can still view the same record simultaneously, but none of them can edit it until the edit process is completed. At that point one other user can gain access to the record for the purpose of editing.

There are a few requirements to successfully implement a multi-user environment. First, and most obvious, multiple systems in a network environment are required. Just about any Windows capable network, wired or wireless, will do the job. Second, a separate copy of TMG must be installed on each system that will access the shared project(s). *Note that Wholly Genes requires a separate license for each system in the network that is being used simultaneously.* The file folder(s) that contain the project(s) to be shared must have "Sharing" turned on. To find the shared project(s) select **File > Open** from the **Main Menu** bar and navigate to the file by using My Network Places.

Multi-user environments are ideal for family reunions, user groups, training, researcher collaboration and family history societies that are automating access to their data.

Project Management Functions

Some Project Management functions are accessed from the Welcome screen *(see Figure 2-1)*. You may *access s*everal others by selecting **File** from the **Main Menu** bar. A description of each of these key functions is contained in the following sections.

Creating a New Project

Select [New] from the initial TMG **Welcome** screen, or

Select **File > New Project** from the **Main Menu** bar to open the **Create New Project Window**.

Select a location for the new project. The screen defaults to the value defined for Default Project Path in **File > Preferences**. If you have retained the initial value set during TMG installation it will be C:\Program Files\The Master Genealogist\Projects\. *While it is not mandatory to store each project within its own file folder, it is prudent.* A good place

to locate the sub-folders for each project is under the Default Project Path defined in Preferences *(see Chapter 4, Customizing the Program)*.

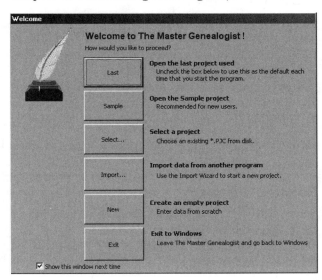

Figure 2-1: Welcome

Enter a name for the Project File and select [Create] to create a new project. Once your new project has been created you will be asked, "What do you want to do with it?"

Select [Import] to launch the Import Wizard and import data from another application *(see Chapter 3, Importing Data)*, or Select [Data Entry] to begin entering data manually.

Opening a Project

Select **File > Open Project** from the **Main Menu** bar, or press <Ctrl>+O to open a project. You will be asked if you want to close the current project if there is one already open.

Select [Yes] to close the current project and open the file selection window, or

Select [No] to leave the current project open and open the file selection window, or

Select [Cancel] to exit the Open Project routine.

Select a file from the file selection window and click [Open]. TMG will launch an additional instance of itself with the newly selected project if you selected [No] above. When used in conjunction with custom layouts, this feature provides a convenient method to compare and contrast data from different projects that are on the screen simultaneously.

Closing a Project

Select **File > Close Project** from the **Main Menu** bar to close the project currently in use. If you work with multiple projects during a single session, it is advisable to back up your project prior to closing if you have made additions and/or revisions to it since TMG will back up only the current project upon exit (see *the Backup section later in this chapter).*

> TMG will not prompt you to back up a project when you Close a Project.

Deleting a Project

Select **File > Delete Project** from the **Main Menu** bar to open the file selection window.
Select a project and click [Delete]. You will be asked to confirm that you want to delete the project *forever.*

> *A project currently in use cannot be deleted.*

Click [OK] to delete the project, or [Cancel] to exit. If you click [OK] you will be given one final chance to change your mind.

Click [Yes] to delete the project, or [No] to exit.

> *Caution, this process cannot be undone!*

Copying a Project

Select **File > Copy Project** from the **Main Menu** bar to open the file selection window.

Click on the project to be copied and click [Select]. Click [OK] when asked to specify the new project location and name to which it will be copied.

Select, or create, a new file folder, and enter the new project name. Click [Create]. When the new project has been successfully created, TMG will open a small window with that indication. Click [OK] to close the window.

Renaming a Project

Select **File > Rename Project** from the **Main Menu** bar to open the Rename Project window.

Click on the project to be renamed and click [Select].

> *A project currently in use cannot be renamed.*

Click [OK] when asked to specify the new project location and name to which it will be renamed. If you want to keep the project in its original folder simply enter the new project name and click [Create]. When the project has been successfully renamed, TMG will open a small window with that indication. Click [OK] to close the window.

Merging Projects

The Merge Projects routine will do a total merge of two projects. It will not attempt to identify or eliminate duplication.

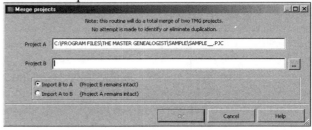

Figure 2-2: Merge Projects

Select **File > Merge Projects** from the **Main Menu** bar to open the Merge Projects window *(see Figure 2-2).* This screen defaults to the project currently in use (Project A).

Click the […] button to search for the second project (Project B).

Select the desired project and click [Open].
You can either,
    Import B to A, or
    Import A to B

If you select Import B to A, Project B remains intact, and a copy of its data set(s) are merged, or added, to the data set(s) already contained in Project A.

If you select Import A to B, Project A remains intact, and a copy of its data set(s) are merged, or added, to the data set(s) already contained in Project B.

> Note: It is strongly recommended that you have a backup of both projects prior to merging them. Then if you don't like the results of the merge you may restore the original projects.

Displaying a Project Summary

Select **File > Project Summary** from the **Main Menu** bar to display the **Project Summary** screen *(see Figure 2-3)*. The screen provides a brief statistical snapshot of data types contained in the current project, and can be filtered to reflect data from a specific data set in a multi-data set project, from all data sets, or from all unlocked data sets.

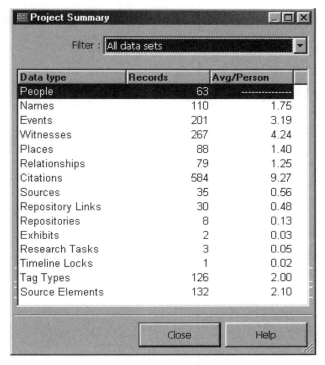

Figure 2-3: Project Summary

Data Set Manager

Select **File > Data Set Manager** from the **Main Menu** bar to open the Data Set Manager screen *(see Figure 2-4)*.

Data Set Manager provides the functionality that allows you to control and manage data sets contained in the currently active project, including Add, Edit, Delete, Import, Refresh, Merge, Export, Enable, Disable and Unlock.

The frame at the top of the Data Set Manager window identifies the current status of each data set in the project by data set ID number. It places a check mark next to each data set that is enabled, and a padlock next to each data set that is locked. It also displays the name of the data set, and the date and time of import for those data sets that were

imported. The full file path of the original file is displayed below this frame, and the data set memo frame below that.

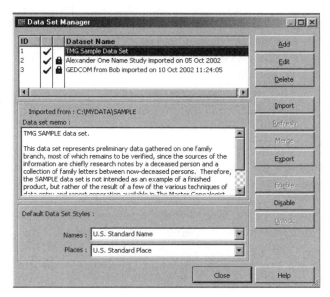

Figure 2-4: Data Set Manager

.You can set the default Name Style and default Place Style for each data set if you are using those advanced features (see *Chapter 5, Customizing the Data)*

Adding a Data Set

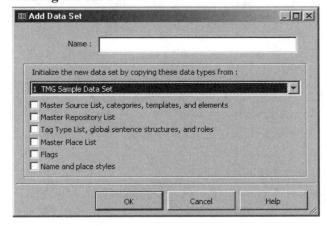

Figure 2-5: Add Data Set

Select **File > Data Set Manager** from the **Main Menu** bar and click [Add] to open the Add Data Set window *(see Figure 2-5)*.

Enter a name for the new data set.

You can initialize the new data set using TMG's default options, or you can select from a specific data set already in the project and optionally copy several data types from it into the new data set. These include:

- Master Source List, categories, templates, and elements
- Master Repository List
- Tag Type List, global sentence structures, and roles
- Master Place List
- Flags
- Name and place Styles

Renaming a Data Set

Select **File > Data Set Manager** from the **Main Menu** bar, highlight a data set by clicking on its name, and click [Edit] to open the Edit Data Set Name window. This window contains two fields – Name and Imported from – the contents of which are displayed on the Data Set Manager window. Make any necessary changes to either field and click [OK] to save, or [Cancel] to close the window without saving.

Deleting a Data Set

Select **File > Data Set Manager** from the **Main Menu** bar, highlight a data set by clicking on its name, and click [Delete] to delete the data set. If the data set is locked you will be given a warning to that effect. Select [Yes] to continue, or [No] to stop. If the data set is not locked, you will be given a warning asking if you are sure that you want to delete the data set. Select [Yes] to continue, or [No] to stop.

> The Delete data set function, unlike the Delete Project function, does not give you a second, more serious, warning, so use caution when deleting data sets!

Importing a Data Set

Select **File > Data Set Manager** from the **Main Menu** bar and click [Import] to open the Import Wizard. See *Chapter 3, Importing Data* for a detailed discussion on importing.

Refreshing a Data Set

One of the powerful new features in TMG v5.x is its ability to refresh a data set. If the original data set from which an import was made has changed, it may be desirable to refresh its contents in the project. This feature will be especially useful for users who collaborate with other genealogists by exchanging data on a regular basis.

> You can only refresh a data set that is locked. Once a data set is unlocked it cannot be locked again!

To refresh a data set, select **File > Data Set Manager** from the **Main Menu** bar, highlight one by clicking on its name, and click [Refresh].

Merging Data Sets

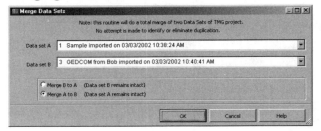

Figure 2-6: Merge Data Sets

Select **File > Data Set Manager** from the **Main Menu** bar and click [Merge] to open the Merge Data Sets window *(see Figure 2-6)*.

Select the two data sets (Data set A and Data set B) from the drop-down boxes.

You can either:
Merge B to A, or
Merge A to B

If you select Merge B to A, the original copy of Data set B remains intact, that is, all data plus the ID numbers for individuals, Source numbers and Repository numbers in Data set B remain unchanged. A copy of the data from Data set B is merged, actually appended, to the data already contained in Data set A. The ID numbers for individuals, Source numbers and Repository numbers for this data will be changed and increment from the next available number in Data set A.

If you select Merge A to B, the original copy of Data set A remains intact, that is, all data plus the ID numbers for individuals, Source numbers and Repository numbers in Data set A remain unchanged. A copy of the data from Data set A is merged, actually appended, to the data already contained in Data set B. The ID numbers for individuals, Source numbers and Repository numbers for this data will be changed and increment from the next available number in Data set B.

Exporting a Data Set

Select **File > Data Set Manager** from the **Main Menu** bar, highlight a data set by clicking on its name, and click [Export] to open the Export Wizard. See *Chapter 15, Exporting Data* for a detailed discussion on exporting.

Disabling a Data Set

There may be times when you want to make the contents of a data set in a multi-data set project invisible to the Project Explorer and Picklist. To do so, select **File > Data Set Manager** from the **Main Menu** bar, highlight a data set by clicking on its name, and click [Disable]. The data is not only invisible, but it is unavailable for reports as well.

Enabling a Data Set

The rest of the program cannot access information contained in disabled data sets because its contents are not visible on the Project Explorer and Picklist. To make the contents of a locked data set visible, select **File > Data Set Manager** from the **Main Menu** bar, highlight a locked data set by clicking on its name, and click [Enable].

Unlocking a Data Set

Information contained in a locked data set can be viewed and reported on, but not changed or amended. To unlock a locked data set select **File > Data Set Manager** from the **Main Menu** bar, highlight a locked data set by clicking on its name, and click [Unlock]. You will be warned that once the data set is unlocked, you cannot lock it again.

Click [Yes] if you are sure that you want to unlock it. The data set will unlock.

Click [No] to cancel.

> The Refresh data set feature works only with locked data sets. If you plan to use Refresh with a particular data set, do not unlock it!

Import (project)

(See *Chapter 3, Importing Data* for a complete discussion of TMG import capabilities.)

Export (project)

See *Chapter 15, Exporting Data* for a complete discussion of TMG export capabilities.

Language

Select **File > Language** from the **Main Menu** bar to select the desired language from the following:

English	Norwegian
English2	Norwegian2
French	Dutch
German	Finnish
Spanish	Italian

Select **Customize** to open the Languages window.

The English language selection cannot be edited, nor deleted. The English2 language can be edited, but it cannot be deleted. All other languages can be edited, or deleted, by the user.

Customized languages are stored in a file called Strings.DBF. *This file is not backed up by TMG's Backup utility.* Be sure to back it up separately if you have made changes to it (see *the Backup section later in this chapter).* In addition, users who are connected to the Internet can check the Wholly Genes web site for updates to TMG v5.x. An updated version of the file Strings.DBF may be included with an update from time to time. Be sure to decline the option to download Strings.DBF if you have customized languages, otherwise your changes will be overwritten and lost.

Performance Considerations

Computers and database applications, like well-engineered automobiles, require tuning and regular maintenance to achieve optimum performance. A sluggish TMG environment could be the result of internally related factors such as the choices made in **Preferences**, or the natural growth in the size of the database through the addition, deletion and/or merging of records. Turning off the Age column and/or selecting the Simple Picklist rather than the Expanded Picklist, for example, may improve performance.

If you are using a screen layout that does not include the Project Explorer (PE), make sure that it is *not* linked to other windows. When it is linked,

TMG must update the PE and Details windows simultaneously to keep them synchronized. This action can degrade performance dramatically, especially in large projects, even if the PE is closed! To check its status, open a custom layout that includes the PE, right-click on a name in the PE, and make sure the line 'Link Project Explorer to other Windows' does not have a check mark next to it.

A sluggish environment can also result from interaction with external factors including hardware (speed of the CPU and amount of memory installed), operating system and availability of resources. Most sluggish environments will benefit from faster CPUs, the addition of memory and even faster hard disk drives. System performance can also be enhanced by limiting the number of programs that are running at the same time, including those that are visible on the Task Bar at the bottom of your screen, or System Tray area on the bottom right side of your screen.

Select **File > Maintenance** from the **Main Menu** bar to access TMG's performance tools.

Select **Performance Recommendations** to have TMG analyze your system and recommend steps to improve its performance. The resulting analysis is saved as a text file, Speed.TXT, in your main TMG program folder for later printing.

Select **Reindex** to sort or re-index the current project. This procedure may become necessary to properly sort, or alphabetize, data according to international standards for handling accented or diacritic characters if the Language selection has been changed.

Select **Optimize** to recover wasted space that accumulates in your data files over time by eliminating records that are no longer needed and reducing file size in the process.

It is a good idea to run **Optimize** after an import or data set merge to remove duplicate place records. *To succeed, the entries in every field of both place records must be identical.* What appears to be a duplicate place may actually have spaces or non-printable characters embedded in one or more of the fields. If **Optimize** fails to remove what appears to be a duplicate place, select **File > Tools > Master**

Place List, find and manually edit the suspected duplicates to be exactly the same, and run **Optimize** again.

Validate File Integrity

Select **Validate File Integrity (VFI)** to validate and repair suspected file damage that may occur due to system freezes and/or inadvertent hardware shutdown. VFI is also used to restore broken links within TMG that should point to external exhibit files.

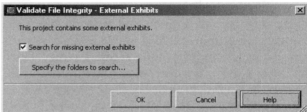

Figure 2-7: Validate File Intergrity – External Exhibits

When you run VFI and your project has external exhibits, the Validate File Integrity – External Exhibits screen will appear *(see Figure 2-7)*. Select the 'Search for external exhibits' check box and click the [Specify the folders to search...] button. This will open the 'List of folders for location' screen *(see Figure 2-8)*.

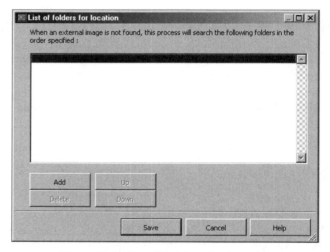

Figure 2-8: List of Folders for Location

You want to add to the search window the path for each folder where you have exhibits stored. Click the [Add] button and use the file dialog to browse to a desired folder. Click the [+] button to expand the folder tree as necessary until you find the target folder. Highlight it and click the [Select] button.

You can add as many search paths for searching as you wish.

VFI starts the search from the selected path at the top of the list, and proceeds down the list until each path has been searched. If the same file is found in more than one folder, VFI will restore only the first copy that it finds. You can control the order of the search by highlighting a path and using the [Up] and [Down] buttons to change its position on the list relative to the other paths. A [Delete] button lets you remove paths from the list.

Once you are finished adding paths, click the [Save] button to save the folder list. You then click [OK] and VFI will run, search each folder defined on the list for your exhibits, and restore the broken links to the exhibits that are located.

When the process completes a small window is displayed stating the number or errors that may have been found and corrected. If errors were found and corrected, run **Optimize** then run **VFI** again until a report of zero errors is displayed at the conclusion

---

*Running **Optimize** between successive **VFI** runs eliminates the issue of running **VFI** multiple times and getting the same 'nn possible errors fixed' message over and over.*

Flag Manager

Flags are one-character fields whose values can be used to classify people in a data set. There are two types of flags – standard and custom. Standard flags are built into every TMG data set and include SEX, LIVING, BIRTH ORDER, MULTIPLE BIRTH, ADOPTED, ANCESTOR (Interest) and DESCENDANT (Interest). These flags cannot be modified by, or deleted from, the Flag Manager. They can be disabled, however, so they will not show on the Flags layout window.

The BIRTH ORDER flag holds special significance within TMG. It is used to record evidence about the order of birth when birth dates are unknown. When used, the BIRTH ORDER flag will set the proper order for children displayed on the Children layout window and printed in reports. Unless there is conflicting evidence, the BIRTHORDER flag should not be used if birth dates for the children are

known. If used together, the BIRTHORDER flag will override the birth date order on the Children layout window and in reports.

Select **File > Flag Manager** from the **Main Menu** bar to open the Flag Manager (*see Figure 2-9*).

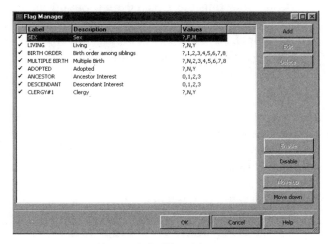

Figure 2-9: Flag Manager

Select [Add] to create a custom flag (*see Figure 2-10*).

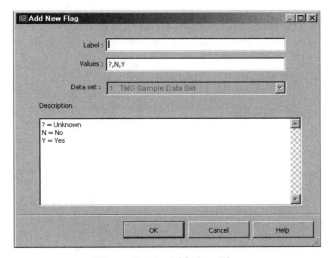

Figure 2-10: Add New Flag

Enter a name for the new flag in the Label field.

Enter the flag values, each separated by a comma and no space.

In a multi-data set project, select a data set from the drop-down box for which this new flag should apply.

Enter a description, or definition, for each value.

Select [OK] to create the new flag, or [Cancel] to exit the Add New Flag window.

A flag's value can be set manually, one person at a time, or it can be set for groups of people defined by setting an appropriate focus in the List of People report and selecting the Change Flag option under Secondary Output. See *Chapter 10, Customizing Reports* for **List of People** report options, and *Chapter 11, Filtering and Sorting* for details on creating and setting custom flags.

Accent

The Accent feature controls the color of each person's name on the screen based on flag and/or data characteristics associated with each person. Its uses are virtually unlimited, and can be used to color code people by:

- Ancestor, or descendant lines
- Any flag, such as a custom Cleaned flag
- Character strings contained in Memo fields
- Data set ID
- Date or location information for any event
- Name
- Thousands of other combinations

Select **File > Accent** from the **Main Menu** bar to open the Accent Definition screen *(see Figure 2-11)*.

The Accent feature has three states:

- Accent OFF
- Accent names by the FIRST matching condition
- Accent names by ALL matching conditions

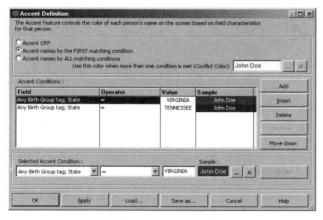

Figure 2-11: Accent Definition

Select **Accent OFF** to disable the Accent feature and other options on the Accent Definition window. When **Accent names by ALL matching conditions** is selected, you have the option to define a separate (conflict) color to be used when more than one condition is met.

Select [Add] to add a new Accent definition.

Click the down-arrow on the **Selected Accent Condition** drop-down box to display an extensive list of conditions. Scroll through the list and select the desired condition.

Select an operator and assign a value, if appropriate. Modify the background color and text color.

Click [Update] to reflect the changes in the Accent conditions panel.

Repeat the process until all desired Accent conditions are defined.

Click [Apply] to apply the Accent conditions to the TMG screens.

Once defined, an Accent condition can be saved for future use, or to be shared with other users of TMG v5.x.

Click the [Save as] button to open the **Save an Accent definition file** window.

Enter a file name and click [Save].

Saved Accent definitions can quickly and easily be enabled by clicking [Load] on the Accent Definition screen, selecting the desired Accent definition from the list and clicking [Load] again.

Preferences

See *Chapter 4, Customizing the Program* for a complete discussion of setting user preferences.

Preserving Your Data

Backing Up Projects

The Master Genealogist™ v5.x provides the facility to back up your Project(s) and to restore them as well. But, it does not provide a convenient method to back up several other types of configuration files that may be required to completely restore the look and feel of your TMG v5.x operation in the case of a disaster. This section covers the traditional Backup and Restore, plus an overview of related TMG v5.x configuration files that should be backed up separately using the Windows File Manager, or similar backup tools.

TMG backup files have an SQZ extension and are stored in the path and folder defined in the Backups field on the Advanced screen under Current Project Options on the Preferences window. For example, the first backup of the Sample project would produce a file named sample__1.SQZ. If a numeric value is entered in the Loop through ___ backups field, TMG will increment the number in the file name for each subsequent backup until it reaches the Loop through value, at which point the series will start over. So subsequent backups would be named sample__2.SQZ, sample__3.SQZ and so on. An automatic reminder to back up the *current* project upon exiting TMG can be set by checking the Prompt for backup option on the Startup and Exit screen under Program Options on the Preferences window.

Caution: the automatic backup reminder applies only to the project open at the time of program exit. If you have updated other projects during the program session you will not be prompted to back them up. You must instead use the manual backup process discussed in the next section.

To make a backup while in the program:
Select **File** > **Backup** from the **Main Menu** bar.

Note: there must be at least one Project open, otherwise the Backup option will be disabled.

The **Backup Project** screen will appear (*see Figure 2-12*).

Select project

The backup process will default to the active project. You may either use the default, or select a different project by manually typing the drive, path, and name of the project, or click on the Select […] button to locate the desired project.

Select backup file

The backup process pre-fills the file name and backup location based on the parameters stored in **File** > **Preferences** > **Current Project Options** > **Advanced** > **Backup**. You may either use the default settings, or target a new file name and/or location by manually typing it, or by clicking the Select […] button to search the Windows directory.

Caution: if you manually enter a folder that does not exist, Backup will create the new folder without prompting you to do so. Use care to ensure that you are typing the folder name correctly.

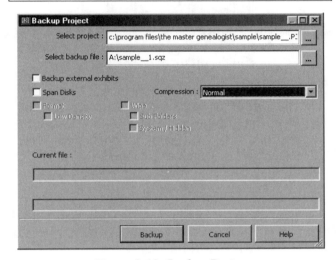

Figure 2-12: Backup Project

Backup external exhibits

When this option is checked TMG will include in the backup (*.SQZ) file all external exhibits that are connected to the project. This could substantially increase the backup file size, and time to back up, if the project contains either a large number of exhibits, or exhibits that are themselves large in file size.

Span disks

When this option is checked TMG will split the backup beyond a single diskette if needed.

Format

This option is available if the Span disks option is checked. Select this option to have TMG format the diskette prior to writing backup data to it.

Low Density

This option becomes available when the Format option is selected, and allows low density formatting of the diskette when checked.

Wipe

This option is available if the Span disks option is checked. Select this option to wipe (delete) files from backup diskettes prior to writing backup data without formatting them.

Sub Directories

Select this option to wipe all folders in addition to files on the diskette.

System / Hidden

Select this option to wipe system / hidden files on the diskette.

Compression

The size of the backup (*.SQZ) file and speed to produce it can be controlled somewhat by selecting one of these six options: None, SuperFast (Minimal compression), Fast, Normal, Slower (More compression), Slowest (Maximum compression).

Click the [Backup] button to start the backup.

You will be asked to insert a disk (or the first disk of a multi-volume set).

Insert a disk and click on [OK].

The backup will begin and you will be able to watch the progress bars.

When you receive the Backup is complete message, click on [OK].

Note: if you use a disk that is too full to hold the backup, you may get an error message that says, "Temporary file failure... (Error code 10)" or "Output file write failure...". Simply use a different disk that is not so full or check Span disks.

Restore

To restore a project from a backup:

Select **File > Restore** from the **Main Menu** bar to open the Restore Project From Backup Window *(see Figure 2-13)*.

Select the backup (*.SQZ) file by typing its name, including its directory path, in the Select backup

file field, or click the select button to the right of the field to locate the backup file in the directory of your system or network.

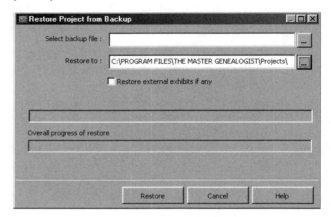

Figure 2-13: Restore Project

Select the restore to location by accepting the default which is defined on the Program Options, General screen of Preferences, or by pointing to a different location by clicking the select button to the right of the Restore to field to locate the desired path and folder, or by typing the directory path and folder in the Restore to field. If you type a path name that does not exist, TMG will inform you that it does not exist and give you an option to create the folder.

Check Restore external exhibits if any to include them.

Click on [Restore].

If a project by the same name already exists, you will be warned "You are trying to restore backup over your existing data! Are you sure that you want to continue?"

Select [Yes] to overwrite your existing data.

Select [No] to either change the restore location, or to cancel the process.

If you have chosen to restore external exhibits, you have multiple choices on overwriting external exhibits:

Yes/Yes to All/No/No to All.

The data will be restored and the original data overwritten. When you get a message that the data has been successfully restored, click on [OK].

Restoring the Paths to External Exhibits

TMG allows for exhibits to be stored internally, as data within a project, or externally in their native file format(s). In the latter case, TMG stores a link to the folder location for each external exhibit. *(See Chapter 12, Multimedia for a complete discussion of exhibits.)* Since they are stored outside of a TMG project, it is possible for external exhibits to become unlinked from the focus subject to which they were originally attached. This may occur, for example, due to any of the following circumstances:

- the exhibit file has been deleted.
- the exhibit file has been renamed.
- the exhibit file has been moved to a different folder (and, possibly, renamed as well).
- the exhibit file was corrupted.
- the link to the exhibit file was originally imported with a tilde "~" notation short form of a long file name, e.g., from TMG v4.x or some GEDCOM files.
- the exhibit file on the backup was stored on removable media such as a diskette, CD-ROM or memory stick and was not present during the restore process.

If any part of the project to be restored was originally imported from a previous version of TMG (version 4.x or earlier), and that data set had external exhibits, then there may be a possibility that the links to these external files will be become broken or mismatched. This will only be a problem if the external files in that earlier version had long file names that had to be stored in their short form name in that prior version of TMG. To check for this, examine the path that is shown for each exhibit in the Exhibit Log.

How exhibits get restored

- If exhibits were originally stored in the default exhibit folder for the program, e.g., C:\Program Files\The Master Genealogist\Pics\, then these exhibits will be properly restored and linked to the default exhibit folder for the program, even if the program was installed to a different path, e.g., C:\Tmg\Pics\. *This applies only to files in that folder and not to files stored in its sub-folders.*

- If exhibits were originally stored in a folder other than Pics, and the path to this folder is common to both the backup and restoring systems, e.g., C:\Program Files\The Master Genealogist\ Pics\Wills\, then these exhibits will be properly restored and linked to the appropriate folder, e.g., C:\Program Files\ The Master Genealogist\Pics\Wills\. If a folder tree with sub-folders is involved, the folder tree and every sub-folder within the tree must exist on the restoring system for the restore process to recreate the exhibits exactly as they were on the backup system. *The restore process does not create folders!*

- If exhibits were originally stored in a folder other than Pics, and the path to this folder is unique to the backup system, e.g., C:\My Unique Folder\, then these exhibits will be restored and linked to the default exhibit folder for the program, e.g., C:\Program Files\The Master Genealogist\ Pics\. If a folder tree with sub-folders is involved on the backup system, that folder tree organization will be lost as each exhibit will be restored to a single folder, the default exhibit folder mentioned previously, and linked to the appropriate exhibit record in the restored project.

Symptoms of unlinked exhibits

An obvious symptom of unlinked exhibits is the discovery that an exhibit that was supposed to be included as part of the report output is missing. This suspicion can be confirmed in one of three ways.

- Open the Exhibit Log and set the focus to all exhibits. Unlinked exhibits may be displayed as a *frowny face* icon.

- An exhibit may be unlinked, but still be displayed in the Exhibit Log without a *frowny face* because the Exhibit Log displays a different representation of the exhibit. This can occur when the 'Save image thumbnails' option is selected in the Current Project Options / Advanced screen of Preferences. If you suspect this to be the case, open the Exhibit Log, right-click on the questionable exhibit and click the **Properties** menu option. If the exhibit is found, the [Save As] button will be accessible and the path to the exhibit's file name will be displayed to the right of it. If the exhibit is not found, the [Save As] button will not be accessible (it will be dimmed) and the path to the unlinked exhibit will be displayed to the right of it followed by the message "(not found)".

■ The 'Save image thumbnails' option noted above is selected by default. When TMG is opened and this thumbnail option is active, the program searches for all external exhibits for the current project. This process creates a Thumbs.LOG file in the current project folder. A list of the invalid paths for all missing exhibits is added to this log file. This is a text file and you can view it with a text editor to determine which exhibits are missing. Select **Tools > Text Editor** from the Main Menu bar to use TMG's internal editor.

Remedies to restoring exhibit links

Case 1 – The brute force method. Once you have identified an exhibit with a broken link, open the Exhibit Log, right-click on the exhibit, click the **Properties** menu option and click the [Load] button. Use the file dialog to browse to the correct image, if available, click on the file name to select it, and click [OK] to create a new link.

Case 2 – When you restore a project to a new computer and the external images were not included in the backup file – assume for this case that you moved the exhibits to the new computer by some other means – the exhibits might be located on the new computer at a different folder location from that used on the original computer. To restore the exhibit links using the new folder location select **File > Preferences > Current Project Options > Advanced** from the Main Menu bar, enter the new path in the Exhibit folder field, click the [Apply] button, then [OK] to close Preferences. The new exhibit folder location will be enabled and the exhibit links will be restored after you exit then restart TMG.

Case 2 applies only to exhibits that are stored in the same base folder, and not to exhibits that are stored in sub-folders of the selected base folder.

Case 3 – This is an extension of the previous example. Perhaps you have totally restructured the folder organization for your exhibits, and the brute force method described in Case 1 above will be too time consuming to pursue. The remedy described in Case 2 above will not work because you have created multiple sub-folders to store exhibits. In this case, the optimum method to restore the exhibit links is to run Validate File Integrity (VFI), which includes a tool to find exhibits no matter where the files are located. *(See the **Validate File Integrity** section earlier in this chapter.)*

Preserving Configuration Settings

The following question often arises, "How do I recreate my working environment?" This may be due to disaster recovery, or simply the desire to duplicate an existing environment on a different computer. The Master Genealogist™ (TMG) contains many advanced features, some of which may never be customized by the typical user. If this is the case, a simple back up to a TMG SQZ file and restore when required should do the job.

But, what if you do take advantage of advanced features within TMG that involve the creation, or modification, of its associated system files? If this is the case, there potentially are several different file types that are not backed up by the standard TMG backup facility.

Table 2-1 on the following page reflects these file types and their typical locations relative to your main TMG v5.x program folder. The default installation folder C:\Program Files\The Master Genealogist\ is represented in the table below as C:\…\..

Type	Extension	Example	Location
Advanced Settings	*.INI	App.ini	C:\…\
Color Names	*.XLS	Colornames.xls	C:\…\
Custom Buttons	*.BMP	Accent.bmp	C:\…\Buttons\
Custom Frames	*.EMF	Balls(30T).emf	C:\…\Frames\
Custom Graphics	*.BMP *.ICO	French.bmp Tmg5.ico	C:\…\Graphics\
Custom Languages[1]	*.DBF	Strings.dbf	C:\…\
Custom Layouts	*.LO	Standard.lo	C:\…\
Custom Reports	*.RPT	Eol.rpt	C:\…\Reports\
Custom Toolbar	*.TBR	Custom.tbr	C:\…\
Filter Definitions[2]	*.FL*	Is an ancestor of Frank Alexander.flp	C:\…\Sample
GEDCOM Export Files	*.XPT	Sample.xpt	C\…\Reports\
Help Annotations – TMG	*.ANN	Tmg.ann	C:\Windows\Hlp\
Help Annotations – VCF2	*.ANN	Vcf2.ann	C:\Windows\Hlp\
Slideshows		Everything in the slideshow folder	C:\…\Slideshow*
Spell check Dictionary[3]	*.DBF	Words1.dbf, Words2.dbf, Words3.dbf	C:\…\
Spell check Dictionary (External, e.g. MS Word)	*.DIC	Custom.dic	C:\…\
TMG Backups	*.SQZ	Sample.SQZ	A:\
Timelines	*.DBF *.DBT *.DOC	Epidemic.dbf Epidemic.dbt Epidemic.doc	C:\…\Timeline\
Visual Chartform Charts	*.VC2	Ancestor Chart.vc2	C:\…\Reports\
Web Other	*.TXT	Webother.txt	C:\…\
Web Places	*.TXT	Webplaces.txt	C:\…\

Table 2-1: Backup File Types

NOTES:

1. If the Custom Languages option is selected during installation, and if the user later modifies one or more of them, care should be taken to back up the file Strings.DBF. In addition, a team of translators updates this file frequently, so if you accept the option to update Languages during an on-line update of TMG, changes that you make to this file *will be lost*. There is currently no method to synchronize your changes to Strings.DBF with those made by Wholly Genes.

2. Custom Filter Definitions are stored in the same folder as their associated project and have a file name suffix starting with "FL".

3. Users have a choice between using an internal dictionary, or Microsoft Word. If Word is selected, the user can also set an option to have TMG check grammar. These options are found by selecting **File > Preferences > Program Options > Data Entry**, Spell Checker.

Chapter 3 - Importing Data

By Jeffry L. Clenard

General Overview

Most genealogy applications provide two methods to input data – manual data input and GEDCOM (Genealogical Data COMmunications) import. In addition to these two methods, TMG supports the import of data *directly* from several popular genealogy programs without the limitations inherent in GEDCOM. This chapter covers importing data, starting with an outline of the import process, continuing with a brief discussion of considerations for an effective import strategy and post import cleanup, and closes with a detailed discussion of advanced import options.

Those who have transferred data between genealogy programs using GEDCOM know that it is a weak standard that is implemented differently by almost every program. Hence, incorrect placement or interpretation of data, and even loss of data is not uncommon. The "art" of GEDCOM transfers typically involves customizing the GEDCOM file with a text editor to achieve desired results. While TMG does support GEDCOM transfers, it also employs an exclusive technology called GenBridge™ with which you can import data directly from several popular genealogy programs. You should achieve superior results with less effort and without having to manually edit a GEDCOM file by utilizing GenBridge™.

GenBridge™ employs an Import Wizard approach to guide you through the import process. The process is similar for each of the supported applications including GEDCOM. In general, the steps are:

1. Welcome - select from a Simple Wizard where GenBridge™ will make import decisions for you, or from an Advanced Wizard to exercise more control over the process.
2. Import From - select from any of the supported file types *(see Table 3- 1).*
3. Import To - you can import the file into a new project, or append it to an existing project as a separate data set.
4. Options screens - each of the supported file types noted above may cause one or more Options screens to appear during the import process. Some of the Options screens are identical across some file types; others are unique to a file type due to the unique data type capabilities it contains.
5. Finish - to start the import.

Software Application	File Type	Backup File
The Master Genealogist™ v4.x or earlier	*.TMG	*.SQZ
Family Origins®	*.FOW	*.ZIP
Family Tree Maker®	*.FTW	*FBK
GEDCOM	*.GED	
Generations™	*.UDS	
Legacy Family Tree™	*.FDB	*.ZIP
Personal Ancestral File® v3-5.x	*.PAF	*.ZIP
The Roots Family of Products		
Family Gathering®	*.PRO	*.SQZ
Roots IV™	*.PRO	*.SQZ
Roots V™	*.PRO	*.SQZ
Ultimate Family Tree®	*.PRO	*.SQZ
Visual Roots™	*.PRO	*.SQZ

Table 3-1: Import File Types Supported by GenBridge™

The length of time to import depends upon many factors including, but not limited to:

- Hardware characteristics such as processor speed, amount of memory, storage capacity, etc., and
- Software characteristics such as the operating system (Windows 98™, Windows ME®, Windows 2000™, Windows XP®, etc.), the size of the data set to be imported including number of people, events, notes, sources, exhibits, etc., and the complexity of the data structure of the target file type.

General Strategy

If you have a large GEDCOM file, or large data set to import, you should not jump right in and expect the initial import to meet your full expectations. Even though Wholly Genes has taken great strides to ensure the quality of the transfer via GenBridge™ the developer cannot take into account all possible permutations of how users might store data in other applications. If you, or the owner of the target import file, have been creative in the use of fields in the target application, the data in those fields may or may not transfer in an expected manner.

With this in mind it is typically best to start with a smaller data set, or representative subset from your target application. By using a small data set for your testing, you will be able to refine your methodology and run multiple imports in a relatively short period of time. Start with the Simple Wizard and check to ensure that your data was imported as expected including event data, relationships, sources, repositories, exhibits and research tasks if applicable. Select and print a number of reports to ensure that the printed output meets your expectations. If you are not satisfied with the results when using the Simple Wizard try the Advanced Wizard (see the appropriate import file type in the sections that follow).

Try the default options in the Advanced Wizard first. In most cases, they will provide the best results. If you are still not satisfied, begin making changes to the advanced options. You may find, in some cases, that certain data just does not import the way you would want. This may be due to the creative use of a field to store data in the exporting application where it is not intended to be stored. In these cases, it may be easier to make a simple change to the data in the target application before attempting your final GenBridge™ import. Once you are satisfied with the trial, import the large data set and validate the results as above, but *do not edit or add data until you are satisfied that you have achieved the best result.*

Conclusion - Cleanup Ideas

GenBridge™ not only ameliorates a typical GEDCOM import, it dramatically improves the quality of the import result with its direct transfer capabilities because it can capture those unique, application specific data types. But, even a "successful" GenBridge™ import may require some clean up. Immediately after import you should open the Master Place List to ascertain the position of all place elements (Detail, City, County, etc.). You should also validate the data in the Master Source List and Master Repository List. It is always a good idea to check all data associated with all of the people included in the imported data set. This can obviously be quite time consuming, especially if you have imported a large data set. But, with TMG you do not have to do it all at once.

Start the record cleanup by first creating a custom "Cleaned" flag with values "N" and "Y" –"N" being the default. Change the flag value to "Y" as you validate the information for each person in your new data set. If you exit TMG and wish to return to the cleanup at a later time or date, you can easily identify those people whose "Cleaned" flag value is equal to "N" by setting a filter for the Project Explorer. In addition, you might use the "Cleaned" flag to drive an accent – preferably making it the first condition, so the desired conditions cannot be seen until the cleanup is completed and the flag value changed to "Y".

See *Chapter 11, Filtering and Sorting* for details on creating and setting custom flags and filtering the **Project Explorer**.

For those remaining import oddities try out John Cardinal's TMG Utility that can be downloaded from:

freepages.genealogy.rootsweb.com/~johncardinal/TMG/.

File Type \ Import Step	Welcome	Import From	Import To	Tag Type Options	External Exhibit Options	Finish
The Master Genealogist™	1	2	3		4	5
Family Origins®	1	2	3	6	4	7
Family Tree Maker®	1	2	3	4		6
GEDCOM	1	2	3	7	4	8
Generations	1	2	3	4	5	6
Legacy Family Tree™	1	2	3	4	5	6
Personal Ancestral File®	1	2	3	5		6
Roots Family of Products	1	2	3	7		9

Table 3-2: Common GenBridge™ Import Steps

The following section provides an overview of GenBridge™ Advanced Wizard steps that are common to several import file types (*see Table 3-2*).

The GenBridge™ Import Wizard

To import a data set, backup file, or GEDCOM:

From the Welcome screen click on [Import], or if TMG is already running,

Select **File > Data Set Manager** and click on [Import], or

Select **File > Import**, from the menu bar.

The **Import Wizard** will appear.

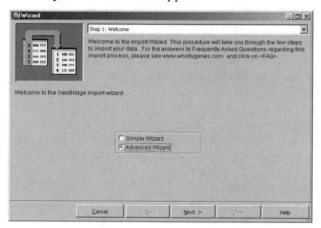

Figure 3-1: Import Wizard, Welcome Screen

Step 1: Welcome *(see Figure 3-1)*

Select Simple Wizard to have the Import Wizard make import decisions for you, or

Select Advanced Wizard to customize the import process, then

Click [Next].

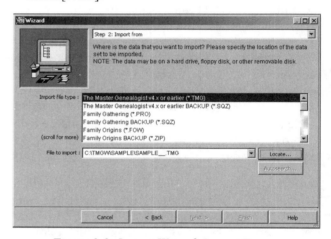

Figure 3-2: Import Wizard, Import From...

Step 2: Import from *(see Figure 3-2)*

Select the Import file type by highlighting the description that matches the data file to be imported (see *Table 3-1*)

Select the File to import by:

Entering the path and file name in the field provided,

Clicking [Locate] to find the file manually, or

Clicking [Autosearch] to have the Import Wizard build a list of all files of the type selected. A scrollable file list can be viewed by clicking on the down arrow to the right of the File to import field.

Once you have located and selected the import file type, TMG will check its structure to ensure it is a complete and valid database or data set based on the type of file. If TMG indicates the import file type is invalid, check to ensure you have a complete set of all files associated with the data set, and that TMG supports the version of the program whose data you are trying to import.

Click [Next] to define the import location.

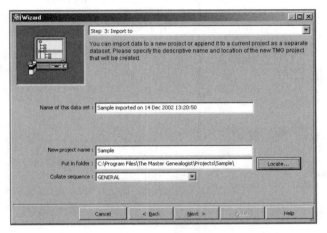

Figure 3-3: Import Wizard, Import To...

Step 3: Import to *(see Figure 3-3)*

The **Import Wizard** auto-fills the new Name of this data set in the field provided. You can either retain this name, or change it to one of your liking.

Select [Add it to the current project] if you intend to import to the currently active project, or

Select [Create a new project] if you intend to add it to a new project. If this is the case,

Enter a name of your liking for the new project, or retain the default.

You may either use the default folder location, or target a new location by manually typing it or by clicking [Locate] to search the Windows® directory. (*If you manually enter a folder that does not exist, the Import Wizard will prompt you to create the new folder.*)

Select the preferred Collate sequence (language) by clicking the down arrow to the right of the list box. The Collate sequence defines the order in which alphanumeric

characters are sorted in your project. Select the language that best matches the language you will be using in your project. Use General for English and all other languages not listed.

Click [Next] to define tag type options.

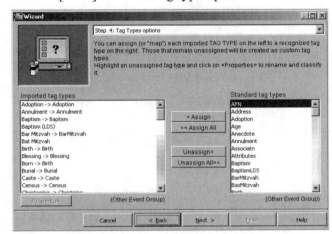

Figure 3-4: Import Wizard, Tag Type Options

Step 4: Tag Types Options *(see Figure 3-4)*

The Import Wizard analyzes the target data set and displays a list of all tag types to be imported. Many of the imported tag types will be pre-assigned to TMG's standard tag types (see Adoption - > Adoption in *Figure 3-4*, plus other tags separated by "- >"). You can re-assign, or map, unassigned tag types on the left to a standard tag type on the right by highlighting a tag from each list and clicking [< Assign]. An individual tag can be unassigned by highlighting it and clicking [Unassign >]. All imported tag types can be unassigned by clicking [Unassign All >>]. The standard tag type can be re-assigned to each by clicking [<< Assign All].

TMG allows the user to classify tags by pre-defined groups to aid in searching, sorting and reporting. Unassigned tags default to the 'Other Event Group' upon import. Highlight an unassigned tag type and click on [Properties] to rename and classify it to the preferred group. Unassigned tag types will be created as custom tag types in the new data set. *(For additional information on custom tags and tag groups see Chapter 4, Customizing the Data.)*

Click [Next] to continue.

Step 5: External Exhibit Option *(see Figure 3-5)*

When an external exhibit is found, you may Import it as an internal exhibit,

Import the link to the file's current location, or

Copy and link the exhibit to a different location defined by you.

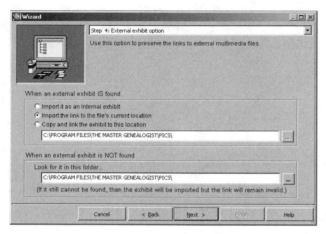

Figure 3-5: Import Wizard, External Exhibit Option

When an external exhibit is not found, you may Specify a specific folder where the Import Wizard should look. (If it still cannot be found, then the exhibit will be imported but the link will remain invalid requiring the user to correct it later.)

Click [Next].

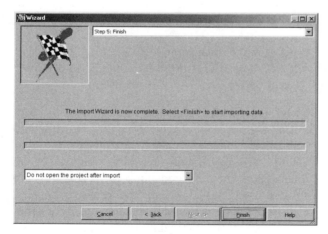

Figure 3-6: Import Wizard, Finish

Step 6: Finish *(see Figure 3-6)*

If you selected Add to existing project in Step 3 above, simply click [Finish] to start the import.

If you selected Create a new project in Step 3 above rather than Add to existing project, the Finish screen gives you three options to continue. Select one of the options by clicking the down arrow to the right of the list box:

Do not open the project after import

Close current project and open imported project

Open imported project as separate window

Click [Finish] to start the import.

TMG displays a small window notifying the user when the import completes, and asking what type of data set it should be, e.g., Locked or Unlocked *(see Figure 3-7).*

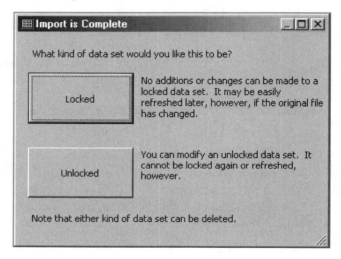

Figure 3-7: Import is Complete

The following sections provide an overview of GenBridge™ Advanced Wizard steps that are unique to each import file type *(see Table 3-1)* including some import considerations to help achieve a better result.

The Master Genealogist™

Import Considerations

TMG v4.x and earlier versions hold ancestor data in a number of different files that make up a data set. It is possible to create and maintain several separate data sets with these versions as some researchers who are investigating multiple lines may do to support their efforts. While ancestor data is kept separate in this environment, some program data is shared among all data sets. For example, researcher information and accent definitions apply to *all* data sets in a TMG v4.x environment.

TMG v5.x implements a fundamental design change that gives the user the ability to associate unique researcher information and/or accent definitions to each and every project. Care should be taken when importing a TMG v4.x or earlier data set if it is desirable to retain this program data.

TMG v4.x stores researcher information and some accent information (colors) in a file named TMG.MEM. An initialized (blank) version of this file is created automatically by earlier versions of TMG, and is typically found in the TMG v4.x or earlier program directory, the default being c:\tmgw\. This information will *not* get imported into v5.x if the Import Wizard cannot find TMG.MEM.

The Import Wizard locates TMG.MEM relative to the location of the TMG data set that is to be imported—in the same folder, or in a parent folder up the directory path from the data set. So, if your target TMG v4.x or earlier data set is not stored in the TMG program folder, or one of its sub-folders, the researcher information and accent definitions may *not* be included when you import into v5.x. The solution is to copy TMG.MEM from the TMG v4.x or earlier program folder, either into the target data set folder, or one of its parent folders.

In the case of a *.SQZ file, the Import Wizard has no knowledge of its origin. If you send or receive a *.SQZ file, and want to include the researcher and accent information, you will need to ensure that the TMG.MEM file accompanies it, and is copied into the *same* folder prior to import.

The Import Wizard

To import a data set from The Master Genealogist™ v4.x or earlier, or from a TMG Backup:

Steps 1-3: Welcome, Import from, Import to
(See Steps 1-3 in the GenBridge™ section)

Steps 4-5: External Exhibit Option, Finish
(See Steps 4-5 in the GenBridge™ section)

Family Origins®

Import Considerations

The Family Origins® fact type AKA is stored as a string of alphanumeric characters. GenBridge™ imports this data as a Name-Var tag with some, but limited flexibility because of the nature of the data (see *Step 5, "AKA" facts on the following page*). Some cleanup of Name-Var tags may be required after import if your Family Origins® data includes AKA facts that have a name suffix such as Sr., Jr., III, etc.

The Import Wizard

To import a Family Origins® data set or Family Origins® Backup:

Steps 1-3: Welcome, Import from, Import to
(See Steps 1-3 in the GenBridge™ section)

Step 4: External Exhibit Option
(See Step 5 in the GenBridge™ section)

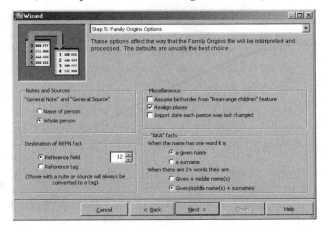

Figure 3-8: Import Wizard, Family Origins® Options

Step 5: Family Origins® Options (*see Figure 3-8*)
The options on this screen affect the way that the Family Origins file will be interpreted and processed by GenBridge™. The defaults are usually the best choice.

Notes and Sources
Select where a "General Note" and "General Source" should be applied; to either the

Name of person, or

Whole person

If Name of person is selected, GenBridge™ imports the Note as a Memo to the primary Name-Var tag in TMG, and the Source as a citation attached to the same tag. If Whole person is selected, GenBridge™ imports the Note as a Note tag associated to the person, and the Source as a citation attached to the Note tag.

Destination of REFN fact

A REFN fact can be applied to one of two places.

Reference field, or

Reference tag

If the Reference field is selected, you may use the dial-box to the right of the Reference field option to set the preferred field length. If the REFN fact contains either a note or a source, it will always be converted to a tag.

Miscellaneous

Select whether, or not, you want the Import Wizard to:

Assume birth order from "Rearrange children" feature: Checking this box will set the Birth Order flag in TMG according to the birth order assigned by using the "Rearrange children" feature.

Realign places: Checking this box will prompt you to open the Master Place List to realign places when the import completes.

Import date each person was last changed: Checking this box will set the Last Edited date field displayed in the Other Info Box in the top right corner of the Details Window, Person View.

"AKA" facts

Decide how you want the Import Wizard to handle names derived from "AKA" facts.

When the name has one word in it, select whether it should be either:

A given name, or

A surname

When there are 2+ words they are:

Given + middle name(s), or

Given/middle name(s) + surnames

Click [Next] to continue.

Step 6: Tag Types Options

(See Step 4 in the GenBridge™ section)

Step 7: Finish

(See Step 6 in the GenBridge™ section)

Family Tree Maker®

Import Considerations

TMG v5.x does not import a true Family Tree Maker® (FTM) backup file – the compressed file that is created by running a backup in FTM – which is a *.FBC file type. The backup that can be imported is a *.FBK file type, and is the one that FTM creates automatically every time you start or exit FTM.

FTM *Facts* are roughly the equivalent of TMG's event tags, and allow the user to input either place information or comments in the Comment/Location field. GenBridge™ allows the user to specify which one to assume for each *Fact* type, and the correct answer depends on how the data was entered. So, if the first import does not meet your expectations, try again with different options. Multiple tries may be necessary to find the best tradeoff.

Most notes in FTM, that is text too extensive to enter in the small comments field of the *Facts*, must be entered in a single Notes field for each individual. There is no provision for sourcing of this field, so the only way a user can record source information is as text in the body of the Notes text. Upon import to TMG, the entire Notes field for an individual, which may be extensive, will be placed in the Memo of a single Note Tag. Usually, the user will want to break this into several TMG tags, move any embedded source information to "proper" sources, and edit the text to accommodate the "He/She" prefix provided by the [P] in the Note sentence structure. (Actually, changing the tag to Anecdote is a good solution in many cases.) One useful trick in breaking up the Note tag, if that's desired, is to use **Edit > Copy Tag**, then edit out different parts of each copy, and change the tag types if desired.

The Import Wizard

To import a Family Tree Maker® data set or Family Tree Maker® Backup:

Steps 1-3: Welcome, Import from, Import to

(See Steps 1-3 in the GenBridge™ section)

Step 4: Tag Type Options

(See Step 4 in the GenBridge™ section)

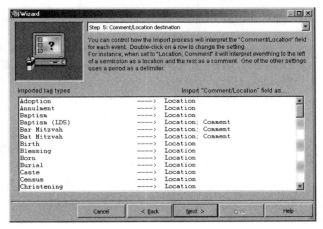

*Figure 3-9: Import Wizard,
Comment/Location Destination*

Step 5: Comment/Location Destination
(see Figure 3-9)

You can control how the import process will interpret the "Comment/Location" field for each event by double-clicking on a row to change the setting. Continuing to double-click on the same row will step you through the four possible import options *(see Figure 3-9)*.

Import "Comment/Location" field settings include:

Location – Interprets everything as a location.

Comment – Interprets everything as a comment.

Location; Comment – Interprets everything to the left of the semicolon as a location and the rest as a comment

Location. Comment – Interprets everything to the left of the period as a location and the rest as a comment

Click [Next] to continue.

Step 6: Finish

(See Step 6 in the GenBridge™ section)

GEDCOM

Import Considerations

The GEDCOM Standard was developed by the Family History Department (FHD) of the Church of Jesus Christ of Latter-Day Saints to facilitate the transfer of genealogical data between researchers. The Standard was originally designed to meet the needs of the FHD, not those of the commercial genealogy software market. It became accepted as a standard in the commercial market because it filled a void, not only to facilitate data exchange between different researchers, but more importantly between different genealogy applications.

The potential for data loss as the result of data exchange is inherent in the GEDCOM Standard from two perspectives. First, much of the GEDCOM Standard is loosely worded and/or open to interpretation. Different interpretations of the Standard lead to different implementations of import and export rules. So when developers who are free to interpret the Standard to best meet their own commercial needs interpret the Standard differently, and they do, users are at risk of losing data during exchange. Second, many of the genealogy applications currently being sold in the commercial market include advanced features and data types that are not supported by the specifications of GEDCOM.

As of this printing, TMG v5.x supports GEDCOM v4.0 and GEDCOM v5.5, both official releases of the FHD. It does *not* support several interim draft releases, most recently GEDCOM 5.0 and 5.4, that were not approved for commercial release by the FHD, but which are known to be in use by some commercial applications.

The Import Wizard

To import a GEDCOM v4.0 or v5.5 file:

Steps 1-3: Welcome, Import from, Import to

(See Steps 1-3 in the GenBridge™ section)

Step 4: External Exhibit Option

(See Step 5 in the GenBridge™ section)

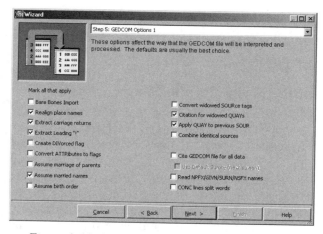

Figure 3-10: Import Wizard, GEDCOM Options 1

Step 5: GEDCOM Options 1 *(see Figure 3-10)*

TMG offers a number of options to control the way that the GEDCOM file will be interpreted and processed. You might start by accepting the default options for a trial import. You can always come back, change a few options, and re-import if the initial results do not meet your needs.

Select all of the options that apply:

Bare Bones Import

When this option is selected, TMG imports *only* the following including associated dates, places and memos:

> Primary Name
> Primary Birth
> Primary Death
> Primary Marriage(s)
> Primary Divorce(s)
> Reference Field
> Flags (Sex, Living...)
> Person Changed Date

And it excludes the following:

> Non-primary names
> Non-primary events
> Other Tag Types
> Sources
> Surety/Quality
> Exhibits

Realign place names

Select this option if you want the Import Wizard to remind you to audit the interpretation of place elements using the Master Place List. Since the

GEDCOM format does not mandate a standard or consistent form for place names, TMG place elements (Detail, City, County, …) may or may not be properly aligned as you might expect after import.

(For a discussion of the Master Place List, see Chapter 5, Customizing the Data.)

Extract carriage returns

Long field values such as notes and memos can be broken into shorter lines during the GEDCOM export. Some applications may use a subordinate CONC tag to indicate that the following value is concatenated to the previous line value without saving the carriage return (see *CONC lines split word on the following page*). Other applications use a subordinate CONT tag to indicate that the following value is concatenated to the previous line value, saving the carriage return. Selecting this option will strip the carriage returns from a note or memo from those applications that use a CONT tag.

Extract Leading "!"

Select this option to have the Import Wizard eliminate an exclamation point that may precede a note or memo in the GEDCOM file.

Create DIV flag

Some programs store divorce data as a tag, or event that includes additional information such as date, place and memo information. Other programs store divorce data as a flag that can typically be set to one of three options, ?/Y/N.

The Import Wizard can handle divorce data that is exported either as an event or as a flag. In both cases, the divorce is recorded in the GEDCOM file with a "DIV" tag. Divorces that are exported as events are ignored by this option since they are imported as events. Divorce data that is exported as a flag will also be imported as an event unless this option is selected. Such events will be mostly empty since the exporting program only stores a Y/N or Yes/No value. If checked, the Import Wizard will create a Divorced flag in the new data set with values ?/Y/N and the value "?" set as the default. Any time the Import Wizard encounters "1 DIV Y" in the GEDCOM file it will set the Divorce flag to "Y". The flag will be set to "N" any time it encounters "1 DIV N".

Convert ATTRibutes to flags

The GEDCOM specification allows ATTRibutes such as physical description, employment, religion, etc. to be recorded similar to events. Leave this option unselected to import the attribute as an event. Select this option to have the Import Wizard create a unique flag for each attribute that it encounters in the GEDCOM file.

Assume marriage of parents

Select this option to have the Import Wizard create a marriage event tag for those couples in the GEDCOM file who do not have one, but who have a family record specifying that they are Husband and Wife.

Assume married names

While many applications allow for the recording of multiple names for an individual such as nicknames, TMG is unique in offering powerful search features such as the Project Explorer and Picklist that display all of the names attributed to each individual in the data set, allowing the user to easily navigate to an individual by clicking on any one of the names. Select this option to have the Import Wizard create a Name-Marr tag with the husband's surname for every married woman in the GEDCOM file so that you can search for a woman by her maiden name or married name.

Assume birth order

The Birthorder flag is one of seven standard flags in TMG. It is typically used to record the birth order of siblings when known, but where there may be a discrepancy or other information missing about them, such as birth dates or perhaps one or more missing siblings. The sequence of the children in the family section of the GEDCOM file may be an implicit recognition of the birth order depending upon the exporting application. Select this option to have the Import Wizard set the Birthorder flag according to this sequence. The Birthorder flag will not be set if the option is left unselected

> TMG uses birth dates to sequence children. The Birthorder Flag, when set, will override that order.

Convert widowed SOURce tags

Widowed source (SOUR) tags are created by an exporting program that mistakes a note or memo as a source. Such notes or memos may get lost during the import process because the SOURce tag is not attached to a real source. Select this option if you want the Import Wizard to identify SOURces of this type and place them in the Memo field of a NOTE event.

Citation for widowed QUAYs

A quality/surety QUAY tag is "widowed" if the exporting program assigns it to a date or place without specifying any particular source. Select this option to have the Import Wizard cite the submitter of the GEDCOM file as the basis for the surety assessment. The Import Wizard will create an "Unknown Source" if no submitter is found. Widowed QUAY tags will be ignored if this option is unselected.

Apply QUAY to previous SOUR

A quality/surety QUAY tag could be processed incorrectly if the exporting program records it in the GEDCOM file at the same level as the source citation. Select this option to have the Import Wizard apply these QUAY tags to the source citation immediately preceding them.

Combine identical sources

Select this option to have the Import Wizard attempt to combine identical sources into a single record. These identical sources may have been exported as though they were distinct from one another.

Cite GEDCOM file for all data

Select this option to have the Import Wizard create a citation for each data element that is imported, using the submitter name, if included, as the source of the data. If the submitter is unknown, the source will be called GEDCOM.

Use Default Surety (next screen)

Select this option to have the Import Wizard use the default surety value on the next screen under Custom Values when citing the GEDCOM file for all data.

Read NPFX//GIVN/SURN/NSFX names

Select this option if the exporting program used these labels in the GEDCOM file. Leave it unchecked if you are uncertain. If you find that you are missing names after the import, try the import again with the option checked.

CONC lines split words

Select this option to have the Import Wizard insert a space between the first word of the CONC line and the last word of the preceding line.

Click [Next] to continue.

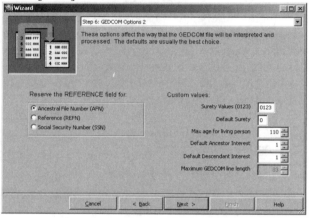

Figure 3-11: Import Wizard, GEDCOM Options 2

Step 6: GEDCOM Options 2 *(see Figure 3-11)*

Reserve the REFERENCE field for:

Ancestral File Number (AFN)

Select this option to have the Import Wizard insert the contents of an Ancestral File Number (AFN) tag into the Reference field.

Reference (REFN)

Select this option to have the Import Wizard insert the contents of a Reference (REFN) tag into the Reference field.

Social Security Number (SSN)

Select this option to have the Import Wizard reserve the Reference field for a Social Security Number (SSN).

Custom Values

Surety Values (0123):

Surety values, also know as quality values or QUAY tags in the GEDCOM specification, convey the researcher's certainty assessment of a piece of information based on the available evidence. TMG implements surety values according to the specification, rating them on a scale of 0 (unreliable evidence, or estimated

data) to 3 (primary evidence, or dominance of the evidence). Some applications use a different scale. Selecting this option allows you to map a different surety scale to TMG's scale.

Default Surety:

Selecting this option will assign a default surety value for those sources that have not been assigned a specific surety value by the exporter or exporting program. In addition, *if you specify a default surety value, any data records with a lower value will not be imported.*

Max age for living person:

The Import Wizard will set the Living flag to "N" for those individuals who are computed to be older than the value entered here, determined by the presence of a valid date in a Birth group tag at the date of import. The value will not be set if a Living tag is also found in the GEDCOM file for the individual.

Default Ancestor Interest:

TMG and many other applications allow researchers to measure their level of interest in acquiring additional information about a subject's ancestors on a scale of 0 (very low interest) to 3 (high interest). Selecting a default value here will set the Ancestor Interest flag at that value for each person in the GEDCOM file who does not have a defined value.

Default Descendant Interest:

TMG and many other applications allow researchers to measure their level of interest in acquiring additional information about a subject's descendants on a scale of 0 (very low interest) to 3 (high interest). Selecting a default value here will set the Descendant Interest flag at that value for each person in the GEDCOM file who does not have a defined value.

Maximum GEDCOM line length:

The default value usually provides a sufficient balance between import processing time and accommodation of data. If you find after import that some data was truncated, select a higher value and re-import the GEDCOM file.

Click [Next] to continue.

Step 7: Tag Type Options

(See Step 4 in the GenBridge™ section)

Step 8: Finish

(See Step 6 in the GenBridge™ section)

Generations™

Import Considerations

Generations™ files having a *.UDS file extension are supported for direct import by GenBridge™. Not supported are files from Generations™' predecessors and allied products including Reunion® for Windows® and Reunion® for Macintosh®. These files must first be imported into a version of Generations supported by GenBridge™ to take advantage of its direct import features. The resulting Generations™ file(s) can then be imported into TMG. GEDCOM can be used as a less attractive alternative.

Generations™ notes can have unlimited embedded source citations. After import to TMG, the source citations from a given note will be linked to the appropriate tag in TMG. They are not embedded because linked citations are more flexible and useful in TMG.

If you wish to retain embedded source citations, some preparation will be required before import, followed by some cleanup afterwards. In Generations™ notes, each embedded source citation appears as a number (the actual source number). In other words, an embedded citation to source number 17 would appear as a specially formatted '17' in the note. Before import, enter a text number into the notes where each embedded source citation is located corresponding to the number of the cited source. After import, embedded source citations can be created at each marker in the TMG memo.

GenBridge™ treats the 'Location of Source' field as a source memo rather than as a repository because Generations does not distinguish the meaning of 'Locality' from 'Location of Source', and there are users who use them interchangeably. Generations™ includes Library/Archive and Repository fields, both of which are imported by GenBridge™ as repositories. But, no default Generations™ source type uses these latter two fields. If it is desirable to import 'Location of Source' as a repository, simply edit the appropriate

sources in Generations™ and replace Location of Source with Library/Archive or Repository.

The Import Wizard

To import a Generations™ data set:

Steps 1-6: Welcome, Import from, Import to, Tag Type Options, External Exhibit Option, Finish

(See Steps 1-6 in the GenBridge™ section)

Legacy Family Tree™

Import Considerations

As of this printing, Legacy Family Tree™ continues to be a "work-in-progress" with new features and capabilities added from time-to-time. On occasion, a new feature may require Legacy's file structure to be reorganized. When this occurs GenBridge™ may become "out of date" with respect to Legacy until release of an update from Wholly Genes takes the new file structure into consideration. If your Legacy import fails, or if it appears that some data is missing or out of place, it may be because of an updated Legacy file structure. Check for a TMG v5.x update to ensure that you are running the most current version.

The Import Wizard

To import a Legacy data set or Legacy Backup:

Steps 1-6: Welcome, Import from, Import to, Tag Type Options, External Exhibit Option, Finish

(See Steps 1-6 in the GenBridge™ section)

Personal Ancestral File®

The Import Wizard

To import a Personal Ancestral File® data set or Personal Ancestral File® Backup:

Steps 1-3: Welcome, Import from, Import to

(See Steps 1-3 in the GenBridge™ section)

Step 4: PAF options *(see Figure 3-12)*

Interpret tagged notes

Check this option if you want properly formatted tagged notes to be imported into the memo field of the appropriate tag.

Import empty custom events

Check this option if you want to import custom events for which there is no detail.

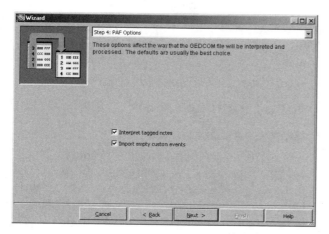

Figure 3-12: Import Wizard, PAF Options

Step 5: Tag Type options

(See Step 5 in the GenBridge™ section)

Step 6: Finish

(See Step 6 in the GenBridge™ section)

The Roots Family of Products

Import Considerations

For the purpose of this section, the Roots Family of products includes Family Gathering®, Roots IV™, Roots V™, Ultimate Family Tree®, Visual Roots™ and the backup file formats for each. GenBridge™ does not support a direct import of Roots III™ data to TMG v5.x. Use GEDCOM instead. Please note that *regardless of which Roots Family product you select, the TMG v5.x Import Wizard Options screens will all reflect Ultimate Family Tree®.*

Ultimate Family Tree® (UFT) and its predecessors incorporate several advanced features for storing data that is not supported by GEDCOM. UFT users who take advantage of those features risk substantial data loss when transferring data to other applications via GEDCOM, including that method of transfer into TMG v5.x. Using GenBridge™ technology instead will maximize flexibility to import UFT data and minimize data loss.

See the FAQ section on the Wholly Genes web site (*www.whollygenes.com*) for a comprehensive comparison chart/white paper on *Transferring data from UFT with GEDCOM and GenBridge™*

The Import Wizard

To import a data set from one of the Roots Family of products or Backup:

Steps 1-3: Welcome, Import from, Import to

(See Steps 1-3 in the GenBridge™ section)

Step 4: Ultimate Family Tree® Import Option I *(see Figure 3-13)*

The options on this screen affect the way that the Roots Family file will be interpreted and processed by GenBridge™. The defaults are usually the best choice.

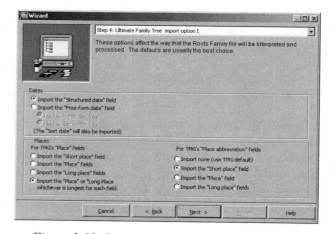

Figure 3-13: Import Wizard, UFT Import Option I

Dates
Import the "Structured date" field

Import the "Free-form date" field

Read as month day year
Read as day month year

The "Sort date" will also be imported

Places
For TMG's "Place" fields
Import the "Short place" field
Import the "Place" fields
Import the "Long place" fields
Import the "Place" or "Long place" whichever is longest for each field

For TMG's "Place abbreviation" fields
> Import none (use TMG default)
> Import the "Short place" field
> Import the "Place" field
> Import the "Long place" field

Click [Next] to continue.

Step 5: Ultimate Family Tree® Import Option II
(see Figure 3-14)

Individual Research Notes can be imported in one of three ways:

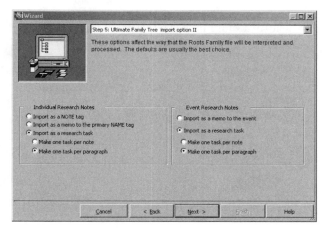

Figure 3-14: Import Wizard, UFT Import Option II

Import as a NOTE tag

Import as a memo to the primary NAME tag

Import as a research task to take full advantage of the advanced features of the Research Log. If you select this option, you may

> Make one task per note, or

> Make one task per paragraph.

Individual Event Notes can be imported in one of two ways:
> Import as a memo to the event.

> Import as a research task to take full advantage of the advanced features of the Research Log. If you select this option, you may

>> Make one task per note, or

>> Make one task per paragraph.

Click [Next] to continue.

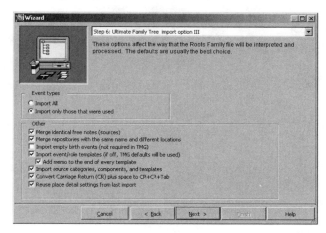

Figure 3-15: Import Wizard, UFT Import Option III

Step 6: Ultimate Family Tree® Import Option III *(see Figure 3-15)*

Event types

You have a choice to either,

> Import all tags, or

> Import only those tags that were used

Other

Additional import options include:
> Merge identical free notes (sources)

> Merge repositories with the same name and different locations

> Import empty birth events (not required in TMG)

> Import event/roll templates (if off, TMG defaults will be used)

>> Add memo to the end of every template

> Import source categories, components, and templates

> Convert carriage return (CR) plus space to CR+CR+Tab

> Reuse place settings detail from last import

Click [Next] to continue.

Step 7: Tag Type Options

(See Step 4 in the GenBridge™ section)

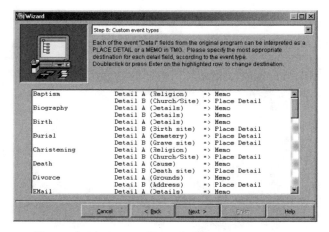

Figure 3-16: Import Wizard, Custom Event Types

Step 8: Custom Event Types *(see Figure 3-16)*

Each of the event "Detail" fields from the original Roots Family file can be interpreted as a Place Detail or Memo in TMG. The Import Wizard provides the control to specify the most appropriate destination for each detail field, according to the event type. Double-click, or press <Enter> on the highlighted row to change the destination.

Click [Next] to continue.

Step 9: Finish

(See Step 6 in the GenBridge™ section).

Family Origins® is a trademark of Parsons Technology, Inc.

Family Gathering® is a registered trademark of Palladium Interactive, Inc.

Family Tree Maker® is a registered trademarks of Broderbund Software, Inc.

Ultimate Family Tree® is a registered trademark of Mattel, Inc.

Generations™, Roots IV™, Roots V™, and Visual Roots™ are all trademarks of Genealogy.com.

Personal Ancestral File® is a registered trademark of the Corporation of the President of the Church of Jesus Christ of Latter-Day Saints.

Legacy Family Tree™ is a trademark of Millennia Corp.

Reunion® is a registered trademark of All-Night Media, Inc.

Macintosh® is a registered trademark of Apple Corp.

Chapter 4 – Customizing the Program

By Dorothy Turner

The Master Genealogist™ offers various ways for you to customize the program. Most are of a personal preference regarding data/screen displays. Others will have a significant effect on your data and will be noted where applicable.

This chapter will discuss the default options as well as suggested options for first-time users. As you feel more comfortable with the initial setting you should take a look at the various other options and try them to see how they affect the program.

Customizing TMG begins the first time you run the program (see *Figure 4-1*). It is advisable for new users to choose the "Beginner" option. This can always be changed later as stated on the bottom of the window.

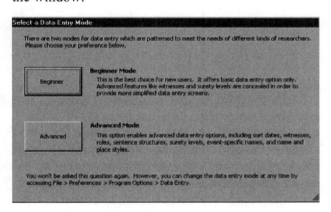

Figure 4-1: Select a Data Entry Mode

The four major area of customizing TMG that will be covered in this chapter are:
1. Preferences
2. Toolbar Customization
3. Screen Layouts
4. Other Info Box

Also language customization will be briefly discussed.

1. Preferences (see Figure 4-2)

This is the first place you may want to visit before bringing your data into TMG. Here you will find the options for the display of your data, the format for data entry, and many other useful options.

Note: You will need to have a project (such as SAMPLE open when setting your preferences.

There are two main sections to Preferences: **Program Options** and **Current Project Options**.

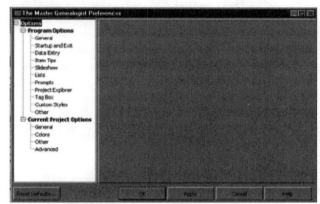

Figure 4-2: Preferences

The **Program Options** selections are passed on from one project to another and affect any new projects opened or imported. Also the settings are kept is the file APP.INI. Keeping a backup copy of this file is highly recommended.

The **Current Project Options** affects the project that is currently open. These options are saved with the project at the time of backup.

Don't worry about making choices that you find you don't like. The defaults can be reset for either the Program Options or the Current Project Options. Or both can be reset by clicking on the Reset Defaults… button at the bottom left of the Preferences window.

To save the selections you make, click on Apply, then OK or just click on OK to return to the main program. If you wish, you can always select the Cancel button and return to the main program without saving the changes.

The old saying "all roads lead to Rome" can be said about Preferences. The window is easily accessible by right clicking on any object in the Layout windows.

Program Options

General (see *Figure 4-3*)

This window has options for navigation aids as well as data display and helpful prompts.

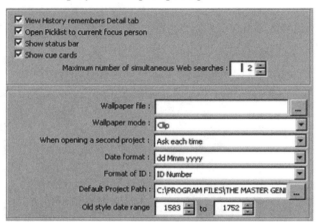

Figure 4-3: Program Options General Window

View History remembers Detail tab

If this item is checked, the view (Person, Family, or Tree) is given after the name of the person (see *Figure 4-4*). If the option is not selected, the display will not include the view (see *Figure 4-5*).

Figure 4-4: View History with Detail tab

Open Picklist to current Focus person

The Picklist will open to the person who is currently the subject or focus person.

Show status bar

If this option is selected, the window's status bar will be displayed at the bottom of the screen (above the Windows™ Taskbar).

Figure 4-5: View History without View tab

Show Cue Cards

When this is selected, a Cue Card window will pop open when executing functions for the first time on different screens. The Cue Card displays helpful information about the function such as "What is the Purpose of this window". *Figure 4-6* is the cue card for Preferences.

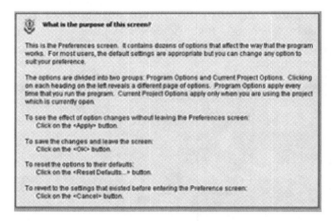

Figure 4-6: Cue Card

Maximum number of simultaneous Web searches

You may enter a number between 1 and 99. The default here is 10.

Note: If you have a dial-up connection to the Internet, it is suggested that you keep the number small. Also take into consideration your computer resources (amount of RAM, etc.).

Wallpaper File

Here you may select an image to be displayed in the background window. It is recommended that you use a jpeg, bitmap, or gif image.

Wallpaper Mode

This instructs TMG how the wallpaper file will be displayed. Of course, this will be your personal preference. Since this is a Windows™ function there are four typical choices: clip, stretch, stretch isometric, or tile.

When opening a second project

There are three options:
1. Close the current project
2. Keep both projects open
3. Ask each time

Note: Before choosing Option 2, take into consideration your system resources. Option 3 could become a nuisance if you open other projects often.

Date format

Here is where you make you selection of the way date information is entered and displayed. This has no effect on the way the information is stored, therefore this may be changed at any time. The default selection is "dd Mmm yyyy."

Formats offered:

A value entered in:	Will be displayed as:
mm/dd/yyyy	04/20/2002
yyyy.mm.dd	2002.04.20
dd/mm/yyyy	20/04/2002
dd.mm.yyyy	20.04.2002
dd-mm-yyyy	20-04-2002
Mmm dd,yyyy	Apr 04,2002
MMM dd,yyyy	APR 04,2002
dd Mmm yyyy	20 Apr 2002
dd MMM yyyy	20 APR 2002

Format of ID

You have the choice of displaying the person's ID number next to their name or the Reference Number or both separated by a comma.

An example of the Both option is:
Frank Alexander (1, S08)

Default Project Path

This is the path of the folder where all projects will be created and stored unless otherwise chosen at the time of import. The default path is:

C:\PROGRAM FILES\THE MASTER GENEALOGIST\PROJECTS

Old Style Date Range

The default for Old Style dates is 1583-1752, the date span over which the Gregorian calendar was adopted for England and her colonies. This can be used for other countries also. You can change these dates by dialing the dates you want to use.

Note: You might want to change this if much of your research is in countries that changed to New Style dates at a time other than the default.

Startup and Exit (*see Figure 4-7*)

During Startup

Options that can be selected are:
- Show Welcome Window
- Show Tips and Hints

Both of these are useful for new users. As you become more proficient with TMG you may want to de-select them.
- Length of Splash Screen

The Splash Screen is TMG's information window displaying the user name, e-mail address, and serial number as well as which version is installed. The default is 4 seconds and may be set from 1 to 99 seconds.
- Check the web site for updates every NNN days.

This will automatically check to see if an update to TMG has been released. If there has been an update, it will download it and apply it. You can disable this by selecting zero days. You may then check for updates via Help > Check for an update.

Note: LAN users will need to verify their proxy settings (see your system administrator) by clicking on the "Advanced" button at the time you check for an update. Also, it is recommended that those AOL users who have a problem when downloading an upgrade use Internet Explorer instead of the AOL browser.

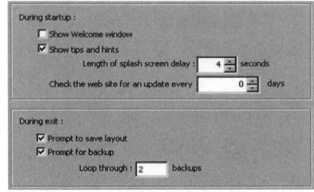

Figure 4-7: Startup and Exit

During Exit
- Prompt to save layout

If you design your own layouts, this option should be selected to remind you to save a changed layout when exiting TMG.

- Prompt for Backup
  o Loop through NNNNN backups

You can set the number of separate backup volumes. TMG will number them through the number you select, then it will start numbering again starting with number one.

It is a good ides to have at least five or six backups in case you need to restore your project from a particular date. It is highly recommended that backups be made on other media than your hard drive (see *Current Project Options > Advanced tab*).

Data Entry (see *Figure 4-8*)

Data Entry Mode

When you first opened TMG after installation, you were prompted to select which mode you wanted for data entry. If you chose Beginner mode, this is where you can change to the Advanced mode.

With the selection of Advanced you can customize the Place Labels and Name Labels. Both have the following options:
- Disable
- Enable
- Available only with Mouse

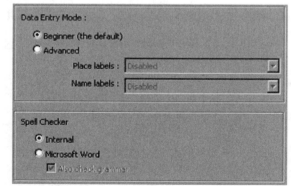

Figure 4-8: Data Entry Mode

When enabled a drop down menu will appear for each such Label allowing you to select your customized choices for name/place labels as you tab from one name/place to another. The third option may be a better choice if you want to have access to the label field and tab through the data fields without tabbing into the labels.

Unless you have customized name/place labels, it is best to choose the Disable option. Creation of customized name/place labels is covered in *Chapter 5, Customizing the Data*.

Spell Checker

These radio buttons allow you to select either the Internal TMG dictionary or to use Microsoft Word with the added option to also check the grammar.

The Microsoft Word selection may be your best choice if you have it installed and if you have made additions to that dictionary.

Item Tips (*Figure 4-9*)

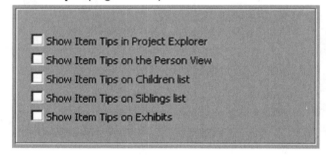

Figure 4-9: Item Tips

In TMG, there are five areas that you can select to display Item Tips. Item Tips is similar to Tool Tips in that when the mouse cursor hovers over a data field a small box containing the information in the field appears. This is very helpful when the columns are narrow and you cannot see the complete information.

Figure 4-10 shows how a Date column Item Tip would appear while *Figure 4-11* is an example of the Memo field Item Tip. Depending on the length of the Memo field, all of the Memo field data may not appear in the Item Tip.

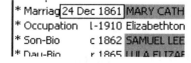

Figure 4-10: Date Column Item Tip

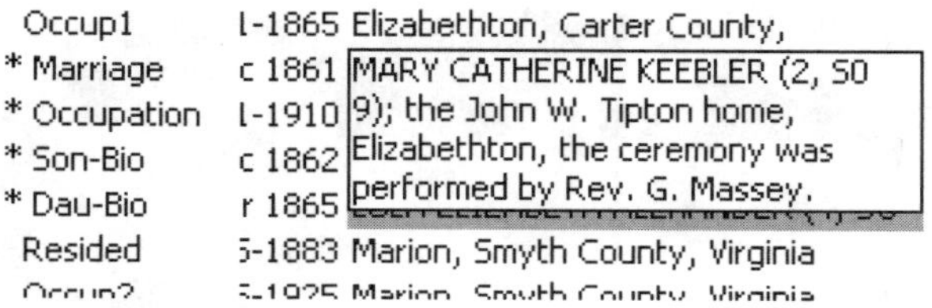

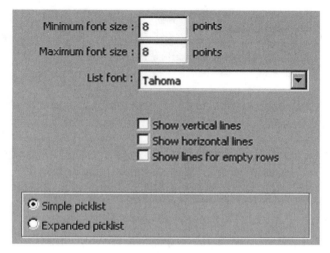

Figure 4-11: Memo Field Item Tip

The Person View and the Project Explorer are good to have selected especially when verifying information.

Slideshow *(see Figure 4-12)*

The default options for "PLAY" in the Slideshow Manager are set here. The system defaults are Self-running, Full Screen, and Effects. See *Chapter 12, Multimedia* for further details.

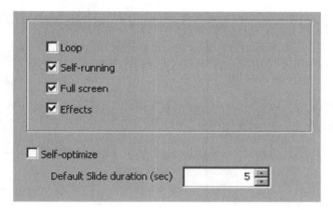

Figure 4-12:Slideshow

If you have limited RAM, you should leave the Self-Optimize option unselected and run Optimize occasionally to clean up the Slideshow Manager.

Lists *(see Figure 4-13)*

The display options regarding the font as well as the minimum and maximum font size for the Detail, Children, Sibling, and Flag windows of TMG may be selected here.

The selections to display lines are as follows:
- Show vertical lines
- Show horizontal lines
- Show lines for empty rows

Figure 4-13: Lists

When all three options are selected, the display will look like a spreadsheet that may be easier to read for some.

Also you may choose which type of Picklist you prefer: Simple or Expanded. This again is personal preference. The Expanded Picklist gives you more options but can also reduce the performance of TMG due to lack of system resources, especially RAM. The Simple Picklist, which cannot be changed, is shown in *Figure 4-14*.

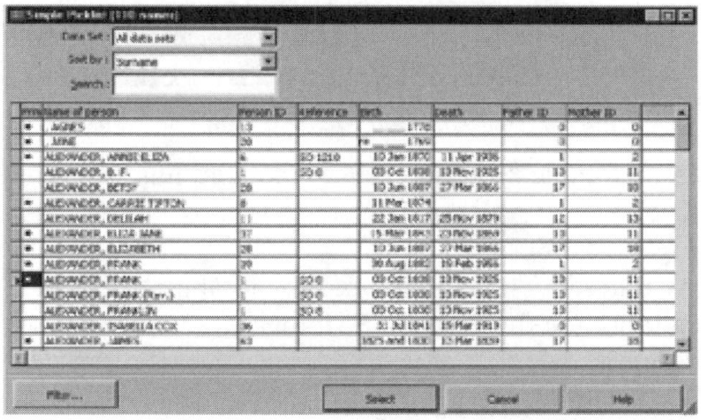

Figure 4-14: Simple Picklist

On the other hand, the Expanded Picklist can be customized. *Figure 4-15* shows columns to the left and the details of the Focus person on the right. In addition, you may select which events (tags) are to be displayed by clicking on the Options button.

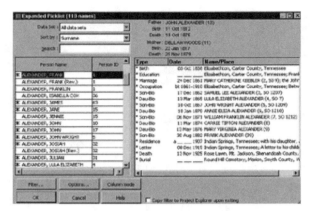

Figure 4-15: Expanded Picklist, Event Mode

Or you can have the Expanded Picklist display in columns similar to the Simple Picklist by clicking on the Column Mode button (see *Figure 4-16*).

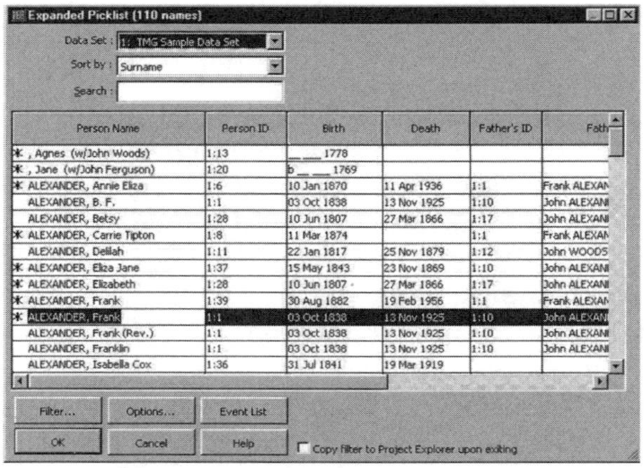

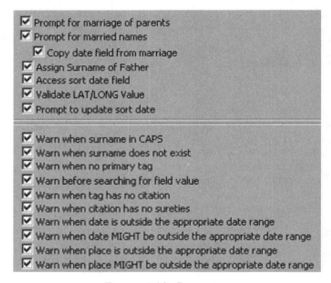

Figure 4-16:Expanded Picklist, Column Mode

In this mode, you may select the columns you wish to display by clicking on the Options button (see *Figure 4-17*).

Also here, you may choose how to apply the accent settings for the Father's, Mother's, and/or Spouses column.

Prompts *(see Figure 4-18)*

Prompts can helps you when entering/saving data. All the options here are selected by default. It is recommended that you look through them and de-select the ones that you feel will not serve you best.

The following options are only effective if you have selected the Advanced mode during Startup or in the Data Entry tab above:
- Access sort date field
- Prompt to update sort date.

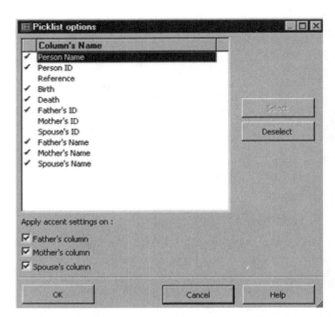

Figure 4-17:Expanded Picklist, Columns Options

If you chose Beginner mode during Startup or in the Data Entry tab above then all options will apply if selected.

Figure 4-18: Prompts

The following options are ones at which you might wish to take an extra look:

Validate LAT/LONG value

Depending on the availability of system resources for your computer, selecting this option can be time consuming. Also, if Lat/Long coordinate data is not being entered, or if British Ordnance Map coordinates are to be entered, then this should be deselected.

<u>Warn when date MIGHT be outside the appropriate date range</u>

When modifiers such as after, before, circa, between, and from-to are used in the date field they can cause a date to fall outside the appropriate date range.

<u>Warn when place is outside the appropriate date range</u>

For this option to be applied, you must have entered a "start year" and "end year" for a place on the Master Place List. See *Chapter 5, Customizing* the Data for more on the Master Place List.

<u>Warn when place MIGHT be outside of the appropriate date range</u>

This is also applicable to the "start year" and "end year" fields noted above. Otherwise see the earlier comment on when the date might be outside of the appropriate date range.

Project Explorer *(see Figure 4-19)*

Display settings for the Project Explorer window such as font, font size, background, and Identifying Primary names with **bold** or an asterisk "*".

Other available settings are:
- Display locks
- Multiline text
- Display ID Numbers

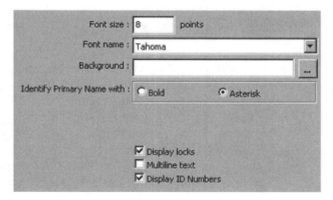

Figure 4-19: Project Explorer

When working with more than one data set in a project, Display Locks and Display ID Numbers can be very helpful.

The fonts settings here will also affect the Focus Group and Preference windows.

Tag Box *(see Figure 4-20)*

This is where you will select the display options for the tag box for the Focus Person in the Details window.

Figure 4-20:Tag Box

The options below preceeded by an asterisk "*"are recommended for first time users.

<u>Number of rows per tag</u>

Depending on the resolution of your monitor, you may want to display more than one row for each tag. This is good if you have events with long-name places.

<u>Undated tags sorted</u>

Tags without a date can be sorted at the:
- *Top
- Bottom
- None (not sorted)

<u>Name tags sorted</u>

Name tags can be sorted at the:
- *Top
- Bottom
- Or by Sort Date

<u>Identify primary event with **Bold** or asterisk "*"</u>

I find the asterisk "*" easy to recognize and it is also the symbol that is used in the Toolbar to indicate an item is primary.

Show only basic events

The basic events are birth, marriage, death, and burial.

*Show children

Show witnessed events

This will display events that the subject witnessed such as a bridesmaid in a wedding.

*Show non-primary events

Show excluded data

*Show Date instead of Sort Date

Show Surety column

Show History Events for Unlinked People

This option will show History events for people who are not linked to them. When it is selected you will be given a Warning message saying this option may have a negative impact on system performance asking are you sure.

*Show Age column

This is the age of the subject at the time the event took place.

Show Timelines with color

Select the text and background color of Timeline events.

*Enter key accesses the Tag Entry screen

Pressing the [Enter] key while the cursor is on a tag in the Tag Box causes the Tag Entry screen to open.

Custom Styles (see Figure 4-21)

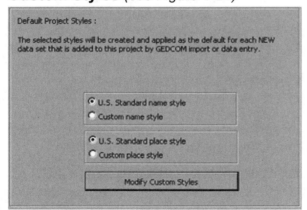

Figure 4-21:Custom Styles

The default styles for each new data set that is added to this project by GEDCOM are selected

here. The U.S. Standard name/place styles cannot be modified.

A Custom place style is useful if you do not want to use the U.S. Standard. An example would be if you live in a country that doesn't have States but does have Provinces.

To make this change first select "custom place style" then click on the button, "Modify Custom Styles, the Customized Modification window will be displayed as in *Figure 4-22*.

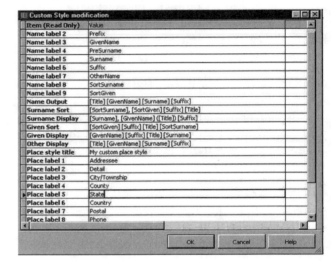

Figure 4-22: Custom Style Modification

Scroll down to Place Label 4, which is State, and change to Province then click the "OK" button at the bottom of the window. See *Chapter 5, Customizing the Data* for more information on Custom Styles.

Reports

You can have TMG prompt you regarding the output file in reports, the options are:

Never ask; do not open the file

Reports will be generated and the file created and saved and you will be returned to the main TMG screen.

*Always ask

After each report is generated, you will be asked if you want to open the file in the appropriate program — word processor, spreadsheet, etc. Note that this is the default and recommended setting.

Never ask, always open the file

After each report is generated, the file will be opened in the appropriate program.

Other *(see Figure 4-23)*

This window has the option to change the font size for the Family View and Tree View. Also, you may set the color and font for Merge Candidates.

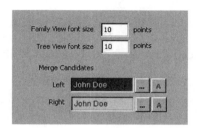

Figure 4-23: Program Options, Other

Current Project Options

General *(see Figure 4-24)*

This displays information for the path of the current project and the date that it was created.

Also this is the place to enter the Researcher's Information. This information can be printed on the reports.

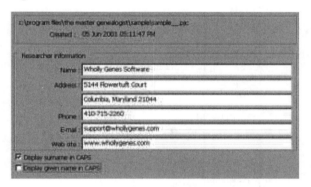

Figure 4-24: Current Project Options, General

Check boxes for:
- Display surname in CAPS
- Display given name in CAPS

This is for display only on the different views. When it comes to reports you will also have a choice.

Note: When entering data it is best to enter your names in mixed case like, John Doe. Using this and report options, you may display of print names in caps or otherwise emphasize them.

Colors *(see Figure 4-25)*

These are settings for the background [...] and text [A] colors for Names and Witnessed events displayed on the different views.

Figure 4-25: Current Project Options, Colors

Other *(see Figure 4-26)*

Source Categories

You have a choice of the following:
- as drawn from "Evidence" (E. S. Mills)
- as drawn from "Cite Your Sources" (R. S. Lackey)
- Custom

The first two options above refer to citation style manuals and their suggested models. See *Chapter 7, Sources* for further information on Sources and Source Categories. The third option allows you to create your own Source Types usually starting from one of the other two.

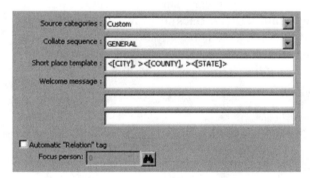

Figure 4-26:Current Project Options, Other

Collate sequence

This is the order in which letters of your chosen alphabet will appear in lists. Changes in the collating sequence are necessary to properly sort diacritics, umlauts, etc. Your choices are: Dutch, General, German, Iceland, Machine, NORDAN, Spanish, SWEFIN, and UNIQWT. If you are using English, you need not change anything. GENERAL applies to English and all other languages not listed. Note: After you change the collate sequence, it is necessary to re-index the project.

Short Place Template

This is an additional way of referring to places. It does not include all of the place fields and is used primarily in charts and other places where the entire set of place fields will not fit. The default is [CITY], [COUNTY], [STATE] *(see Chapter 5, Customizing the Data)*.

Welcome Message

You can enter three lines of data; this data will be displayed at time of startup of TMG with an "OK" box to be clicked before continuing. This is not to be confused with the Splash Screen option as seen on *Figure 4-7* regarding Startup and Exit Options.

Automatic Relation Tag

The first tag in the Person View will identify the blood relationship of each person in the data set to the target person. It will also include adoptive or foster relationships if the relationship between parent and child is primary. The default for this feature is OFF, and the Focus ID is 0 (zero).

NOTE: Using this feature can reduce performance if you have a large project.

Advanced *(see Figure 4-27)*

This is where you can change your default paths for the Exhibit Folder, Backups, Timelines, GEDCOM, and Reports. To change any of them, you can either type in the path or click on the [...] button which will open the Select Folder window.

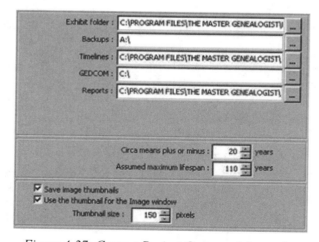

Figure 4-27: Current Project Options, Advanced

In addition to folder settings, you can also adjust the number of years for the following:
- Circa means plus or minus

The default is 20.
- Assumed maximum life span
The number of years that the program assumes the maximum life span of a person if no death event is included. The default is 110.

Save image thumbnails

TMG allows exhibits to be saved as thumbnails by selecting this option. This will increase performance when working with the Exhibit Log.

Use the thumbnail for the Image window

This allows you to select the pixel size of the display for the thumbnail.
Note: Choosing these last two options for the first time can be time consuming depending on how many exhibits you currently have.

2. Customizing the Toolbar

As with most Windows™ programs you can customize the toolbar to your liking and the same can be said about TMG. The main toolbar contains groups with related items.

The default groups and their contents (each shown left to right) are:

Standard *(see Figure 4-28)*

Figure 4-28: Standard Toolbar

- Open project
- Find Person by ID
- Picklist of People
- Last Viewed Person
- Add New Person
- Quick Search on the Web
- Research Log
- Exhibit Log

Layout *(see Figure 4-29)*

Figure 4-29: Layout Toolbar

- Project Explorer window
- Details window
- Flags window
- Children window

- Sibling window
- Image
- Focus Group
- Save Custom Layout

Tag Box *(see Figure 4-30)*

Figure 4-30: Tag Box Toolbar

- Add tag
- Delete tag
- Toggle Primary mark on current tag
- Filter for tags of this type
        (that belong to the same tag group)
- Filter for Primary events
- Toggle Timelines

Other available Toolbars are:

Easy Search *(see Figure 4-31)*

Figure 4-31:Easy Search Toolbar

Clicking on any of the letters will take you to the first person that has the surname that begins with the letter clicked on for all windows except Project Explorer. If the Project Explorer is linked to the other windows then the focus of the Project Explorer will also change to this person.

Bookmark *(see Figure 4-32)*

Figure 4-32:Bookmark Toolbar

- Bookmark current person
- Open Bookmark Manager
  (This allows you to edit the bookmarks)
- Clicking on the down arrow key allows you to access the drop-down list of people that have been bookmarked.

Note: This is an excellent navigational tool.

Reporting *(see Figure 4-33)*

Figure 4-33: Reporting Toolbar

- Individual Narrative preview
- Individual Narrative Preview with sources

- List of source preview
- Create a Fan Chart
- Create Descendant Chart
- Create Ancestor Chart
- Create Hourglass Chart

The first three reports noted above will be displayed to the screen for the Focus Person. Selecting one of the charts will bring up the Report Definition Screen for that particular chart.

Text Editing *(see Figure 4-34)*

- Undo last editing
- Redo last editing
- Cut selected text
- Copy selected text
- Paste text from clipboard
- Spellchecker
- List field values
- Repeat field values
- List recent field values

Figure 4-34: Text Editing Toolbar

Custom

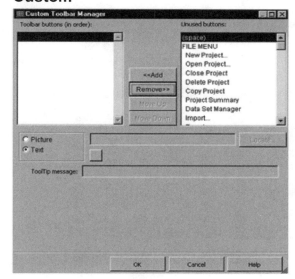

Figure 4-35: Custom Toolbar Manager

The Custom toolbar allows you to create a toolbar of your favorite shortcuts. You can use it along with the standards or replace the standards with yours.

If you wish to create or modify a custom toolbar, click on the **View > Toolbars > Customize** option of the **Main Menu**. The Custom Toolbar Manager (*see Figure 4-35*) will be displayed.

Let's create a custom toolbar with buttons for the Master Source List (MSL), Master Place List (MPL) and the Master Repository List (MRL), see *Figure 4-36*.

Figure 4-36: Custom Toolbar

In the right panel, scroll down to the Tools Menu section, select Master Source List, and click on Add, in the middle of the window, to move this to the left panel. Now change the text to MSL. Finish up by selecting the other two (Master Repository List and Master Place List) in the same way and edit appropriately. The window should look like *Figure 4-37*.

You may prefer to use a picture (icon) instead of text. If so, click on the **Picture** option and click on the [Locate] button to the right of the text field to browse for the desired file.

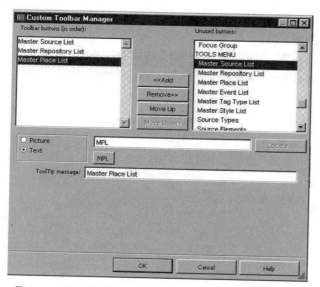

Figure 4-37: Toolbar Manager with Custom Toolbar

Click on OK. Note you may be prompted with a question: "The custom toolbar is not active, would you like to activate it now?" Answer Yes to see the results as in *Figure 4-38* below (to the right and under the Help menu option).

*Figure 4-38: **Main Menu** with Toolbars and Custom Toolbar*

3. Screen Layouts

With TMG you can create different screen layouts in addition to the default standard shown in *Figure 4-39*.

Windows that are available for the layout can be found under the **Window** menu item and they are:

- Project Explorer
- Details
- Flags
- Children
- Siblings
- Image
- Focus Group

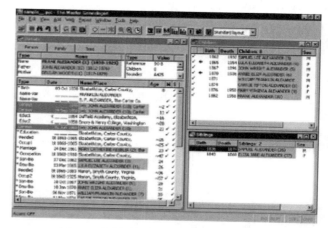

Figure 4-39:Default Standard Layout

To create a new Layout I would recommend closing all open windows leaving you with an empty screen. Before you start adding windows you may want to consider what kind of work you will be doing. Maybe you will be starting a new project and hand entering all your data. A layout that contains the following windows might by helpful:

- Details
- Flags
- Siblings
- Children

Open all four windows, then resize and organize them to fill up the screen in a way that suits your needs.

Since the toolbar is part of the Layout you might want to choose the tools that will be useful. I suggest:

- Standard
- Layout
- Tag Box
- Text Editing
- Custom (the one that we just created)

Once you have the Layout to your liking you can save it by **View > Layouts > Manage Layouts**. The Layout Manager window will open (see *Figure 4-40*).

Enter a Layout name, such as Data Entry. You may also want to add a comment telling more about the layout. Then click the Save button.

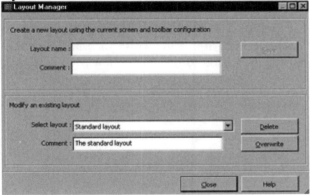

Figure 4-40: Layout Manager

Now when you click on View, Layout you will find the Data Entry layout that you just created.

Your customized layout should be similar to the one in *Figure 4-41* on the next page.

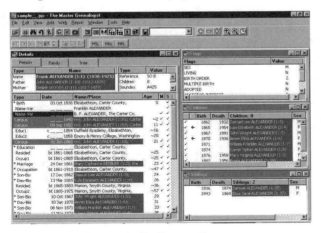

Figure 4-41: Custom Layout

4. Other Info Box

The Other info box is located in the upper right corner of the Details window on the Person View. You can customize this box to include or exclude these fields: Reference (number), Children (count), Soundex, Tag count, Age (at death), and Last edited (date) as well as their order and height.

To edit the 'Other info' box on the Person View:
Right-click on the box and select Customize 'Other info' box. Fields can be customized as follows:

1. Enabled/Disabled by double clicking on the check mark or highlighting and choosing the appropriate [Enable] or [Disable] button.
2. Order by highlighting the item and choosing the appropriate "Move up" or "Move down" button.
3. In addition to the above, the length of the Reference field can be altered by highlighting and choosing the "Customize" button. You need to be aware that while you can increase the length of the Reference field up to 250 characters, you may not be able to see all of the field due to screen space.

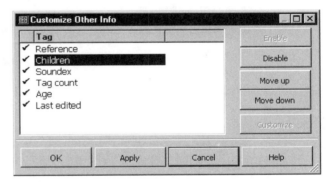

Figure 4-42: Customize Other Info

To save the changes and exit the window, click on [Okay].

Click on the [Apply] button see how the change(s) will appear in the Other Info box without closing the window.

Click on [Cancel] to exit without making any changes or to discard the changes that you have made.

Language

TMG has the capability of displaying the Menus as well as reports in another language besides English.

The following languages are included in TMG: French German, Spanish, Norwegian, Norwegian2, Dutch, Finnish, Danish, and Italian.
The English language cannot be changed but there is an English2 language that you can modify.
Also, you can create other languages by choosing File, Language, and Customize.

When installing TMG you will have the option to choose to install the Language feature. It is not automatically installed until you select it.

You should be aware that when upgrading to a newer version, you will be warned about overwriting the language files. So if you have modified a language, you may not want to allow the upgrade to overwrite your modifications.

Final Note

As noted through the chapter your system resources especially the amount of RAM and the speed (mhz) of your computer will play an important role in selecting the preferences within TMG5.

You may also want to run **Performance Recommendations**. This option is located under File > Maintenance from the **Main Menu**. This option will analyze your current project and your system making recommendations that may result in improved program performance.

Also, you will find **Reindex**, **Optimize**, and **Validate File Integrity** listed there, all of which may help in performance and prevent problems with your project.

The **Reindex** command rebuilds all the index files associated with the current project. This may be useful if your lists are not in correct order. The Optimize command will help to reduce the size of your files by eliminating records no longer needed. The Validate File Integrity gives you a way to check the integrity of the TMG files in the current project. It is good to run this option when you may have had a computer glitch or a power failure.

Chapter 5 – Customizing the Data
By John Cardinal

Introduction

Chapter 4 described customizing TMG's user interface to suit your needs. The focus of this chapter is customizing data to achieve particular results. Some tips and techniques will be discussed in detail in this chapter. Other, more complex techniques will be introduced in this chapter and then explained in greater detail in a subsequent chapter.

Some of the customizations described here produce effects that are similar to customizations covered in Chapter 4 in that they change the behavior of the program. An important distinction is that the customizations described in this chapter are specific to a particular project and/or data set whereas the customizations in Chapter 4 are not. Other than that exception, however, you do not have to concern yourself with the difference.

Why Customize?

How Versus Why

Intermediate users understand *how* to customize TMG. Expert users understand *why*. Both intermediates and experts alike will strive to follow sound genealogical practices and both will have a specific goal in mind. The expert, however, will also consider the abstract or more general goal. TMG is a very powerful program and there is often more than one way to achieve a certain result. Knowing the more general goal is often the best way to choose from among the available methods.

The following is my list of abstract goals. Yours may differ. I will explain mine in hopes that it will help you discover or define yours.

Consistency
Efficiency
Usability
Practicality
Cultural Suitability
Personal Suitability

Consistency

Customizations often improve consistency. Done properly, they capture the result of a thought process that yields the best or most appropriate way to achieve a result and help you easily achieve the same result in the future. Consistency only for consistency's sake is unwise,[1] whereas consistency for the purpose of conveying a particular meaning is fundamental to genealogy.

Efficiency

Any customization that improves efficiency leaves you more time to do other tasks.

Practicality

Some results can only be achieved through customization. In other cases, a customization is the easiest way to achieve a result.

Cultural Suitability

TMG has many features that can be customized to produce culturally appropriate results.

Personal Suitability

If you want TMG to work a particular way for no reason other than it makes you happy, that's a great reason for a customization!

Customization Basics

One of the most basic questions is, how much customization is too much? When should you customize, and when should you run away and return to customize another day? In general, you should review the standard ways of doing things to make sure that you are not reinventing the wheel. Take advantage of the knowledge of TMG's designers and beta testers!

Once you decide that a customization is the best way to achieve the goals, you should test the

---

[1] Consistency is often attacked using a partial quote from Ralph Waldo Emerson, "consistency is the hobgoblin of little minds". His sentence actually began, "A foolish consistency is the hobgoblin of little minds," and the missing word "foolish" changes the meaning considerably.

various possibilities. Testing helps you hone your "how" skills, so that the decision whether to customize is not based solely on the time it will take to implement the customization. Easy customizations are not necessarily better. More importantly, though, testing will help you determine whether using the customization will improve your results, and/or make you more efficient, and so on. When there are multiple ways to achieve a result, testing will help you pick the option that fits your needs the best.

Most experienced users have a test project that they use to experiment. If you do not have one, make one. A good approach is to create a test project from a subset of people in your main project. I suggest you choose a subset that includes familiar people that are a focus area for your research. Your test data should include people with many tags, rich source and citation data, etc.

Many customizations are only available when Data Entry Mode is set to Advanced. Use the **File > Preferences** command and then select Data Entry under Program Options to change Data Entry Mode.

Some customizations are available via right-click menus, for example, you can right-click on a Place Label on the Tag Entry screen to temporarily enable or disable the Place Label pull-down menu.

Custom Flags

TMG provides a set of one-character fields called Flags that the program uses to codify information about a person or classify individuals into categories. You can define Custom Flags to augment the set of standard flags provided by TMG. You use the **File > Flag Manager** command to manage existing Flags or add new Custom Flags. If you need to classify individuals into categories, a Custom Flag is the most efficient method to do so, and for that reason, the Accent feature and reports provide robust support for Flags. Some of the capabilities of both the Accent feature and the reports are only possible through the use of Flags.

Focus Groups are another way to classify individuals into groups. See *Chapter 11, Filtering and Sorting*, it describes Focus Groups in detail.
In order to decide whether a Custom Flag is the proper way to record a piece of information, you should consider the difference between Flags and Tags. A Tag is a collection of data fields describing a name, event, or relationship, whereas a Flag is a one-character field. If you need to record more than one character of data, then a Custom Flag is not appropriate. If you want to include the data in a narrative type report, a Custom Flag is not appropriate because Flags do not have an associated sentence.

Common Uses for Flags

As mentioned above, the Accent feature and reports make good use of Custom Flags. See *Chapter 10, Customizing Reports*, and *Chapter 11, Filtering and Sorting*.

- Many TMG users define Custom Flags to track the progress of research or cleanup tasks. For each task, you define a Custom Flag with the values "N" and "Y", where the default is N. When you complete the task for a specific person, you change the flag to Y. Some users set the default so "Y" for cleanup tasks because all new additions to the data set will be clean, i.e., they will be entered properly and will not need further review. If you choose that approach, use a List of People report to set the flag to "N" for all existing people before manually setting the flag for a particular person.

- Custom Flags may be used to divide a single TMG data set into logically distinct groups such as ancestor branches. If you use a Custom Flag for each group, a single person can easily be a member of two or more groups. If you use a single flag, a person may only be a member of a single group because only a single value may be stored in a flag. If group membership is mutually exclusive, a single flag is appropriate.

- A Custom Flag may be appropriate to record a characteristic that is present in multiple people, but is not associated with a particular time and place. For example, the presence or absence of an inherited health condition is a good candidate for a Custom Flag. On the other hand, the first appearance in a particular person of the symptoms associated with the health condition is an example of data that should be stored in an Event Tag.

- External tools, such as my TMG companion programs, use Flags to identify a subset of the data set. This allows the user to control the external program using the familiar and powerful Focus criteria provided by TMG.

Custom Tags

Tags are used to record information about the events, names, and relationships associated with a person or persons in your data set. TMG includes more than 100 Standard Tags[2], and TMG also allows users to define their own Custom Tags. Custom Tags are real tags and include all the features and capabilities of Standard Tags.

Custom Tags are powerful tools that are used to achieve various goals. As a result, the benefits vary. A typical goal is to specify a sentence definition that fits a particular situation more closely than the best alternative standard tag. Such a tag improves consistency because the sentence will be the same whenever the circumstances are the same, and it improves efficiency because you do not have to enter the customized sentence each time you add the tag. Other reasons to add Custom Tags are described below in the *Common Reasons to Add Custom Tags* section.

Don't Get Tag Happy!

It happens to everyone, I'm afraid. Seduced by the power and versatility of Custom Tags, we define so many that we forget what they all do. A cure is possible, but the treatment is painful!

Seriously, before you add a Custom Tag, review the list of Standard Tags to see if a good option already exists. You may change the Standard Tag sentence, and add Roles, and that may be a good choice. If not, ask yourself approximately how many times you will use the Custom Tag. How many is enough to justify a Custom Tag? You decide.

---

[2] The Master Tag List includes all the tags defined in a project. The List of Tag Types report will also produce a list of tags. Appendix B includes a list of the Standard Tags as well as the Roles defined for those tags.

Tag Groups

When defining a new Custom Tag you must select a Tag Group. The Tag Group Summary (Table 5-1) lists the ten available Tag Groups.

Tag Group	Contents of Tags in Tag Group
Name	One principal, name of that person or name variation, date, memo, and sentence
Parent/child relationship	Two principals related by blood, memo
Birth	One principal, date, place, memo, and sentence
Death	One principal, date, place, memo, and sentence
Burial	Two principals, date, place, memo, and sentence
Marriage	Two principals, date, place, memo, and sentence
Divorce	Two principals, date, place, memo, and sentence
History	Witnesses only, date, place, memo, and sentence
Address	Two principals, date, place, memo, and sentence
Other	Two principals, date, place, memo, and sentence

Table 5-1: Tag Group Summary

Each of the groups has a fairly specific use, with the exception of Other (see the group-specific sections below). In all cases, you should be aware of that intended use before you create a Custom Tag because you cannot change the Tag Group after the tag is defined.

If you are unsure which Tag Group to use, a good approach is to decide which existing tag most closely resembles the Custom Tag you want to define and use the same Tag Group as that tag. The resemblance should be based more on the behavior associated with the tag than with the name or sentence.

Name Group Tags

A Name Group tag is used to record a name or name variation for a person. Tags in this group are limited to a single principal and you cannot add witnesses. You cannot define roles. You can customize the sentence. If a Name Group tag is primary, the sentence is ignored, as all reports have a predefined treatment for the primary name.

A common convention among TMG users is to begin the label for a Name Group tag with "Name-", e.g., "Name-Var", "Name-Marr", etc. I recommend that you follow this convention, even though the Master Tag Type List introduced in TMG Version 5.0 reduces the need for this convention by providing a means to filter the Tag Type list by Tag Group. (Use the **Tools > Master Tag Type List** command or <F4> to open the Tag Type List; use the Filter pull-down menu to restrict the list to tags in a specific Tag Group).

I will return to the topic of custom name tags in the Custom Name Styles section later in this chapter.

Parent/Child Relationship Group Tags

A Parent/Child Relationship Group Tag is used to record a blood relationship between parent and child. Tags in this group are limited to the two principals and you cannot add witnesses. You cannot define a sentence and you cannot define roles. These tags define relationships, and they affect the contents of reports such as Journal reports and Pedigrees, but they do not appear in Individual Narratives or the narrative section of other reports. Despite the availability of "Ado" (for Adopted) and other suffixes that imply a non-blood relationship, TMG treats people linked by Parent/Child Relationship tags as blood relatives for the purposes of standard genealogical reports and other generation-to-generation processing.[3]

When these tags appear in the program, such as in the Person View of the Details screen, the Label includes a prefix such as "Father-", "Dau-", etc., and a suffix of "Bio", "Ste", etc. The Label field on the Tag Type Definition screen, however, only includes the suffix. This is an important clue to how these tags work: a *single tag links the parent and child.* When it is displayed in the Person View of the parent, the parent's prefix is used, "Mother-" or "Father-". When the same tag is displayed in the Person View of the child, the child's prefix is used, "Dau-" or "Son-".

Relationship tags do not have dates. The date shown in the Person View for a relationship to a child is the primary Birth Group date of the child.

The Parent/Child Relationship Group tags supplied by the program include most if not all of the relationship types that are in common use. Many users, however, add a Custom Tag in this group with the label "Can" ("Mother-Can", "Dau-Can", etc.) meaning *candidate.* The tag is used to indicate that there is scant or questionable evidence of the relationship or possibly more evidence for an alternate relationship. The quality of the evidence regarding the relationship should also be recorded in the surety fields of the citations linked to the tag, but the "Can" suffix provides an additional, highly visible indicator of the questionable link.

Event Tags

Tags Types in the remaining groups, Birth, Marriage, Death, Burial, Divorce, History, Address, and Other, are Event tags. They have much in common, such as fields to store dates, places, memos, and custom sentences. They can be linked to witnesses, and they support roles. Most of the Custom Tags you define will be in one of the Event tag groups.

Birth, Marriage, Death, Burial, and Divorce Group Tags

Tags in the Birth, Marriage, Death, Burial and Divorce Groups represent the most commonly recorded genealogical data. When you define a Custom Tag in one of these groups, you are telling TMG that you want the tag to be treated like the other Tag Types in the group; your new tag will share the special behaviors implied by the name of the group. For example, if you define a Custom Tag in the Birth Group, TMG will use that tag to calculate a person's age relative to another tag's date if the custom tag is marked Primary.

A person can only have one primary tag in each of the Birth and Death Groups. A person can have one primary tag for each unique combination of principals in each of the Marriage, Divorce, and Burial Groups. So, person "A" can have a primary

---

[3] This topic has been debated many times by TMG users.

Marriage Group event with both spouse "B" and spouse "C".

History Group Tags

History Group tags differ from all other Tag Groups because no principals can be recorded for a History Group tag. These tags are used to link people to historical events. Being linked to such an event does not imply participation in the event, but rather, that the event had a special significance for the individual.

The History tag, or any tag in the History Group, can be used to make a one-event timeline. See the Timeline section in *Chapter 8, Concepts*.

Address Group Tags

Address Group tags are intended to record mailing addresses. Address Group tags are intended to record the *current* address of a person, whereas the Residence tag in the Other Group is intended to record *historical* addresses.

Other Group Tags

The Other Group includes all the Tag Types that do not fit into any of the previous groups. In practice, most custom event tags will be defined in this group. Unlike the other groups, there can be a tag marked primary for each tag with a unique combination of principals within a set of tags with the same Tag Type.

Common Reasons to Add Custom Tags

Adding More Specific Tags

The most common reason to add a Custom Tag is to make a tag uniquely address a specific set of circumstances that occurs frequently in your data. You can write a sentence that is appropriate—write it once and forget it—and you can assign a label that distinguishes the event from other similar events.
One of the first Custom Tags I added was a "Milit-Serv" tag. TMG's standard "Milit-Beg" and "Milit-End" tags are used for the start and end of military service, respectively, but I had many cases where the evidence only revealed that the person was a member of a certain regiment, or participated in a battle, on a particular date.

Output from the Milit-Serv tag in Table 5-2 might be "Tyler Hopewell served in the military in the Union Army at the First Battle of Bull Run on 21 July 1861 at Manassas, Virginia."

Field	Value
Label	Milit-Serv
Principal Sentence	[P] <and [PO]> served in the military <[M]> <[D]> <[L]>
Witness Sentence	[W] witnessed the military service of [P] <and [PO]> <[M]> <[D]> <[L]>

Table 5-2: Milit-Serv Tag Summary

Adding Variations to Allow Multiple Primary Tags

TMG includes an Occupation tag. Many people have multiple occupations over the course of their life, or practice their profession at multiple locations. If you enter multiple "Occupation" tags, you must set the "Events:" option to "All variations" or "All events and witnessed events" on the Tags tab of the Report Options screen. That will work under some circumstances but is not desirable when you have other non-primary tags that you do not wish to include in reports.

One solution is to add a series of Custom Tags such as Occupation2, Occupation3, etc. One tag of each Tag Type can be marked primary and they will appear in reports even when you set the "Events:" option to "Primary events" (*see Chapter 9, Controlling Narratives*).

Adding Tags to Support Data Inclusion/Exclusion and Sequencing

You may use Custom Tags to control the inclusion or exclusion of data in reports. Consider this example. TMG includes a standard Will tag. If you store the text of the will in the memo field of the Will tag, then all reports that include that tag will also include the text of the Will. That may not be desirable. It's true that you can exclude *all* memo data from the report, but that's "throwing out the baby with the bath water."

Even if you wish to include the text of the will in all reports that include the Will tag, you may not want that text to be in the chronological sequence defined by the date of the will because the text may break the flow of the narrative in an undesirable way.

Field	Value
Label	Will-Text
Principal Sentence	[PGS] will <dated [D]>:[:CR:][M]
Witness Sentence	--

Table 5-3: Will-Text Tag Summary

A flexible approach to this problem is to add a custom Will-Text tag (*see Table 5-3*). You record the date, place, and witnesses, etc. in the Will tag, but you store the text of the will in the Will-Text tag. Assign a sort date to the Will-text tag that places the text in the narrative at its optimal position. When running reports, the Will and Will-Text tags can be included or excluded independently.

I used the [PGS] (possessive given name) variable for my Will-Text tag, but you could substitute [PS] (possessive name) or [PP] (possessive pronoun) to suit your tastes. See *Chapter 6, Sentence Structures*, and *Chapter 9, Controlling Narratives*, for more details related to sentence construction.

How Come My Custom Tag Did Not Appear in a Report?

This is a frequent question in on line TMG discussion lists and forums. A likely reason is that the "Tag types:" option on the Tags tab of the Report Options window is set to Selected, but the new custom tag is not checked in the associated tag list.

Other Custom Tag Ideas

The possibilities for Custom Tags are limitless. See *Table 5-4, Custom Tag Ideas* for a list of some tags used by other TMG users.

Label (group)	Description
Land-Buy, Land-Sell (Other)	Used to show land ownership changes.
CauseDeath, COD (Other)	Used to record the cause of death as an alternative to using the memo in the Death Group event.

Label (group)	Description
Obituary and Obit-Text (Other)	Use it to record a published obituary. If desired, create an Obit-Text tag for the same reasons as described for Will-Text.
"-Alt" (various)	Some users define tags with labels that include the suffix "-Alt" (Birth-Alt, Death-Alt, etc.) to capture cases where there is conflicting evidence and they want to include the alternative in narratives, etc. They assign a sort date that makes the "-Alt" version appear immediately after the other tag that represents the more likely case. The "-Alt" sentence should include qualifying statements like "was also reported as".
CensusYYYY (Other)	If you create a custom census tag for each census year, i.e., Census1870, Census1880, etc., you can record multiple primary census events.
Liaison, Partner (Marriage or Other)	Used to capture marriage-like relationships. If you include the tag in the Marriage Group, then it will be treated exactly like a Marriage, whereas if you put it in the Other Group it will not. Perhaps you'll want one of both. See the *GEDCOM* sections of Chapter 3, *Imporing Data*, and Chapter 15, *Exporting Data*, for more details.
Research (Other)	Use it to store research notes. Start the default sentence with the double-exclusion marker "--'" if you do not want the tag to appear in reports.
Researcher (Other)	With Researcher and Researchee roles, use it to capture which genealogists are researching which ancestors.
SamePerson or Duplicate (Other)	Use it to record the possibility that two people in your data set may actually be the same person. You may or may not want this tag to print in narratives.

Label (group)	Description
Name-Std (Name)	Use it to record a standardized spelling of a name. This is primarily a research device used to add the standardized version of the spelling to the Picklist. Unlike the alternative approach of correcting the spelling in the "SortSurname" or "SortGiven" fields, this method adds an entry to the Picklist so that the person may be found using one of several names. Start the default sentence with the double-exclusion marker "--'" if you do not want the tag to appear in reports.
Picture, Photo, Image (Other)	Use it to describe a photograph or image stored as a TMG exhibit and linked to the event. You may want to add multiple Custom Tags, one each for photographs, documents, newspaper clippings, etc. With multiple tags, you can include or exclude the image exhibits by image type.

Table 5-.4: Custom Tag Ideas

GEDCOM Implications

When you define a Custom Tag, you have the option of entering a specific GEDCOM tag[4] label, or using the generic GEDCOM "EVEN" tag.

If you are making a variation of an existing TMG tag and you want it treated the same with regards to GEDCOM exports, set this option the same as the other tag. If you are familiar with the GEDCOM specification, you may know which GEDCOM tag is best suited for the data. In all other cases it is best to choose the "1 EVEN/2 TYPE" option. TMG will export the data using EVEN tags and include a TYPE tag containing the label of the Custom Tag.

If you plan to export your data via GEDCOM, perform a test to verify that the results match your expectations. GEDCOM is a problematic data transfer method and in some cases it may be difficult or impossible to transfer your data completely and accurately (*see Chapter 16, Exporting Data*).

Changing Standard Tags

In addition to defining your own Custom Tags, you have the option of changing the definition of Standard Tags. In some cases, there are subtle implications that you should consider before making the change.

The Birth, Marriage, Death, Burial, and Name-Var tags are associated with standard control-key combinations (<Ctrl>+<B>, etc.). The mapping of the key combination to these Standard Tags cannot be redefined, and no matter how you change them, they retain their basic meaning.

Standard Tags are assigned the proper GEDCOM tag, and changing those tags will change the results of importing and exporting GEDCOM data.

Roles

Roles are yet another powerful feature of TMG. Roles are used to record the specific nature of a person's participation in an event. For common events with well-known roles, such as a marriage and the members of its bridal party, assigning a role implies a set of behaviors and indicates that other relationships may exist among the various participants. Situations vary with time and culture, but those factors can be considered when the role is assigned.

Standard Tags define a limited set of Roles. You may define new Roles for Standard Tags or Custom Tags. Like Custom Tags, roles encourage consistency and efficiency. In combination with Custom Tags, roles can be used to achieve outcomes that are difficult or impossible to achieve any other way.

Without using roles, it is difficult to construct sentences that identify how participation varied from witness to witness. With roles, it's easy.

Roles also can be used to provide a sentence "library" where you can choose a specific role solely to use an alternative sentence. In those cases, the person's participation in the event does not vary but the language used to describe it does.

---

[4] GEDCOM tags are not the same as TMG tags; see the GEDCOM 5.5 Specification that is available from various sources for more information.

Chapter 6, Sentence Structures, describes the interplay between roles and sentences in detail.

The Display Witnessed Tags option and Display Roles option on the Tag Type Definition screen affect how data is displayed in the Person View and in some reports.

Role-Related Options for Principals (Table 5-5) and Label- and Role-Related Options for Witnesses (Table 5-6) show the effects and interplay between the options.

Display roles for Principals	Label:	Detail:
Checked	<label>	<role>;
Unchecked	<label>	

Table 5-5: Role-Related Options for Principals

Places

TMG has very flexible and complete storage of place data.

Place records include support for 10 different data fields; the *Field Labels and Styles* section and the *Custom Place Field Labels and Place Styles* section —both of which are later in this chapter— describe those data fields and how you can customize them.

Display witnessed tags	Display roles for Witnesses	Label:	Detail:
Using the label	Checked	<label>	<role>;
Using the label	Unchecked	<label>	(w);
As "Witness"	Checked	Witness:	<role>; <label>:
As "Witness"	Unchecked	Witness:	<label>:

Table 5-6: Label- and Role-Related Options for Witnesses

When you enter the data for a place, TMG determines whether the data represents a new place or an exact copy of an existing place. The result is that TMG has a single record for each unique place. Each place record includes the place style and the ten data fields that are set via the Tag Entry

window. TMG's place data includes four other fields that are described in Table 5-7 below.

Use the **Tools > Master Place List** command to review the list of unique places and edit the Short Place, Start Year, End Year, and Comment data associated with each unique place.

Review the Master Place List periodically to find and correct accidental inconsistencies in your place data.

Use the **File > Maintenance > Optimize** command to remove duplicate places created by editing the Master Place List.

Please note that TMG will not consolidate places unless the place records are exactly the same for both places. This includes all the place sub-fields as well as the Place Style, Short Place, Start Year, End Year, and Comment.

A technique used by many TMG users is to add the single- or double-exclusion marker to the beginning of certain place sub-fields. That avoids displaying the full place when that would be unnecessarily repetitive but retains the full data as part of the recorded evidence.

Field	Description
Short Place	Holds the rule for specifying the short version of the place data. It usually does not include all the place sub fields and can be used in charts or reports where the full version of the place will not fit or is undesirable for other reasons.
	The default is [CITY], [COUNTY], [STATE], but that can be changed for a specific project via the *Short place templat*e field on the Other tab of **File > Preferences > Current Project** Options.
Start Year, End Year	Controls place data validation. TMG will warn you when a place is used in an event and the event date falls outside the range specified in the Start Year and End Year fields.
Comment	Holds your comments about a place.

Table 5-7: Place Record Data

Field Labels and Styles

Genealogical data is filled with examples of variations in the structure and interpretation of data. Place data and name data are two prominent examples. As your research leads you back through time or across cultural boundaries, you discover that the names of place fields vary, that people didn't always have surnames, that some cultures adopted different naming structures, and so on.

TMG's Place Field Labels and Name Field Labels allow you to change the label assigned to a Place Field or Name Field. Through custom labels, the label becomes a part of the data, and provides a location to store a precise interpretation of the data. Custom field labels only affect the display of the information within TMG, but the alignment between the label and what is stored in the field makes the display more accurate. That will improve your data entry consistency and accuracy.

Place Styles and Name Styles allow further customization of the treatment of place data and name data. Both define a collection of field labels that you can easily assign to a place or name, and both allow you to change the display of the data. More details are provided in the Place- and Name-specific sections below.

I highly recommend creating styles to define a set of field labels. If you do not choose a style, and instead simply change a field label, TMG will create a style for you but it will not give the style a meaningful name.

The Master Place List (**Tools > Master Place List**) is a list of all the Place Styles and Name Styles defined in the project. Use the Master Place List to add or modify styles. You can define new field labels in the Edit Place Style window or Edit Name Style window. You can also define a new field label by right clicking on a label in the Tag Entry window.

You can set the Tag Entry screen's default Place Style or Name Style using the Data Set Manager.

Custom Place Field Labels and Place Styles

Place Fields and Place Field Labels

TMG provides ten place fields. Each place field has a standard label as well as a default label. The standard labels are the same as the historical names for the fields prior to the introduction of Place Field Labels. The default labels are the same as the standard labels unless you are using a special edition of TMG that has been customized by Wholly Genes for a particular locale.

You are not constrained to using the place fields for the same level of information as are represented by the standard place fields. For example, you could change the label of the "Temple" place field to a political subdivision such as "Ward", and place it between "Detail" and "City" in the output template.

When writing sentences for events with custom Place Field Labels, use the [L1] through [L10] place variables rather than the place variables that use the standard place names. Another sentence writing tip: if you reference a single place field directly by its variable name, that field will not be included in the value of [L].

Output Template

Place Styles support a single template that defines the place fields that are included in the output format and their sequence.

The contents of the Place Style Output template resemble a sentence. Like sentences, you may include conditional brackets and literals. Use place labels in brackets, for example, "[City]", to include a place field in the Output template.

The place fields in the Output template of the "U.S. Standard Place" style are all conditional, i.e., they are surrounded by the "<" and ">" characters. I can't think of any reason to make place field unconditional, and I believe the conditional notation is only used to provide a means to control punctuation.

Speaking of punctuation, in the Output template of the "U.S. Standard Place" style, a comma follows all the place fields except the last. You may use other punctuation when defining your own custom Place Styles.

Place Styles and Reports

The Output template is used in reports when the "Place:" option is set to "Use place styles." The Output template is ignored when the "Place:" option is set to either "Use Short Place field" or "Use selected place fields".

The Output template does not affect the display of the place data on the Person tab of the Details window.

Custom Name Field Labels and Name Styles

TMG provides nine name fields. The standard fields include GivenName, Surname and five other fields whose data would usually be included in charts and reports.

Two additional fields, SortSurname and SortGiven, are designed to hold data that is only used when names are sorted, similar to the Sort Date field in tags. You should understand the benefit of sort-specific fields before you omit them from a Name Style.

You may change the label of any field, and you may choose to change the purpose of any of the nine fields, with one exception: the indexing features of the Report Definition screen ([Options] button) only process the Surname and GivenName fields, regardless of any changes to the field labels, etc.

Before you create your own Name Field Labels or Name Styles, you should understand the intended uses of the standard fields. Standard Name Field Labels (Table 5-8) describes the standard name fields.

You may or may not agree with the descriptions in *Table 5-8*, but the beauty of TMG is that you don't have to agree. You only have to decide how you want to use the name fields, and then follow your own convention.

Label	Description
Title	The person's title, often used for inherited or honorific titles. Example: "Sir"
Prefix	Word or words that precede the given name or surname, often used for military ranks or professional titles. Examples: "General", "Dr."
GivenName	The person's given name.
PreSurname	A word or words that follow the given name but precede the surname. Example: "von" as in "Maria von Trapp". See *Using the PreSurname Field*.
Surname	The person's surname.
Suffix	Words that follow the surname, such as academic degrees and/or professional certifications. Example: "MD"
OtherName	Another name field that may be used to capture nicknames or elements of the name that do not fit in the other fields. Example: "Betty" in "Elizabeth 'Betty' Smith"
SortSurname	The surname for sorting purposes. See *Sorting Names*.
SortGiven	The given name for sorting purposes. See *Sorting Names*.

Table 5-8: Standard Name Field Labels

Name Style Templates

Many actual names have a different structure than is implied by the standard Name Field Labels. You are free to change the field labels, but more importantly, you can define Name Styles and customize the six templates that control the appearance and sort order of names. Each template defines which fields are used in a certain context and in what sequence. *Table 5-9, Name Style Templates*, describes the six templates.

The contents of Name Style templates resemble a sentence, but they are quite different. You use name labels in brackets, for example, "[Surname]", to include a name field in a template, and that is the same as the variable-reference notation in sentences. Unlike the Place Style Output template, however, Name Style templates do not support conditional brackets; name fields are always conditional.

Template	Use
Output template	Controls the appearance of the name in reports, charts, and in most TMG windows
Surname sort template	Defines the sequence of the name fields when TMG sorts names by surname, such as in the Project Explorer.
Surname display template	Controls the appearance of the name when it has been sorted using the surname sort template, such as in the Picklist or Project Explorer.
Given sort template	Defines the sequence of the name fields when TMG sorts the name by given name, such as in the Picklist or Project Explorer.
Given display template	Controls the appearance of the name when it has been sorted using the given name sort template.
Children/Sibling display template	Controls the appearance of the name in the Children and Siblings windows.

Table 5-9: Name Style Templates

Literals in Name Style templates always appear in the output, with one exception. Parentheses around a name field reference are omitted if the name field is empty.

Using the PreSurname Field

The PreSurname field is intended for words that precede the surname such as "von", "van", "dit", etc. There are cases, of course, where those words are considered part of the surname. A good indicator that the word belongs in the PreSurname field is the existence of people who have dropped the word from their names.

The U.S. Standard Name style does not include the PreSurname in any of the templates, so you need to create a custom Name Style before you will see the PreSurname in any display.

Sorting Names

Name variations are one of the more difficult problems in genealogy. As genealogists we are caught between conflicting goals: we are taught to record the data as we found it on the source, but it is difficult to find someone in an index or database when there are multiple versions of the name because of spelling variations or other cultural naming practices.

The default Name Style includes the SortSurname and SortGiven fields to help deal with that problem. The method entails storing a standardized variation of the surname and given name in the SortSurname and SortGiven fields. The Surname sort template and the Given sort template use those fields as the most significant parts of the sort key. By carefully choosing the values you store in the SortSurname field or SortGiven field, you can make names that are spelled differently appear together in a list or index.

Let's consider two examples to reveal how using the SortSurname field can help with some common problems. Along the way we'll use Custom Name Field Labels and Custom Name Styles.

Sorting Names: Dealing with Spelling Variations

The surname Millet appears in records spelled a variety of ways, including Millit, Mylit, and Mylett. Millett is very common, and may be more numerous today than Millet. If people with those names are sorted by surname, people with the same

Surname, Given
Millet, James
Millet, Joan
Millet, John
Millet, Joseph
Millett, Joan
Mylet, Jn.

Table 5-10: Sort by Surname, Given

given name but a variant of the surname will not sort together. If, in all cases, the SortSurname was set to "Millet", sorting results will improve dramatically.

Table 5-10, Sort by Surname, Given and *Table 5-11, Sort by SortSurnam, SortGiven* show the difference between sorting by Surname and GivenName versus sorting by standardized values in SortSurname and SortGiven. TMG sorts the names in bold in a more useful sequence using SortSurname and SortGiven.

Surname, Given	SortSurname, SortGiven
Millet, James	Millet, James
Millet, Joan	Millet, Joan
Millett, Joan	Millet, Joan
Millet, John	Millet, John
Mylet, Jn.	Millet, John
Millet, Joseph	Millet, Joseph

Table 5-11: Sort by SortSurname, SortGiven

Another way to record spelling variations is to enter two name tags, one with the name as specified in the source document, and one with a standardized spelling. The advantage of this approach is that both names appear in the Picklist. The disadvantage is the extra data entry involved. See the "Name-Std" tag in the *Other Custom Tag Ideas* section earlier in this chapter.

Where the spelling variation occurs may help you decide between the two methods. In the examples given in Table 5-10, the names are not in strict sequence, but the difference is small. If a SortSurname was used to sort "O'Callahan" under "Callahan", however, the large difference in position may make the sorted list harder to use.

Sorting Names: Dealing with Cultural Naming Practices

The SortSurname field also helps when dealing with difficulties caused by certain cultural naming practices. In Norway, for example, patronymic names varied by gender. A further complicating factor is that many Norwegians included a farm name after the patronymic, and if they moved, the farm name changed. The daughter of Knut Oleson could be named Anna Knutsdatter, whereas his son might be named Iver Knutson. If they lived on the

Hopland farm, they would be known as Iver Knutson Hopland and Anna Knutsdatter Hopland. If the family moved to the Botten farm, they would be known as Iver Knutson Botten and Anna Knutsdatter Botten.[5]

Here's one suggestion for how we might combine three of TMG's name-related features to record this information. First, we'll use multiple Name-Var tags; there is no satisfactory way to capture all the data with a single name record. We'll also use two Custom Name Styles with Custom Name Fields.

The two Custom Name Styles are "Patronymic" and "Farm". Each has Custom Name Field Labels like:

Style	Standard Field Label	Custom Name Field Label
Patronymic	OtherName SortSurname	Patronymic SortPatronymic
FarmName	OtherName SortSurname	Farm SortFarm

Table 5-12: Example Name Styles for Norwegian Names

In both cases, the Surname sort template would be customized as shown in *Table 5-13: Surname Sort Templates for Norwegian Name Style* on the next page.

It is also necessary to modify the display templates to include the Patronymic or Farm name.

Style	Surname Sort Template
Patronymic	[SortPatronymic] [SortGiven] [Suffix] [Title]
Farm	[SortFarmName] [Surname] [SortGiven] [Suffix] [Title]

Table 5-13: Surname Sort Templates for Norwegian Name Style

If we use those name styles, as well as the Default style, we could create four tags for each of the two children as shown in Table 5-14 and Table 5-15.

---

[5] Names in this example taken from posts to the TMG-L mailing list in February and March of 2002 in a thread titled "Recording Norwegian Names."

The extra tags take time and effort to enter, but the searching-related advantages are considerable. Using Custom Name Styles reminds you—via the Custom Name Field Labels—what to record and where to record it. The Custom Name Field Labels define what the fields represent in an unambiguous and consistent manner that you will understand when you revisit the data in the future.

#	Name and Style	Field Labels and Values
1	Iver Knutson (Style=Default)	Given=Iver Surname=Knutson SortSurname=Knutson
2	Iver Knutson (Style=Patronymic)	Given=Iver Surname=Knutson Patronymic=Knut SortPatronymic=Knut
3	Iver Knutson Hopland (Style=Farm)	Given=Iver Surname=Knutson Farm=Hopland SortFarm=Hopland
4	Iver Knutson Botten (Style=Farm)	Given=Iver Surname=Knutson Farm=Botten SortFarm=Botten

Table 5-14: Name Tags Using Custom Name Styles (Male)

#	Name and Style	Field Labels and Values
1	Anna Knutsdatter (Style=Default)	Given=Anna Surname=Knutsdatter SortSurname=Knutsdatter
2	Anna Knutsdatter (Style=Patronymic)	Given=Anna Surname=Knutsdatter Patronymic=Knut SortPatronymic=Knut
3	Anna Knutsdatter Hopland (Style=Farm)	Given=Anna Surname=Knutsdatter Farm=Hopland SortFarm=Hopland
4	Anna Knutsdatter Botten (Style=Farm)	Given=Anna Surname=Knutsdatter Farm=Botten SortFarm=Botten

Table 5-15: Name Tags Using Custom Name Styles (Female)

Conclusions

There are almost as many ways to customize TMG data as there are reasons to do it. Used with care, Custom Flags, Custom Tags, Name and Place Styles, and the other customizable data structures discussed here and in subsequent chapters can help you enter data consistently, improve the speed of your research and analysis, support cultural variations, and achieve results that are impossible any other way. I hope this chapter has helped you understand the functions these structures are intended to support so that when you deviate from them you will do so knowingly, rather than the alternative.

Chapter 6 – Sentence Structures

By Terry Reigel

In TMG data is entered in Tags, and within those Tags, it is entered in individual fields. The data fields for an event include those that identify the participants, Date, various place fields, and one for a Memo. The Sentence Structures in each Tag are templates, or maps, which tell TMG how to assemble the information in those fields to generate narrative style reports. Charts and other styles of reports do not use Sentence Structures, but have their own systems for formatting the information from selected tags. Nor are Sentence Structures used to create TMG screens.

Table 6-1 may help you determine how Sentence Structures fit into your method of using TMG, or even if they do at all.

If Table 6-1 suggests that managing Sentence Structures would help achieve your objectives in using TMG, this chapter may help you master this feature. The first part of the chapter covers general concepts and principles that are useful to understand if you want to become comfortable working with Sentences Structures. Following that are sections that discuss in detail the various elements that are used in their construction.

If you …	then you …
are mainly interested in viewing your data on screen, or in non-narrative reports like Pedigree and Dependency Charts, Family Group Sheets, and Box Charts,	can ignore Sentence Structures.
use narrative style reports, but want to keep your data entry simple, without having to know anything about Sentence Structures,	can enter all details beyond basic events related to birth, marriage, and death into Anecdote Tags, entering complete sentences into the Tag Memo field.
want a bit more structure, but still to keep it simple and have your information appear in reports without undue regard for style,	can use the default Sentence Structures, choosing the Tag Type for each event that records the information in an acceptable fashion with minimal attention on your part.
want to record a rich variety of information and have it displayed in narrative Reports in a reasonably readable fashion,	should customize the Sentence Structures of default Tag Types and create custom Tag Types to express what you have in mind, probably using Roles, and occasionally customizing the Sentence Structures of individual Tags to address specific or unusual cases.
want to get the information recorded, with the intent of later polishing the text when you publish it,	should use a combination of default Tags and customized Sentence Structures as required to adequately record your information, then polish the text in your word processor when you get to the publishing stage.
want to be able to create and update at any time reports or web pages that contain polished prose, including the variation in flow that distinguishes good prose from computer-generated text,	Should use customized Sentence Structures for default Tag Types, custom Tag Types, including use of Roles, and heavily customize the Sentence Structures of individual Tags to achieve the quality of prose you desire.

Table 6-1: Deciding How to Use Sentence Structures

Basic Concepts of Sentence Structures

Before we discuss those general topics, we should pause for a moment and get a basic idea of what Sentence Structures are. First, some key concepts:

- TMG consults the Sentence Structures in a Tag when narrative reports are generated.
- The Sentence Structure is used when the report writer is creating the sections of the report related to a person entered in the Tag.
- If a Tag has, for example, two Principals and one Witness, and the report being generated includes sections on all three people, the Sentence Structures of that Tag will be used three different times.
- Each time TMG uses the Sentence Structure appropriate for the person whose paragraph was being created at that instant.

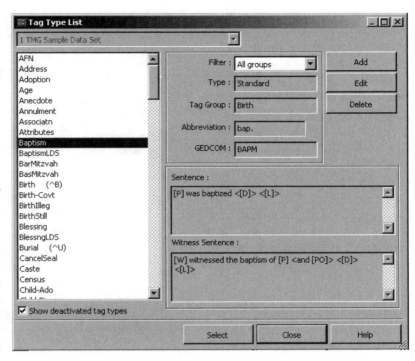

Figure 6-1: Use the Tag Type List to preview Sentence Structures

Now we will look at some of the basic ideas used in creating and applying Sentence Structures before moving to the details later in the chapter.

Elements of a Sentence Structure

If you are new to Sentence Structures, open the Tag Type List to preview them (**Tools > Master Tag Types List** on the menu). In the Sentence area, just below the center on the right side, you can see the Sentence Structure for Principals and Witnesses in the Tag Type that is selected in the list on the left side of the screen. Click on several Tag Types in turn, or click on one and use the up and down arrows on the keyboard to scroll through the list, observing how the Sentence Structures differ for various Tag Types.

To get a general sense of how Sentence Structures work, let's examine the default Sentence Structure for the standard Baptism Tag:

[P] was baptized <[D]> <[L]>

Notice that it is made up of three types of elements:

- **Variables** – these are the letters enclosed by square brackets. Variables tell TMG where to place information that is to be taken from data fields in this tag, or in some cases

information from other tags. In this Tag Type, the variables are:

- o **[P]** – represents the current Principal of the tag. Either a pronoun (he or she) will be used, or the full name will be obtained from a Name Tag, depending on the placement of this sentence in the narrative.
- o **[D]** – represents the Date. The information in the Date field of the Tag will be inserted here.
- o **[L]** – represents location. Information from the place fields will be inserted here.
- **Text** – ordinary text, in this case the phrase "was baptized." Text included in the Sentence Structure is simply included without change in the Report. Note that while it is not present here, text may include punctuation marks.
- **Conditional Variables** – these are codes that control how the Sentence Structure will be applied in certain conditions. Here the angle brackets "< >" appear around the date and location variables. These are called Conditional Brackets, and indicate that these

variables should be ignored if the data field they refer to is empty.

Global and Individual Sentence Structures

Sentence Structures are used at two different levels in TMG – I call them Global and Individual. TMG Help refers to them as changing the default Sentence Structure for a Tag Type and changing it for an individual Tag. While the same rules and "grammar" of Sentence Structures are used in both levels, the results of changing the two are quite different. It is important to understand the differences.

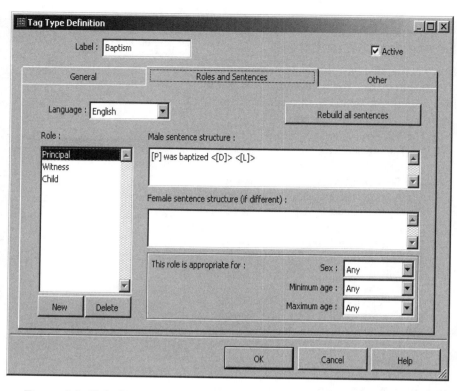

Figure 6-2: Global Sentence Structures are created or edited in the Tag Type Definition screen

Global Sentence Structures apply to all tags of any one Tag Type. That is, to all Birth Tags, all Note Tags, or all Occupation Tags, as examples. Each standard Tag Type (those provided with the program) is supplied with a default Sentence Structure. Each Custom Tag Type that is created by GenBridge™ during data import will have a Sentence Structure defined by GenBridge™. You must define a Sentence Structure for each Custom Tag Type that you create.

When you modify a Global Sentence Structure, that is the Sentence Structure of a Tag Type, the new structure will apply to any new Tags added of that Type. The New structure is also applied to all existing Tags of that Type, *except for tags whose Sentence Structures have been customized individually as described next.*

Individual Sentence Structures apply only to one specific Tag when it is attached to a person. That is, it applies to the Birth Tag you add for Frank Alexander, or the Burial tag you add for Mary Catherine Keebler, for example.

When you add a new Tag you must select a Tag Type – say Birth, Note, or Burial. The new Tag initially takes its Sentence Structure from the Global Sentence Structure for that Tag Type. At any time you may modify the Sentence Structure for that individual tag, thus creating an Individual Sentence Structure. Once you do, any future changes to the Global Sentence Structure of the Tag Type will not apply to that individual tag.

Global changes to Sentence Structures are made on the Roles and Sentences tab of the Tag Type Definition screen (see Figure 6-2). Changes to the Sentence Structures of individual Tags are made from the Tag Entry screen, by clicking the [Sentence] button to open the Sentence Structures screen (see Figure 6-3).

If you are not sure if you have created an Individual Sentence Structure for the Principals of a particular Tag, look on the Basic tab of the Tag Entry screen, next to the [Sentence] button. If there is an Individual Sentence Structure for that tag it will appear to the right of he button. If that space is blank, the Global Sentence Structure applies.

After you create an Individual Sentence Structure for a Tag, you may sometimes then want to change

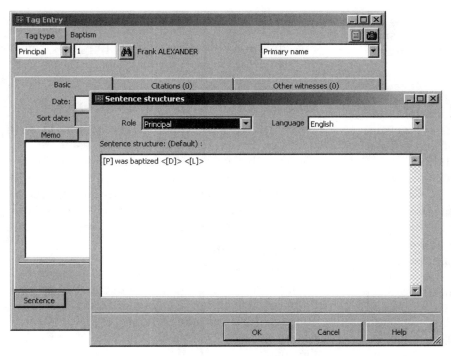

Figure 6-3: Individual Sentence Structures are created or edited from the Tag Entry Screen, by clicking the [Sentence] button

When you define Sentence Structures for a Tag Type you are creating what I called Global Sentence Structures above. You create a Sentence Structure for Principals, and another for Witnesses. Actually, you may optionally create a gender specific versions of each – see the following section.

When you add a Tag, the global Sentence Structure from the Tag Type you select is applied as the default for the new Tag. You can customize this Sentence Structure if you like, creating what I call an Individual Sentence Structure. You can create one Individual Sentence Structure for Principals, which will apply to both Principals. However, for each Witness you can create an Individual Sentence Structure for that particular Witness. So you might, for example, edit the Sentence Structure for one Witness to include the fact that this Witness was the executor, while editing the Sentence Structure for another Witness to reflect that this person was an heir.

it back to Global Sentence Structure for the Tag Type. To do that, simply delete all text from the Sentence Structure field of the Tag, and close the Sentence Structure screen. The Global Sentence Structure from the Tag Type is then applied, as you can see by re-opening the Sentence Structures screen.

Principals and Witnesses

As you create Sentence Structures, you need to have clearly in mind which person will be the subject of the Sentence you are constructing. They fall into two categories:

Principals – those people most involved in the event. Most Tags in TMG can refer to two Principals. Most commonly they will be husband and wife, but they can be any two individuals that you want to describe as involved in a single event.

Witnesses – may include any other people somehow linked to the event. In a will Tag they might be witnesses in the legal sense, but they could also be heirs or perhaps the executor. In a census Tag the Witness feature might be used to record other members of the household enumerated on the census. Tags may have any number of Witnesses.

Sentence Structures with Gender Specific Variations

When you create or edit the Global Sentence Structures there is an option to create Sentence Structures for each gender. In most cases the Sentence Structure works fine without using this option. But it is very useful if you include pronouns or other terms that differ by gender in your Global Sentence Structures. Relationship terms, like son or daughter, and some position titles, like executor and executrix, are examples of gender specific terms you might occasionally use in your Sentence Structures.

When you add Tags based on a Tag Type having separate male and female versions the appropriate version is automatically applied when reports are generated using those Tags. Note that if you choose to create Individual Sentence Structures for Principals in such a Tag, only one version will be maintained – that is, the Tag will no longer have separate male and female Sentence Structures for Principals. This is not an issue for Witnesses, since each Witness has it's own Individual Sentence Structure.

The Function of Roles

TMG uses the optional concept of Roles to define the part played by various participants in an event. Each Tag Type can have its own set of Roles. Roles can be used in two separate but related ways:

As "Libraries" – of Sentence Structures available for selection by name. This is easier to grasp from an example than from the description, so consider this example. Suppose you want to record as Witnesses the executor and heirs in Will Tags. As mentioned above, you could manually modify the default Sentence Structure for each Witness to reflect the part of each person involved. Or, you could create Roles for executor and heirs in your Will Tag Type, each with appropriate Sentence Structures. Then, instead of manually modifying the Sentence Structure each time you add such a Witness, you just select the appropriate Role and the corresponding Sentence Structure is automatically applied.

As "Handles" – to more conveniently refer to specific participants as you create Sentence Structures. For example, in the Will Tag, say you are constructing the Sentence Structure for the Principal – the person who wrote the will. And suppose you what to include in the text generated for that person a statement that "…he named as executor …" followed by the name of the Witness who was the executor. Without Roles, you cannot distinguish between Witnesses who were heirs and those that were executors. But if you give one Witness the Role of executor, you can than refer to that Witness specifically. Details of how this is done are discussed below in the section on Role Name Variables.

The use of Roles is completely optional. You can simply ignore them if you prefer. A few of the standard Tag Types have Roles defined, but they all have the same Sentence Structure as the Principal. So as a practical matter, if you want to use Roles you have to define them and create Sentence Structures for them that suit your own needs.

Note – while you can modify the Sentence Structures for Roles in individual Tags, you cannot add new Roles to an individual Tag. Roles can only be created for Tag Types.

Using the Sentence Elements

Now that we have explored the general idea of Sentence Structures, and reviewed some of the concepts that need to be considered when we are editing or creating them, we are ready to discuss in more depth the individual elements that are used to write Sentence Structures. The remaining sections of this chapter cover each of those elements in turn.

Name Variables

We will start with those Sentence Variables that identify the participants in an event. I've loosely grouped them in the category of Name Variables, although that is not a term used in TMG's documentation. The Name Variables cause either the name of a participant, or an appropriate pronoun, to be inserted in the Report text.

Note that the name that is generated by a Name Variable is not actually taken from the Event Tag whose Sentence Structure we are discussing. The Event Tag refers to individuals by ID Number. So when the Name Variable is evaluated by TMG to generate a Report, a Name Tag for that person is consulted to obtain the actual name of the individual. Since any individual in the Data Set may have an unlimited number of Name Tags, TMG needs to be guided to the Name Tag you have in mind. By default, the Primary Name Tag (the one marked as Primary, and thus appearing at the top of that individual's Person View) is used. Using other Name Tags is discussed under "Specifying Name Variations" below.

Name Variables for Principals

TMG offers a long list of Variables for the names of Principals. The different Variables allow you to choose which of the two Principals is used (for Tags that have two), which Name Elements to include, and options to use the possessive form. There are three different ways to specify which of the two Principals are to be used, and it is important to understand the difference in order to get your desired result. They are:

Current Principal / Other Principal Method. This method is based on how the individuals relate to the report being generated. The Current Principal is the subject of the paragraph that is being constructed in a report. Say we have a Marriage Tag, in which John Jones and Mary Smith are the two Principals. When a report is generated, in the paragraph about John, he is the Current Principal and Mary is the Other Principal. If there is another paragraph about Mary, the positions are reversed. Note that it doesn't matter which one is listed first in the Tag. The primary variables for this method are:

    [P] – Current Principal
    [PO] – Other Principal

First Principal / Second Principal Method. This method is based on the positions in which the two principals are entered in the Tag, that is, as the first or second Principal. The primary variables for this method are:

    [P1] – First Principal
    [P2] – Second Principal

Using Roles. This method is based on the use of Roles to identify the Principals. Principals can be assigned Roles just as Witnesses can. See the section on Name Variables for Roles, below, for details on this method.

In most cases, the Current Principal / Other Principal method works best. Using it, the order of the Principals in the resulting narrative automatically adjusts according to which principal is the focus of the paragraph, as shown in the example above.

But occasionally you don't want the Principals to be exchanged. Say you add a tag to record the fact that Tom Smith was the godson of William White. You certainly don't want that turned around so it says William was Tom's godson! You can control that by using the First Principal / Second Principal method, making sure you enter the each person into the proper Principal field to match your Sentence Structure. This works well if you are customizing an individual Tag. But if you are creating a customized Tag Type, you have to be careful when you use it to remember the order in which the

Principals are to be named. In this case, using Roles is a more reliable method, as you have the Role names available it easier to be sure that the two individuals are properly identified.

Once you have decided how to indicate which Principal you have in mind (if you have decided not to use Roles), you can select the Variable that produces the format of the name that you have in mind from Table 6-2.

For Tags with only one Principal, use the forms for Current Principal. The full name forms are most commonly used. But customizing individual Tags by using other variations can add variety to the narrative that helps it to not read like computer-generated text.
produces the format of the name that you have in mind from Table 6-2.

For Tags with only one Principal, use the forms for Current Principal. The full name forms are most commonly used. But customizing individual Tags by using other variations can add variety to the narrative that helps it to not read like computer-generated text.

Name Variables for Witnesses
There are two Name Variables available for referring to Witnesses, with no options for partial names or possessive variations:

    [W] or **[W+]** – Current Witness (see section on Pronoun Substitution, below)
    [WO] – Other Witnesses

Some special considerations apply to the use of these variables:
- The [W] form, Current Witness, may only be used in Sentence Structures for Witnesses. If you try to use it in a Sentence Structure for Principals it will be changed to [P] when the Sentence Structure is saved. In Sentence Structures for Principals the [WO] form must be used. This works well if there is only one Witness, or if you want all of them listed. But if you only want to refer to one of several, Roles must be used to specify the desired Witness.

Name Form	Current Principal	Other Principal	First Principal	Second Principal
Full Name	[P] or [P+]*	[PO]	[P1]	[P2]
Given Name	[PG]	[POG]	[P1G]	[P2G]
First word of Given Name	[PF]	[POF]	[P1F]	[P2F]
Possessive Full Name	[PS]	[POS]	[P1S]	[P2S]
Possessive Given Name	[PGS]	[POGS]	[P1GS]	[P2GS]
Possessive First word of Given Name	[PFS]	[POFS]	[P1FS]	[P2FS]
*See section on Pronoun Substitution, below				

Table 6-2: Name Variables for Principals

- The form [WO] produces a listing of the "other" witnesses, if there are more than one, separated by commas and with the word "and" before the last one, like this: "…John Jones, Mike Jones, and Mary Smith." When used in a Sentence Structure for Principals, it lists all Witnesses. However, when used in a Sentence Structure for Witnesses, it lists all the Witnesses except the Current Witness, that is the person who is the focus of that section of the report.

It may be helpful to reflect that Name Variables for Witnesses are used in two rather different ways. They may be used in a Sentence Structure for a Witness, to refer to that Witness. For example, say that Mary White was a bridesmaid at the wedding of Tom Smith and Sue Jones, and you entered her as a Witness in Tom and Sue's Marriage Tag. In creating the Sentence Structure for Mary as a Witness, you might use [W] Variable to refer to Mary, producing a sentence like "She was a bridesmaid in the wedding of …" in a narrative report focusing on Mary.

Continuing with this example, you might also want to include mention of Mary's role in a narrative report focusing on Tom or Sue. In that case, when creating the Sentence Structure for Principals you would refer to Mary with the Variable [WO], producing a sentence like "… with Mary White as bridesmaid." These two applications of the Witness Name Variable are independent – you can use either or both, as serves your purpose.

Name Variables for Roles

The Name Variables for Roles consist of two parts – the first part shows which form the name is to take, and the second part tells to which Role it refers. For example, the variable [RG:Heir] would produce the Given Name of a person with the Role of "Heir." A variety of name forms, similar to those for Principals, are available. In the following list, the term "Rolename" represents the name you would actually assign to your Roles:

[R:*Rolename*] or **[R+:*Rolename*]**– Full Name of Person (see section on Pronoun Substitution, below)

[RG:*Rolename*] – Given Name of Person

[RF:*Rolename*] – First word of Given Name of Person

[RP:*Rolename*] – Nominative Pronoun of Person (he, she, or they)

[RS:*Rolename*] – Possessive Pronoun of Person (his, her or their)

[RM:*Rolename*] – Objective Pronoun of Person (him, her or them)

When a Tag has more than one person with the same Role, the first three forms generally produce a list of names, separated by commas, like the [WO] Variable. But there is an important exception – the first form ([R:*Rolename*] and [R+:*Rolename*]) behaves differently if the person who is the *focus* of the narrative being constructed is *assigned to that Role*. When the focus person is assigned that Role, this Variable behaves like the Variables for Principals, and refers only to the focus person.

An illustration may help. Say you add a Will Tag to record that William Smith left a will naming his children John, Mary, and Sue as heirs. And, you created the Role "Heir" and assigned it to the children, who were entered as Witnesses. Say you created this Sentence Structure for the Principal:

[P] left a will naming [R:Heir] as heirs

This will produce in a narrative the sentence "He left a will naming John Smith, Mary Smith, and Sue Smith as heirs." But, if you applied the same approach to Sentence Structure for John, intending to obtain a listing of all the other heirs, you might be tempted to use the Sentence Structure:

[W] was named in the will of [P], along with [R:Heir]

But instead of what you expected you would get "He was named in the will of William Smith, along with John Smith." Note that John himself is named, but his sisters are not – not your intent.

As a general rule, I find it safer to avoid using a Role Name Variable in Sentence of the Role of the same name. That is, don't use [R:Heir] in the Sentence Structure for the Role "Heir." Instead, I use the Variable [P] or [W], whichever applies. Note that using the [P] or [W] Variables this way in Sentence Structures for Roles means that the same Role name cannot be used for both Principals and Witnesses in the same Tag Type. But I think it is generally a good practice when you create a Role in any one Tag Type to do so planning to use that Role either for Principals or Witnesses, not both.

The fact that the first three forms generally produce a list of names is also a concern if you intend to refer to only one of several people assigned that role. The solution generally is to create a separate Role for that person. Say you have several individuals with the Role "Heir" in a will Tag, but you only want to refer to one of them in the text for the Principal of the Tag. You might create a new Role of Heir1 for that person in order to be able to do that. (Remember you have to do this for the Will Tag Type; you cannot for just the one Tag you are adding).

Sometimes Role Name Variables Are Not the Best Way

You do not need to use the Role Name Variables just because you have assigned Roles. In fact, in some cases it is much better to not use them. The following example shows a case where even though Roles are used the use of Role Name Variables is not a good solution. Note that this example also provides an example of the use of Roles as a "Library" of Sentence Structures from which the desired one can be easily selected.

Suppose you want to recognize multiple marriages by inserting the traditional words "first," "second," "third" etc. You could do this by editing the Sentence Structures individually in the marriage tags involved. But you could instead modify the default Marriage Tag to add the following Roles, with the Sentence Structures shown:

Role	Sentence Structure
First	[P] married first [PO] <[PARO]> <[D]> <[L]>
Second	[P] married second [PO] <[PARO]> <[D]> <[L]>
Third	[P] married third [PO] <[PARO]> <[D]> <[L]>

Now for people with multiple marriages, assign these Roles instead of the default Principal "Role." Note that any Role could be assigned to either Principal, and both Principals could have the same Role. (If one Principal in a Tag is assigned a Role the other must be too; TMG will not allow the other Principal to remain with the default "Role" of Principal. So in this case if one spouse had only one marriage, or you do not know which marriage this is for that person, assign the standard Role of Bride or Groom to that spouse).

In this case if you were to try to use Role Name Variables to refer to the "other" spouse, which Role would you use? There are a considerable number of possible combinations, which you can ignore by using the Name Variables for Principals instead, as shown in this example.

Using Principal and Witness as Roles

The default Roles "Principal" and "Witness" are genuine Roles, and can be used in all the Role Variables. This can be useful, for example, in obtaining name forms not supported by the standard name variables. Suppose you wanted to have a Witness referred to by first name, a form not offered in the Witness name variables. You can achieve that result by using the variable

[RF:Witness]. Similarly, this method can produce pronoun forms not otherwise available.

Other occasionally useful applications include displaying the age of a Tag's Principal in a paragraph in which a Witness is the focus. The variable [RA:Principal] used in a Witness' Sentence Structure will produce the age of the Principal, which cannot be produced with other variables. But use caution in Tags with two Principals, as unexpected results may occur.

In summary, Roles and Role Name Variables are powerful tools, enabling you to create many useful customized Tag Types. But the Sentence Structures do need to be constructed with care, and the results tested in order to be sure you get the results you had in mind.

Name Variables for Parents

Name Variables for Parents are ordinarily used in Marriage Tags, but can be used in any Event Tag. Variables for Parents work only for the Principals in a Tag, and always use the Parent's Primary Names. There is no option to use any name variations for the Parents. The Variables are listed in Table 6-3.

The "Parents" forms are generally used because they provide both parents (if both exist) with a single Variable, and also provide the connecting phrase in the form ", son of Mary Smith and John Jones." The [FATH] and [MOTH] variables are best used when only one parent is desired. They provide only the actual names of the parents – you must supply any connecting language, such as "…son of [FATH]."

Aside from their default use in Marriage Tags, perhaps the most useful application for Parents Name Variables would be in Birth Tags, if you prefer to use narrative report types that do not make the parents obvious, like the Individual Narrative.

The Parents Name Variables are generally not useful in Sentence Structures for Witnesses. The [PAR1] and [PAR2] Variables may be placed in Sentence Structures for Witnesses, but will provide the names of the parents of the Tag's Principals, not the parents of the Witness. (If you try to enter [PAR] or [PARO] they will be converted to [PAR1] and [PAR2] respectively when you close the Sentence Structures screen.) The [FATH] and [MOTH] variables, if used in Witness Sentence Structure, always produce the names of the father or mother of the first Principal in the Tag.

Pronoun Substitution

To avoid the monotonous repetition that would result from repeating the name of a paragraph's subject in every sentence, writers often substitute a personal pronoun in place of the name. TMG does this automatically for certain situations, using the following rules:

- The nominative pronoun (he or she) is used in place of the name.
- Applies only to the focus person of a section of a report, not to any other person who may appear in that section, even if that person appears in several sentences.
- Applies only if the name variable appears before any other variable in the Sentence Structure.
- Does not apply to the first sentence of a new paragraph (exception: does apply to the second paragraph automatically produced in Journal reports).

The only Name Variables that have the pronoun substitution feature are:

[P] – Current Principal

[W] – Current Witness

[R:*Rolename*] – Full Name of Rolename

This is a powerful feature that has a major impact on how Name Variables function when generating reports. By default, most tags have a Sentence Structure beginning "[P] was…" or something similar. As a result of Pronoun Substitution, the vast majority of those Tags will produce sentences starting with a pronoun rather than with the person's name. Generally, the name of the subject of the report

	Current Principal	Other Principal	First Principal	Second Principal
Parents of …	**[PAR]**	**[PARO]**	**[PAR1]**	**[PAR2]**
Father of …	**[FATH]**	–	–	–
Mother of …	**[MOTH]**	–	–	–

Table 6-3: Name Variables for Parents

section will appear only once, in the first sentence, unless you create paragraph breaks as described below under "Embedded Format Codes."

Pronoun Substitution generally works well, but can cause problems in special cases:

Wrong Reference – consider, for example, a Tag that contains a lengthy Memo that includes one or more sentences whose subject is another person. Say you have an ancestor who served under a famous general, and you include a sentence or two describing the general. If the next Tag were, say, an Occupation Tag that produced a sentence like "He was a farmer after the war" this second Tag would appear to refer to the general instead of your ancestor. Use one of the methods below to solve the problem.

Obscuring Name Variation – if you have specified that a Tag use a name variation other than the Primary Name, Pronoun Substitution may obscure that by using a pronoun instead of the selected name. Depending on your intent, than may or may not be satisfactory. If your application requires that the selected name variation be used instead of the pronoun, use one of the methods below to suppress Pronoun Substitution.

Wrong Case – if the sentence construction calls for objective case – him or her – a grammatical error will be generated. The solution is to reformat the sentence so that nominative case is correct, change to a form that does not use the substitution feature, or use an Objective Pronoun Variable as described below.

There are several ways to suppress Pronoun Substitution when it is not desired. They are:

- Use the special forms of the variables that explicitly suppress substitution:
  [P+] for Principals
  [W+] for Witnesses
  [R+:*Rolename*] for Roles

- Use a Name Variable form that does not use the substitution feature, such as a Given Name Variable.

- Use Embedded Format Codes to create a new paragraph for the next tag. See the section of that name later in this chapter for details.

- If your sentence structure permits, position the name variable after another variable.

The Pronoun substitution feature is generally helpful in improving the flow of narratives, but can cause issues in some cases, as we have seen. In addition, the repetitive string of pronouns can itself become monotonous. For more readable narratives, try adding some variety by choosing alternate name forms for some Tags, or rearranging the flow of the some sentences.

Pronoun Variables

You can force use of a pronoun, for the Current Principal or for persons assigned to Roles, by using these Variables:

- **[PP]** – Possessive Pronoun of Current Principal (his or her)
- **[OBJ]** – Objective Pronoun of Current Principal (him or her)
- **[RP:*Rolename*]** – Nominative pronoun of the person in the role (he or she)
- **[RS:*Rolename*]** – Possessive pronoun of the person in the role (his or her)
- **[RM:*Rolename*]** – Objective pronoun of the person in the role (him or her)

Specifying Name Variations

Each individual may have used several different names, including nicknames, middle names in lieu of first name, married name, and alternate spellings, especially at time of immigration to a new country. By default, the various Name Variables we've discussed use the Name from the Primary Name Tag – the one at the top of the Person View Screen. But TMG allows you to specify a different Name variation to use for each Event Tag.

There are two cases where you cannot select a variation other than the one in the Primary Name Tag. One case is the variables for parents' names, which always use the names in their Primary Name Tags. The second is in the titles of reports, which likewise take the name of the focus person from the Primary Name Tag.

For Principals, you select the desired name variation with the drop-down box in the upper right of the Tag Entry screen (see Figure 6-3). For Witnesses, there is a similar drop-down box on the Add Witness screen. In either case, if you want to use a name other than the Primary one, just click on the down arrow button and select the name you want to be used for that Tag. When you select name variations in a tag, all Name Variables that refer to Principals or Witnesses within that tag will use the selected name variations.

Note that the list shows the names from all the Name Tags previously entered for that individual. They are displayed, as they will appear in Reports, according to the Name Style selected in each Name Tag (see *Chapter 5, Customizing the Data*, for more on Styles). The default Name Style uses the Name Elements: Title, Given Name, Surname, and Suffix. When a Name Tag other than the Primary one is selected, and if that Tag has no Given Name or no Surname, as commonly is the case with married names and nicknames, the missing element will be replaced by the same element from the Primary Name Tag. If you do not want this to happen, enter a single or double Exclusion Marker (one or two hyphens) in place of the empty name, or use a custom Name Style that omits the undesired name element.

Also note that you are not actually selecting the name shown on the list, but you are choosing the associated Name Tag. Therefore if you subsequently change the name in that Tag, the new version will appear in reports. If you subsequently delete a Name Tag that is selected as the "Report Name" in event Tags, the Primary Name Tag will be substituted.

And one final caution – if your Sentence Structure uses one of the name variable forms that call for given name, the appropriate given name will be used and any conflicting formatting of the selected name variation by use of Name Styles will be disregarded.

Having now explored all the variations of Variables used to refer to individuals, we can now turn our attention to the other types of Variables

Date Variables

There are only two Variables for dates:
- **[D]** – Date of the Event
- **[DD]** – Date of the Event, preceded by the day of the week

The options for using Dates in tags would appear to be simple. But in reality there are a number of subtle factors that control how dates are shown in reports:

Date Format – "Regular" dates are formatted according to the Date Format selected in the Program Options – General section of Preferences. If the date is "Irregular" the date is always shown exactly as entered. Regular Dates are those entered in a format recognized by TMG (for details, search Help for "Date: Incomplete or Irregular").

Automatic Prepositions – TMG prefixes Regular Dates enclosed in Conditional Brackets (written <[D]>) with the preposition "in" or "on" by default. TMG supplies "in" if the date contains only year or month and year, and "on" for full dates. If you insert anything, even just a space, between the first conditional bracket and the Date Variable, the automatic preposition is omitted so that you can supply your own prefix. Generally, letting TMG insert the preposition works best. So you should generally enter Date Variables with the Conditional Brackets, taking care to avoid any character between the opening Conditional Bracket and the Date Variable. But remember that you do have the ability to override TMG's prepositions for special situations.

The form [DD] only applies if the date is both Regular, and complete, meaning that day, month and year are all included. If these conditions do not both apply, it produces the same result as the [D] form. The day of the week will be abbreviated or spelled in full, depending on the setting for the "Months spelled out" option in the Report Definition, on the Dates tab of Options.

Additional special conditions apply to Journal Reports. Those Reports have an option to control how dates appear in birth, marriage, death and burial (BMDB) Tags, partially overriding the Sentence Structure of those Tags. For details, see the *Special Options for Journal Reports* section in *Chapter 9, Controlling Narratives*.

Despite their apparent simplicity, Date Variables are complex enough to require some care to obtain the results you have in mind, particularly if you use the Journal Reports and like the abbreviated options for "BMDB" Tags. Experimenting and testing with your favorite style of reports will produce the best results.

Location Variables

Place or location information in event tags may be recorded in as many as ten different fields. These fields are intended to represent different levels of detail about the location. By default, the levels are assigned names based on common U.S. terminology, for example Detail, City, County, State, etc. However, these are simply labels, and data can be entered in any field that suits the user's needs. Further, as described in *Chapter 5, Customizing the Data*, the default labels can be customized. Regardless of the labels used, the value of the separate fields is that in reports they can be placed in any order, or some omitted, as suits the users' needs.

Printing all Location Elements

Most often, we want to have all the location fields that contain data output for reports. The easiest way to do this to use the "standard" location variable:

[L] – includes all location fields

By default, all location fields that contain data will be output. However, if you have constructed and used custom Place Styles, the [L] variable will produce only the elements specified in the selected Place Style. Place Styles are discussed in detail in *Chapter 5, Customizing the Data*.

Report options also impact how place information is produced. The Narrative report definitions have options three options on the Places tab of Report Definition Options:

- **Place Styles** – applies the default Place Style or any custom Place Styles you have specified for each Tag.
- **Short Place Template** – applies the Short Place name from the Master Place List for each place. (Open the Master Place List, select a place and click the [Edit] button to see this field.) If none has been entered for a

place, uses the Template specified in Preferences to construct one.
- **Selected Place Fields** – allows selection of specific place fields that are then applied to every tag.

The selected option is applied to every Tag used to create the report. Selecting the last two options will override any Place Styles you have applied to individual Tags. But these options apply only when the [L] variable is used; if you specify specific location elements as described below, they will be used regardless of the settings of these options.

Using Specific Location Elements

Sometimes we want to have only specific location elements produced in reports, even though others may appear in the Tag. For example, you might want a census tag to produce a sentence like "He appeared in the 1880 census of Hamilton Co., Ohio…" even though the tag may contain additional location elements. You can do this by using the Specific Location Variables listed in Table 6-4.

Element	Numeric Form	Short Form	Long Form
1	[L1]	[LA]	[ADDRESSEE]
2	[L2]	[LD]	[DETAIL]
3	[L3]	[LCI]	[CITY]
4	[L4]	[LCN]	[COUNTY]
5	[L5]	[LS]	[STATE]
6	[L6]	[LCR]	[COUNTRY]
7	[L7]	[LZ]	[ZIP]
8	[L8]	[LP]	[PHONE]
9	[L9]	[LL]	[LATLONG]
10	[L10]	[LT]	[TEMPLE]

Table 6-4: Specific Location Variables

The three forms on each row are equivalent. You can use which ever is most convenient. Users who are keeping the default "U.S. Standard" place names may find the short or long forms easiest to remember. Users who have created custom place labels may find it easier keep track of the desired element using the numeric forms.

If you use these level specific variables in a tag that also uses a Place Style, the variable overrides the Place Style. That is, the specified element will be produced if it exists, and only that element, regardless of the Place Style.

If you use a specific location variable such as [LD] and also use the overall location variable [L] in the same Tag, the specific element will not be repeated by the [L] variable. For example, if you placed the cemetery name in the detail location element in a burial tag, and had a Sentence Structure "[P] was buried <in [LD]> near <[L]> <[D]>" the cemetery name would appear only once.

Location Prepositions

The Narrative Reports have an option to specify what preposition, if any, will precede the name of a place produced by a Location Variable. The choices are **at, in,** or **none**. However, the option applies **only** if the Location Variable is enclosed in Conditional Brackets (written <[L]>). And, as with the Date Variables, even if the Brackets are used, anything (including a space) placed between the first conditional bracket and the Location Variable causes the preposition to be omitted.

Working with Memos

The Memo field of a Tag may contain anything from a brief phrase to flesh out the details of a Tag to extensive paragraphs of text. There are two inter-related ways to control how, or if, the text in a Memo field will appear in Reports. The Memo text may be included in Reports by using the Memo Variables described here in the Sentence Structures of Tags.

Alternatively, the contents of the Memo field can be displayed in a specific Report using options in the Report Definition for that report. However, if any of the Memo Variables are present in the Sentence Structure of a Tag, those Report Definition options will be ignored for that Tag. See the *Tricks with Memos* section in *Chapter 9, Controlling Narratives*, for details of this option.

Normally, the whole content of the Memo field is treated as a single unit of text. But if you wish, you can create up to nine separate sections, each of which can be referred to individually in the Sentence Structure. This is sometimes called using "Split Memos."

The Memo Variables are:
- **[M]** – includes the entire Memo field (same as [M1] if the Memo is split).

- **[M1]** through **[M9]** – includes the corresponding sections of a split Memo.
- **<[M0]>** – includes nothing, but prevents the Memo field from being included through use of the Memos options in Report Definitions (note the variable is written with the number zero, not the letter O).

Splitting the Memo field is done by separating the segments with the code || produced with two vertical lines. (The vertical line character is above the backslash key on most keyboards, and usually appears on the key with a break in the middle.) Any segments not referenced with a Memo Variable are ignored.

The Variable [M0] must always be enclosed in Conditional Brackets (written as <[M0]>) because it is actually a request to include Memo segment number 0, which by definition is empty. So if the Conditional Brackets are not included an "unknown value" phrase will be inserted.

This Variable is not, strictly speaking, required if you never use the Report Definition Memo options. If there is no Memo Variable, and the Memo options in the Report Definition are not turned on, the text in the Memo field will not print. However, many users include it, out of caution, when a Memo entry will exist in a Tag but they do not want it to print in reports, just in case they later find a use for the Memo options. Should you later want to use one of the Report Definition options, this saves going back and adding the <[M0]> variable to perhaps hundreds of tags.

This most commonly occurs in Sentence Structures for Witnesses, when the Memo entry is intended for use only for the Principals. In such cases, the <[M0]> variable is included in the Sentence Structures for the Witnesses to be sure the Memo text will not print for the Witnesses should the user later decide to use the Report Definition Memo options.

The Age Variables

There are several Variables to produce the age of a participant of an event. One of them is included in the Sentence Structure of the default Death Tag, but may be included in any Tag if you like. The age is calculated from the date on the Primary Birth Group Tag. The forms available are listed in Table 6-5.

The "Age" forms produce the person's age in whole years attained. If the age is less than one year, the phrase "at an unknown age" is produced unless Conditional Brackets (like this: <[A]>) are used.

The primary purpose of the "Exact Age" forms is to produce the age in years, months, and days. For this result, both the Primary Birth Group Tag and the Tag in which the variable is used must contain a full date (day, month, and year). However, the "Exact Age" forms, unlike the "Age" forms, will also produce the age in years when partial dates appear in either of those Tags.

If you enclose the variables in Conditional Brackets both forms supply the phrase "at age" so you do not have to include them. Like prepositions for Date and Location Variables, if any text, including a space, is placed within the Conditional Brackets, the phrase is omitted. The "Exact" form includes units, that is, "years," "months" and "days."

To avoid the risk of producing the "at an unknown age" message, and to include the supporting phrasing, Age Variables should always be enclosed in Conditional Brackets.

	Current Principal	Other Principal	First Principal	Second Principal	Roles
Age	[A]	[AO]	[A1]	[A2]	[RA:*Rolename*]
Exact Age	[AE]	[AOE]	[A1E]	[A2E]	[RE:*Rolename*]

Table 6-5: Age Variables

If you want to generate the ages of children who died in their first year, you need to use the Exact Age form rather than the more general form.

The Age Variables for Roles will produce a list of ages of all persons with that Role, if there are more than one such person – something like "...at age 23, at age 34, and at age 32..." Since this is seldom the intended result, generally that form should only be used if you expect only one person to be assigned the Role in any one Tag.

Variables Used in Name Tags

Sentence Structures are not used for the Primary Name Tag. The Primary Name Tag never generates a sentence in a report by itself, but instead the Name in that Tag is used in conjunction with other Tags and the structure of the report itself. However, non-Primary Name Tags, which might contain married names, nicknames, spelling variations, and the like, can be used to produce narrative text, using Sentence Structures. These Tags have access to a limited set of the Variables used by Event Tags, plus one Variable unique to Name Tags. These Variables, as interpreted in Name Tags, are:

- **[P]** – Primary name of the Current Principal
- **[N]** – Current Name (the name in this Tag) of the Current Principal
- **[PP]** – Possessive Pronoun of Current Principal (his or her)
- **[OBJ]** – Objective Pronoun of Current Principal (him or her)
- **[M]** – entire Memo field
- **[M1]** through **[M9]** – section of a split Memo
- **<[M0]>** – prevents the Memo from being included through use of the Report Definition Memo options.

These variables generally work as described in the preceding sections. The one perhaps needing some comment is the [N] variable. As noted in the "Choosing Which Name Variation Is Used" section above, when a Name Tag omits either the given name or surname then, in some contexts, the omitted name is replaced by the one from the Primary Name Tag. However, the [N] variable always produces only the names actually contained in that Name Tag; it does not pick up missing name elements from the Primary Name Tag.

More on Conditional Variables

Conditional Variables allow us to create Sentence Structures that produce different text depending on the conditions that occur in our data. This allows for more general Sentence Structures that work without having to be customized for every use.

Dealing with Missing Elements

The most common condition is dealing with missing data elements in the Tag. For example, the default Sentence Structure for the Birth Tag is:

[P] was born <[D]> <[L]>

Note the angle brackets around the date and place Variables. They are known as Conditional Brackets, and indicate that if the associated fields are empty, the variables should be ignored. In the absence of Conditional Brackets, an empty field produces a phrase such as "an unknown value" in the report text. Note that the Brackets are not placed around the Name Variable, since the Tag must have a Principal. But it is quite likely that the date or place of birth may be unknown. Using the Conditional Brackets this Sentence Structure produces the desired text both with and without all the elements.

You should always include Conditional Brackets when you create Sentence Structures that may be used in situations where elements may be absent in some cases. In addition, Conditional Brackets are useful in managing the automatic insertion of prepositions (see discussions in the "Date Variables" and "Location Prepositions" sections above).

One or Two Principals

Most Tag Types allow for either one or two Principals. A vertical bar within Conditional Brackets allows us to write Sentence Structures that work with one or both Principals present. For example, the default Sentence Structure for the Adoption Tag is:

[P] <was|and [PO] were> adopted <[D]> <[L]>

The vertical bar between "was" and "and" indicates that the word "was" is to be inserted if there is only one Principal, but the phrase "and (name of other Principal) were" is to be used if both Principals are present.

Principal Living or Not

Conditional Variables can also be used to produce different output depending upon whether the subject of the paragraph is living or not. For example, you might want to have a living tag produce the text "He is living at..." for people who are living, but have it produce "He was living at..." for those who are not. To use this feature, you create two separate Sentence Structures, and joint them with a double vertical bar, such as:

[P] was living <[L]>|| [P] is living <[L]>

The part before the double bars is used if the Living Flag for the Principal is set to "N" while the part after the bars is used if the flag is set to "Y" or "?." Note that the Living Flag of the Principal who is the focus of the paragraph being generated is used, even though the Sentence Structure may use variables referring to other people. You must use care with this feature in tags with two Principals, or containing Witnesses, as unexpected results can be produced in those cases.

Punctuation and Connecting Phrases

In addition to the variables discussed above, Sentence Structures provide the connecting phrases and punctuation needed to properly express the data contained in the various fields of the Tag in narrative reports. For example, in the default Sentence Structure for the Birth Tag –

[P] was born <[D]> <[L]>

the phrase "was born" is needed to convey the significance of the date and location information. This phrase is simply repeated in the narrative unchanged. In more complex Sentence Structures, punctuation may be needed, and spaces between variables, and between variables and text, must be considered.

Some of these elements are provided automatically:

Period – is automatically supplied at the end of the text produced by the Sentence Structure. But double periods are suppressed, for example when a period after an abbreviation in a data field falls at the end of a sentence. For this reason you may enter a period at the end of the Sentence Structure or not – the result is the same.

Commas – are placed after each location field when the variable **[L]** is used, except one that falls at the end of the sentence. Thus you should not put a comma between **[L]** and any variable that follows it in a Sentence Structure, because a double comma would result. These results are produced by the default Place Styles. If you create custom Place Styles, or choose an option on the Places tab of the Report Definition

Options other than "Use place styles," you may see different results. In those cases, be sure to verify that your results are as intended.

Variables that produce lists, such as **[WO]**, place commas appropriately to separate the items of the list, but not at the end of the list. And a comma is automatically inserted by the "Parent" name variables at the beginning of the phase ", son of ..."

Spaces – are automatically placed between text items produced by separate variables, provided that the variables are enclosed in conditional brackets. As long as you use the conditional brackets, multiple spaces are suppressed, so you can safely to include them in Sentence Structures if in doubt. But if conditional brackets are not used TMG uses exactly the spaces you include, so you must include all needed spaces but no extras.

These provisions generally produce correctly punctuated text without much attention by the user, except for the need to remember to not place a comma after the variable **[L]**. However, when you create more complex Sentence Structures, especially when they involve conditional terms, some care is required. This is particularly true when you want a comma or period to appear only if a specific data field is used. In this case, the punctuation must be within the conditional brackets.

For example, suppose you want to create a custom Tag Type for Army enlistments that may or may not contain information in the Memo field about the enlistee's rank. But if the rank is in the Memo field, you want it to be set off by a comma. You might create the following Sentence Structure:

[P] enlisted <[D]> in the Army, < [M]>, <[L]>

But the resulting text would be something like "He enlisted on 1 Jun 1856,, in Richmond" when the rank is omitted, with undesired extra commas. What is needed is:

[P] enlisted <[D]> in the Army <, [M],> <[L]>

Note that the commas are placed inside the conditional brackets. This would correctly produce "He enlisted on 1 Jun 1856 in Richmond" when the

rank is omitted, and "He enlisted on 1 Jun 1856, as a private, in Richmond" when it is included.

With some thought and practice, and by occasionally testing the results in a Preview Report, you can create Sentence Structures that produce correctly structured text in a wide variety of circumstances.

Embedded Format Codes

TMG offers a variety of Embedded Format Codes, often call "Printer Codes," which allow you to change the way text will appear in reports. These codes work together with the settings in Preferences and those in the Report Definitions to control various aspects of the final text. We cover these codes here because of their utility in Sentence Structures, but most of them can also be used in output templates for Sources, and in many of the data entry fields for Tags and Source Definitions.

Available Codes

The available codes can be divided into four groups:

Special Characters

- **Carriage Return** – to start a new line. If the Enter key is used to create a new line in a Sentence Structure, it is removed when the editing screen is closed. Use this code instead if a new line (paragraph) is needed. See *Chapter 9, Controlling Narratives*, for suggestions on using these codes to control paragraphs in Narrative Reports.
- **Tab** – a tab character cannot be entered with the Tab key, as that key is used to move between fields in data entry screens. When a tab is desired in the output, use this code.
- **Non-breaking Space** – to create a space that cannot be left at the end of a line of text by the word wrap feature of the report generator or your word processor. Useful, for example, to keep a house number and street name from appearing on separate lines. This code is more useful in Memos and other data fields than in Sentence Structures.

Formatting Text

This group directly controls the font formatting of the indicated text. This group includes the following normal text formatting styles:

- **Bold**
- **Underline**
- **Italics**
- **Superscript**
- **Subscript**
- **Caps**
- **Small Caps**

Note – The codes above are designed for use in Memos and Citation Detail fields, and in Source Templates. They are not recommended for use in Sentence Structures because of adverse interaction with Report Font Coding (see next section).

The following special codes are also available:

- **Hidden Text** – the included text will be visible in TMG screens, but will never be included in reports. This is useful in data fields but generally not in Sentence Structures.
- **Index** – allows you to create an index entry, for use when an index is created in a report. This function is generally used in Memos, rather than in Sentence Structures. See Help, under "Index(es)" for details.
- **Point Size** – allows you to specify the size of the font to be used. Specify the desired point size after the opening code, followed by a semicolon. For example: [SIZE:]8; *applicable text*[:SIZE].
- **E-mail** – allows e-mail addresses to be included.
- **HTML** – allows HTML codes, the language of web pages, to be included. See Help under "HTML Embedded Codes" for details.
- **Web Link** – allows Internet links to be included.

Report Font Coding

Report Definitions allow you specify the font type, style (regular, bold, Italic), and size separately for each of ten types of data. Examples include Surnames, Given Names, Dates, Places, etc. These specifications can be set independently for each report you create (see *Chapter 10, Customizing Reports*, for details). The embedded codes for "Font" allow you to have any text you mark to take on the characteristics specified for the corresponding type of data when you create reports.

By using this feature, rather that using the codes listed above to specify the font size and attributes like bold or Italics directly, you can easily change the font specifications for groups of text when you create reports, or even have them appear differently in different reports. In addition, you can control the actual font, or typeface, with this feature, which you cannot do with the other codes. However, some attributes, such as superscript and small caps, cannot be applied with this coding.

Embedded Citations

This special purpose code allows a source citation to be placed at the point in a report corresponding to where the code is placed. This function is generally used in Memos, rather than in Sentence Structures. For details on its use, see *Chapter 7, Sources*.

Entering Embedded Codes

Many fields that support use of embedded codes have the appropriate codes listed on a right-click menu. You can either enter them by using the right-click menu, or type them in directly. Note that the codes in the Special Characters group consist of a single code, in the form [:TAB:]. All the rest are paired codes, placed in pairs around the text to which they apply. They take the form [ITAL:]*applicable text*[:ITAL]. For these paired codes, when you are applying them to existing text, select (highlight) the text to be included before choosing the code from the right-click menu.

Sentence Structures and GEDCOM Export

Sentence Structures are **not** exported in GEDCOM files. Therefore if you commonly export GEDCOM files you should not embed significant information in Sentence Structures. For example, suppose you created a "No Children" Tag, to mark couples without issue. You might create a Sentence Structure of "[P] and [PO] had no children." If this Tag was included in a GEDCOM export the intent would be lost to the recipient. However, if instead you used an Anecdote Tag and entered in the Memo "They had no children" the full meaning would likely be transmitted in the exported file.

Similarly, use of Roles and their associated Sentence Structures is not reflected in GEDCOM exports. So information that might be contained through Roles, such as the multiple marriage example shown in the above section "Sometimes Role Name Variables Are Not the Best Way" will not be communicated by GEDCOM exports. For further details on the limitations of GEDCOM see *Chapter 15, Exporting Data.*

Tip – Create a Customized Preview Report

Many factors impact the text produced in various reports by a given Sentence Structure. They include which person is the focus of the Report (in tags linked to more than one person), the position of the resulting sentence in the narrative, the options selected for the Report, and even the specific Report you use. Many users find it takes some practice to learn how to create Sentence Structures that produce the results they have in mind. The best way to be sure your efforts create the results you want is to check them by using a "Preview" report.

There is a very helpful "Individual Narrative Preview" report available on the Reports Toolbar. This report is a quick and easy way to verify that the Sentence Structures you create work generally as you intend. The default settings for each of the dozens of available report options may not match your preferences, but you can change those options to match your own favorite settings. To apply your own settings, open the Individual Narrative Report from the Reports menu, and select the "Individual Narrative Preview" configuration on the Report Definition Screen. Then make any changes to the Options you would like, and save them by clicking the Save button. After that, the Preview Report toolbar button will produce reports with the options that you have selected.

However, many users prefer the Journal style narrative reports, which arrange text in a different layout. Others prefer to see how their data will appear in multi-generation formats such as the Descendant Indented Narrative or the Ahnentafel reports. If you prefer a report style other that the Individual Narrative, you can obtain a more accurate preview by creating a custom preview report in your preferred style. You can attach that report to the Custom Toolbar for easy access (see *Chapter 9, Controlling Narratives*, for more on specific narrative reports, and *Chapter 4, Customizing the Program*, for details on attaching a report to the Toolbar).

A Case Study – Using Sentence Structures as Part of an Overall Strategy for Data Management

This chapter covers techniques for using Sentence Structures to meet a range of user needs; some fairly basic and others quite complex. The techniques that work best for you will depend on just what you want TMG to do for you, and particularly what you expect in data output.

As a way of illustrating a range of output expectations and how different expectations lead to different practices, I outline my own practices. You can perhaps see how your own expectations agree or differ, and thus choose a strategy that works well for you.

I've found that my expectations for output fall in three stages, linked to my progress in documenting a specific line.

In the first stage, I want to document everything I find. But I also want to maintain my data in a form that will allow me to create narratives for any line that I can send to a newfound cousin without editing, and without being embarrassed by the result. I want the output to be grammatically correct, but style is not much of an issue. So at this stage I:

- Use Global Sentence Structures that produce grammatically correct output for the majority of the cases, and customize Individual Sentence Structures when needed. For example my customized Census Tag Type deals with children living with mother, father, or both parents, but I have to customize individual Tags when I find elderly parents living with their children, or nieces, nephews, grandchildren, or the like in the household.

- Cite every source in detail. This includes such "questionable" sources as Ancestral File™ and any sort of index if I don't immediately access the original source, and even web sites I find.

- Record conflicting data with abandon, using custom Birth-alt tags (with a Sentence Structure of "[P] has also been reported to have been born< [D]>< [L]>< [M]>"), custom note tags, and similar means. I tend to record each item of information independently, disregarding how the separate Tags may cause choppy narratives. For example I may use a new occupation tag for every time if find someone's occupation.

- Every time I run a report and find spelling or grammar errors, or data entry errors, I fix the data in TMG. I then either rerun the report or make the same change in the word processor. That way I don't have to make that correction again.

In the second stage, when the line begins to get fairly solidly documented, I begin to think of sending "finished" reports on portions of it to selected relatives, especially to the cousins who have provided help with various branches. At this stage I'm still not looking for compelling reading, but I want the story of each person to flow reasonably well – not just one fact after another but a smooth flow from one subject to another. This stage seems to be precipitated by the need to send a report to someone special, so I create the report and start polishing it up as follows:

- Try to resolve conflicting information, often getting rid of the Birth-alt and similar Tags, transferring the citations to the remaining Tags and adding notes documenting my thinking in choosing the information I think most likely correct.
- Add Exclusion Markers to citations of low quality sources if I've found better ones, so they won't print in reports.
- Change Sort Dates so the paragraphs flow better. Sometimes I put all comments on a subject together rather than making everything chronological. Census and other tags related to the family's' movement may be put together, then a discussion on occupation changes over time, then public service, etc.
- Modify Tags to add context. For example, four occupation tags from three census and a death certificate may get combined into a single tag, with wording added that the initial occupation was as "a youngster working in his father's shop" but then he "became a salesman as reported in the 1920 and 1920 census" and finally was reported "in his death certificate to be a ...." so the reader knows why we only have three or four snapshots. I

do this with a combination of adding text in Memos and customizing Sentence Structures.

- Always make all these changes in TMG, not in the word processor. Because the next cousin I write to will likely need a different report, with perhaps two thirds of the same people but one third new ones, and I don't want to edit the same people again.

Finally, step three is somewhat hypothetical at this point. It's "the book" that every genealogist hopes to one day write. My one attempt to issue a "mini-book" leads me to see that it can start with the output from the previous stage. But I need to weave in a story to make it more interesting reading. I don't really expect to do that in TMG. I suspect the addition of a story line, more polished flow, and final formatting all need to be done in a word processor.

Conclusion

With just a little care in the selection of Tag Types as you enter your data, the default Sentence Structures will produce understandable, but hardly polished, narratives. In many cases the text will seem repetitive and a bit stilted, perhaps a bit like the computer-generated text it is. If your intent is to communicate information rather than create a linguistic work of art, you may be satisfied with only a little attention to the finer points of editing Sentence Structures.

By contrast, high quality writing requires substantial human editing, no matter how sophisticated the computer program that generates the draft. This can be done by extensive customizing of the data within TMG, or by editing your reports in a word processor.

Many users have expectations somewhere between these two extremes. My own objectives and techniques, as outlined in the previous section, illustrate some points in this range.

Other users want to produce reports, or more likely web pages, that contain high quality narratives, and they want to be able to re-generate those outputs regularly to incorporate new information they include in their data. TMG also supports this way of working quite nicely. If this is your objective, you should pay more attention to the Sentence

Structures of Tags as they are entered, and consider how they will fit with surrounding Tags. Sentence Structures will have to be edited to provide the variety we expect in good writing. Such techniques as rearranging elements, and using a variety of Name Variables help produce text that reads as we expect in better writing.

Decide what your objectives are, and then use the ideas in this chapter to help you obtain them. If you want something more than basic communication, you can achieve it with attention and practice. Create a customized preview report, and use it often. With practice, your skills become polished, and getting the results you want becomes progressively easier.

Chapter 7 - Sources

By Jim Byram

Next to collecting data in your genealogical research, the second most important task is to document the origins of your data. Data without accompanying source documentation is little better than hearsay and lacks credibility. The primary value of documenting your data is to provide a record that can be passed on to others and that will allow your readers or other researchers to reconstruct your research process by being able to review the data that you used. In addition, the quality of your source documentation facilitates your own research by allowing you to review and reconsider your own work and by giving you a tool to analyze the value of the data obtained from a particular source.

A Quick Overview of Sources

Many people using TMG for the first time are confused by sources and source citations and how all of the pieces fit together. Here is a simplified overview of how sources are defined, cited and used in reports.

Let's begin with four definitions:

- **Source** – The original material from which you obtained data (a book, a census schedule, a birth certificate).

- **Source citation** – A link connecting the data to the source (a source citation could indicate that you obtained birth data for a person from a certain book).

- **Citation Detail** – Where in the source the data was found (a page in a book, a census sheet).

- **Repository** – The institution or person in possession of the source from which you obtained data (a library where the book was found).

You go to the library (a repository) and use a book (a source) to obtain information about one of your ancestors… for example, his birth (an event). You have the birth (a fact) and some data about the birth (the date and place). The information came from one page in the book. In TMG, you are going to record several different types of information and tie them all together. Let's do the steps in the following order:

- **Create a repository record.** Open the Master Repository List (**Tools > Master Repository List**), click [Add] to open the Repository Definition screen and record the details about the library that you visited. Save this new repository.

- **Create a source record.** Open the Master Source List (**Tools > Master Source List**), click [Add] to create a new source definition, and [Select] a source type of Book (Authored). This opens the Source Definition screen (SDS) with the General tab showing. You will see a field to enter an abbreviation and other fields where you will record the information about your book (Title, Author, Date, Publisher, etc.). Record the appropriate details. You might add text to the Comments field on the Supplemental tab.

- **Link the source to the repository.** Select the Attachments tab and from this screen link this source to the repository you created. You click the [+] button next to the repository field, click the 🔍 button to open the Master Repository List, highlight the repository entry for your library and click [Select]. Click [OK] to save this repository link.

- **Take a look at the Output Form tab.** This tab of the Source Definition screen has several *Ibid* options and three default templates that determine how the full footnote, short footnotes and bibliography will appear when you create a report that uses this source. Save your source by clicking [OK].

- **Record the birth using a Birth tag.** Go to the individual's Person View in the Details window and add a birth tag (<CTRL>+<B> or **Add > Birth**). With the Tag Entry screen open, you will edit the tag and record the birth date and place.

- **Create a Source Citation to link the Birth tag to the source.** Select the Citations tab on the Tag Entry screen for the Birth tag and add a citation to the source that you just created. You click the [+] button next to the citations field, click the 🔍 button to open the Master Source List, highlight the source entry for your book and click [Select]. You enter the page number into the empty Citation Detail field and save the citation by clicking [OK]. Save the birth tag by clicking [OK].

Looking back, you have created a repository entry, created a source entry and linked this source to the repository, added an event tag and created a source citation with citation detail linking the birth tag to your new book source. In other words, you have recorded various types of data and have tied all of these pieces of data together. At this point, it's important to note that you can add source citations to facts (using name, relationship and event tags) about a person, not to the person directly. You can add as many source citations as you wish to any tag and you can cite a given source from as many tags as you wish. Likewise, a repository can be linked to multiple sources.

So, you've recorded source information for this birth. How will that data be used? Let's assume that you produce an Individual Narrative report about this person (**Reports > Individual Narrative**). You select the appropriate options for the report on the Report Definition Screen so that your report will include sources. Click on the [Options] button and select the Sources tab. You could choose to generate footnotes or endnotes. From the Publication Tools tab, you can choose to add a bibliography. After selecting the desired options, you click [OK] to save your settings and [Print & Save] to generate the report.

Here's where the templates that you saw on the Output Form tab of the Source Definition screen are used. During the printing of the report (report generation), all of the tags linked to that person are processed and the report text is created. Footnotes (or endnotes) are created 'on the fly' as the source links for each tag are processed. The source templates determine the information that will be

added to the footnotes and are comprised of 'Source Elements' that correspond to the fields where you entered your source data on the General tab of the Source Definition screen.

The full footnote template is used the first time that a footnote is created. The short footnote template is used for subsequent citations of the same information. The *Ibid* options on the Output Form tab determine whether the short footnote will be repeated or whether *Ibid* is used. The bibliography template is used for creating the bibliography entries. Repository data will be included in the footnotes if a given template has elements referring to the repository data. Remember that we chose a 'source type' of Book (Authored) as appropriate for our book. Each source type has a unique set of templates appropriate for that source type (book, census, tax list, will, etc.).

When a report is output, the report generator follows *who, what, and how* rules to determine what to include in the report.

- *Who* – Who are the individual(s) to be included in the report.

- *What* – What data is included in the report (all or selected tags, sources, etc.)

- *How* – How is the report formatted (fonts, sources as footnotes or endnotes, etc.)

These *who, what, and how* rules come from:

- the settings on the Report Definition Screen and

- the data and settings on the Source Definition screen.

As you can see from our walk-through above, source data and applicable options are found in a number of locations in TMG:

- the Master Source List (**Tools > Master Source List**) – define sources and enter source data, link to repositories, edit/review the templates that control report output.

- the Master Repository List (**Tools > Master Repository List**) – define repositories and enter repository data.

- the Tag Entry screen Citations tab (open a tag on the Person view of the Details window and select the Citations tab) – create citations linking tags to sources.

- the Source Types screen (**Tools > Source Types**) – manage and create Source Types and their templates (used for report output).
- the Source Elements screen (**Tools > Source Elements**) – manage and create Source Elements (these make up the source type templates).
- various Report Definition screens (Reports, then select a report type) – specify whether the report will include sources and set various details.

Lastly, you might wonder why I did the walkthrough in a seemingly backwards way – repository, then source, then event, then citation. Your normal inclination might be to create the event, citation, source and repository in that order. Or, if we're discussing sources, why not go to the Master Source List first? I wanted each section of the puzzle to be completed before it was added to the big picture. And the 'backwards' walkthrough is easier to explain. Once you are comfortable with how the parts work, you can enter your data in the order that you prefer.

Important Source References

Two books have been published specifically to give genealogical researchers some guidance in using and documenting sources.

- Lackey, Richard S. *Cite Your Sources. A Manual for Documenting Family Histories and Genealogical Records.* Jackson, Mississippi: University Press of Mississippi, 1980.

- Mills, Elizabeth Shown. *Evidence! Citation & Analysis for the Family Historian.* Baltimore, Maryland: Genealogical Publishing Company, 1997.

TMG includes templates for report output modeled after the examples in each of these books (see below). Both of these books take a 'U.S.-centric' approach but offer lessons that can be applied to any locale. The style guides give both guidance on what elements to include in various types of source citations and also suggest the form (including order and punctuation) for footnotes and bibliographic entries. The first half of Ms. Mills' book consists of an extensive treatment of the citation of genealogical sources and the analysis of genealogical data. At the least, every TMG user who uses the standard templates should have a copy of Ms. Mills' book on your bookshelf and should make frequent use of it.

Lumpers vs. Splitters

Lackey is what you might call a 'lumper' providing only fourteen very general-purpose categories, one of which can be applied to any type of source. A frequent complaint is that Lackey does not specifically address modern 'electronic' sources although one of his categories can be used to record even those types of sources.

Mills, on the other hand, is a 'splitter' dividing her examples into over 100 much more specific categories. People are frequently searching for just the right fit for a given source into one of Ms. Mills' categories. They miss the point that these various categories are, in fact, examples intended to help guide the researcher in constructing their own source categories as the need arises.

The important point about using either of these two style guides is that one of your responsibilities as a researcher is to understand what is required to properly document a source and, then, to use your creativity in accomplishing that goal. The examples in Ms. Mills' book are the current standard for documenting genealogical data and her examples provide much more handholding and insight into what sort of data is required to document sources.

TMG and Sources — Some Background

Wholly Genes, Inc. has made the documentation of sources easier for you by building into TMG two sets of source categories modeled after these two style guides (*see Appendix F, Source Templates*). It is important to note that the source types and the templates for each source type are the particular interpretation by Wholly Genes of these style guides and "are not intended to suggest endorsement on the part of their authors" nor to "warrant that they accurately reflect the intentions of those authors."

TMG also has a third set of source categories called 'Custom' that in TMG5 are initialized to one of the above two sets of source categories (modeled after the categories in either the Lackey or Mills style guides) as the starting point. Custom categories are the default selection for new projects and for projects imported from a source other than from an older version of TMG or from Ultimate Family Tree (UFT). A project based on an imported TMG data set will use the set of categories selected in the original data set. A project imported from a UFT data set will use custom source categories imported with the UFT data set. The Custom source categories should probably be the starting point for most researchers.

The set of source categories used for a particular **project** is selected on the **File > Preferences > Current Project Options > Other** tab using the Source Categories selection box. You can select 'as drawn from "Evidence" (E.S.Mills)', 'as drawn from "Cite Your Sources" (R.Lackey)' or Custom. If the project is set to Custom, a **new data set** will be set to source categories modeled after the Mills style guide. Each data set in a project using Custom source categories can be independently initialized to source categories following either the Mills or the Lackey style guides.

Important tip… If you change your Source Categories setting from Lackey or Mills to Custom, afterwards, you should go to the Source Types screen (**Tools > Source Types**) and explicitly [Initialize] each data set in the project to the source categories type that you plan to use for that data set. *This step is required to initialize to Lackey source categories but is also recommended if you plan to use Mills categories.*

Initializing the sources to the templates modeled after the Lackey or Mills style guides sets or resets all of the global output templates associated with that set of source categories to the default template designs. Initializing does not change any output template that had been customized at the source definition level.

Since the choice of source categories is set on a project basis, data sets imported into an existing project will have their source categories converted into the corresponding selections already in use. If you import a TMG data set using source categories modeled after Lackey or Mills and wish to retain those source types, you should go to the Source

Types screen and [Initialize] that data set to the source categories modeled after Lackey or Mills respectively. Custom source types, elements and templates will be retained.

If you plan to switch from Lackey to Mills source categories or from Mills to Lackey source categories, Appendix D, *Translation of Source Categories* shows how the source types for the two sets of source categories are translated from one to the other.

Terminology – An Explainer

Some find the 'Source Categories' and 'Source Types' terminology confusing. TMG allows the user to select and thus implement either of two sets of Source Categories modeled after the categories in the Lackey and Mills style guides. Source categories are like buckets and source types are like apples that you put into the buckets. Some buckets (source categories) hold only one apple (one source type) whereas others can hold more than one apple (several source types could fall into that category).

In TMG, *each source category from the Lackey and Mills style guides is represented by a specific source type* that exemplifies a particular collection of data elements that can be used to document one or more different source types. There are obviously many thousands of potential source types that can be divided into a smaller number of source categories.

Using Lackey source categories, the source type representing each source category is very broad and is named just like the category would be named (census record, family bible, letter, etc.)

The source types representing the Mills source categories are much more narrowly defined and the name used for each representative source type may not give you a clear picture of how to visualize the broader source category that the particular example represents.

For example, the source category example in Ms. Mills book named "Photograph (Private Possession) (Annotated, with Provenance)" actually represents a broader collection of objects that could be called "Family Memorabilia." This particular category can be used to document any of the wide variety of items that constitute family memorabilia. In discussions on the TMG Mailing List (TMG-L), Ms. Mills has pointed out that the critical elements in documenting these items of family memorabilia are "the 'type' of object, the inscription (on the object), a description (of the object), the provenance (where the object came from), and the current location (of the object)". The TMG source type 'Photograph (Private Possession) (Annotated, with Provenance)' is representative of the family memorabilia category of sources and can be used to document any item of family memorabilia used as a source.

Looking around me, I see several photographs of family members, several photographs taken by family members, a ceramic made by one of my sisters, a cartoon, a print of an electron micrograph, an Indian water pipe and a brass mortar. The objects represent at least several distinct source types. These objects all fall into the source category of family memorabilia and each may be documented using the 'Photograph (Private Possession) (Annotated, with Provenance)' source type that represents the broader Family Memorabilia source category.

You may find that none of the existing source types can fit well for a source that you need to document and that you will want to add a new custom source type (see below).

Master Source List Management

If you begin by importing a data set into TMG from a program or data source other than TMG, your first introduction to sources will be when you open the Master Source List (MSL) (**Tools > Master Source List**).

This is a time to stop and reflect on the chaos that most likely greeted you at that point. The 'Less' view of the MSL is typically sorted by the source Abbreviation. The source abbreviation is entered or edited in the Abbreviation field on the General tab of the Source Definition screen. You open the Source Definition screen by selecting a source and clicking the [Edit] button on the MSL. The source abbreviation helps you locate any particular source in the list on the Less view of the MSL, shows on the Tag Entry Citations tab and Citations screen, and, optionally, is output on the List of Sources.

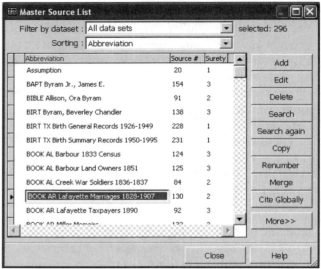

Figure 7-1: Master Source List, Less View

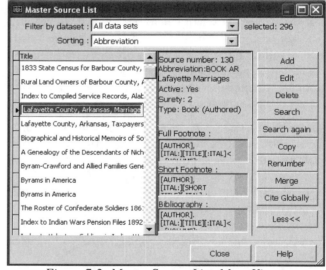

Figure 7-2: Master Source List, More View

To help manage your MSL, it's important to give some thought to how to structure the 50-character source abbreviation. Several schemes have been described using a 3- or 4-character keyword at the beginning of the field to order your sources. The keyword is followed by information appropriate to the particular source (place abbreviations, a name, a surname, a few words of a title, etc.). I personally use a mix of 3-6 letter keywords and some words. Some examples follow.

- Assumption
- BAPT Byram Jr., James E.
- BIBLE Allison, Ora Byram
- BIRT Byram, Beverley Chandler
- BOOK AR Lafayette Marriages
- CEME LA Bossier Rocky Mount
- CENSUS 1880 U.S. LA Bossier
- DEAT Gardner, Ike
- EMAIL Byram, J. 1999/05/18
- FGS Watson Jr., William B.
- GEDCOM Dalrymple (79492)
- LAND Patent AL 4250_.430
- LETT Byrom, Jack E. 1997/01/20
- LIST Byram Reunion 1999
- MARR AR Union Marriages B
- MILI LA Confederate Pensions
- MISC Barnett Affidavit
- NEWS Bossier Banner
- OBIT Klock, Robert Eugene
- PROB Byram, J.C. (estate 2)

Jeri Steele has described a system based on the abbreviation of the locality in reverse order (US Cen Pop Sched 1850, TX SmithCo Tyler City Directory, UK Camb Vitals of Cambridgeshire England, etc.). In addition, Jeri uses FAM for family sources and PER for person sources. Others have described a variety of different approaches to MSL organization.

Source Types, Source Element Groups and Source Elements

Source data are entered on the Source Definition screen (*see Figure 7-3*).

When you add a new source from the MSL, you click the [Add] button and select a Source Type. If you chose to use the source categories modeled after Lackey, you have available 14 source types. If you chose to use the source categories modeled after Mills, you have available 96 source types. Additional custom source types can be added when using Custom source categories. Once you select the source type, the Source Definition screen is opened to the General tab where the source data is entered. After you enter a default surety value and the abbreviation, you proceed to enter the actual source data. The particular Source Type that you have selected will determine the labels for the Title field and the lower 14 fields. No pre-constructed source type actually uses all 14 lower fields.

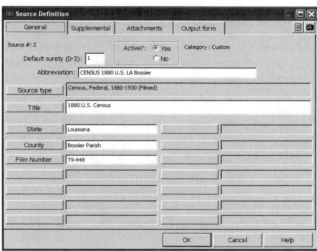

Figure 7-3: Source Definition screen, General tab

If we look 'under the hood,' here's how the 15 fields work. Source data is broken down into 30 Source Element Groups and each Source Element Group is represented by one or more Source Elements for a total of 130 Source Elements (*see Appendix E, Source Element Groups and Source Elements*). There are two very important concepts underpinning the structure of the source data.

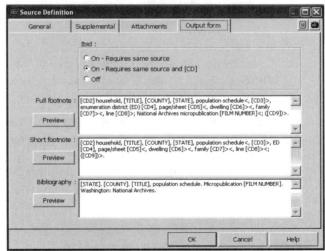

Figure 7-4: Source Definition screen, Output form tab

First, you are actually storing data in fields representing the Source Element Groups. The Source Elements are aliases for the Source Element Groups to make the field labels on the General tab and the elements used in the Source Templates on the Output Form tab more user-friendly.

It makes a lot more sense if the elements for a particular source type use terminology appropriate for that source type. For a book, for example, you would expect to see fields on the General tab and use elements in the templates on the Output Form tab named something like Author, Publish Date, Publisher and Publisher Address.

Second, and this is important… Each Source Element Group can be used only once for a given source record. In other words, each field used on the General tab and each corresponding Source Element used in the templates on the Output Form tab must come from a different Source Element Group. You need to keep this in mind when you add custom Source Elements for your custom Source Types.

Not all Source Element Groups and their Source Element aliases will show up in the fourteen lower fields on the General tab.

- The Comments Source Element Group is used for the source memo field (labeled 'comment', 'Comment' or 'Memo' depending on the source type in use) on the Supplemental tab of the Source Definition screen. The comments field can be used for comments or for recording the source text.

- There are two Source Element Groups that use the Citation Detail and the Reference fields from Tag Entry Citation screens. We will come back to the Citation Detail Source Element Group CD element later.

- Three Source Element Groups are used for repository data. Two of these use data from fields on the Repository Definition screen and one uses data from the Reference field on the Repository Link Entry Screen that is accessed from the Attachments tab of the Source Definition screen.

Further Notes Regarding the General Tab of the Source Definition Screen

Default surety field – This field is used to record a number (0-3) reflecting your evaluation of the general worth of the source. This entry is used nowhere else in TMG. Surety entries on the Citation screen linking a given data tag to a source (see the Citations section below) are entered independent of this value.

Title field – The 'Title' field is unique in that it remains even if you delete the [TITLE] (or equivalent) Source Element from the templates on the Output Form tab. The Title field will always be used for the Title Source Element Group and its label will change depending on which title Source Element is used by the templates.

Fields allowing name entry – The data entry fields representing the Source Elements used in templates accept alphanumeric data; however, fields used for the four Source Element Groups that are used for name entry differ. These Source Element Groups are Author, Compiler, Second Person and Subject. Fields used for Source Elements representing these four Groups allow entry of a name in two different forms:

- As a name in text – For example, 'Smith, John' or 'John Smith'. See the discussion about Lastname/Firstname order below.

- As an ID number – In other words, you can enter the ID number of a person from the data set to which the source belongs. An ID number is entered as a number only. If the number represents a person in the data set, the person's name will appear when you save the field (for example, by tabbing to the next field).

Names entered into the name fields representing the Author, Compiler and Second Person Source Element Groups should be entered in the form 'Lastname, Firstname' with semicolons (;) separating the names of multiple persons. Multiple names entered as ID numbers are also separated with semicolons. The report output for certain source types following the Mills style guide requires that the order of the Lastname and Firstname differ in footnotes and in the bibliography. The program will create text with the name parts in the correct order when the Author's name is entered as described above.

Names entered as 'Lastname, Firstname' into name fields representing the Subject Source Element Group are also processed as above. This results in name formatting that differs from the examples in the Mills style guide (for example, Birth Registration (State Level). If you enter the name into these Subject Group Element fields in

'Firstname Lastname' form, you will get report output of names like the Mills examples.

The short footnote output for some source types, following Mills' examples, uses only the author's last name. An example would be the 'Book (Authored)' source type. If you have multiple sources from authors of the same surname, the report output might be confusing so you need to modify the short footnote template to include author's full name. This can be done by direct entry of the author's name into the template on the Output Form tab or by adding an element from a different Source Element Group such as [SUBJECT]. You can then enter the name in 'Firstname Lastname' format into the Subject field on the General tab. An alternative used by some TMG users is to use a Lastname Initial form or other short coding to help distinguish similar authors. For example: SmithJ, SmithL, or SmitJ and SmitL.

Field label display conventions – Several display conventions are used for the lower 14 field labels (on the buttons) used on the General tab. The labels reflect the Source Element names used in the templates on the Output Form tab. Conditional Source Elements in a template show up on the General tab of the Source Definition screen enclosed in '<   >' (for example, '<Edition>'). If you do not enter data into those fields, they will not show up in your report as 'missing…'. If a Source Element has been removed from the templates (by deletion on the Output Form tab), the field name will be displayed in lower case (for example, 'edition'). If you either save the source or change the source type, the out-of-date empty field will be removed with one exception. *If the field for the missing element on the General tab contains data, the label for the field will again be displayed in lower case and the field will remain on the General tab until the field contents are cleared.* In the last case, if you change to a source type that uses this deleted element, the out-of-date field will be rejuvenated.

Source Templates

Each source type has three templates that determine how the source data will be formatted in full footnotes, short footnotes and the bibliography when a source assigned to this source type is used

in a report (*See Appendix F, Source Templates*). The Source Elements used to compose those templates determine the data-entry fields available on the General tab of the Source Definition screen for a source assigned that particular source type. A template is simply a text construct consisting of Source Elements, punctuation & spaces, conditionals (< >) and formatting codes (such as [ITAL:] [:ITAL]). Any portion of a source template enclosed in conditionals will be omitted from report output if the data-entry field represented by the included element is empty.

Source Templates are defined at two levels:

- Globally – When you define a new source type, you construct the three templates. These templates will apply globally to all sources assigned to that particular source type. If you edit the template(s) for an existing source type from the Source Types screen, those edits will apply to all sources using that source type.

- Individually – The templates for any given source type definition can be edited for that particular source entry on the 'Output form' tab of the Source Definition screen. 'Locally' edited templates are marked as 'Overridden' on the 'Output form' tab. The edited template(s) will replace the default global templates when the source is used in a report. Any subsequent changes to the global templates will have no effect on the overridden template(s) for that particular source. Simply erasing the overridden template(s) can restore the global template(s) for any given source.

There is one template design limitation… Citation detail Source Elements such as [CD] and the citation reference element [CREF] cannot be used in the Bibliography template. If you enter one of these elements in a Bibliography template, it will not be processed and the element text (for example, '[CD]') will show up in your report bibliography. The reason that you can't use these Source Elements in a Bibliography template is that there can be many different citations attached to a given source, each with its own citation detail and reference entry.

How Do You Know What Each Source Element Represents?

There have been several questions on The TMG Mailing List (TMG-L) asking if there is a dictionary of Source Element definitions. The answer is no. Look at the templates of the Source Type that you are concerned about. Open Ms. Mills' book and compare her example(s) to the templates. There will not necessarily be a one-to-one correspondence but, in most cases, you will be able to quickly determine the intent of the TMG implementation and understand how to fit your source data into the fields on the General tab of the Source Definition screen. There may well be more than one way to record your data. Don't be afraid to edit and innovate until you are comfortable with the results. Don't forget about the source memo (Source Definition screen > Supplemental tab) and the Citation Detail to record details that need to be spelled out more fully.

An Overview – Creating New Source Types and Source Elements

If you are using the Custom source categories, it won't be too long before you find a new source that just doesn't fit any of the pre-constructed source types. You might approach this task in the following way.

Look at the existing source types on the Source Types screen and at comparable examples in Ms. Mills' book. Have at hand, the list of Source Element Groups with their Source Elements (*See Appendix E, Source Element Groups and Source Elements*). Think through the design of the new source type.

- First, if necessary, create any new custom Source Elements from the Source Elements screen. In most cases, you will find that the default Source Elements will suffice. Keep in mind that no two Source Elements from the same Source Element Group can be used in the same source definition. In other words, you can't have two Source Elements from the same Source Element Group used for two different fields on the General tab or in the templates on the Output form tab of the Source Definition screen.

- Second, create the new custom source type from the Source Types screen. More than likely, one of the existing source types can be copied and the templates edited.

- Third, apply your new custom source type to an existing or new source definition. Enter your source data into the fields on the General tab of the Source Definition screen. Test your new source output by using the Preview buttons on the Output Form tab. Select the appropriate *Ibid* choice (see below) on this screen.

- Fourth, link this source to a tag on the Detail screen of an individual by creating a citation and entering the citation detail if required.

- Fifth, test the output for your new source using a narrative report. Configure and generate an Individual Narrative or other narrative report. The report definition should include source and bibliography output. Make liberal use of the on-screen report previews. I often check source output using a custom Journal report set to 1 generation and send the report to a Microsoft Word file. Check the report output to see how your source type templates worked.

- Sixth, if any refinement is necessary, walk through each step of the process once again to make any necessary edits. Repeat the cycle until you are satisfied with the result.

Creating New Source Types

You create your new custom source type from the Source Types screen (*see Figure 7-5*).

The Source Types screen can be accessed in one of two ways. If you want to create a new source type from scratch, you should use the Source Types option on the Tools menu (**Tools > Source Types**).

Or, if you want to create a new source type for an existing source, you could open the Master Source List (**Tools > Master Source List**), select the existing source and click the [Edit] button. On the General tab of the Source Definition screen, click on the [Source type] button to open the Source Types screen.

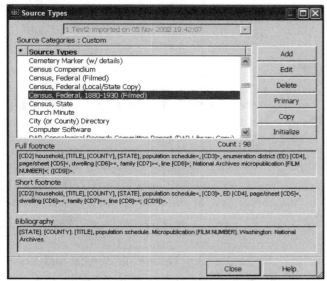

Figure 7-5: The Source Types screen

Once you get to the Source Types screen, there are two ways to create a new source type. You can click the [Add] button and start with a clean slate – the name and the three template fields will be empty. Alternatively, you can select an existing source type, make a copy by clicking the [Copy] button and, then, edit the name and existing templates. In most cases, the [Copy] alternative is the method of choice.

The 'is most similar to' setting is used during source types initialization. Any custom source type is reset to one of the default source types during initialization. It would be typically set to the Mills (or corresponding Lackey) source type most similar to the custom source type that you are editing. If your custom source types include none of the default source types modeled after Mills or Lackey, then you could set the 'is most similar to' setting to any existing source type.

Creating New Source Elements

The Source Elements screen can be accessed in one of two ways.

If you want to create a new Source Element from scratch, you should use the Source Elements option on the Tools menu (**Tools > Source Elements**).

Or, if you want to create a new source type for an existing source, you could open the Master Source List (**Tools > Master Source List**), select an

existing source and click the [Edit] button. On the General tab of the Source Definition screen, click on any blank button next to one of the 14 data fields in the lower half of the General tab to open the Source Elements screen.

Figure 7-6: The Source Elements screen

Note that when you open the Source Elements screen from the General tab, Source Elements from any Source Element Group that is already being used in your source definition will not show in the list.

You might also want to change an existing Source Element for a new or different Source Element. Clicking on one of these 14 buttons will open the Source Elements screen. After adding or changing a Source Element for a field on the General tab, you would want to edit the appropriate template(s) on the Output form tab to add the new or different Source Element.

Creating a new custom source type from scratch

The procedure for doing this in TMG5 is much simpler than it was with TMG4. First, **if necessary**, open the Source Elements screen (**Tools > Source Elements**) and add any required new Source Elements. You need to carefully plan the addition of Source Elements to Source Element Groups so that you will not attempt to use two Source Elements from the same Group in the same source type definition.

Next, open the Source Types screen (**Tools > Source Types**) and [Copy] an existing source type or [Add] a new source type. In most cases, you will probably use the first and simpler route of copying an existing source type. Name your new source type appropriately and create your new templates or edit the existing templates. If copying and editing an existing source type, be sure to edit the name!

After these two steps, you can go to the MSL (**Tools > Master Source List**) and [Add] a new source selecting your new source type.

Replacing the source type for an existing source with a new custom source type

I would recommend creating the new Source Elements and new source type as described above and then go to the MSL (**Tools > Master Source List**) and open the existing source by double-clicking on the source abbreviation or by selecting the source and clicking the [Edit] button. Click on the [Source Type] button on the General tab of the Source Definition screen and select the new custom source type. Then, enter the appropriate data into the new fields on the General tab. You would also want to move or delete data from the now unused fields on the General tab. Empty unused fields will be removed when the source is saved.

The alternative pathway for creating new source types

In TMG, there are always other possibilities. You can open the Master Source List, create a new source with the [ADD] button and select an existing source type. From the General tab of the Source Definition screen, you can click on the [Source Type] button and open the Source Types screen. You can [Add] or [Copy] and define a new source type and edit the name and templates of the new source type. Select the new source type and return to the General tab. Add new Source Elements if required and enter data. Save your new source definition.

Further Possibilities

The following was not possible in TMG4 but is possible in TMG5.

Create a new tag. Enter data into the tag fields. Select the Citations tab and click [+] to add a citation to the tag. Type <F2> or click [Binoculars] to open the Master Source List. Click [Add] to define a new source and click [Select] for an existing source type. From the General tab of the Source Definition screen click [Source Type], click [Add] to create a new custom source type, save and [Select] it. Add new custom Source Elements by clicking on blank buttons. From the Attachments tab of the Source Definition screen click [+] to add a new repository. From the Repository Link Entry Screen, type <F2> or click [Binoculars] to open the Master Repository List. [Add] a new repository using the Repository Definition screen and click [OK] to save. [Select] the new repository. Click [OK] to save the repository link. Click [OK] to save the new source definition. Click [Select] to select the new source. Enter the citation detail and surety values. Click [OK] to save the citation. Click [OK] to save the tag.

Modifying the templates for an existing source

You can modify the templates for any particular existing source without changing the global templates for the source type. Go to the MSL (**Tools > Master Source List**). Open the existing source by double-clicking on the source abbreviation or by selecting the source and clicking the [Edit] button. If you first need to create new Source Elements, start from the General tab of the Source Definition screen. Click on any of the blank fields in the lower half of the screen to open the Source Elements screen. Add a new element by clicking the [Add] button. Again, use forethought as to the Source Element Group to which you assign the new element. After saving the new element, save it and select it from the Source Element screen. You are returned to the General tab where you can add the data for the new field. Repeat this procedure if you need to add additional elements.

Next, select the Output Form tab and edit the three templates as required adding any new elements that you have created and deleting any elements that you choose not to use. Test each revised templates with the Preview button. Revised templates should be marked to the left of the template fields with the

(Overridden) notation. Be sure to change the *Ibid* setting if required. When you are finished, save your new source definition by clicking the [OK] button.

When you save the revised source definition, any fields on the General tab no longer being used in the templates defined on the Output Form tab will be removed. The next time that you open this particular source definition for editing, you will see that these unused elements have been removed from the General tab and that the remaining fields on the General tab will be ordered based on the order of the elements used in the templates shown on the Output Form tab.

The 'Ibid.' Selections on the Output form tab

First, let's define *Ibid. Ibid* means literally 'in the same place'. The use of *Ibid* is a document convention used to keep from repeating the full text of the same footnote or endnote over and over. Depending on the setting chosen (see the examples below), *Ibid* is used in place of the text to be repeated when the *next* footnote output by the report generator is for the same source and the citation detail may or may not be identical.

The Output Form tab of the Source Definition has three settings to determine how and when *Ibid* is used when you generate footnotes or endnotes with a narrative report. Three examples will make the point. In these examples, the second citation has a page number (p. 44) in the Citation Detail that differs from the page number (p. 33) used in the Citation Detail of the other three citations.

In this first example, *Ibid* is used for the additional citations and the differing page number is included.

On – Requires Same Source

[1]Frank M. Cochran Jr., *Lafayette County, Arkansas, Taxpayers, 1890* (Bradley, AR: Privately published, 1986), p. 33. Hereinafter cited as *1890 Lafayette Co. AR Taxpayers.*

[1]Ibid., p. 44.

[1]Ibid., p. 33.

[1]Ibid.

In this second example, *Ibid* is not used when the Citation Detail differs.

On – Requires Same Source and [CD]

[1]Frank M. Cochran Jr., *Lafayette County, Arkansas, Taxpayers, 1890* (Bradley, AR: Privately published, 1986), p. 33. Hereinafter cited as *1890 Lafayette Co. AR Taxpayers.*

[1]Cochran Jr., *1890 Lafayette Co. AR Taxpayers*, p. 44.

[1]Cochran Jr., *1890 Lafayette Co. AR Taxpayers*, p. 33.

[1]Ibid.

In this third example, *Ibid* is never used.

Off

[1]Frank M. Cochran Jr., *Lafayette County, Arkansas, Taxpayers, 1890* (Bradley, AR: Privately published, 1986), p. 33. Hereinafter cited as *1890 Lafayette Co. AR Taxpayers.*

[1]Cochran Jr., *1890 Lafayette Co. AR Taxpayers*, p. 44.

[1]Cochran Jr., *1890 Lafayette Co. AR Taxpayers*, p. 33.

[1]Cochran Jr., *1890 Lafayette Co. AR Taxpayers*, p. 33.

In the above examples, the number of footnotes or endnotes generated and the information conveyed to the reader is the same in all three cases. One caveat for the first example – If split CDs are being used, the entire Citation Detail string is tested, but if a difference occurs in any CD element, the *Ibid* is used but only the text from the first CD element (CD1) is appended. So, particularly when using 'generic' sources and split CDs to convey detail, it will be important to use the 'Requires Same Source and [CD] choice (see below).

Repositories

Each source that you use comes from a particular location – a 'repository.' This location may be the Family History Library in Salt Lake City, the National Archives in Washington, D.C., your local library or historical society or your personal file cabinet or bookshelf.

A repository entry is linked to a source from the Attachments tab of the Source Definition Screen. To add a repository link to this source, you click the

'+' button next to the 'Repositories for this source' field. This opens the Repository Link Entry Screen.

Figure 7-7: The Repository Link Entry Screen

From this screen, you can enter a repository Reference number of up to 30 characters and can click the ![binoculars] button to select a repository from the Master Repository List. You select an existing repository by highlighting the repository and clicking the [Select] button (not shown in *Figure 7-8)*. Alternatively, you can click the [Add] button to add a new repository definition (see below), save the new repository and [Select] it. Selecting a repository returns you to the Repository Link Entry screen and clicking [OK] returns you to the Attachments tab of the Source Definition Screen.

Note that the [Select] button only shows on the Master Repository List screen when the MRL is opened from the Repository Link Entry Screen. It does not show when the MRL is opened from the Tools menu.

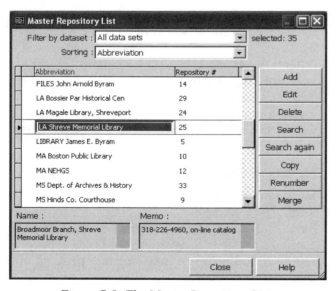

Figure 7-8: The Master Repository List

The Master Repository List – The Master Repository List (MRL) allows you to record and

manage these repositories (**Tools > Master Repository List**).

You click the [Add] button to create a new repository entry.

The Repository Definition screen – Repository details are entered on the Repository Definition screen. The Abbreviation field is used only for listing the repositories on the Master Repository List. As with sources, you should design meaningful repository abbreviations to allow you to quickly locate a repository on the MRL.

The name of the repository can be a person linked from a data set using the Name – ID# field or can be a person or place name or title entered into the Name – Other field. The Source Element [REPOSITORY] uses the contents of these fields in source templates.

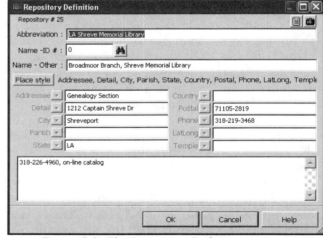

Figure 7-9: The Repository Definition screen

The remaining Repository Definition fields are place fields labeled according to the chosen place style. Using the U.S. Standard Place style, the fields include Addressee, Detail, City, County, State, Country, Postal, phone, LatLong and Temple. The [REPOSITORY ADDRESS] and [REPOSITORY INFO] Source Elements use the contents of these fields, except for LatLong, in source type templates. The Repository Definition screen also includes a memo field but there is no Source Element corresponding to this field. The repository memo field is provided for the user's notes (maybe directions on how to get there or a description of the environment (e.g., "the records are not well-maintained…").

You need to keep in mind how this data will appear in a report when entering data into these fields. Only certain of the default source type templates use these Source Elements. You might want to add the [REPOSITORY] and/or [REPOSITORY ADDRESS] Source Elements on a source or global basis to other templates.

Note that when you link a repository to a source, the Repository Link Entry Screen includes a repository Reference field (**Tools > Master Source List**, select a Source, click [Edit] to display the Source Definition screen > Attachments tab, select a repository from the list and open by double-clicking to display the Repository Link Entry Screen). The [REPOSITORY REFERENCE] Source Element uses the contents of this field in source templates.

Citations

Tags are linked to sources by adding a 'source citation' to the tag from the Citations tab of the Tag Entry screen (*see Figure 7-10*).

From this screen, you add citations by clicking the [+] button opening the Citation screen (*see Figure 7-11*) and remove citations by selecting a citation and clicking the [-] button.

The Citation screen has a field at the upper left showing the source number. A new citation shows '0' in this field. To link the source to the citation, you enter a source number or click the button, highlight a source on the Master Source List and click [Select].

The large text field is where you enter Citation Detail. Whereas the repository is where you locate a source, the citation detail provides a record of where *in the source* the data is located. At the simplest, this field might contain a page number. At the other extreme, the citation detail might point you to where a single household or even a person is located on a microfilm of a U.S. census population schedule. This field is also where you might enter comments about the data in the source. For example, I've found a household in the U.S. census split onto two pages that were microfilmed out of

order and separated from one another and recorded that information as part of the citation.

The Citation Detail field can contain one piece of data or can hold up to 9 discrete data elements (split CD elements, discussed below).

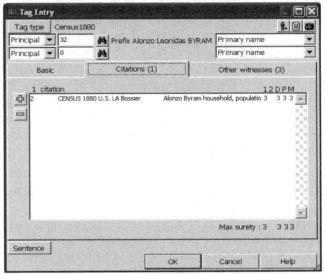

Figure 7-10: Tag Entry screen, Citations tab

The Citation Reference field accepts up to 30 characters of alphanumeric data and can be used, for example, to relate the source citation to a file or book location in your data filing system.

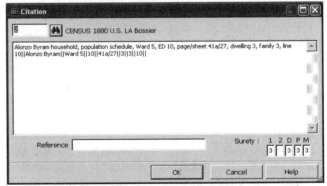

Figure 7-11: The Citation screen for a census tag. The large field is used to enter the Citation Detail.

You use the Surety fields to record your evaluation of the quality of the data in the source cited by this source citation. The five surety fields are for the Principal 1, the Principal 2, the date, the place and the memo field. The user enters their qualitative evaluation of the data using a scale of -, 0, 1, 2, or 3. For example, entering a surety value for the P1 for the primary name tag might indicate whether you judge that the name is complete and accurate. A surety value for the P1 of a birth tag might indicate whether you judge that this data applies to this person. A surety value for the date of the birth tag might indicate whether you judge that the date is accurate.

The hyphen or dash '-' represents negative surety and is used when the data is known or suspected to be false. '0' reflects that the quality of the data is unknown. '1' might indicate that another source for this data needs to be found. '2' might be used for secondary sources and transcriptions. '3' is normally used for original sources recorded close to the time of the event.

Each surety entry is subjective and is the user's evaluation of the data and source quality. Some users find entering surety to be a waste of their time and don't use this feature. I primarily use surety to indicate what data came from what source and as a visual guide to work that needs to be done.

How to Make Use of Split CDs

An example would be a census microfilm where you are recording data from various households. Ms. Mills' book contains an example, Census, Federal, 1880-1920 (Filmed). We will construct a custom source type that can serve as this example. In the process, we will both adhere to the layout of the Mills example and extend the utility of our TMG source type.

The first step is to create a new custom source type by copying the default 'TMG Census, Federal (Filmed)' source type. We will name the custom type 'Census, Federal, 1880-1930 (Filmed).' In this example, two new Source Elements are needed. From the **Tools > Source Elements** screen, we will add the Source Elements State to the Location Group and County to the Second Location Group. Edit the templates for our new source type as follows and save the source type definition. The 'Is most similar to' field will point to Census, Federal (Filmed).

If the citation detail has multiple CD elements, only CD1 is exported to GEDCOM files. Also, if a report is generated using the using the 'unique endnotes' feature (see below), only CD1 is printed.

For these reasons, in this example, CD1 is reserved for a complete listing of the citation detail.

Footnote

[CD2] household, [TITLE], [COUNTY], [STATE], population schedule<, [CD3]>, enumeration district (ED) [CD4], page/sheet [CD5]<, dwelling [CD6]><, family [CD7]><, line [CD8]>; National Archives micropublication [FILM NUMBER]<; ([CD9])>.

Short Footnote

[CD2] household, [TITLE], [COUNTY], [STATE], population schedule<, [CD3]>, ED [CD4], page/sheet [CD5]<, dwelling [CD6]><, family [CD7]><, line [CD8]><; ([CD9])>.

Bibliography

[STATE]. [COUNTY]. [TITLE], population schedule. Micropublication [FILM NUMBER]. Washington: National Archives.

Note that if you plan to use John Cardinal's Second Site web page generator with your TMG database, all CD elements must be enclosed in conditionals. These extra conditionals will have no effect on the report output from TMG.

Footnote (modified for Second Site)

<[CD2] household, >[TITLE], [COUNTY], [STATE], population schedule<, [CD3]><, enumeration district (ED) [CD4]><, page/sheet [CD5]><, dwelling [CD6]><, family [CD7]><, line [CD8]>; National Archives micropublication [FILM NUMBER]<; ([CD9])>.

Short Footnote (modified for Second Site)

<[CD2] household, >[TITLE], [COUNTY], [STATE], population schedule<, [CD3]><, ED [CD4]><, page/sheet [CD5]><, dwelling [CD6]><, family [CD7]><, line [CD8]><; ([CD9])>.

Create a new source definition from the Master Source List choosing our new source type 'Census, Federal, 1880-1930 (Filmed).' Enter data into the fields on the General tab of the Source Definition screen as appropriate to the census data. The remaining fields were entered as follows:

Abbreviation – CENSUS 1880 U.S. LA Bossier

Title – 1880 U.S. Census

State – Louisiana

County – Bossier Parish

Film Number – T9-448

Switch to the Output Form tab of the Source Definition screen and set the *Ibid* option to 'On – Requires Same Source and [CD].'

Create a new repository definition from the Master Repository List. The fields on the Repository Definition screen are completed as appropriate. In this case...

Abbreviation – US NARA--New England Region
Name - Other – National Archives--New England Region
City – Waltham
State – MA

Be sure to return to the Attachments tab of the Source Definition screen an link this Repository to your new Source.

When a narrative report is generated using this data, we'll see the following results.

Bibliography

Louisiana. Bossier Parish 1880 U.S. Census, population schedule. Micropublication T9-448. Washington: National Archives.

Footnote

Alonzo Byram household, 1880 U.S. Census, Bossier Parish, Louisiana, population schedule, Ward 5, enumeration district (ED) 10, page/sheet 41a/27, dwelling 3, family 3, line 10; National Archives micropublication T9-448.

Short Footnote

Alonzo Byram household, 1880 U.S. Census, Bossier Parish, Louisiana, population schedule, Ward 5, ED 10, page/sheet 41a/27, dwelling 3, family 3, line 10

Short Footnote (different household)

J. N. Gardner household, 1880 U.S. Census, Bossier Parish, Louisiana, population schedule, Twp. 22, ED 9, page/sheet 4a/7, dwelling 66, family 66, line 12.

The last example is very important. When our report is generated, there will be one footnote/endnote from this source and, possibly, many short footnotes. The short footnotes may very well pertain to different households and, thus, different heads of household. By using the techniques above, we were able to adhere to the examples in Ms. Mills' book as well as documenting each different household.

Some Additional Tips Regarding Split CDs

Using the second *Ibid* option on the Output Form tab of the Source Definition screen (On – Requires Same Source and [CD]), all parts of a split CD (in other words, the entire contents of the Citation Detail field) are compared during report generation to determine if *Ibid* or the short footnote should be used.

If you generate a report using the unique endnotes feature (**Report Definition Screen > Options > Sources tab > Endnotes radio button > Unique checkbox**), only the first Citation Detail element (CD or CD1) is printed in the endnotes.

Missing split CD elements – How do you edit the Citation Detail when the data is not available for one of the inner split CD elements? Say that the citation detail consists of three CD elements – CD1||CD2||CD3 and no data is available to enter for CD2. Either one of two methods work – CD1||||CD3 or CD1|| ||CD3. In other words, in addition to the normal '||' delimiter between the CD elements, add one delimiter set '||' for each missing CD element. One or more spaces are allowed between the delimiters where the missing element would go. The extra space or spaces aren't printed in report footnote/endnote output.

Trailing delimiters for split CD elements that are used in the templates but are unused in a given Citation Detail field can be dropped. Example – If your normal CD field consists of eight CD elements and you have no data for CD6, CD7 or CD8, you only need to enter CD1||CD2||CD3||CD4||CD5.

Use text macros as templates for frequently used split CDs. For example, for a particular census source type, you use a nine-part split CD.

CD1||CD2||CD3||CD4||CD5||CD6||CD7||CD8||CD9

You could construct a Text Macro (**Tools > Text Macros**) such as this example. Remember from the census example above that CD1 is used for the full listing for GEDCOM export or for report output using the 'unique endnotes' feature.

HOH household, population schedule, Tn, ED n, page/sheet n/n, dwelling n, family n, line n ||HOH||place||ED||pg/sh||house||family||line||comment

Insert the text macro into the Citation Detail field and replace the tokens with data. The tokens only need to understandable by you so keep them as short as possible to reduce editing. Using a template may take longer than direct entry but provides standardization and a visual prompt for the task at hand as well as reducing your data entry error rate and, thus, taking less time in the long run.

Specialized Source Types – 1

Many people use specialized sources such as Assumption, Inference, Speculation or Conclusion. You might want to add data to your data set based on 'reading between the lines' of the data reported from one or more sources. Since this new data will not be supported by explicit proof, you will want to document your thought process. An example of this is used in the SAMPLE data set. You can define a custom source type to facilitate using this source in reports. The following is an example of an Assumption source type.

Your source will have a default Surety of 0, an abbreviation of 'Assumption' and a title of 'Assumption.' You might wish to elaborate the title. The *Ibid* selection on the Output form tab should be set to 'On – Requires same source and [CD].'

The source type is titled 'Assumption' and the templates are as follows:

Footnote
[TITLE]<, [CD]> (alternatively, use [TITLE]<, [CD1]>)
Short Footnote
[TITLE]<, [CD]> (alternatively, use [TITLE]<, [CD2]>)
Bibliography
--

Enter your notes into the Citation Detail field of the tag. Using a 0 surety for the citations will allow you to exclude these sources from reports, if desired, by specifying that the reports should not include citations with sureties less than 1. You can enter full notes plus an abbreviated note for the Short Footnote template by using split CDs. The double exclusion marker (--) prevents any entry for this source in the bibliography of your reports.

Specialized Source Types – 2

The following example serves two purposes. The source categories drawn from the Mills examples lack a 'miscellaneous' all-purpose source type such as the 'Unpublished / Miscellaneous' source type seen in the categories modeled after Lackey. In addition, some people simply prefer not to use a variety of source types and their accompanying data

entry fields on the General tab of the Source Definition screen. There are many ways to construct such a source type and this source type can be used in a generic fashion.

The source abbreviation would be appropriate for the Master Source List and the source Title field would contain the source entry in its entirety. The *Ibid* selection on the Output form tab should be set to 'On – Requires same source and [CD].'

The Source Type is titled 'Miscellaneous' and the templates might be constructed as follows:

Footnote
[TITLE]<, [CD]>
Short Footnote
<[CD]><. Hereinafter cited as "[SHORT TITLE]">.
Bibliography
[TITLE]

The tag Citation Detail would contain the data specific to one record.

In a message on The TMG Mailing List (TMG-L), Birdie Holsclaw described a source entry for Social Security applications along these lines using what she calls her 'all-purpose free-form' source type. The source title is the full reference to the SS-5 form. The CD contains the applicant name, date and application number.

Be aware that when you choose to use free-form sources, you are bypassing two of TMG's internal checks on using sources – consistency of data input as encouraged by the input fields on the General tab of the Source Definition screen and standardization of output as controlled by the templates on the Output Form tab.

Embedded Citations

So far, we have been discussing source citations linked to name, relationship and event tags. There is another way to link source citations to your data. That is by embedding citations in event tag memos. To add an embedded citation, you open the memo for editing, position your cursor exactly where you wish for the citation to be inserted, right-click your mouse and select 'Embedded Citation.' The Master Source List is opened. You select the appropriate source (or add a new source) and then click the Select button. A Surety screen appears. You enter a surety value if you wish and click OK. The citation is embedded into your document.

Example with surety value:
    and they were married[CIT:]9:3;[:CIT] by Sallie's grandfather, Rev. Allen Winham

Example without surety value:
    and they were married[CIT:]9;[:CIT] by Sallie's grandfather, Rev. Allen Winham

You can enter citation detail after the semicolon (;).

Example with surety value and citation detail:
    and they were married[CIT:]9:3;page 3[:CIT] by Sallie's grandfather, Rev. Allen Winham

The embedded citation is text delineated by [CIT:][:CIT] codes and will be processed during report generation to create a footnote or endnote depending on your report options. Any part can be omitted (source number, colon and surety value, or semicolon and citation detail). If a source number is present, a bibliographic entry will be generated for that source. If the [CIT:][:CIT] codes contain only text, that text will be inserted as a footnote or endnote.

Example with a comment and no source, surety or citation detail:
    and they were married either at her parent's house or in the adjacent church[CIT:]Where her father was the minister[:CIT].

Citations can also be embedded in four additional data fields:
    – the 'Sentence structure' field of event tags.
    – the 'Topic' field on the General tab under properties of images linked to individuals in the Exhibit Log.
    – the field on the Description tab under Properties of images linked to individuals in the Exhibit Log.
    – the narrative report 'Living text' field on the Miscellaneous tab of the Report Options under the Report Definition Screen.

Embedded citations in these four fields are not announced features of TMG and should be used with caution since they will not necessarily work in future versions of the program. Embedded citations are contrary to the normal conventions for using the sentence field and the recommendation is to **not** use them there. Embedded citations can be particularly useful in an image caption in the Description field

and in the narrative report 'Living text' field.

Note that split CD elements **are not supported** in embedded citations. Any '‖' delimiters within embedded citations would be interpreted as delimiters for split memo elements.

Project/Data Set Merges and Source Types

Merging two projects using differing default source categories (**File > Preferences > Options > Current Project Options > Other > Source Categories**) brings up potential complications.

For example… Consider that you have two projects. Project A has one data set and uses Lackey source categories. Project B has one data set and uses Mills source categories. If you merge Project B into Project A, you will discover that the newly added data set that had been using Mills source categories is now using Lackey source categories. This will create quite a mess with the sources for this data set.

The recommendation is to convert projects and data sets to Custom source categories before any merger. If a data set used Lackey source categories, after changing the Preferences setting to Custom source categories, open **Tools > Source Types** and initialize the data set to Lackey source categories. Likewise, if a data set used Mills source categories, after changing the Preferences setting to Custom source categories, open **Tools > Source Types** and initialize the data set to Mills source categories.
Following the above procedure, after you initialize your data sets to Lackey or Mills, you will find that your data is intact with your source types and sources just as you began. The only change will be in the source categories type (now Custom). When you merge two data sets using Custom source categories (whether initialized to Lackey or Mills or customized by you), you will find that the resulting data set has all of the unique source types and unique Source Elements of the original two data sets.

Understanding the above allows you to create a data set with Custom source categories and both Lackey and Mills source types. Say that you have a data set using Custom source types originally initialized to Mills. You would like to use some of the Lackey source types. Rather than create new custom source types one at a time, you can add the fourteen Lackey source types at once with no editing. Here's how. Open the Data Set Manager (**File > Data Set Manager**) and [Add] a new data set. Initialize the new data set to Lackey source categories (**Tools > Source Types**). Be sure to select the correct data set from the list box before clicking [Initialize]. Then return to the Data Set Manager and merge the new empty data set into your original data set. You have just added the 14 Lackey source types.

Here's an alternative procedure. As usual, in TMG5 there is more than one way to accomplish a task. Create a new data set. Initialize the new data set to Lackey source categories (**Tools > Source Types**). Add a dummy person to the new data set. Go to the Master Source List and add 14 dummy sources, each using a different source type. Link the 14 sources to the name of your dummy person by adding 14 source citations. Copy the dummy person from this new data set to your original data set. The fourteen Lackey source types will be copied along with the dummy person.

Note that there are philosophical and design differences between Lackey and Mills source type templates in regard to the order of the Source Elements in the templates and other details. For example, compare the bibliography templates of the Lackey Civil Vital Record source type and the equivalent Mills Baptismal Record source type. If you combine both Lackey and Mills custom source types in one data set, you would need to do some source type editing so that your report output is consistent.

The procedures described above can be used to move custom source types to any data set. UK users might want to add Caroline Gurney's UK source types (*see Chapter 1, Introduction,* Web site section) by importing the TMG4 data set to your project and merging the imported data set into your data set. At the time this was written, Caroline had developed eighty-two UK-specific custom source types and twenty-eight custom Source Elements. The 'dummy person' technique allows you to move *selected* source types. You could also use these methods to exchange custom source types with other users until a better method is added to the program.

Chapter 8 - Concepts in TMG
By Allen Mellen

TMG is designed to assist the researcher in recording and later examining data about people and their relationships -- the underlying subject of all our research. The data is generally organized around a **focus** person or **Subject.**

Five of the seven windows available in the TMG Window menu relate to the **Subject --** they are the Details, Flags, Children, Siblings, and Image windows. Chief of these is the Details window, which has three views, the Person View, the Family View and the Tree View.

Tags and Flags[6]

Most of the information about the subject appears in the Person View and is recorded in **tags.** A major exception is the sex of the subject, which is recorded in a **flag** rather than a tag, and appears in the Flag window[7] rather than the Person View of the Details window. Some other bits of information such as Birth Order may also be recorded in flags.

In general, *tags* have several fields and each can be linked to more than one person. All people in the data set have the same *flags,* but usually different people have different sets of *tags.* Except for Sex, *flags* are not generally useful for basic information about the subject but are used in analysis of your data. For example, flags can serve to simplify the grouping of people for accents and filters (see *Chapter 11, Filtering and Sorting).*

You can enter a source for a tag but not for a flag, so sometimes it is useful to have *a tag in addition to a flag.* For example, if you need to enter a source for Sex, you can use a custom Sex tag (in the Other event Group) to supplement the Sex flag.

TMG has **Name** tags, **Relationship** tags, and **Event** tags. On the Tag Type List, tags are classified into ten Tag Groups. Name and Relationship tags each have their own Group. The remaining eight groups are collectively called Event tags but do not necessarily record real events in the ordinary sense

of the word "event." Five event groups chronicle life events -- the four "BMDB" groups (Birth, Marriage, Death and Burial) and the Divorce Group. The other three groups of Event tags are the Address Group, the History Group and the Other Group (see *Chapter 5, Customizing the Data).* Tag groups are significant in the context of filtering (see *Chapter 11, Filtering and Sorting).* Later in this chapter, some implications of using particular Tag Groups are discussed.

The **automatic 'relation' tag** that can be selected in **File > Preferences > Current Project Options > Other** is not really a tag, even though it displays in the tag box.

Principals, Witnesses and Events

Event tags are used to record information other than a Name or a Relationship[8]. Except for History tags, Event tags have at least one **Principal** and some may have two. All Event tags may have one or more **Witnesses.** History tags have **Witnesses** only; they do not have a Principal.

A **Principal** is a person who is a chief participant in an event. '**Principal**' is the default Role[9] on the Tag Entry screen for Event tags. While for some purposes a Principal is included in the term 'witness,' a **Witness** in TMG is primarily *a person who is associated with an event tag in some way other than as a Principal* and is not necessarily an actual witness to an event. A Witness is entered on the **Other witnesses** tab of the Tag Entry screen. Note that '**Witness**' is also the default Role on the Add witness screen.

---

[6] See also *Chapter 5, Customizing the Data.*

[7] The Flag window is not part of the Standard layout. It can be contained in a custom layout, or can be accessed from the **Window** menu.

---

[8] Strictly speaking, even names and relationships can be recorded in a tag in the Other event group. However, TMG will not process tags in the Other event group in the same manner as Name tags or Relationship tags.

[9] Roles are a powerful feature of TMG and are discussed in Chapters 5, *Customizing the Data* and 6, *Sentence Structures* and *in TMG Help.*

Table 8-1 lays out the various expressions that use the word "witness" in TMG.

As the table shows, there are certain places in TMG where the term witness is used to signify *anyone* associated with a tag, either in the role of a Principal or the role of **Witness.**

Projects and Data sets

TMG 5, like its precursor, Family Tree SuperTools, introduces TMG users to the concept of projects. A project contains one or more sets of data, which are called data sets. In the majority of instances, the data sets within a project are insulated from each other.

Some specific issues and possible pitfalls and solutions

For most tag groups, a Principal can have only one Primary tag. Primary tags can be used to customize output *(See Chapters 10, Customizing Reports and Chapter 14, Working With Charts in Visual Chartform™ Options).* Following are some observations and tips relating to particular Tag Groups, along with some ways to get around the restriction on Primary tags. The Tag Groups are presented in the order they appear in the filter of the Master Tag Type List.

a) Name Group. The primary name of the subject appears in the upper left box of the Person View. The Primary name is contained in the Primary Name Group tag, usually a Name-Var tag. If either the GivenName or Surname[10] of another Name tag that is not Primary is missing, TMG will infer the missing name based on the Primary Name tag.

On the Tag Entry screen, a specific name can be associated with each Event tag for use in reports. The Primary name will be used in those reports where the tag Sentence is not used, including Family Group Sheets, Ahnentafels, Charts, and the first paragraph of Journal reports. One way to change the Primary name is to select a Name tag and then choose **Edit > Toggle Primary.**

b) Relationship Group. The only relationship that TMG recognizes is the Parent-Child relationship. The Primary father and mother of the subject appear in the upper left box of the person View. The

---

[10] That is, for U.S. Standard Name Style.

Primary parent-child relationship is contained in Primary Relationship Group tags, usually XXX-Bio tags.

Expression	Where found	Includes Principals?
Any Witness	List of Witnesses; List of Events	Yes
Number of Other Witnesses	Any Report	No
Number of Witnesses	Any Report	Yes
1 more witness *or* <u>n</u> more witnesses	Tag Entry screen	No
Other Witnesses	Accent Clauses; Picklist and Project Explorer Filter Clauses; Tag Entry screen	No
Witnessed Events *or* Witnessed ... Tag	Accent Clauses; Picklist and Project Explorer Filter Clauses	No
Witnesses (in title)	List of Witnesses	Yes
Witness (as in Witness ID#)	List of Witnesses	Yes
Witnesses	Project Summary; Data Set Information	Yes

Table 8-1: Witness Expressions

TMG uses the Primary Relationship Group tags for all generation-to-generation processing, including the determination of lineages and kinship. Caution must be used in recording **non-blood relationships.** The standard -bio tags are intended to cover most parent-child relationships. TMG provides other relationship tags, however, for use in special situations involving adoption, foster, step or godparent relationships. These are the -Ado, -Fst, -God, and -Ste tags. Use of any of these tags means that the program treats the relationship **for all purposes** exactly like a -Bio tag.

For example, if the -Ado tag is used (and is made Primary) the adopted child would appear

on the adoptive parent's view as of the child's date of birth, not her adoption date[11].

In standard genealogical reports and in other generation-to-generation processing, TMG uses only Primary Relationship tags (see *Chapter 5, Customizing the Data*). Non-Primary Relationship tags can appear in only two places in reports — in the parent section of Family Group Sheets and in Individual Detail reports.

If you desire to have adopted, foster, or stepchildren appear in reports as if they were biological children, you need to use a relationship tag and make that relationship Primary. If your data includes both the biological parents and, for example, the stepparents of the children, you might have to generate two sets of reports, one with each set of parents marked as Primary[12]. In this case, if output is sent to a word processor you can assemble a composite report.

If you do not want to record non-biological children as if they were biological, you might use instead an Event tag and appropriate roles.

- **Adoption.** There is a standard Adoption tag. Enter the child as a Principal(s) and the adopting parent(s) as Witnesses with appropriate roles.
- **Foster relationship.** TMG does not provide a standard tag. You can make a custom Foster tag,[13] modeled after the Adoption tag.
- **Step relationship.** This might well be considered a role connected to a Marriage. The stepchildren would be entered in the Other witness section of the marriage tag. Another approach is to make a custom Step tag, modeled after the Adoption tag.

- **Godparent.** If you use the -God tag, the godparents will appear on a Family Group Sheet if All Variations is selected for parents[14]. Consider using a role in a Baptism or Christening tag if you do not need to have the godparent appear on the Family Group Sheet. The godparent would be entered in the Other witness section of the tag.

c) Birth group. The Birth group contains both a standard Baptism tag and a standard Christening tag because in many instances evidence of baptism or christening can be found where evidence of birth is lacking. In these instances, the date of baptism or christening is used by TMG as a substitute for a date of birth. Since only Primary tags can appear on some charts and reports, it is **not** possible on those reports to show both birth **and** baptism if the standard tags are used. You may wish to make a custom tag in the Other event group so that a baptism or christening can be recorded as a Primary event. Most other religious events are already in the Other event group — including BarMitzvah, BasMitzvah, and ordinances of the Church of Jesus Christ of Latter Day Saints (LDS events).

d) Death Group. Cause of death can be entered in the memo of the Primary Death tag. It is wise to avoid making custom tags in the Death group, except as a way of providing an alternate sentence (see *Chapter 6, Sentence Structures).*

e) Marriage Group. For any pair of Principals, there can be only one Primary tag in the Marriage group. TMG has several standard tags in the Marriage group. For **unmarried parents** and **marriage-like partnerships** special treatment may be needed. While it is not necessary to enter a Marriage Group tag for unmarried parents, on Family Group Sheets the relationship will appear as if it were a marriage regardless of whether there is a Marriage Group tag. For this case and for other partnerships, some users have found it useful to make a custom Liaison tag in the Marriage Group. If you choose to do this, you might want to adjust

---

[11] This discussion also applies to the -Fst, -Ste, and -God tags and to any custom tags in the Relationship group.

[12] This would also be true of adoptive and step relationships.

[13] In a discussion among the beta testers and developers for TMG v5.0 there was no consensus as to an appropriate name for the tag for a foster relationship.

[14] The other tags in the Relationship group (-Ado, -Fst, and -Ste as well as any custom tag) also appear in the same place.

the sentence for this tag, since TMG treats all Primary tags in the Marriage Group the same way.

f) Divorce Group. Despite the name of this tag group, a custom tag could be made in this group for any end of a marriage (or any relationship recorded in a Marriage Group tag,) however that may occur.

g) History Group. The History group was designed with a special purpose. A History tag can be used to document a single historical event. Then persons in your data set can be attached as Witnesses to the tag. The History tag might be thought of as a one-event Timeline *(See below)*. However, unlike Timelines History tags are specific to a particular data set and so cannot be shared – either within or among projects or among users. Moreover, Witnesses must be attached to History tags explicitly. It should be noted that since History tags do not have Principals, they can never be Primary.

h) Address Group. The Address tag is designed to hold a current address for people in your project and only one tag in the Address group can be Primary. To record past addresses, you can use a Residence tag (in the Other event group). If you wish, you might make a series of custom tags in the Other events group, so that each one could be Primary. They might be called Resided1, Resided2, and so forth.

i) Other Event Group. In the Other event group, there can be only one Primary tag of each type for each principal (or pair of principals).

Timelines

Timelines provide a way of showing the historical context within which your ancestors and other people in your data set lived. A Timeline is a small database consisting of dates and text describing events. Timelines can be shown on the Person View for all persons. To be shown, a Timeline must be selected in the Timeline Manger (**Tools > Timeline Manager**). There are a number of ways to choose the option to show selected timelines including a checkbox in the Timeline Manager, a right-click option in the Tag Box, **Tools > Show Timelines** on the Person View, and in Preferences. There is also a shortcut key combination, <Ctrl> + <\>.

It is also possible to "lock" a timeline to one or more particular individual persons. The timeline will then show on the Person View of those individuals, regardless of the setting for the Project as a whole. In TMG 5, timelines can be locked and unlocked for individuals using Secondary Output on the List of People report (see *Chapters 10, Customizing Reports, and Chapter 11, Filtering and Sorting)*.

When timelines are shown on the Person View, only certain events from the selected timelines are shown - those that fall within the person's lifetime adjusted by the **Circa means** value from the Advanced section of Preferences (see the entry 'Life Span Calculation' in Help for details).

Several timelines are provided with TMG. These can be viewed in the Timeline Manager. From time to time TMG users make new timelines available. These can usually be found at *www.tmgtips.com*. There is a link to this resource at *www.whollygenes.com*. If you wish to make your own timeline, it is a relatively easy process. In the Timeline Manager, you can add a new timeline and then add events to it. The Help topics: "Add New Timeline" and "Edit Timeline," provide complete instructions. In brief, the process consists of entering dates and descriptions of events, one at a time. You can also edit an existing timeline in the Timeline Manager. An individual timeline event can be edited from the Tag Box, as if it were a regular tag.

A timeline can also be created from the events in your data set. The process requires a database manager that can produce dBase III/IV files and is described in an article by Lee H. Hoffman entitled "Auto-Creation of Timeline Files," found at *www.tmgtips.com*.

Special Considerations

Conflicting Evidence. One of the strengths of TMG is its ability to accommodate conflicting evidence. For example, if different sources for an event give conflicting dates, you can enter a tag with each date. If you follow that approach, you might make Primary the one you consider most likely to be correct. If additional evidence later leads you to reach a different conclusion, it is easy to change the Primary designation to a different tag.

Sometimes it is simpler to record conflicting evidence in the Citation Detail of a tag. You can also use the tag's surety fields to indicate which is more likely (see *Chapter 1, Introduction*).

Another approach is to use a 'Conclusions' tag, that is, a custom tag in the relevant tag group with a tag name like Birth-Conc. In this approach, you can place your reasoning in the Citation Detail or the Memo.

Making non-people. Many users have found inventive ways to use TMG. One of the cleverest is to enter data for entities or even concepts that are not people. At *www.tmgtips.com* is a link to Diana Begeman's site where a method of using a 'Census person' to link together actual people found in a census may be found.[15]

Some people have used the second principal in a Burial tag to enter a 'Cemetery person,' that is, to record the name and location of the cemetery. Cemetery information should probably also be entered in the place fields of the Burial tag.

The use of such 'non-people' is a way of linking people. For example, if you have several people buried in the same cemetery, it is easy to find them all if the cemetery is entered as a 'person' on the death tag. You simply go to the Person View for the cemetery, and you see all the people buried there.

Since the cemetery (or the census) is not recorded as related to anyone in your data, it will never turn up inappropriately in a report.

---

[15]   There is also a link at *www.tmgtips.com* to Terry Reigel's site where a different method of entering census data is described.

Chapter 9 – Controlling Narratives
By Terry Reigel

TMG offers an extensive set of tools for controlling the content and format of narrative reports. Many of them are options selected at the time a report is generated. But others are based on options selected and methods employed when the data is recorded. Since many significant features of report output depend on, or are at least interactive with, the way data is recorded, it is important that you consider the kind of reports you would like to generate when deciding how to record information in TMG.

This chapter covers both the issues you need to consider as you enter data and the options available when narrative reports are generated. In it we will discuss the techniques for producing the narrative reports you have in mind, using the following steps:

Selecting the Desired Format – Choosing the report format you want.

1. **Controlling Who is Included** – Defining which individuals to be included.
2. **Selecting Tags** – Managing which information appears about them.
3. **Controlling the Text Layout** –Managing how the text is arranged.

What Do We Mean by Narrative Reports?

TMG produces a wide variety of Reports and Charts. In this chapter we will discuss only the group of Reports classified as narratives. What they have in common is that they provide the information in full sentences, or narrative style. This is in contrast to Charts, which show brief

Journal	This report, or more properly group of reports, is arranged in the rather formal styles used by the journals of the major US genealogical societies. Reports in these styles are sometimes called Journal Narratives, or not entirely correctly, Register reports.
	Both descendants and ancestors versions are offered. There is a set of detailed style options to produce reports similar to each of the major societies' publications, or the user can select options individually to produce a custom style.
	Individuals are arranged by generation. All members of a generation are listed, together with brief listings of children of each, before moving to the next generation.
Individual Narrative	This report describes, in narrative style, a single individual.
Descendant Indented Narrative*	This report includes an individual and his or her descendants.
	Individual narratives are arranged in outline style, with each generation indented and numbered as in an outline. All descendants of each individual are listed before moving to that individual's siblings.
Ahnentafel*	As its name implies (Ahnentafel means "ancestor table"), this is an ancestor report. It includes an individual and his or her ancestors. The individual narratives are listed in numerical order, using traditional Ahnentafel numbering.
Ahnentafel – Direct Line*	This is a special case of the Ahnentafel Report, in which only those ancestors in the direct line of from one individual to a specified ancestor are included.
*The last three Reports can be thought of as collections of Individual Narratives, arranged and numbered in various ways to depict relationships between the individuals included.	

Table 9-1: Types of Narrative Reports

information about individuals arranged in a diagram fashion, usually with graphic elements to display relationships, and Forms, such as Family Group Sheets, which provide more information, but in a highly structured format using brief phrases rather than full sentences. The Narrative Reports produced by TMG are listed in Table 9-1.

Selecting the Desired Format

Perhaps the most fundamental step in controlling the output of a narrative report is to select the basic layout, which is done by choosing the appropriate report for your purposes. If you want only the details for a specific person, the Individual Narrative Report is probably a good choice. And if you want to show only the direct line from an individual to a specific ancestor, the Ahnentafel - Direct Line Report is a likely choice.

But for general ancestor and descendant reports, there are two separate decisions to make – report "style" and "direction." First we will consider the "direction." Do you want an Ancestor report – the ancestors of a specified individual, or Descendant report – the descendants of one individual? Ordinarily, this is obvious from what you have in mind. But one special case it may not be so obvious. If you are thinking of an Ancestor report, but want to include collateral relatives beyond the siblings of various ancestors, the best choice may be a group of Descendant reports. Each report in the group would start with a different "end of line" ancestor of your target individual. See the section on "Combining Multiple Lines" below for details.

Once the direction (Ancestor or Descendant) of the report is

selected, you can select the style, which controls the way individuals and information are arranged within the report. In addition to the way that the individuals are arranged in the reports, there are differences in the way the information within each person's narrative is organized. You can choose from two quite different formats – the formal Journal styles, or the somewhat simpler Descendant Indented Narrative or Ahnentafel. Refer to Table 9-2, Descendant Reports and Table 9-3, Ancestor Reports for illustrations of the two formats.

Journal (Descendants)

Generation One

1. FOCUS PERSON
   Children:
      i. FIRST CHILD
   2. ii. SECOND CHILD
      iii. THIRD CHILD
   3. iv. FOURTH CHILD

Generation Two

2. SECOND CHILD
   Children:
      i. FIRST GRANDCHILD
      ii. SECOND GRANDCHILD
3. FOURTH CHILD
   Children:
   4. i. THIRD GRANDCHILD
   5. ii. FOURTH GRANDCHILD

Generation Three

4. THIRD GRANDCHILD
   Children:
      i. FIRST GREAT GRANDCHILD
      ii. SECOND   GREAT GRANDCHILD
      iii. THIRD   GREAT GRANDCHILD
5. FOURTH GRANDCHILD
   Children:
      i. FOURTH   GREAT GRANDCHILD

In this format all members of each generation are grouped together. Children of each descendant are listed under that person.

Joint events for spouses, such as marriage, are reported, and other spouse events, such as birth and death, are optionally included.

Several styles of numbering are available in addition to the one illustrated.

Descendancy Indented Narrative

I. FOCUS PERSON

 A. FIRST CHILD

 B. SECOND CHILD

  1. FIRST GRANDCHILD

  2. SECOND GRANDCHILD

 C. THIRD CHILD

 D. FOURTH CHILD

  1. THIRD GRANDCHILD

   A) FIRST GREAT GRANDCHILD

   B) SECOND GREAT GRANDCHILD

   C) THIRD GREAT GRANDCHILD

  2. FOURTH GRANDCHILD

   A) FOURTH GREAT GRANDCHILD

In this format each line is followed to the last generation before starting with the next descendant, creating an arrangement that some find easier to follow.

*Joint events for spouses, such as marriage, are reported, but other spouse events, such as birth and death, are **not** included.*

Several styles of numbering are available in addition to the one illustrated.

Table 9-2: Descendant Reports

Journal (Ancestors)	Ahnentafel
Generation One	*1st Generation*
1. FOCUS PERSON	1. FOCUS PERSON
Generation Two	*2nd Generation*

2. FATHER
Children:
   i. FIRST SIBLING
1 ii. FOCUS PERSON
   iii. SECOND SIBLING
3. MOTHER
	2. FATHER
	3. MOTHER

Generation Three	*3rd Generation*

4. PATERNAL GRANDFATHER
Children:
   i. FIRST AUNT/UNCLE
   ii. SECOND AUNT/UNCLE
2 iii. FATHER
   iv. THIRD AUNT/UNCLE
5. PATERNAL GRANDMOTHER
6. MATERNAL GRANDFATHER
Children:
   i. FOURTH AUNT/UNCLE
   ii. FIFTH AUNT/UNCLE
3 iii. MOTHER
7. MATERNAL GRANDMOTHER
	4. PATERNAL GRANDFATHER
	5. PATERNAL GRANDMOTHER
	6. MATERNAL GRANDFATHER
	7. MATERNAL GRANDMOTHER

In this format all children of each ancestor are listed under that ancestor. *The numbering shown is only one of several options available.*	*In this format only ancestors are shown, creating a substantially simpler report.*

Table 9-3: Ancestor Reports

In the Journal Reports, all the birth, marriage, and death information is placed in the first paragraph. If there is additional information it all appears in a second paragraph. Then spouse information is shown in descendant reports, if the "Spouse Events" option is selected. Finally there is a list of children. That listing includes only birth and marriage information if that child has children in the report, with full information in his or her own listing. But if that child has no children included, his or her full narrative appears with the parents' listing.

The Descendancy Indented Narrative and Ahnentafel reports by default place all the information about the individual in a single paragraph.

Some techniques to override these defaults are described in the section on "Controlling the Text Layout" later in this chapter.

The choice of format is mostly a personal preference, but do consider who the reader will be. Readers not familiar with genealogy reports may find the styles on the right in Tables 9-2 and 9-3, while users familiar with Journal reports may find that style more comfortable.

Controlling Who Is Included

Once the report type is selected, perhaps the next issue is managing which individuals are to be included. For two of the narrative reports, this is straightforward:

Individual Narrative – by default only includes one person. To use it this way, leave the Subject(s) set to "One person" on the Report Definition screen. If you want to create narratives for several individuals on a single Report you use one of the other options on the Report Definition screen under Subject(s) to specify what group you want to include. See *Chapter 11, Filtering & Sorting,* for details on how to do this.

Ahnentafel - Direct Line – shows the line between a person and a specified ancestor. You identify those two individuals on the Report Definition screen.

The ancestor and descendant reports are a bit different, and frequently the source of confusion. By definition, these reports are designed to start with one Subject, usually called the Focus Person. The report format itself then includes the specified ancestors or descendants, and in some cases spouses and siblings. So for these reports, you specify on the Report Definition screen *only the Focus Person* – that is the starting person – of the report and let the report itself take care of adding all the other people who are supposed to be included. You do not specify all the people in the report. The principal controls used are:

- **Focus Person** – there is generally only one, and the best choice is to leave the Subject(s) set to "Use the Current Focus Person" so you don't have to change that tab each time the Report is run. However, see the section on Combining Multiple Lines below for exceptions to this.
- **Number of Generations** – is controlled by a setting on the General tab of the Report Definition Options.
- **Spouse Events** – is an option only for the descendants version of the Journal Reports. If this option is not selected, spouses are named in connection with marriages and other joint events, but their own events, including births and deaths, are not reported. To include Spouse Events select that option on the Tags tab of the Report Definition Options. That option can only be selected after you choose the Custom format under "Style" on the Options General tab.

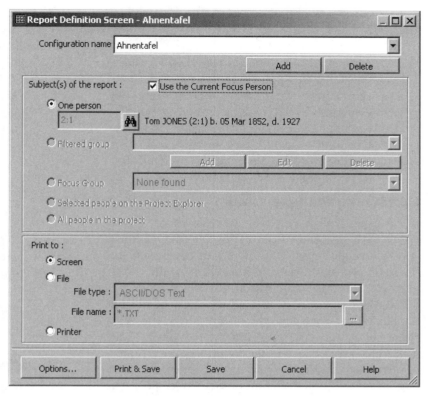

Figure 9-1: Specify the subjects of reports on the Report Definition Screen. For Ancestor and Descendent reports you usually specify only the Focus, or starting person.

Excluding Selected Individuals

Sometimes you want to exclude certain individuals who would normally be included in an ancestor or descendant report. Several tools are available for this task:

- **Using a Temporary Data Set** – is the most powerful tool for excluding individuals, and is particularly useful if there are many to exclude. The idea is to create a temporary Data Set that excludes those individuals who you do not want included in the report. Then run the Report from that Data Set. For details on how to create a temporary Data Set, including tips on filtering to obtain your intended individuals, see *Chapter 11, Filtering & Sorting*.
- **Edit Manually** – in a word processor. Sometimes it is simpler to complete the reports and then edit them in your word processor to remove specific individuals.

- **Follow Surname** – this option causes only people whose surname matches the Focus Person to be included. This can be very useful if it matches your intent. In descendant reports, children whose surname does not match will be included, but their lines will not be followed further. This option is on the Miscellaneous tab of the Report Definition Options for the Journal and Descendancy Indented Narrative reports. Caution – if the spelling of the surname is different for different generations, this option will stop the report at the point of the spelling change.
- **Remove Primary Relationship Tag** – if you want to stop only one or a few lines short of where it would otherwise end, you can temporarily remove the primary status of the parent/child Relationship Tag where you want to break the line. Just remember to restore them later.
- **Surety Options** – if you want to exclude doubtful connections in the lines in a report,

the Surety options may help. For this option to work, you need to have assigned lower sureties for citations in the doubtful parent/child relationship tags than for those you for which you are more confident. You can adjust the Surety options on the General tab of Report Definition Options to exclude connections with lower Sureties. Caution – using this option will also exclude from the report any Event Tags that have the same or lower Surety.

Combining Multiple Lines

Some times you may want to create reports with ancestor or descendant narratives for several lines within a single report. You could, of course, create separate reports for each line. But if the lines intersect, there is a significant advantage of doing them in a single report. Instead of repeating all the duplicate lines each time they occur, the report will show them only the first time they appear, and insert cross references in the narratives for all later occurrences. You do this by setting the Subject(s) options on the Report Definition Screen to specify a group of individuals, each of which will be the Focus Person for one of the lines. You control the order in which the separate narratives will appear (and thus which will contain the full text for duplicate individuals) with the Sort by tab of Report Definition Options. See *Chapter 11, Filtering & Sorting*, for details on how to do this.

Selecting Tags

Now that we have examined who will be included in a report, next we consider what information about them will be included. Recalling that most information about individuals is stored in Tags, the most significant factor in controlling what is included about each individual is to select which Tags to include. Two separate but interdependent options are the primary controls for which Tags are included. But the results they produce is highly dependant on the selection of Tag Types when data was entered, and the choices made in creating and using custom Tag Types. Therefore it is important to consider the various ways you may want to configure your reports before investing a lot of effort in data entry (see *Chapter 5, Customizing the Data,* for details on creating custom Tags).

The two control options are on the Tags tab of the Report Definition Options. The choices available for each are:

Events:

- **Primary Events** – Includes only Tags marked as Primary
- **All Variations** – Includes all Tags in which the individual was a Principal
- **All Events and Witnessed Events** – Includes all Tags in which the individual was either a Principal or a Witness

Tag Types:

- **None** – Includes only Name Tags
- **All** – Includes all Tag Types
- **Selected** – Includes only the Tag Types selected by the user. Once you select this option, a list of Tag Types appears on which you can check those you want to include by double clicking on them.

Choosing Which Options to Use

In deciding how you want to use these two controls, and how you want to enter your data to make those controls produce the results you desire, consider that you may have three categories of data, which I call:

- **Never** – information that you want to include in your Data Set for reference only on screen, to be seldom, if ever, included in reports.
- **Always** – information that you will almost always want to include in narrative reports.
- **Sometimes** – information that you will sometimes want to include, and sometimes not, depending on the recipient and intended use of the report.

There are two common methods for managing which tags are included in a report:

Primary Events Method – marking only selected Event Tags as Primary, and then choosing either the Primary Events or one of the "All" choices in the Events option depending on which set of Tags you want to include. The Tag Types option is normally set to All. "Never" data must be marked with Exclusion Marks or Sensitivity Brackets to exclude it.

Selected Tag Types Method – setting the Tag Types option to Selected, and choosing which Tag Types to include by using the Define feature. The Events option is then set to either All Variations or All Events and Witnessed Events.

In my opinion, Primary Tag Method is unsatisfactory for the following reasons, and should be avoided:

- It offers only two groupings (indicated by the Primary /non-Primary designation) so it will not provide for the three categories listed above. And I find that the "Sometimes" category really includes several subcategories, depending on the use of the report.
- When you are using the Primary choice in the Events option to omit selected Tags, you cannot include Witnessed events.
- Data marked with Exclusion Marks or Sensitivity Brackets can only be included by including all data so marked; it is difficult to select specific items.
- Only one Event Tag of each Type can be marked as Primary for any one set of Principals, so if you want, say, two Note Tags marked Primary, you have to create a custom Tag Type, say Note1, and use that for one of the notes.

Therefore I believe the Selected Tag Types Method is superior, and recommend it. The following sections describe how to use it effectively.

Arranging Your Data for the Selected Tag Types Method

To use this method, you create enough custom Tag Types so that you can mentally assign each Tag Type you use to only one of the three categories. Then, when you enter data consider which category the data falls in and enter it in a Tag Type you have assigned for that category – that is, never put "Sometimes" data in a Tag Type you have reserved

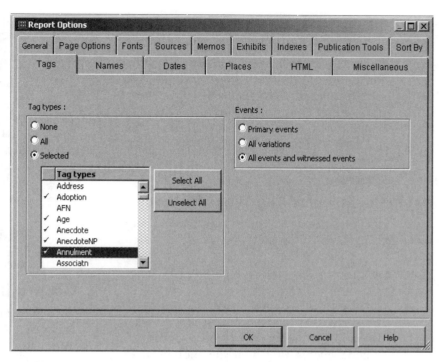

Figure 9-2: Specify the Tags to be included in a report on the Tags tab of the Report Definition Options screen. The Selected Tag Types option shown here is the most powerful and flexible method.

for "Always" data. Some examples may help make this clear:

Example 1: Say you want to record conflicting birth information in separate tags. Further, when you create a report for a non-genealogist sibling you don't want the conflicting information to appear. But when you create a report for a fellow researcher, you want to include all the information, conflicting or not.

Solution: Create a custom Tag Type called Birth-Alt. Enter the information you judge most reliable in the default Birth Tag – this is "Always" data, and you would always include the Birth Tag in reports. You enter conflicting information in your custom Birth-Alt Tag – this is "Sometimes" data and you may or may not include it in a given report.

Example 2: Say you want to record notes on disputed parent-child linkages in a note that you would share with a fellow researcher, but not with your disinterested sibling. And you also want to keep as notes various odds and ends of information that you are unlikely to share with anyone.

Solution: Create a Tag Type, say DispNote, for the notes on disputed information. This is "Sometimes" data and you may or may not include it in a given report. Create another, say ReschNote, for all the odds and ends. While this may be "Never" data, you could include it in a report if you changed your mind.

Using the Selected Tag Types Method

After you've separated your information into separate Tag Types, now how do you get it sorted out in the reports? When you are ready to create your report, open the Report Definition screen for the Report you want to use and:

- Set the Events option to All Events or to All Events and Witnessed Events, depending on whether or not you want to include events in which the individual is recorded only as a Witness.
- Set the Tag Types option to Selected. Then mark those Tag Types you want to include with check marks.
- If this is a set of selections you may want to use again in the future, save the Report Configuration with an explanatory name. For example, for each of the narrative reports that I use frequently, I have one version called "Pretty" and another called "Full Details." The "Pretty" versions exclude conflicting date and place information, notes on disputed ancestries, sources, and other "details" that are of no interest to family members who just want a sense of our family history. The other version includes all this detail, and is for sharing with other researchers. (To save a Report Configuration, click the Add button near the top of the Report Definition Screen, and enter the name you want to use as the File Name in the Save As screen that opens. Excluding Selected Tags.)

The sections above describe the principal means of controlling what Tags are included in Reports, but there are several other tools available that are useful in specific situations. They include:

- **Suppress Details for Living People** – choosing this option on the Miscellaneous tab of Report Definition Options excludes all details other than the name for individuals marked as living in your Data Set. This feature treats as living those individuals whose Living Flag is set to ? or Y. The phrase "is still living," is printed after the name by default. You can enter an alternate phrase in the "Living Text" field of the same tab.
- **Surety Options** – as described above, the Surety options in the Report Definition can be used to exclude information that has been assigned surety settings below a selected value.

Controlling the Text Layout

We've covered how you define which Tags will be included, so now we consider just how the information in those Tags will be arranged within the report.

Certain basic formatting is part of the definition of the reports, and is controlled by the selection of the report type, as covered at the beginning of this chapter. This would include, for example the indenting in the Descendant Indented Narrative, and numbering of individuals (though some report types have several options for numbering on the Report Definition).

Perhaps the most powerful control for the flow of text is the use of Sentence Structures. That subject is so important, and has many variations to consider, that it has its own chapter (see *Chapter 6, Sentence Structures*). Several additional techniques are described in the sections below.

The Sequence of Information

Generally, Tags for an individual appear in reports in order according to their Sort Dates. So to change the order in which events are shown, you need to change the Sort Dates on one or more of the Tags involved until they are listed in the Person View in the order you would like them to be in your narrative reports. Remember that Sort Dates only control the order of Tags, and never appear themselves in reports.

There is an important exception – Journal reports follow the style of the journals of the major US genealogy societies, which is to place birth, marriage, death and burial information in the first paragraph, with all other information in a following paragraph. TMG implements that style by placing the text from Tags in the Birth, Marriage, Divorce, Death and Buried groups in the first paragraph. Within that paragraph, all Tags in the Birth group are placed first, followed by those in the Marriage and Divorce groups, then the Death group, and finally the Burial group, with tags within each group arranged by Sort Date. Tags in the Other Tags groups are placed in a second paragraph, arranged by Sort Date.

This order cannot be changed directly (except by changing to another report type), but can be changed by using Tags in another Group. For example, the default Baptism Tag is in the Birth Group. If you were to want the baptism to appear after a marriage (say for an adult baptism) you could create a custom baptism Tag Type in the Death group. Or if you wanted to move baptisms out of the first paragraph, you could create a custom baptism Tag Type in the Other Group, and use it instead of the default tag. Likewise, if you wanted some information to appear in the first paragraph that is not normally placed there, you could create a custom Tag Type for it on one of the Groups that appear in that paragraph. Caution – substituting custom tags in the Other Group for your Primary Birth and Death Tags will disrupt display of dates in many views, as well as many Forms and Charts, and therefore is generally not a good idea.

Special Options for Journal Reports

There is an option in Journal Reports to further control the format of the first paragraph for each person, producing tightly formatted paragraphs or ones that use more ordinary language. That feature partially overrides the Sentence Structure of those Tags, depending on which of the following options is selected on the Tags tab of the Report Definition Options:

- **He was born in 1861** – produces the text just as specified by the Sentence Structure.
- **born 1861** – places a semicolon after the name, connects all the sentences in the first paragraph into a single sentence separated by semicolons, and removes the word

"was" if present after the Name Variable and the preposition in or on before the date.
- **b. 1861** – same as above, but also changes "born" "married" "died" and "buried" to "b." "m." "d." and "bur."

The following examples, taken from the SAMPLE Project, may help to illustrate the differences. Using the first option produces:

John Alexander was born on 11 October 1812 in Washington County, Tennessee. He married **Delilah Woods**, daughter of **John Woods** and **Agnes ——?——**, on 22 January 1835 in Sullivan County, Tennessee. He died on 18 October 1876 in Marion, Smyth County, Virginia at age 64. He was buried in Round Hill Cemetery, Marion, Smyth County, Virginia

While the third option produces:

John Alexander; b. 11 October 1812 in Washington County, Tennessee; m. **Delilah Woods**, daughter of **John Woods** and **Agnes ——?——**, 22 January 1835 in Sullivan County, Tennessee d. 18 October 1876 in Marion, Smyth County, Virginia at age 64; bur. in Round Hill Cemetery, Marion, Smyth County, Virginia.

Managing Paragraph Breaks

As described above, by default the narrative for each individual will be in either one or two paragraphs, depending on the style of report selected. This works well for short narratives, but when there is extensive text this structure becomes awkward. The solution (other than manually editing the report in a word processor) is to place Embedded Format Codes in some Tags to force a paragraph break (see *Chapter 6, Sentence Structures*, for more details). Two codes are useful – the Carriage Return code [:CR:] and the tab code [:TAB:]. They can be typed in or entered from the right click menu, and can be placed in either the Sentence Structure or in the Memo. The following should to taken into account when using these codes for paragraph control:

- Consider whether you prefer a report style that by default creates a paragraph break after birth, marriage, and death information, or not. Place your manually created breaks to fit the report style you prefer.
- Consider whether your preferred report style uses indented paragraphs or not, and use or omit the tab code accordingly.

- In the Memo field, using the [Enter] key has the same effect as entering the Carriage Return code. But only the embedded codes work for Tabs, or for either in Sentence Structures.

- Placing paragraph control codes in Memos works well to separate paragraphs of long memos. However, placing them at the beginning of the Memo will still leave the first few word of the text generated by the Tag's Sentence Structure in the previous paragraph unless the Memo is the first, or only, data field printed from that Tag.

- Placing paragraph control codes in either the Memo or Sentence Structure so that they are the last item in the text produced by the Tag will result in a period and Source note reference number appearing at the beginning of the next paragraph. So it is generally better to place those codes at the beginning of the Sentence Structure of the Tag that is to start the new paragraph, rather than at the end of the last Tag of a paragraph.

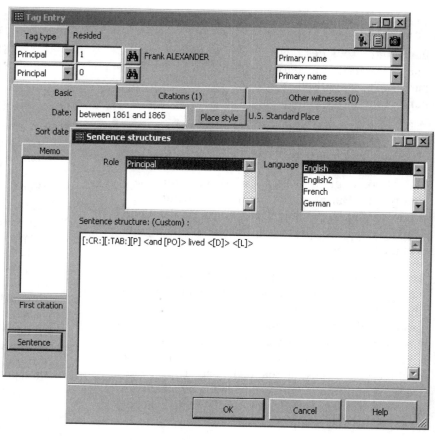

Figure 9-3: Paragraph breaks are best inserted by adding a [:CR:] code at the beginning of the Sentence Structure of the Tag that is to start the new paragraph. Also add a [:TAB:] code if you use the Journal reports, so the new paragraph will be indented to match that report's style.

Some users recommend creating a custom Tag Type to create a new paragraph, containing only the embedded codes for the Carriage Return, and optionally, tab code. The problem is, such a Tag will also create an extra period, which must be removed in your word processor. Instead, you might create versions of several common Tag Types containing the embedded codes, and use them instead of the normal ones when you want a Tag to start a new paragraph. For example, I have a Note-NP Tag Type I use instead of the normal Note Tag Type in such cases.

Excluding Sensitive Information

Sometimes you may have certain information recorded in a Tag that you do not want to show in reports, but you do want the rest of the information in the Tag to be included. For example, you may have recorded the cause of death information in a Death Tag, but not want to show it in reports. But you do want to show the other information in that Tag. TMG provides the following tools to do that:

- **The Exclusion Marker or Double Exclusion Marker**, a single or double hyphen, applies to an entire field. You enter it as the first character in the field to suppress the printing of the information entered in the remainder of the field. It can also be entered in the Sentence Structure of a Tag to suppress printing of the entire Tag.

- **Sensitivity Brackets and Hidden Text Codes** are used within a field, where they suppress only the portion of text enclosed within the marks. Sensitivity Brackets are entered by typing them in like this – the {part in these brackets} will be suppressed. Hidden Text uses codes that can be typed in or entered from the right click Menu in many fields and looks like this – the [HID:] part between the codes [:HID] will be suppressed.

- **Overriding Excluded Text** – Single Exclusion Markers and Sensitivity Brackets can be overridden by the Exclusion options on the Miscellaneous tab of Report Definition Options. The Double Exclusion Marker and Hidden Text cannot be made to appear in reports.

Note: these techniques also apply to Sources and Repositories, where they can be similarly used to suppress specific information.

Tricks with Memos

Normally, the contents of the Memo field of Tags are inserted in the text as directed by the Sentence Structure (see *Chapter 6, Sentence Structures*). However, Memos not specified in the Sentence Structure can still be printed by use of the options on the Memos tab of Report Definition Options. The following options are available:

- **None** – only memos specified in Sentence Structures will appear.
- **Footnotes** or **Endnotes** – this offers a way to have information in the Memo field of a Tag appear as a note rather than in the body of the text.
- **Embedded**, with or without parentheses – this simply embeds the contents of the Memo field in the text generated by the Tag, after the text produced by the Sentence Structure. If you use the option without the parentheses, the Memo text is set off with a semi-colon. This method gives you somewhat less control of the exact placement of the Memo text than use of Sentence Structures, but does give you the option to decide when each report is

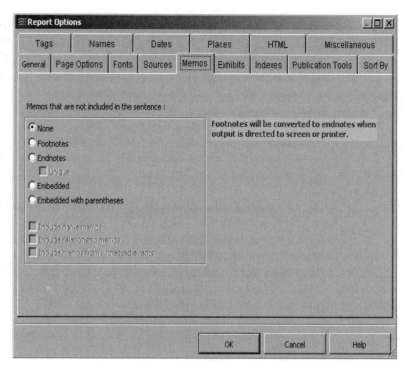

Figure 9-4: Memos not specified to be printed by the Sentence Structures of Tags can be printed using the options on the Memos tab of the Report Definition Options.

generated whether to include the Memo text in that report.

Note that these options have no effect if the Sentence Structure of the Tag contains a variable for the Memo. Also, note that the option applies to the whole report, so it applies to every Tag used to generate the report.

Caution – using either option may also cause Memos to be printed in Witnessed events, which is often not what you had in mind. To avoid this, use the <[M0]> variable in the Sentence Structures for Witnesses, as described in *Chapter 6, Sentence Structures*).

In Conclusion

TMG offers a powerful set of options and controls, which allow you to manage how your data will appear in the reports that you produce. The options available are many and varied and the results depend significantly upon how you enter your data into the program. So if you are concerned about the format of narrative reports you will produce, it is important to explore the report types available and find the ones that you prefer. Then you can manage your data entry in a way that will permit production of the exact report types you have in mind. Creating a custom "Preview" Report Definition in your favorite format, and using it frequently as you make data input decisions, is the key to getting exactly what you want from your reports.

Chapter 10 - Customizing Reports

By Jeffry L. Clenard

General Overview

The Master Genealogist™ (TMG) is well known for its powerful reporting capabilities. TMG offers a wide range of reports in a number of different formats including charts, forms, narratives, lists, publication tools, and statistical. Coupled with the powerful filtering and sorting capabilities and the ability to define and assign an unlimited number of Flags, TMG offers unparalleled flexibility to output

Category	Report Type	
Charts	Descendant Indented	
	Pedigree	
	Pedigree – Compressed	
	Relationship	
	Visual Chartform™	Ahnentafel, Columnar
		Ancestor Box
		Descendant Box
		Fan
		Hourglass Box
Forms	Ahnentafel – Direct Line, Columnar	
	Family Group Sheet	
	Individual Detail	
	Kinship	
	Ahnentafel	
Narratives	Ahnentafel – Direct Line	
	Descendant Indented	
	Individual Narrative	
	Journal	
Lists	Citations	
	Events	
	Names	
	People	
	Places	
	Repositories	
	Sources	
	Tag Types	
	Tasks	
	Witnesses	
Publication Tools	Bibliography	
	Endnotes	
Statistic	Audit	
	Data Set Information	
	Data Set Information	
	Statistical Report	

Table 10-1:Report Categories and Types

the data held within its projects. The reports listed by category in *Table 10-1* are covered on the following pages in alphabetical order except for Visual Chartform™ charts, which are covered in detail in *Chapter 13, Generating Charts For Use in Visual Chartform™* and *Chapter 14, Working With Charts in Visual Chartform™.*

This chapter describes how to create reports using TMG, and is divided into three parts. The first part covers The Report Definition Process, a step-by-step approach to transform your data into useful information that can be displayed on your screen, output to a printer, or saved to one of several industry standard file types including the native format of some popular word processing programs. It also includes an overview of those screens that are common to several reports. The second part covers some General Report Considerations

The third part of the chapter devotes a separate section to each of the standard TMG report types listed in *Table 10-1*. It is organized alphabetically by report with each section containing an overview of the report, the process used to create it and in some cases one or more examples.

The Report Definition Process

The **Report Definition Screen** *(see Figure 10-1)* is your gateway to running standard reports, as well as defining, saving and running custom reports. TMG's standard reports are designed to meet the general needs of most researchers, and can be run *as is* without customization. TMG defaults to the standard version of each report type until you customize and run a different version of it. To run a report, simply select the subject(s), select the report destination and click [Print & Save].

Report Definition Screen

The **Report Definition Screen** is also your key to unlocking TMG's comprehensive customization capabilities. Click the [Options] button to open the

Report Options window, a tabbed guide that serves two basic purposes. First, to identify and filter content to include in the report such as tags, sources, memos, exhibits, an index and/or bibliography. Second, to control how that content is displayed and/or printed by selecting font size and style, page number location and style and date format among others. Customized reports can also be saved and easily retrieved for use over and over again.

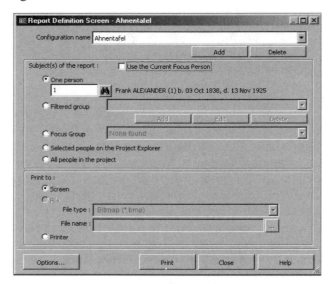

Figure 10-1: Report Definition Screen

The **Report Definition Screen** and **Report Options** window provide a simple, standard interface to report production. Check boxes are used to select one or more options from a group, and are represented by a square box (◘). Option buttons, or radio buttons, are used to select one option from a fixed set of mutually exclusive choices and are represented by a circle (○). Another key distinction is that check box options may stand-alone and have many selected, while radio buttons always occur in a set of two or more of which only one may be selected.

The **Report Definition Screen** includes the following options:

Configuration Name – Each report must have a unique **Configuration Name**, because it also doubles as the Windows™ file name. The report settings associated with an existing report will be lost if you save a custom report to an existing **Configuration Name**. TMG takes advantage of

long file names, so give each of your custom reports a useful name that fully describes its function.

TMG defaults to the version of the appropriate report type that was last used each time you run a report. To select a different configuration, click the arrow on the drop-down box, highlight the desired configuration name and click on it.

> Simply adding a new report and accepting the option to use the default configuration can recreate the default options for any report.

Click [Add] to open the file **Save As** screen.

The location for the new file will default to the folder path stored in **File > Preferences > Current Project Options > Advanced** (see *Chapter 4, Customizing the Program)*

Enter a file name for the new configuration and click [Save].

To delete a report configuration, its name must be visible in the **Configuration name** field. If it is not visible, click the arrow on the drop-down box, highlight the desired configuration and click on it. Click [Delete]. You will be asked if you are sure that you want to delete the selected configuration.

Click [Yes] to delete the configuration.

Click [No] to cancel the delete process.

Subject(s) of the report – Select one of the options listed below to set the report focus on one or more individuals.

    ◘ Use the Current Focus Person – This is the person currently in focus in the **Project Explorer** if it is linked to other windows. If it is not linked, then it is the person in focus on the **Details** window.

    ○ One person – Type in the person's ID Number, or click the binoculars ﹢ to open the **Picklist** to search for a person.

    ○ Filtered group *(See Chapter 11, Filtering and Sorting)*

    ○ Focus Group *(See Chapter 11, Filtering and Sorting)*

- Selected people on the Project Explorer – You can use conventional Windows™ techniques, <Shift>+Mouse click to highlight a range of people, or <Ctrl>+Mouse click to select multiple individuals.
- All people in the project

Print to – TMG uses standard Windows™ "Print to" nomenclature to identify the report destination. When you generate a report you can "print" it to the screen, to a file, or to a printer.

- Screen – Select this option to preview the report on your computer display.
- File – Select this option to create the report and save it directly as a file.

  File type – Click the arrow on the drop-down box to display a list of supported file types. Click on one of the listed file types to select it.

  File name – Name the file and select its location by entering a file name and file path. The file will be created in the folder defined in **Preferences > Current Project Options, Advanced, Reports** if no path is entered. Otherwise click the [...] select button to browse for a specific folder.

- Printer – Select this option to print the report directly to the printer you have selected under the **File > Printer Setup** option of the **Main Menu** *(see Figure 10-18).*

Click [Print & Save] to save the new report configuration and start the report.

If you selected **Print to** File above, TMG will perform one of three file output operations depending upon your setting in **Preferences > Program Options, Reports**. *(See Chapter 4, Customizing the Program.)* After creating the file, TMG will either leave the file closed, prompt you to open the file, or open the file automatically with the application associated with the selected file type.

If you selected **Print to** Printer above, TMG will open the **Printer Setup** window *(see Figure 10-18).* Click [Print] to print the report using the default or selected values or [Cancel] to close the **Printer Setup** window and return to the **Report Definition Screen** without printing.

Click [Save] to save the new report configuration and close without printing.

Click [Cancel] to close the **Report Definition Screen** without saving any changes. Select this option to preserve all existing values in the report definition.

Click [Help] for on-line information about this report.

PDF File Creation

TMG is capable of producing reports in Portable Document Format (PDF) – a universal file format that presserves all the fonts, formatting, graphics, and color of any source document, regardless of the application and platform used to create it – without the requirement of purchasing a separate program.

PDF files are ideal for electronic document distribution because of their broad cross-platform support and small size relative to the source document. PDF files can be e-mailed, posted on Web sites or on CD-ROM and be viewed, navigated and printed exactly as intended with an appropriate reader on Mac®, UNIX or Windows® platforms.

Visit the Adobe Systems Incorporated Web site at *http://www.adobe.com* to download their free Adobe® Acrobat® Reader®.

TMG uses a special PDF printer driver to create PDF files. In most cases, TMG installs a temporary PDF printer driver at report run-time when **Print to** is set to **File** and **File type** is set to PDF. This driver is removed when the report completes. Some systems, however, may be configured in such a way that the temporary installation process fails. When this occurs you will receive an error message similar to "PDF printer cannot be initiated. Please access **File > Printer Setup** and install the permanent PDF printer." *(See the **Setting up the printer** section later in this chapter.)*

Accessing the Report Options Screen

Click [Options] to display the **Report Options** screen and enable report customization. The number of tabs on the **Report Options** screen varies from report to report depending upon the degree of customization that is available for each. All reports have at leave four tabs in common, specifically General, Page Options, Fonts and HTML.

Icon	Label	Function
🖨	Print Report	Select this button to send the entire report to the printer you have selected under the **File > Printer Setup** option of the Main Menu *(see Figure 10-18)*.
📄	Print Current Page	Select this button to print only the current page that is visible on the **Report Preview** window.
←	Restart Report	Select this button to jump back to first page of the report and maximize the **Report Preview** window.
🔍	Zoom In	Select this button to zoom in, or magnify, the size of the preview image.
🔍	Zoom Out	Select this button to zoom out, or reduce, the size of the preview image.
⏮	First Page	Select this button to jump back to the first page from any other page of the report and retain the current size of the **Preview Window**.
◀	Previous Page	Select this button to jump to the previous page of the report.
▶	Next Page	Select this button to jump to the next page of the report.
⏭	Last Page	Select this button to jump to the last page from any other page of the report.
⏸	Pause	It *may* take some time to jump from the first page to the last page on the first attempt for each report run for particularly long reports, especially when run on older computers with limited memory and/or processor speed. Select the Pause button to stop the jump process and display a page prior to the last page.
⏹	Close Preview Window	Select this button to exit the **Report Preview** window without printing the report.

Table 10-2: Report Preview Window Button Functions

The **Report Options** screen may have up to fifteen tabs including; General, Page Options, Fonts, Sources, Memos, Exhibits, Indexes, Publication Tools, Sort By, Tags, Names, Dates, Places, HTML and Miscellaneous. The customization options available on each of these screens are described next.

Some of these options do not apply to some reports, and thus are not shown on their respective screens.

The Report Preview Window

A **Report Preview** window is opened whenever you run a report that has the **Print to** option set to Screen. This window enables you to see on the display screen exactly what will appear when the document is printed. In other words, it provides a visual WYSIWYG (what you see is what you get) representation of the report. In addition, the report "image" retains its proportions if you resize the window, so there is no distortion of the data unless you make the screen too small.

Only one report of each type can be open at the same time in a Report Preview window.

The **Report Preview** window displays the name of the selected report in the window header. The row of action buttons just below the header is used to perform various functions on the report preview *(see Table 10-2)*.

General Tab

The **General** tab *(see Figure 10-2)*, or a subset of it, is included as a **Report Options** tab for all report types. It may include the following options depending upon the report type:

Report title – Type the title as it is to be printed for the report. Several variables may also be used to augment the report title *(see Table 10-3)*.

Output Language – TMG supports several languages, and can do some translation dependent upon the availability of language translations (see *Chapter 2, Project Management, Project Management Functions, Language*). Select the language to be used for the report from the drop-down box. TMG will translate those English words and phrases to the appropriate language if a translation for them is available.

Number of generations – Use the dial box, or type the number of generations for the report. The value for most reports must be between 1 – 250. Some reports, however, are restricted to a lower number such as the **Descendant Indented Narrative**, which is limited to 15 generations.

Variable	Action
[F]	Prints the name of the focus person when the report is for an individual.
[FO]	Prints the name of the second focus person in an Ahnentafel – Direct Line and Relationship Chart, or the name of a spouse in a Pedigree Chart.
[?]	Prompts the user to enter a report title at report run-time.
[PROJECT]	Prints the file name of the current Project, e.g,. SAMPLE__.PJC
[PATHPROJECT]	Prints the path and file name of the current Project, e.g., c:\program files\ the master genealogist\sample\ SAMPLE__.PJC
[DATE]	Prints the date on which the report was generated.
[TIME] or [TIME24]	Prints the time at which the report was generated using the 24-hour clock, e.g., 13:50 rather than 1:50 PM.
[TIME12]	Prints the time at which the report was generated using the 12-hour clock, e.g., 1:50 PM.
[RNAME]	Prints the name of the researcher stored in **Preferences > Current Project Options > Other**.
[RADD1]	Prints the first line of the researcher address stored in **Preferences > Current Project Options > Other**.
[RADD2]	Prints the second line of the researcher address stored in **Preferences > Current Project Options > Other**.
[REMAIL]	Prints the e-mail address of the researcher stored in **Preferences > Current Project Options > Other**.

Table 10-3: Report Title Variables

Surety – You can control which people and events are included in a report by setting a threshold Surety value for the report. Relationship and Event tags subject to exclusion must include a source citation that has a surety value entered for it.

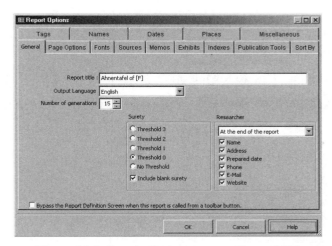

Figure 10-2: Report Options screen, General Tab

For example, if Threshold 2 is selected, then anyone who has a Relationship tag with a Surety value equal to 1 or 0 will be excluded from consideration in the report. Similarly, all Event tags that have a Surety value equal to 1 or 0 will be excluded from consideration in the report.

Select from the following options:
- Threshold 3
- Threshold 2
- Threshold 1
- Threshold 0
- No Threshold
- Include blank surety – Select this option to include all tags for which no Surety has been set.

Selecting a threshold that is "too low" may cause TMG to print "unknown date" or "unknown person" in place of the actual text.

Researcher – Click the down-arrow on the drop-down box to select where the researcher information, as defined in **Preferences**, will print.
- None
- At the end of the report
- In the header or footer

- Bypass the Report Definition Screen when the report is called from a toolbar button.

Select this option to speed report creation for those reports that do not require additional customization.

Page Options Tab

The **Page Options** tab *(see Figure 10-3)* is included as a **Report Options** tab for all report types. It includes the following options:

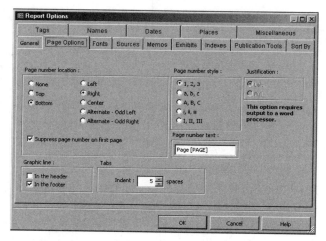

Figure 10-3: Report Options screen, Page Tab

Page Number Location
- ○ None
- ○ Top
- ○ Bottom
- ○ Left
- ○ Right
- ○ Center
- ○ Alternate – Odd Left
- ○ Alternate – Odd Right
- ◘ Suppress Number on First Page

Page Number Style – This option requires output to a supported word processor.
- ○ 1, 2, 3 …
- ○ a, b, c …
- ○ A, B, C …
- ○ i, ii, iii …
- ○ I, II, III …

Page number text – Enter the text that you want to precede the page number. For example:

      Page [PAGE]   would print as Page 17

while

      p. [PAGE]   would print as p. 17

The fields that contain the font name, size, and style are not directly editable. While you can click in one of these fields and select its contents, you cannot do anything with it. You must use the select button to make changes.

Justification – This option requires output to a supported word processor.
- ○ Left
- ○ Right

Graphic Line
- ◘ In the header
- ◘ In the footer

Tabs – Use the dial box arrows to select, or type the value for the number of spaces for indentation. The default value is five spaces.

      Indent _____ spaces

Fonts Tab

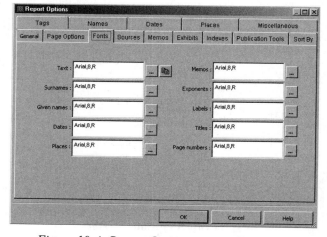

Figure 10-4: Report Options screen, Fonts Tab

The **Fonts** tab *(see Figure 10-4)* is included as a **Report Options** tab for all report types. This screen provides font control for a variety of data types to enhance the printed output, and includes the following options for most report types:

• Text	• Memos
• Surnames	• Exponents
• Given names	• Labels
• Dates	• Titles
• Places	• Page numbers

Click the […] select button to select a different font and style for each data type. To set all fonts and styles alike at once, set the desired font and style for Text and then click the ▦ button to copy the desired font to all other fields

Several reports produce results that are tabular in nature, e.g., most Lists, Project Information and the Statistical Report. These reports use a subset of the

Fonts screen that includes control over only two data types, Titles and Text, since tabular reports tend to look better if a non-proportional font such as Courier is used.

Sources Tab

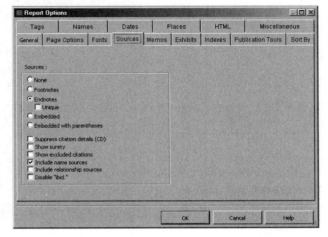

Figure 10-5: Report Options screen, Sources Tab

The **Sources** tab *(see Figure 10-5)* is included as a **Report Options** tab for several report types. This screen provides control over the printing of sources. Options include:

- ○ None – Select this option to exclude all sources from being printed in the selected report.
- ○ Footnotes – When selected, this option will include footnotes in reports that are printed to a file for certain word processors that allow footnotes. Footnotes will be converted to endnotes when output is directed to the screen or printer.
- ○ Endnotes – Select this option to enable the accumulation of endnotes over several different reports.
  - ◘ Unique – This option, when selected, will number and print each source once as an endnote. Additional citations to the same source will reference the same source number, so there will be no *ibid* endnotes. Additional citations to the same source that have different citation details will print as a separate endnote using the short form followed by the citation detail. When output is directed to a word processor file, unique endnotes will print as regular text, so they cannot be updated automatically when changes that may affect them are

made to the document. *It will be necessary to manually update the affected endnotes.*
  - ○ Embedded – Select this option to print the source directly following the tag that is cited.
  - ○ Embedded w/parentheses – This option, when selected, will print the source between parentheses directly following the tag that is cited.
- ◘ Suppress citation details (CD) – Select this option to suppress the printing of citation details with the source. When used in conjunction with Unique endnotes, this option will eliminate all short form endnotes, and refer all citations for a single source to a single source number.
- ◘ Show surety – Select this option to print the sureties between brackets for each source.
- ◘ Show excluded citations – Citations that have an exclusion marker "-" can be included in the report output by selecting this option.
- ◘ Include name sources – Select this option to include citations that are attached to name tags. When this option is selected, the citation will print following the name.
- ◘ Include relationship sources – Select this option to include citations that are attached to relationship tags. When this option is selected, the citation will be printed immediately after the primary name of the child.
- ◘ Disable "ibid." – Select this option to disable the printing of *ibid* and always print the short form of the note instead.

> *Not all word processors support all of TMG's footnote and endnote features. Check your word processor reference manual if you are in doubt.*

Memos Tab

The **Memos** tab *(see Figure 10-6)* is included as a **Report Options** tab for several report types. This screen provides control over the printing of memos. Options function similarly to those on the **Sources** tab and include:

- ○ None
- ○ Footnotes
- ○ Endnotes
  - ◘ Unique
- ○ Embedded
- ○ Embedded w/parentheses

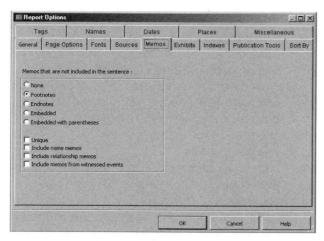

Figure 10-6: Report Options screen, Memos Tab

◘ Include name memos – Select this option to include memos that are in name tags. When this option is selected, the memo will print following the name.

◘ Include relationship memos – Select this option to include memos that are in relationship tags. When this option is selected, the memo will be printed immediately after the primary name of the child.

◘ Include memos from witnessed events – Select this option to include memos that are part of witnessed events. When this option is selected, the memo will be printed after the witnessed event. Leave this option unselected to prevent the same event memo from printing as a footnote, endnote or embedded note for all witnesses to an event. To prevent the memo from printing in the witness sentence replace the <[M]> variable in the witness sentence structure with the <[M0]> variable (see *Chapter 6, Sentence Structures*).

Exhibits Tab

The **Exhibits** tab *(see Figure 10-7)* is included as a **Report Options** tab for several report types. This screen provides control over whether exhibits are printed, or not, and how they are printed. *These options are available only when the Destination option on the Report Definition Screen (see Figure 10-1) is set to file, and the file type is set to Word, WordPerfect, or HTML.*

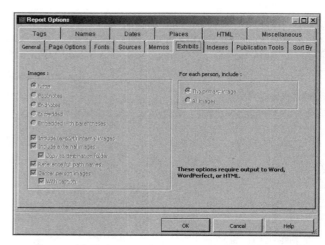

Figure 10-7: Report Options screen, Exhibits Tab

Exhibit options function similarly to those on the **Sources** tab and include:

Images
- ○ None
- ○ Footnotes
- ○ Endnotes
- ○ Embedded
- ○ Embedded with parentheses
- ◘ Include (export) internal images
- ◘ Include external images
    - ◘ Copy to destination folder
- ◘ Reference full path names
- ◘ Center person images – This option becomes enabled when the Images of people option above is set to either Embedded or Embedded with parentheses. When selected, this option will center the image on the printed page directly above the subject's primary record.
    - ◘ With caption

For each person, include:
- ○ The primary image – Select this option to include Exhibit Log images whose Focus is set to *A Person* and is also marked as primary.
- ○ All images – Select this option to include *all* images in the Exhibit Log whose Focus is set to *A Person.*

Indexes Tab

The **Indexes** tab *(see Figure 10-8)* is included as a **Report Options** tab for several report types. This screen provides control over whether indexes are printed, or not, and how they are printed. *These options are only available when the Destination* *option on the Report Definition Screen (see Figure 10-1) is set to file, and the file type is set to a word processor.*

> Not all word processors support TMG's index features. Check your word processor reference manual if you are in doubt

Index options include:

People

- ◘ Surname Index
- ◘ Given Name Index
- ◘ Combined Index – Select this option to combine the Surname Index and Given Name Index into a single larger index.
- ◘ GENDEX File (HTML) – The GENDEX WWW Genealogical Index is a server that indexes thousands of web sites containing genealogical data for tens of millions of individuals, giving researchers the ability to locate and view data from any of these sites without having to visit each separately. Select this option to create a GENDEX-compatible index that can be included on a personal genealogy web site. Once the index is submitted to GENDEX it will become available to anyone using the GENDEX server.
- ○ Show no lifespan
- ○ (Year – Year) – For example: (1905 – 1992)
- ○ (Date – Date) – For example: (05 Jan 1905 – 19 Jun 1992)
- ○ (b. Year – d. Year) – For example: (b. 1905 – d. 1992)
- ○ (b. Date – d. Date) – For example: (b. 05 Jan 1905 – d. 19 Jun 1992)

Places

Select all that should be included.

- ◘ By short place
- ◘ By place detail (L2)
- ◘ By city (L3)
- ◘ By county (L4)
- ◘ By state (L5)
- ◘ By country (L7)
- ◘ Largest element first – Select this option if you want to reverse the place order when the index is printed.

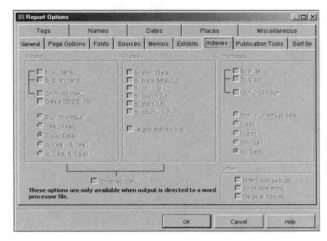

Figure 10-8: Report Options screen, Indexes Tab

The **Indexes** screen defaults to printing the People index and Places index separately. They can be combined into a single index with the People/Place headings by selecting the following option:

- ◘ Combined index

Marriages

- ◘ By bride – Select this option to include a separate index for all females in the report who have a primary Marriage tag.
- ◘ By groom – Select this option to include a separate index for all males in the report who have a primary Marriage tag.
- ◘ Combined index – Select this option to combine the bride index and groom index into a single index.
- ○ Show no marriage date
- ○ (Year) – For example, (1985)
- ○ (Date) – For example, (5 Nov 1985)
- ○ (m. Year) – For example, (m. 1985)
- ○ (m. Date) – For example, (m. 5 Nov 1985)

Other

- ◘ Indent subheadings
- ◘ Count references
- ◘ Merge all indexes – Select this option to combine all indexes into a single index.

Publications Tools Tab

The **Publication Tools** tab *(see Figure 10-9)* is included as a **Report Options** tab for several report types. This screen provides control over the inclusion of a table of contents and bibliography. Options include:

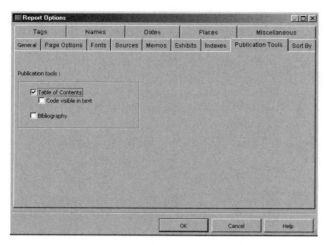

Figure 10-9: Report Options screen, Publications Tools Tab

Publication Tools

- ◘ Table of Contents – Select this option to have TMG generate the appropriate table of contents field codes required by the word processor selected in the **Print to** section of the **Report Definition Screen**. This option is available for output to word processor formats only.
- ◘ Code visible in text – Select this option to display the special field codes used by your word processor that define table of contents entries. This feature can be used to identify and/or troubleshoot entries to the table of contents to better meet your report output expectations.
- ◘ Bibliography – Select this option to accumulate a bibliography for the target report (see *the **Bibliography** report section later in this chapter, for details on accumulating and printing a bibliography for multiple reports*).

Sort By Tab

The **Sort By** tab *(see Figure 10-10)* is included as a **Report Options** tab for several report types whose focus can be more than one person, e.g., a filtered group, a focus group, selected people on the Project Explorer, or all people in the project *(see Figure 10-1, Report Definition Screen, Subject(s) of the report).*

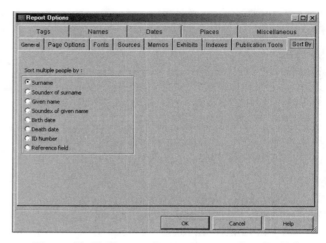

Figure 10-10: Report Options screen, Sort By Tab

This screen controls the order in which the focus people print. Options include:

Sort multiple people by

- ○ Surname
- ○ Soundex of surname
- ○ Given Name
- ○ Soundex of given name
- ○ Birth date
- ○ Death date
- ○ ID Number
- ○ Reference field

Tags Tab

The **Tags** tab *(see Figure 10-11)* is included as a **Report Options** tab for several report types, and controls the inclusion of tags and events in them. Options include:

Tag types

- ○ None
- ○ All
- ○ Selected – When this option is selected, a **Tag types** frame appears displaying a list of active tag types. To find tag type(s) for inclusion in the report use the scroll bar on the right side of the frame, or click once on one of the **Tag types** in the list and use either the <Arrow> keys, or [PageUp]/[PageDown] keys. Double-click on a **Tag type** to include it in the report. Once included, you can unselect a **Tag type** by double-clicking on it a second time. Selected **Tag types** will have a small check mark in the column to the left of the **Tag type** column.

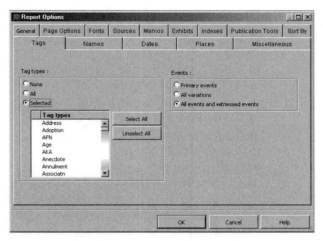

Figure 10-11: Report Options screen, Tags Tab

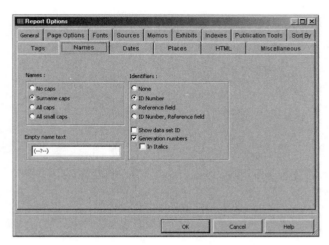

Figure 10-12: Report Options screen, Names Tab

Click [Select All] to select all **Tag types** for inclusion in the report.

Click [Unselect All] to unselect all **Tag types** that are currently selected.

Events
○ Primary events
○ All variations
○ All events and witnessed events

Names Tab

The **Names** tab *(see Figure 10-12)* is included as a **Report Options** tab for several report types, and controls how names and identifiers are printed. Options include:

Names
○ No caps
○ Surname caps
○ All caps
○ All small caps

Empty name text

This option provides the means to define what will print when part, or all, of a name is not known. The value stored in this field will print once for each part of a name that is missing (see *Chapter 5, Customizing the Data,* for a discussion on name styles). Use this option to accept the default value, (--?--), or to define a personal preference. Delete the default value and leave the field blank to print only those parts of the name that are known.

Identifiers
○ None
○ ID Number
○ Reference field
○ ID Number, Reference field
◘ Show data set ID
◘ Generation numbers
   ◘ In Italics

Dates Tab

The **Dates** tab *(see Figure 10-13)* is included as a **Report Options** tab for several report types, and controls the format in which dates are printed. Options include:

Date format:	Examples:
○ mm/dd/yyyy	11/01/1951
○ yyyy.mm.dd	1951.11.01
○ dd/mm/yyyy	01/11/1951
○ dd.mm.yyyy	01.11.1951
○ dd-mm-yyyy	01-11-1951
○ Mmm dd, yyyy	Nov 01, 1951
○ MMM dd, yyyy	NOV 01, 1951
○ dd Mmm yyyy	01 Nov 1951
○ dd MMM yyyy	01 NOV 1951

◘ Months spelled out – TMG supports a number of date formats, but the month is typically printed as either a two-digit number, or three-character abbreviation. Select this option to force printing the month name in full when the date format is set to one of the alphanumeric options.

> *This option will not affect the spelling of months that are stored as part of an irregular date.*

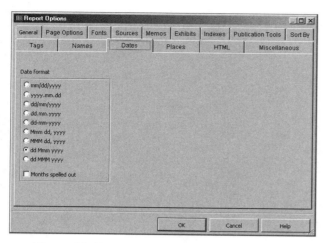

Figure 10-13: Report Options screen, Dates Tab

Places Tab

The **Places** tab *(see Figure 10-14)* is included as a **Report Options** tab for several report types, and controls how places are printed. Options include:

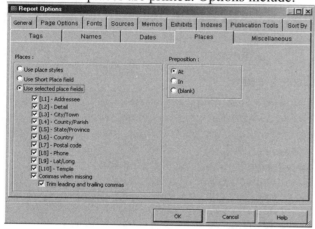

Figure 10-14: Report Options screen, Places Tab

Places

- o Use place styles *(see Chapter 5, Customizing the Data)*
- o Use Short Place field – Select this option to print the place name as defined in the **Short place template** field which is stored in **Preferences, Current Project Options, Other.** This option is used primarily for those reports with limited space for place names, such as charts, but could also be used in narrative reports as a shortcut to selecting individual place fields.
- o Use selected place fields – Select all that apply.

- ◘ [L1] – Addressee
- ◘ [L2] – Detail
- ◘ [L3] – City/Town
- ◘ [L4] – County/Parish
- ◘ [L5] – State/Province
- ◘ [L6] – Country
- ◘ [L7] – Postal code
- ◘ [L8] – Phone
- ◘ [L9] – Lat/Long
- ◘ [L10] – Temple
- ◘ Commas when missing – TMG ignores the commas and spaces between place fields that are missing data when printed. Select this option to include all commas between place fields.
  - ◘ Trim leading and trailing commas

Preposition – Use this feature to select a default preposition that will print for all place names in reports. You may find, however, that a choice of one or the other options does not always generate proper syntax for every use in a report. In those cases, the default preposition can easily be overridden by the construction of effective custom sentence structures *(see Chapter 6, Sentence Structures)*. Preposition options include:

- o At
- o In
- o (blank)

HTML Tab

The **HTML** tab *(see Figure 10-15)* is included as a **Report Options** tab for all report types. The options on this screen are available only when the **Print to** option on the **Report Definition Screen** is set to **File** and **File Type** is set to Hypertext Markup Language (HTML). The default values for the fields may be modified by the user to control the visual aspects of web pages generated by TMG and can include standard HTML tags or the proprietary (HTML) pseudo-tags that are unique to TMG.

Standard HTML tags are used to define paragraph and font styles, and other Web page structure elements. For example, paragraph attributes such as alignment are defined in the tag <P> for "paragraph break" while the appearance of the text is described in tags like <B> for "bold" or <I> for "italic" and <U> for "underlined". The Web page layout is described in other tags such as <TABLE>, used to define "table attributes" and <FRAMESET> used to split the main frame, also known as the documents window, into two or more smaller independent scrollable frames. TMG also employs its own (HTML) pseudo-tags *(see Table 10-4)*. These pseudo-tags are unique to TMG, and are designed to facilitate the inclusion of TMG-specific data types in HTML output. While most standard tags have both a start tag, such as <B> and a corresponding end tag, such as</B>, TMG pseudo-tags do not require an end tag.

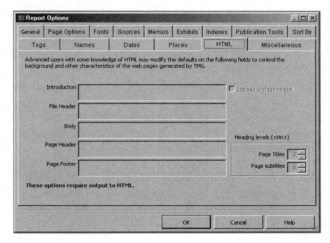

Figure 10-15: HTML Tab

Users can also control the visual aspects of the narrative for a web page. See *Chapter 6, Sentence Structures* for a discussion on *Entering Embedded Codes* into the Tag sentence structure. See also TMG's on-line **Help** under *HTML Embedded Codes*.

A treatise on web page design and HTML coding is beyond the scope of this chapter as there are several current publications available that are dedicated to the subject, some of them at a very low cost. In addition, free tips and hints for HTML coding and web page color mapping can be found by doing an appropriate search on the web. It should be noted that even users who are unfamiliar with HTML can take advantage of these powerful TMG features to create attractive, unique web pages.

Introduction – The contents of this field are included on the Table of Contents web page directly below the page header when the **Table of Contents** option is selected on the **Publications Tools** tab of the **Report Options** screen. The text and any HTML syntax in this field should be enclosed in

off-setting HTML formatting codes as in the example below:

> [HTML:]This text is on the first line.
This text is on the second line.[:HTML]

The above will display on your web page as:

> This text is on the first line.
> This text is on the second line.

Use the HTML code <P> instead of <BR> to force a blank line between paragraphs in your introduction.

> ◘ Instead of page header – Select this option to eliminate the page header, as defined below, from the Table of Contents page.

The following options pertain to all HTML pages.

	Context
File Header	<HTML><HEAD> xxxx </HEAD>
Body	<BODY xxxx >
Page Header	<BODY> xxxx
Page Footer	xxxx </BODY></HTML>

File Header – This option controls the type of information that is included in the File Header section of the HTML source code that defines your web page(s). *The file header information is not actually displayed as part of the web page.* It is intended for information use, and can be viewed with the rest of the page source code via a text editor or by using your browser's feature to view the page source.

The default value for **File Header** is:

> [HTML:]<TITLE><TMGSUBTITLE><TMGTITLE> </TITLE><META NAME="Author" CONTENT= <TMGAUTHOR>"> <META NAME="Keys" CONTENT="<TMGKEYWORDS>"> <!--Subject: <TMGSUBJECT>--><!--Comment: <TMGCOMMENTS>--><!--Creation Date: <TMGDATE>--><LINK REV="made" HREF="mailto: <TMGEMAIL>">[:HTML]

On output, the above pseudo-tags are substituted with data obtained from TMG based on the rules and definitions shown in Table 10-4 below.

Body – The contents of this field control the appearance of the background and text for your web page(s). You can control the color of the background, or point to a tiled image in JPG or GIF format to act as wallpaper for your web page(s). You can also control the color of the text and page links independently.

The default value for **Body** is:
    BGCOLOR="#FFFFC0"
This is the pale yellow background that may be familiar to many TMG users who use this feature.

TMG Pseudo-Tag	HTML Output Substitution
< TMGSUBTITLE>	The label for the appropriate report section associated with its specific web page, e.g., Index, Table of Contents, Endnotes, and Bibliography, when the afore-mentioned pages are selected as Report Options.
<TMGTITLE>	The Report Configuration name found on the Report Definition Screen.
<TMGAUTHOR>	The name(s) found in the Name field on the **Preferences > Current Project Options > General** screen.
<TMGKEYWORDS>	The contents of the Keywords field on the Document Summary Screen.
<TMGSUBJECT>	The subject(s) of the report as defined on the **Report Definition Screen.** This may be a person's name or a reference to a filtered group or focus group.
<TMGCOMMENTS>	The contents of the Comments field on the Document Summary Screen, e.g. "Originally created by The Master Genealogist (TMG) v5.x.
<TMGDATE>	The system date at the time of report generation.
<TMGEMAIL>	The address stored in the E-mail field on the **Preferences > Current Project Options > General** screen.

Table 10-4: TMG Pseudo-Tag HTML Output

Some additional variables that can be added to the body include:
    TEXT="#XXXXXX"
    LINK="#XXXXXX"
    VLINK="#XXXXXX"
    ALINK="#XXXXXX"
    BACKGROUND="FILENAME"

Where XXXXXX is a valid RGB hex triplet color value. The value for LINK defines the color for unvisited links on your web page(s), while the value for VLINK sets the color for visited links. The value

for ALINK sets the color of text marking hypertext links when selected by the user. The actual result varies by browser. Microsoft Internet Explorer® changes the color of the link text as you tab through the links in a document; the current link is set to the ALINK color. The color changes back when you tab to the next link. For Netscape® 6.2 and Netscape® 7, click on a link and hold the mouse button down to see the link text change to the ALINK color.

The value for BACKGROUND must be a valid file name including its JPG or GIF suffix, and can contain one or more file folder prefixes that point to the image's folder location relative to that of the web page. The example below points to a JPG image called mybackground.JPG that is located in the same folder that contains your HTML file(s), and will be used as a tiled background for your web page(s):
    BACKGROUND="mybackground.jpg"

The next example points to a JPG image called mybackground.jpg that is located in a folder called images that is one level up in the directory tree from the folder that contains your HTML file(s). This file will be used as a tiled background for your web page(s):
    BACKGROUND="/images/mybackground.jpg"

Note the backslashes *before and after* the folder name.

Page Header – The contents of this field are displayed at the top of each web page.

The default value is:
    [HTML:]<TMGTITLE>[:HTML]

You can add additional text or pseudo-tags before or after the default, or even delete the pseudo-tag and type a unique header that will be used at the top of each web page. In addition, you can also control the font type plus its size, color and justification by using the appropriate HTML codes.

Page Footer – The contents of this field are displayed at the bottom of each web page.

The default value is:
    [HTML:]
Please send e-mail to: <A HREF= "mailto: <TMGEMAIL>"><TMGEMAIL></A>
Created with <A HREF="http://www.

whollygenes.com">The Master Genealogist for Windows</A> on <TMGDATE> at<TMGTIME> .[:HTML]

As with the **Page Header** option above, you can add additional text ot pseudo-tags to the **Page Footer** before or after the defaults, or even delete them and type a unique footer that will be used at the bottom of each web page. Again, you can also control the font type plus its size, color and justification by using the appropriate HTML codes.

Heading levels (<Hn>)

    Page Titles ____ – This option controls the size of the font for page titles, e.g., Ahnentafel of Frank ALEXANDER. Enter a value between 0 and 6. A value of 0 sets the size of the Page Titles font to be consistent with the normal or default body font. For values 1 – 6, the smaller the value, the larger the font. The default value is 2.

    Page Subtitles ____ – This option controls the size of the font for page subtitles, if any, e.g., 1st Generation, 2nd Generation, etc. Enter a value between 0 and 6. A value of 0 sets the size of the Page Subtitles font to be consistent with the normal or default body font. For values 1 – 6, the smaller the value, the larger the font. The default value is 0.

Miscellaneous Tab

The **Miscellaneous** tab *(see Figure 10-16)* is included as a **Report Options** tab for several report types. The options on this screen vary from report to report, but generally include the following:

Exclusion – The discussion of excluded and sensitive data are integral to the advanced functionality of TMG, but beyond the scope of this chapter. *See Chapter 9, Controlling Narratives* for an in-depth discussion regarding these features.

- Show excluded data – Select this option to print data in your report that carries a single exclusion marker, "-".
- Show sensitive data – Select this option print data in your report that is marked with sensitivity brackets, "{ }".
- With brackets – Select this option to print the sensitive data with brackets "{ }" surrounding it.

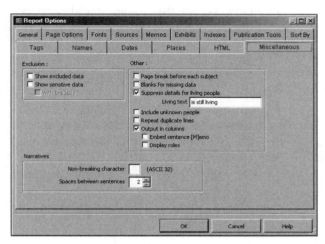

Figure 10-16: Report Options screen, Miscellaneous Tab

Other

- Blank line before each subject
- Blanks for missing data – Many TMG reports can be used as research aids. Select this option to print underline characters where data is missing, e.g., dates, places, names, etc., as a reminder and convenient place to enter new information found during a research effort.
- Suppress details for living people – Select this option to keep information about living people private. When selected, the only information that prints is the person's name and a brief message defined with the **Living text** option in the adjoining field.

    Living text – Use this option to accept the default value *is still living*, or to define a personal message.

> The Living text field accepts embedded citations, so you can document your assertions for living persons in your output. See *Chapter 7, Sources* for tips on using embedded citations.

- Include unknown people – Select this option to include unknown spouses of known subjects in the report.
- Repeat duplicate lines – Duplicate lines occur when cousins procreate – no matter how distantly they are related. TMG will truncate the printing of duplicate lines, and refer the reader back to the initial occurrence of the

duplicate, potentially saving multiple pages of duplicate printed material. Select this option to force printing of the duplicate lines.

◘ Output in columns – This feature is found only on the **Ahnentafel** and **Ahnentafel Direct Line** reports.

◘ Embed sentence [M]emo – Select this option to display the contents of the memo field in the same column, but after the tag date and place information.

◘ Display roles – Select this option if you use roles for Principals and/or Witnesses and you want those roles to be displayed in the columnar output.

Narratives

Non-breaking character ___ (ASCII 32) – Could be a character, a space or ASCII 0160.

Spaces between sentences ___ – The number of spaces that should be used between sentences is often determined by personal preference, or in other cases, by the publisher. In general, traditional mono-spaced fonts require a minimum of two spaces between sentences to look "good" while many modern proportionally spaced fonts can look just as "good" using a single space. Use this option to select the required number of spaces between sentences.

Output Columns Tab

The **Output Columns** tab *(see Figure 10-17)* is found on the following **List of …** reports: **Events**, **Names**, **People**, **Places**, **Tag Types** and **Witnesses**. This screen is used to define the data fields, up to nine, that can be printed in these reports. *Each row on the screen represents one column in the report.* You have control over the following four report characteristics:

Sort Order – Enter a value from 1 to 4 to determine the order in which each line of the report will be sorted.

Column Type – Click the arrow on the drop-down box to display a comprehensive list of fields that are available for inclusion in the report. Each field that is selected will represent a column of information in the report.

Heading – Type a name that describes the information that will be contained in each column of the report.

Width – Enter a value to specify the field width for each column.

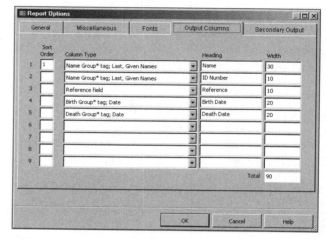

Figure 10-17: Report Options screen, Output Columns Tab (List of… Reports)

To insert a column before an existing column, place the cursor on the row corresponding to the existing column, right-click the mouse and select **Insert Column**. To delete an existing column, place the cursor on the row corresponding to it, right-click the mouse and select **Delete Column**.

General Report Considerations

Setting up the printer

Select **File > Printer Setup** from the Main Menu bar to define your preferred printer settings *(see Figure 10-18)*.

Options include:

[Install PDF printer] – Click this button to install a permanent PDF printer driver. TMG will open a window that describes the normal process to send a report to a PDF file, and notes that this special procedure is unnecessary for most users and should be used only if the normal process fails.

Click [Yes] to install the permanent PDF printer driver. Click [No] to cancel the procedure.

*This procedure is necessary **only** if your system experiences a failure while attempting to install the temporary PDF printer driver which occurs at report run-time when **Print to** is set to **File** and **File type** is set to PDF. In addition, this procedure can only be performed by someone who has logged into Windows® with Administrator Rights.*

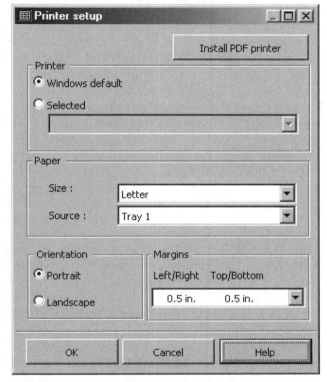

Figure 10-18: Printer Setup

Printer – using the **Windows default**, or **Selected** (a specific printer other than Windows default).

Paper – **Size** (e.g., Letter, Legal, A4) and **Source** (e.g., Tray 1, Tray 2, etc.)

Orientation – Portrait or Landscape

Margins – for **Left/Right** and **Top/Bottom** (e.g., 0.5 in. and 0.5 in. or 1.0 in. and 0.5 in.)

Which report should I use?

A simplistic answer is that it depends upon what information you want to extract, and in what form you want it displayed, e.g. as a chart, form, list, or narrative. The distinction between charts, forms, and narratives is particularly straightforward due to the unique format of each. So, it should be fairly

simple to determine which format is most appropriate to meet your needs.

List reports, however, are another matter. The Master Genealogist™ (TMG) is capable of producing lists from ten categories of data, e.g. Citations, Events, Names, People, Places, Repositories, Sources, Tag Types, Tasks and Witnesses. Each **List** can be narrowly focused by applying up to eight filter expressions, each one capable of referencing several thousand data elements and dozens of Boolean operators giving rise to several million combinations of possible report filters *(see Chapter 11, Filtering and Sorting).*

In some cases, a similar report can be produced using more than one of the above **List** types, because some of the **Lists** support similar data fields for Output Columns. *Availability of the particular data field(s) that you want to include in a report is the key to determining which **List** report is best for your needs.*

For example, which report do you use to print a list of names for people in a project that are married? At first glance you might expect to use either a **List of Names** or **List of People** report. But, neither of these will associate spouses to one another, and display them on the same line in the report. A properly filtered **List of Events** report, however, will do just that. So the key is to determine first which data types should be included in the report, and second which report type is capable of producing the desired output. Then evaluate the filter options for each to determine which report type provides the best focus for your needs.

One Report or Many?

The subject(s) of a report are selected on the **Report Definition Screen.** There is a not so subtle difference between producing multiple subject reports for **Lists** versus other report types. All report types can include multiple subjects as the focus of the report. *List reports will include all subjects in a single report. The other report types, however, will include each subject as the focus of a separate report, but included in the one output.*

For example, say you want to create a single 5-generation **Ahnentafel** report for the individual with ID# 1:1.

The proper approach is to select **One person** as the subject of the report on the **Report Definition Screen** and enter 1:1 as the ID#. Click the [Options] button and enter the value 5 for **Number of generations** on the **General** tab. Click [OK], then [Print & Save] to run the report.

The following is an improper approach. Select **Filtered group** on the **Report Definition Screen** and click [Add]. Select ID number Equals 1:1 as the report filter. At the bottom of the screen, under **And then add their**, check the **Ancestors** box and enter the value 5. Click [OK] and then [Print & Save] to run the report. This approach will print separate **Ahnentafel** reports for the individual with ID# 1:1 <u>and</u> all known ancestors for the next 5 generations.

Sort order of children in reports

The default order for children is controlled by Birth Group tag Dates unless the BIRTH ORDER flag is set for one or more children, in which case the flag controls the sort. So, the BIRTH ORDER flag can be used to control the sort order of children in reports where Birth Group tag Dates are unknown, or where evidence suggests that the order differs from the available dates. This could be the case, for example, where evidence is found of a "missing" unnamed sibling who may have died as an infant.

BIRTH ORDER flag values, when used, will override the sort order for children set by Birth Group tags. If some children in a family have a Birth Order flag value set, and some do not, those with a value will sort first followed by those without a value, even if all children have a Birth Group tag present.

Standard TMG Reports

Ahnentafel

Overview

The term ahnentafel is derived from a German word meaning 'ancestor table'. The **Ahnentafel** report utilizes a numbering system that allows the reader to quickly determine the relationship of an ancestor

with the focus person of the report. The focus, or starting person, is always given the number one regardless of gender. The starting person's father is number two and mother is number three. The father for each parent in each successive generation is always twice that of the child, the mother is twice that of the child plus one. (In other words, given any number N, N's father is 2N and N's mother is 2N + 1.)

The **Ahnentafel** report is typically produced as a narrative version of a **Pedigree** chart. TMG also offers a unique output option for this report that can be printed and used as a handy research aid. This version, called the **Ahnentafel, Columnar**, uses the same numbering scheme, but prints tag information in a format similar to a **Family Group Sheet**. Each tag starts on a separate line under the person's name. The tag name, date and place are printed in separate columns. The place column may wrap to several lines if role and memo information is selected for printing *(see Figure 10-16)*.

The **Ahnentafel** report provides a convenient way to print all of the direct-line ancestors of the focus person. Since it is a narrative, the **Ahnentafel** report can contain substantially more information about the people it includes than does a Pedigree chart. When printed in its columnar version, all of the events in each person's life are conveniently aligned in a table, much like the **Person View** of the **Details** window, so as to provide a simple and quick overview to key information during a research trip. In addition, and unlike the **Pedigree** chart, the **Ahnentafel** report can be defined to include multiple subjects.

Creating an Ahnentafel Report

Select **Report > Ahnentafel** from the **Main Menu** bar to open the **Ahnentafel** Report Definition Screen *(see Figure 10-1)*.

Select the desired report configuration, the subject(s) for the report and the print to location (see *The Report Process, Report Definition Screen*). Click [Print & Save] if you plan to run an existing report configuration without modification, or

Click [Options] to open the **Report Options** screen and enable report customization. This screen has 15 tabs; General, Page Options, Fonts, Sources,

Memos, Exhibits, Indexes, Publication Tools, Sort By, Tags, Names, Dates, Places, HTML and Miscellaneous. The options on each of these tabs are described in this chapter in the section titled *The Report Definition Process*. Please refer to that section for the details.

The **Ahnentafel**, Miscellaneous tab includes these additional options *(see Figure 10-16)*:
- ◘ Output in columns – Select this option to print the **Ahnentafel, Columnar** style report.
- ◘ Embed sentence [M]emo – Select this option to display the contents of the memo field in the same column, but after the tag date and place information.
- ◘ Display roles – Select this option if you use roles for Principals and/or Witnesses and you want those roles to be displayed in the columnar output.

Example

Print an Ahnentafel report of your four grandparents.

Rather than printing four separate **Ahnentafel** reports, in which there may be duplication, select your four grandparents as subjects of the report via the Report Definition Screen *(see Figure 10-1)*. On the **Sort** tab, select **Sort multiple people** by **ID Number**. Click [OK] when you have completed setting options on the **Report Options** screens. TMG will create a single **Ahnentafel** report with four sections that are sorted by your grandparents' **ID Number** when it is printed. In addition, TMG will eliminate any duplicate lines, unless the **Repeat duplicate lines** option is selected on the **Miscellaneous** tab.

Ahnentafel – Direct Line

Overview

The **Ahnentafel – Direct Line** report produces a special version of the standard **Ahnentafel** that associates the direct ancestral line between the focus person and a target ancestor. Like its parent report, the **Ahnentafel – Direct Line** can be printed as either a narrative or columnar report (see **Ahnentafel**).

Creating an Ahnentafel – Direct Line

Select **Report > Ahnentafel – Direct Line** from the **Main Menu** bar to open the **Ahnentafel – Direct Line** Report Definition Screen *(see Figure 10-19)*.

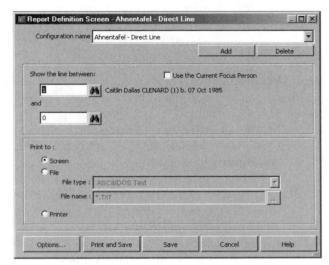

Figure 10-19: Report Definition Screen Ahnentafel - Direct Line

Select the desired report configuration and print to location for the report (see *The Report Process, Report Definition Screen*).

Select the two subjects for whom the report will show the line between.

- ◘ Use the Current Focus Person – This is the person currently in focus in the **Project Explorer** if it is linked to other windows. If it is not linked, then it is the person in focus on the **Details** window.

If you intend to use someone other than the focus person, type their ID number, or click the binoculars ![binoculars icon] to open the **Picklist** to search for a person.

In either case, type the ID number of the second subject, or click the binoculars ![binoculars icon] to open the **Picklist** to search for a person.

Click [Print & Save] if you plan to run an existing report configuration without modification, or

Click [Options] to open the **Report Options** screen and enable report customization. This screen has 15 tabs; General, Page Options, Fonts, Sources, Memos, Exhibits, Indexes, Publication Tools, Sort By, Tags, Names, Dates, Places, HTML and Miscellaneous. The options on each of these tabs are described in this chapter in the section titled *The Report Definition Process*. Please refer to that section for the details.

The **Ahnentafel – Direct Line**, Miscellaneous tab includes these additional options *(see Figure 10-16)*:

- ❑ Output in columns – Select this option to print the **Ahnentafel – Direct Line, Columnar** style report.
  - ❑ Embed sentence [M]emo – Select this option to display the contents of the memo field in the same column, but after the tag date and place information.
  - ❑ Display roles – Select this option if you use roles for Principals and/or Witnesses and you want those roles to be displayed in the columnar output.

Example

Print an Ahnentafel – Direct Line Columnar report.

Select **Reports > Ahnentafel – Direct Line** from the **Main Menu** bar.

Select the subject(s) for the report and the report destination.

Click the [Options] button to open the **Report Options** screen.

Click the Miscellaneous tab and select the option 'Output in columns' which is located in the 'Other' frame.

Select any other desired options and click [OK] to return to the Report Definition Screen.

Click [Print & Save] to print the report.

Audit

Overview

The **Audit** report analyzes the data in your project based on parameters that you define to identify potential error conditions. Individuals for whom more than one error condition exists will print only once, followed by a description of each error. In some cases, a single error condition may cause multiple errors to be reported, not only for the individual, but for other related individuals as well. For example, a birth date entered incorrectly could propagate errors for a person, and for that person's children whose births are compared to that date. The **Audit** report is sorted by **ID Number**. If no errors are found, the **Audit** report will state "nothing to report."

Not all errors listed in the **Audit** report are necessarily real errors. Some may be caused by peculiar circumstances that are accurately documented in the historical record. In these unusual cases, you might consider adjusting and saving the threshold values in a separate report definition where they are not reported as errors.

There are few methods available to add information to a data set – manually, or by importing data from either a GEDCOM file, or directly from another application with GenBridge™. All data, whether entered by you manually, or entered by someone else in another program and imported is typically fraught with errors. Fortunately many of these errors are caught at the time of data entry. But, what if you did not do the data entry? What if you accepted a file from another person that you plan to incorporate into your data? Does this person enter data with the same high standards as you? Regardless of how you entered data into your data set, the **Audit** report analyzes your data set based on parameters that you define to identify *potential* error conditions.

Creating an Audit Report

Select **Report > Audit** from the **Main Menu** bar to open the **Audit** Report Definition Screen *(see Figure 10-1)*.

Select the desired report configuration, the subject(s) for the report and the print to location (see *The Report Process, Report Definition Screen)*.

Click [Print & Save] if you plan to run an existing report configuration without modification, or

Click [Options] to open the **Report Options** screen and enable report customization. This screen has nine tabs; General, Page Options, Fonts, Indexes, Publication Tools, Sort By, Names, HTML and

Miscellaneous. The options on each of these tabs are described in this chapter in the section titled *The Report Definition Process*. Please refer to that section for the details.

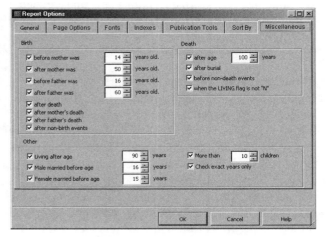

Figure 10-20: Audit Report, Miscellaneous Tab

The **Audit Report**, Miscellaneous tab *(see Figure 10-20)* allows you to narrow your audit to one or more potential trouble areas that deal with birth, marriage and death events. You may either accept the predefined option for any field, or select your own parameters. You may identify people for whom:

Birth

- before mother was ___ years old.
- after mother was ___ years old.
- before father was ___ years old.
- after father was ___ years old.
- after death
- after mother's death
- after father's death
- after non-birth events

Death

- after age ___ years
- after burial
- before non-death-events
- when LIVING flag is not "N"

Other

- Living after age ___ years.
- Male married before age ___ years
- Female married before age ___ years
- More than ___ children
- Check exact years only

Example

*I received a GEDCOM file from another researcher and imported it as the second data set in my master project. How can I use the **Audit** report to validate this data separately from my existing data?*

To run the report, select **Reports > Audit** from the **Main Menu** bar.

Select **Filtered Group** and click the [Add] button next to it.

Click the arrow on the **Field** drop-down box and select **Data Set ID**.

Leave the **Operator** set at "= Equals".

Enter the Data Set ID, in this example 2, in the **Value** field

Click [OK] to close the Report Filter window.

Click [Print & Save] to run the report.

Bibliography

Overview

A **Bibliography** report is an alphabetical list of sources that are referenced in your work. It may be accumulated in the course of generating one, or several different reports from any of the following report types:

- Ahnentafel
- Audit
- Descendant Indented Narrative
- Family Group Sheet
- Individual Detail
- Individual Narrative
- Journal
- Kinship Report
- Pedigree - Compressed
- Relationship Chart

Specify the creation of a bibliography from any of the above reports by checking the **Bibliography** option on the **Publication Tools** tab of the **Report Options** screen. In addition, you must also activate sources on the **Sources** tab of the **Report Options** screen. The output form, and effectively the sort order, for the **Bibliography** report is defined on the **Output Form** tab of the **Source Definition** screen *(see Chapter 7, Sources)*.

A complete and accurate bibliography is required for most professional and academic publications. A printed bibliography also offers a convenient method of sharing your source material with a fellow researcher.

> The accumulation feature for bibliography entries is **system** related, not project related, so a Bibliography will accumulate when running reports across multiple projects.

Creating a Bibliography Report

Select **Report > Bibliography** from the **Main Menu** bar to open the **Bibliography** Report Definition Screen *(see Figure 10-1)*.

Select the desired report configuration and print to location.

Click [Print & Save] if you plan to run an existing report configuration without modification, or

Click [Options] to open the **Report Options** screen and enable report customization. This screen has four tabs; General, Page Options, Fonts and HTML. The options on each of these tabs are described in this chapter in the section titled *The Report Definition Process*. Please refer to that section for the details.

After running the **Bibliography** report you will receive an option to either:

> Erase the bibliography in preparation for the next report
> Select [Yes] or

> Retain the bibliography so it will continue to accumulate
> Select [No].

Descendant Indented Chart

Overview

The **Descendant Indented Chart** relates selected details about a focus individual and his or her descendants in the form of a chart. The chart can run for several pages depending upon the number of generations selected. Multiple charts can be created simultaneously by selecting more than one focus individual.

The **Descendant Indented Chart** gets its name from its appearance. Each successive generation of descendants is further indented by a similar amount from the previous generation. So descendants who are indented by a like amount are in the same generation removed from the focus person. Graphic lines further delineate the generational relationship by connecting families on the report.

Each person included on the chart is printed on a separate line, and details about their life follow, beginning on the same line and wrap to additional lines if required. Details are limited to primary tag(s) in the Birth, Marriage, Death and Burial event groups. The spouse of each descendant, identified by a plus sign (+) before their name, is indented by the same amount and printed on the following line. Their offspring continue indented further on the following lines followed by additional spouses of the parent, if any.

> Birthorder flag values, when used, will override the sort order for children set by Birth Group tags. If some children in a family have a Birthorder flag value set, and some do not, those with a value will sort first followed by those without a value, even if all children have a Birth Group tag present.

Creating a Descendant Indented Chart

Select Report > Descendant Indented Chart **from the Main Menu bar to open the** Descendant Indented Chart **Report Definition Screen** *(see Figure 10-1).*

Select the desired report configuration, the subject(s) for the report and the print to location (see *The Report Process, Report Definition Screen).* Click [Print & Save] if you plan to run an existing report configuration without modification, or

Click [Options] to open the **Report Options** screen and enable report customization. This screen has 14 tabs; General, Page Options, Fonts, Sources, Memos, Exhibits, Indexes, Publication Tools, Sort By, Names, Dates, Places, HTML and Miscellaneous. The options on each of these tabs are described in this chapter in the section titled *The Report Definition Process*. Please refer to that section for the details.

Descendant Indented Narrative

Overview

The **Descendant Indented Narrative** relates selected details about one or more focus individuals and their descendants utilizing the sentence structures associated with selected tags *(see Chapter 6, Sentence Structures)*. The narrative can be quite comprehensive, or very brief, for each individual depending upon the number of **Tag Types** selected for inclusion in the report. Memos, sources and exhibits can be embedded in the narrative, or included as footnotes, or endnotes.

The **Descendant Indented Narrative** is rendered in an outline format, and is limited to fifteen generations including the focus person or focus group if multiple progenitors are selected. The outline can either be un-numbered or numbered using one of the following five styles: Chicago Manual of Style, Modern Languages Association (MLA) Handbook, Henry Numbers, Modified Henry Numbers and d'Aboville System (see Table 10-3)

The Henry Numbering system is named after Reginald Buchanan Henry, who used the system in his book Genealogies of the families of the presidents published in 1935. In his system, the progenitor's first child is numbered 1, the second child is 2, the third child is 3, and so on. The children of 2 are numbered 21, 22, 23, etc. So each person's number starts with his parent's number and adds a digit to represent his position in the family. Thus, if a person has the number 2739, s/he is four generations removed from the progenitor (there are four digits), and s/he is the ninth child of the third child of the seventh child of the second child of the progenitor. If there are more than 9 children in a family, the child's position in the family is enclosed in parentheses, for example 273(10). Modified Henry Numbers use capital letters instead of the numbers enclosed in parentheses. So the tenth child in the previous example would be 273A, the eleventh would be 273B and so on.

The focus generation is left justified on the printed page. Each subsequent generation is indented to line

up with the given name of the parent and is numbered according to one of several industry recognized standards.

> Birthorder flag values, when used, will override the sort order for children set by Birth Group tags. If some children in a family have a Birthorder flag value set, and some do not, those with a value will sort first followed by those without a value, even if all children have a Birth Group tag present.

Creating a Descendant Indented Narrative

Select **Report > Descendant Indented Narrative** from the **Main Menu** bar to open the **Descendant Indented Narrative** Report Definition Screen *(see Figure 10-1)*.

Select the desired report configuration, the subject(s) for the report, and the print to location (see *The Report Process, Report Definition Screen)*.

Click [Print & Save] if you plan to run an existing report configuration without modification, or

Click [Options] to open the **Report Options** screen and enable report customization. This screen has 15 tabs; General, Page Options, Fonts, Sources, Memos, Exhibits, Indexes, Publication Tools, Sort By, Tags, Names, Dates, Places, HTML and Miscellaneous. The options on each of these tabs are described in this chapter in the section titled *The Report Definition Process*. Please refer to that section for the details.

The **Descendant Indented Narrative**, General tab has these additional options.

> **Outline Numbering** *(See Table 10-5)*
> ○ None
> ○ Chicago Manual of Style
> ○ MLA Handbook
> ○ Henry Numbers
> ○ Modified Henry Numbers
> ○ d'Aboville System
> ◘ Numbers bold

Generation/Style	Chicago Manual of Style	MLA Handbook	Henry Numbers	Modified Henry Numbers	d'Aboville System
Progenitor	I.	I.	Not numbered	Not numbered	Not numbered
1	A.	A.	1	1	1
1	B.	B.	2	2	2
2	1.	1.	21	21	2.1
3	a)	a.	211	211	2.1.1
4	(1)	(1)	2111	2111	2.1.1.1
5	(a)	(a)	21111	21111	2.1.1.1.1
6	i)	(1)	211111	211111	2.1.1.1.1.1
6	ii)	(2)	211112	211112	2.1.1.1.1.2
7	(a)	(a)	2111121	2111121	2.1.1.1.1.2.1
6	iii)	(3)	211113	211113	2.1.1.1.1.3
6	iv)	(4)	211114	211114	2.1.1.1.1.4
7	(a)	(a)	2111141	2111141	2.1.1.1.1.4.1
8	i)	(1)	21111411	21111411	2.1.1.1.1.4.1.1
9	(a)	(a)	211114111	211114111	2.1.1.1.1.4.1.1.1
10	i)	(1)	2111141111	2111141111	2.1.1.1.1.4.1.1.1.1
11	(a)	(a)	21111411111	21111411111	2.1.1.1.1.4.1.1.1.1.1
12	i)	(1)	211114111111	211114111111	2.1.1.1.1.4.1.1.1.1.1.1
13	(a)	(a)	2111141111111	2111141111111	2.1.1.1.1.4.1.1.1.1.1.1.1
14	i)	(1)	21111411111111	21111411111111	2.1.1.1.1.4.1.1.1.1.1.1.1.1

Table 10-5: Descendant Narrative Outline Numbering Styles

The Miscellaneous tab has this additional option.

- Follow surname only –Select this option to restrict output *to the exact spelling* of a single surname for each progenitor defined as a subject of the report on the **Report Definition Screen**. For example, if the subject of a 5-generation report was named Siméon Clénard it would print him and his children and stop because their descendants dropped the accent on the "e" in Clenard.

Example

I would like to share some information with a fellow researcher who prefers to use Henry Numbers. How do I accommodate him?

Select **Reports > Descendant Indented Narrative** from the **Main Menu** bar.

Select the subject(s) for the report and the report destination.

Click the [Options] button to open the **Report Options** screen.

On the General tab select the Henry Numbers option that is located in the 'Outline Numbering' frame.

Select any other desired options and click [OK] to return to the Report Definition Screen.

Click [Print & Save] to print the report.

Distribution of People

Overview

The **Distribution of People** report is a statistical report that allows you to see how people are distributed in your data set according to a specific value. You can define a report to analyze all people in the data set, or select a specific subset of people by creating a Filtered Group on the Focus Tab. The report can be sorted by the value of the field that is distributed, or by its frequency of use.

Statistics for the focus person(s) can be generated based on any of the following fields:
- Any Flag
- Age at Death
- Age Today
- Birth* (primary tag)
- Death* (primary tag)
- Parent's Name(s)
- ID Number
- Last Edited Date
- Several fields relating to Mother's Name(s)
- Several fields relating to Name* (primary tag)
- Number of Children, Daughters, Exhibits, Incomplete Tasks, Sons, Spouses and Tasks
- Reference

Creating a Distribution of People Report

Select **Report > Distribution of People** from the **Main Menu** bar to open the **Distribution of People** Report Definition Screen *(see Figure 10-1)*.

Click [Print & Save] if you plan to run an existing report configuration without modification, or

Select [Options] to open the Report Options screen. This screen has seven tabs; General, Page Options, Fonts, Output Columns, Publication Tools, HTML and Miscellaneous. The options on each of these tabs are described in this chapter in the section titled *The Report Definition Process*. Please refer to that section for the details.

The **Distribution of People**, Output Columns tab allows for one column, and so does not include a sort by column option.

Example

How can I create a list of all the surnames in my project?

To run the report, select **File > Reports > Distribution of People**.

Click the [Options] button.

Click the Output Columns tab.

Click the arrow on the Column/Field Contents drop-down box.

Select Name* from the list.

Select Surname

Click the Sort tab.

Select Sort by: Value to sort the surnames alphabetically.

Click [OK] to close the Report Options screen

Click [Print & Save] to generate the report.

Endnotes

Overview

An **Endnotes** report is a numbered list of references to your work that appears at the end of the report rather than at the bottom of each page that holds the reference, as in the case of a footnote. Sources, memos and exhibits may be sent to endnotes in the course of generating one or several different reports from any of the following report types:

- Ahnentafel
- Descendant Indented Narrative
- Family Group Sheet
- Individual Detail
- Individual Narrative
- Journal
- Kinship Report
- Pedigree - Compressed
- Relationship Chart

Specify the creation of endnotes from the above reports by checking the **Endnotes** option on the **Sources**, **Memos**, and/or **Exhibits** tabs of the **Report Options** screen. *Note, sending exhibits to endnotes requires report output set to Word, Word Perfect or HTML.* In addition, you must also activate sources on the **Sources** tab of the **Report Options** screen in order to send sources to endnotes.

Endnotes are not automatically printed when report output is directed to the screen or printer. They are accumulated instead until the **Endnotes** report is run. In addition, footnotes will be converted to endnotes when output is directed to the screen, printer or non-word processor file, so they will accumulate as well.

Run the **Endnotes** report to print endnotes for one or more reports, after running the desired report(s) from the list above. Run it before running the desired report(s) from the list above to ensure that endnotes from a previous, perhaps unwanted, accumulation have in fact been erased.

> The accumulation feature for endnotes is system related, not project related, so Endnotes will accumulate across multiple projects.

Creating an Endnotes Report

Select **Report > Endnotes** from the **Main Menu** bar to open the **Endnotes** Report Definition Screen *(see Figure 10-1)*.

Select the desired report configuration and print to location (see *The Report Process, Report Definition Screen)*.

Click [Print & Save] if you plan to run an existing report configuration without modification, or

Click [Options] to open the **Report Options** screen and enable report customization. This screen has four tabs; General, Page Options, Fonts and HTML. The options on each of these tabs are described in this chapter in the section titled *The Report Definition Process*. Please refer to that section for the details.

The **Endnotes** report, General tab contains a subset of the standard options for this tab. They include the Configuration name and Print to options.

After running the **Endnotes** report you will receive an option to either:

> Erase the endnotes in preparation for the next report
> Select [Yes], or

> Retain the endnotes so they will continue to accumulate
> Select [No]

Family Group Sheet
Overview
The **Family Group Sheet** is a form that relates information about a family – their relationships and the events in their lives. The subject of each **Family Group Sheet** in TMG is an individual. Also included on the form are the subject's spouse, their common children and their parents. The type of information displayed for the subject, subject's spouse and their children is controlled by the user and can include all **Tag Types**, selected **Tag Types** or none. Information can be restricted for each of the above to birth, marriage, death and burial events simply by checking an option button. The parents' lifespan, if selected, can be displayed using one of several formats.

> Birthorder flag values, when used, will override the sort order for children set by Birth Group tags. If some children in a family have a Birthorder flag value set, and some do not, those with a value will sort first followed by those without a value, even if all children have a Birth Group tag present.

If the subject has more than one spouse, or children by more than one partner, a separate **Family Group Sheet** will print for each family.

Creating a Family Group Sheet

Select **Report > Family Group Sheet** from the **Main Menu** to open the **Family Group Sheet** Report Definition Screen *(see Figure 10-1)*.

Select the desired report configuration, the subject(s) for the report and the print to location (see *The Report Process, Report Definition Screen)*.

Click [Print & Save] if you plan to run an existing report configuration without modification, or

Click [Options] to open the **Report Options** screen and enable report customization. This screen has 15 tabs; General, Page Options, Fonts, Sources, Memos, Exhibits, Indexes, Publication Tools, Sort By, Tags, Names, Dates, Places, HTML and Miscellaneous. The options on each of these tabs are described in this chapter in the section titled *The Report Definition Process*. Please refer to that section for the details.

The **Family Group Sheet**, General tab *(see Figure 10-2)* includes the following additional feature:

Title position
- ○ None
- ○ Left Justifies
- ○ Centered
- ◘ Blank line above and below

The **Family Group Sheet**, Fonts tab *(see Figure 10-4)* includes the following additional feature:

Use SURNAMES and GIVEN NAMES font for
- ◘ Subject
- ◘ Subject's parents
- ◘ Spouse
- ◘ Spouse's parents
- ◘ Children
- ◘ Child's spouses
- ◘ Child's in-laws
- ◘ Child's children
- ◘ Other people

The **Family Group Sheet**, Exhibits tab includes the following feature:

Exhibits
- ○ None
- ○ Small Images
- ○ Large Images
- ◘ Borders for missing images

The Tag Types and Event options found on the **Family Group Sheet**, Tags tab are discussed in detail at the beginning of this chapter in The Report Definition Process, Tags Tab section.

The **Family Group Sheet**, Tags tab *(see Figure 10-21)* includes the following features:

Subject
- ◘ Restrict to BMDB events – Select this option to print only birth, marriage, death and burial events for the subject.
- ◘ Include parents – The subject's parents, if known, will be printed if this option is selected.
- ◘ Isolate shared events – Select this option to collect all events in which both subject and spouse are principals into a single section and printed after the subject's information.

◘ Assume married – Select this option to print a marriage event for a subject and spouse even if one does not exist.

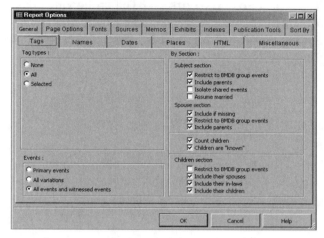

Figure 10-21: Family Group Sheet, Tags Tab

Spouse
- ◘ Include if missing – Select this option to reserve space on the form for the spouse, even if not known.
- ◘ Restrict to BMDB events – Select this option to print only birth, marriage, death and burial events for the subject's spouse.
- ◘ Include parents – The spouse's parents will be printed if this option is selected.
- ◘ Count Children – Select this option to count the number of children associated with the subject and subject's spouse. The number of children will print on the line immediately preceding the first child, e.g. Six Children.
- ◘ Children are "known" – Select this option to print the word "known" for the number of children, e.g., Six Known Children.

Children
- ◘ Restrict to BMDB events – Select this option to print only birth, marriage, death and burial events for each child included on the form.
- ◘ Include their spouses – When this option is checked, the spouse(s) of each child included on the form will be included as well.
- ◘ Include their in-laws – Select this option to include the parents of each child's spouse(s) that are included on the form.
- ◘ Include their children – When this option is checked, the children of each child included on the form will be included as well.

The **Family Group Sheet**, Dates tab *(see Figure 10-13)* includes the following additional features:

Lifespan of parents – The following date options are available when the 'Include parents' option is selected on the Tags tab under Subject or Spouse:
- No Lifespan
- (Year – Year)
- (Date – Date)
- (b. Year - d. Year)
- (b. Date - d. Date)

The **Family Group Sheet**, Miscellaneous tab *(see Figure 10-16)* includes the following additional features:

Other
- BMDB when missing – Select this option to print labels and reserve space on the form for birth, marriage, death and burial information when it is not known.
- Birthorder of children – Select this option to print the birthorder for children. If the BIRTHORDER flag is not set, TMG will print a question mark next to each child.
- Space for unknown children – The **Family Group Sheet** can be used as a convenient form upon which to write information gleaned from sources during research. Select this option to reserve additional space on the form for unknown children.
- Asterisks indicate primary tags – Select this option to distinguish primary tags from non-primary by an asterisk (*) instead of a colon (:).
- Roles – When this option is selected, TMG will include role information, if available, for each tag included on the form.

Parents
- Primary Only – Select this option to print only the primary parent for each subject.
- All Variations – Select this option to include all parents for each subject who are marked primary or non-primary.

Individual Detail

Overview

The **Individual Detail** report provides the means to print all tags, or a selection of tags, in the context of a form for one or more focus individuals. The output is similar to the information contained on the **Person View** of the **Details** window. The subject is displayed at the top of the form. The subject's parents, if known, are displayed with their lifespan, if selected, on the next two lines. The body of the report follows just below in three columns representing from left to right, the **Tag Type** label, date of each event, and location of each event. Sentence memos can be embedded with each tag. History tags and Timelines can also be included to provide an historical frame of reference for the events surrounding the focus individual(s).

Creating an Individual Detail Report

Select **Report > Individual Detail** from the Main Menu bar to open the Individual Detail Report Definition Screen *(see Figure 10-1)*.

Select the desired report configuration, the subject(s) for the report and the print to location (see *The Report Process, Report Definition Screen)*.

Click [Print & Save] if you plan to run an existing report configuration without modification, or

Click [Options] to open the **Report Options** screen and enable report customization. This screen has 14 tabs; General, Page Options, Fonts, Sources, Memos, Exhibits, Indexes, Publication Tools, Sort By, Names, Dates, Places, HTML and Miscellaneous. The options on each of these tabs are described in this chapter in the section titled *The Report Definition Process*. Please refer to that section for the details.

The **Individual Detail**, Fonts tab *(see Figure 10-4)* includes the following additional feature:

Use **SURNAMES** and **GIVEN NAMES** font for:
- Subject
- Subject's parents
- Other people
- Name variations
- Spouse
- Children

The **Individual Detail**, Exhibits tab includes the following feature:

Exhibits
- None
- Small Images
- Large Images
- Borders for missing images

Lifespan of parents
- No Lifespan
- (Year – Year)
- (Date – Date)
- (b. Year - d. Year)
- (b. Date - d. Date)

The **Individual Detail**, Miscellaneous tab *(see Figure 10-16)* includes the following additional feature:

Timelines
- Globally selected – Select this option to include Timelines that are activated via **Tools > Timeline Manager** on the **Main Menu** bar.
- Locked to ID – Select this option to include Timelines that are locked to individuals via the Lock Timelines option on the Secondary Output tab of the **List of People** report.

Individual Narrative

Overview

The **Individual Narrative** report relates selected details about one or more focus individuals. The narrative, which is printed in the form of a single paragraph, subject to embedded codes *(see Chapter 9, Controlling Narratives)*, can be quite comprehensive, or very brief, depending upon the number of **Tag Types** selected for inclusion in the report. In this regard, the **Individual Narrative** is similar to the **Descendant Indented Narrative**. But it differs in that no individuals are linked, if multiple subjects are selected.

The **Individual Narrative** produces a concise report that can be used to quickly analyze the narrative flow of your tag sentence structures. The **Individual Narrative Preview** with sources is an excellent means to quickly check all sources associated with an individual.

Creating an Individual Narrative Report

Select **Report > Individual Narrative** from the **Main Menu** bar to open the **Individual Narrative** Report Definition Screen.

Select the desired report configuration, the subject(s) for the report and the print to location (see *The Report Process, Report Definition Screen)*.

Click [Print & Save] if you plan to run an existing report configuration without modification, or

Click [Options] to open the **Report Options** screen and enable report customization. This screen has 15 tabs; General, Page Options, Fonts, Sources, Memos, Exhibits, Indexes, Publication Tools, Sort By, Tags, Names, Dates, Places, HTML and Miscellaneous. The options on each of these tabs are described in this chapter in the section titled *The Report Definition Process*. Please refer to that section for the details.

Example

How can I quickly check the narrative flow of my tag sentence structures and associated source citations?

The default TMG installation includes two special reports to meet this requirement – the **Individual Narrative Preview** and the **Individual Narrative Preview with Sources**. In addition, TMG provides two convenient ways to access both reports – from the Reporting Toolbar, or from the **Report** option on the **Main Menu** bar.

Select **View > Toolbars > Reporting** from the **Main Menu** bar to activate the Reporting Toolbar if it is not already active. The Toolbar includes an icon to launch each of these reports.

Or, select **File > Report > Individual Narrative** from the **Main Menu** bar to open the **Report Definition Screen**. Click the arrow on the Configuration Name drop-down box and highlight the desired report name to select it. Select 'Use the Current Focus Person' as the Subject of the report. Click [Print & Save] to run the report.

Journal

Overview

The **Journal** report is often used to create a book, or journal article. The Master Genealogist™ (TMG) supports three industry recognized styles including the **Register Format** from the *New England Historical and Genealogical Register* (NEHGR), the **Record Format** from the *National Genealogical Society Quarterly* (NGSQ), and **The American Genealogist** (TAG) from the publication by the same name. In addition, TMG supports a fourth, **Custom Format**, that allows the user to add or delete several options to any one of the three standard styles.

The **Journal** is a narrative report that utilizes the sentence structures associated with each tag *(see Chapter 6, Sentence Structures)*. Memos, sources and exhibits can be embedded in the narrative, or included as footnotes, or endnotes. The **Journal** can be oriented in either descendant or ancestor directions spanning 1 – 250 generations.

> Birthorder flag values, when used, will override the sort order for children set by Birth Group tags. If some children in a family have a Birthorder flag value set, and some do not, those with a value will sort first followed by those without a value, even if all children have a Birth Group tag present.

Creating a Journal

Select **Report > Journal** from the **Main Menu** bar to open the Journal Report Definition Screen *(see Figure 10-1)*.

Select the desired report configuration, the subject(s) for the report and the print to location (see *The Report Process, Report Definition Screen)*.

Click [Print & Save] if you plan to run an existing report configuration without modification, or

Click [Options] to open the **Report Options** screen and enable report customization. This screen has 15 tabs; General, Page Options, Fonts, Sources, Memos, Exhibits, Indexes, Publication Tools, Sort By, Tags, Names, Dates, Places, HTML and Miscellaneous. The options on each of these tabs are described in this chapter in the section titled *The*

Report Definition Process. Please refer to that section for the details.

The **Journal**, General tab *(see Figure 10-2)* has these additional options.

Style – The default report definition for each of the first three styles listed below conforms to a specific industry recognized style. When one of these is selected, several options on the Miscellaneous tab are preset, and cannot be changed. Several other options may be grayed out and unavailable. Select the Custom format to access all options on the Miscellaneous tab.

- ○ Register Format (NEHGR)
- ○ Record Format (NGSQ)
- ○ The American Genealogist (TAG)
- ○ Custom Format

> *Select the Custom Format to maximize control over what is included in the Journal report.*

The **Journal**, Tags tab *(see Figure 10-11)* has these additional options.

BMDB Abbrev – The following options control the form in which birth, marriage, death and burial tags are printed in the first paragraph.
- ○ He was born in 1861
- ○ born 1861
- ○ b. 1861

The **Journal**, Names tab *(see Figure 10-12)* has these additional options.

Parent Names
- ○ No Caps
- ○ Surname Caps
- ○ All Caps
- ○ All Small Caps

Child Names
- ○ No Caps
- ○ Surname Caps
- ○ All Caps
- ○ All Small Caps
- ◘ Include Surname
- ◘ Honor Name Font Styles

Other Identifiers:
- ◘ Back Reference Generations – Select this option to include the name(s) of male

predecessors between parentheses following the name of each ancestor or descendant.
  - Names in Italics
  - Include Middle Names

The **Journal**, Miscellaneous tab *(see Figure 10-16)* has these additional options:
Direction
  o Descendants
  o Ancestors
    - Use Ahnentafel Numbers – Select this option to compute and display ahnentafel numbers for direct line ancestors of the focus person(s).
    - Siblings show BMDB only – Select this option to restrict sibling output to birth, marriage, death and burial information.

Master Document File(s) – The following options are available when the Report Definition Screen, Print to option is set to File and the word processor supports Master Documents.
  o Off – Select this option to print the entire report to a single file. Since some word processors can only open files of a limited size, the following two options provide a convenient approach to split the **Journal** report into several files, each of a smaller, perhaps more, manageable size.
  o One file per generation – When this option is selected, one file will be created for each generation defined on the General tab of the Report Options screen.
  o One file per progenitor – This option, when selected, will create one file for each subject when multiple subjects are selected on the Report Definition Screen.

Miscellaneous
  - Indent subject – Select this option to indent each subject from the prior generation.
  - Section numbers bold – Each section of a **Journal** report includes a subject, the subject's spouse and their children, if any. Select this option to set the section number, that is, the number associated with the subject, to a bold-faced font.
  - Missing spouse – Select this option to print "and an unknown spouse" after the subject.

  - Number all children – Select this option to number all children using the defined numbering scheme.
  - Period after child number
  - Count Children – Select this option to count the number of children in each family. The number will be printed on the line immediately preceding the first child, e.g. the six children of …
  - Children "known" – Select this option to print the word "known" for the number of children, e.g., The six known children of …
  - Group common birth places – If all children from one union share a common birth place, that birth place can be printed once on the line preceding the first child rather than several times, once following each child.
  - Suppress Name-Marr from Text – TMG will typically print a sentence in the narrative for each female bearing a Name-Marr tag. "Her married name was Clenard." Select this option to prevent this sentence from printing.
  - Follow surname only – Select this option to restrict output *to the exact spelling* of a single surname for each progenitor defined as a subject of the report on the **Report Definition Screen**. For example, if the subject of a 5-generation report was named Siméon Clénard it would print him and his children and stop because their descendants dropped the accent on the "e" in Clenard.
  - Blank Line Before Each Subject
  - Blank Line Before Each Family

Example

Print a Descendant Journal report of your end-of-line male ancestors.

Select **Reports > Journal** from the **Main Menu** bar.

Rather than printing several separate **Journal** reports, in which there may be duplication, use a filtered group that defines your end-of-line ancestors as subjects of the report via the **Report Definition Screen** *(see Figure 10-1) (see also Chapter 11, Filtering and Sorting).*

Click the [Options] button to open the Report Options screen.

Click the **Sort** tab and select **Sort multiple people** by **Surname**. Click [OK] when you have completed setting options on the **Report Options** screens.

Click [Print & Save]. TMG will create a single **Journal** report with sections that are sorted alphabetically by your end-of-line ancestor surname. In addition, TMG will eliminate any duplicate lines, unless the **Repeat duplicate lines** option is selected on the **Miscellaneous** tab.

Kinship Report

Overview

The **Kinship Report** produces a list of all people in the data set related to the focus person. The people in the list are categorized by the type of relationship and can include ancestors, cousins, descendants and the spouses of each.

The **Kinship Report** provides a convenient format to see the first, or nearest, relationship between the focus person and other individuals in your data set. Consider creating a personalized **Kinship Report** for every family member attending a family reunion.

Creating a Kinship Report

Select **Report > Kinship Report** from the **Main Menu** bar to open the **Kinship** Report **Report Definition Screen.**

Select the desired report configuration, the subject for the report and the print to location (see *The Report Process, Report Definition Screen).*

Click [Print & Save] if you plan to run an existing report configuration without modification, or

Click [Options] to open the **Report Options** screen and enable report customization. This screen has 12 tabs; General, Page Options, Fonts, Sources, Memos, Exhibits, Indexes, Publication Tools, Names, Dates, HTML and Miscellaneous. The options on each of these tabs are described in this chapter in the section titled *The Report Definition Process.* Please refer to that section for the details.

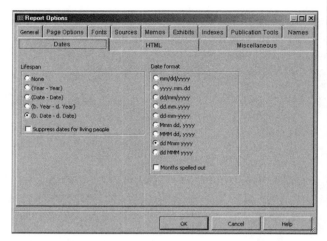

Figure 10-22: Kinship Report, Dates Tab

The **Kinship Report**, General tab has these additional options:

Include – Select all relationships that you wish to apply.
- Ancestors
  ____ Generations - Use the dial box, or type the number of generations for the report. The value must be between 1 – 250.
- Cousins
- Descendants
- and their Spouses

The **Kinship Report,** Dates tab *(see Figure 10-22)* also includes:

Lifespan – Select one of the following options to print lifespan dates after each person.
- None
- (Year – Year)
- (Date – Date)
- (b. Year – d. Year)
- (b. Date – d. Date)
- Suppress dates for living people

Date format – *(See the discussion following Figure 10-13)*

List of Citations

Overview

The **List of Citations** report identifies selected citations that are attached to a specific tag. The report focus can be either all citations, or a focus group defined by up to eight filters selected from an extensive list *(see Chapter 11, Filtering and Sorting).* The report is sorted by source number.

Each citation occupies two or more lines in the report and is separated from the following citation by a blank line. The first line includes the source number, the source name abbreviation, citation detail, if any, and surety. The second and additional line(s) include the tag label, date of the event, name and ID number of the principal(s), plus event place information (if selected) and tag memo information (if selected).

The **List of Citations** can be filtered to produce a highly focused report in a large project to assist in finding a specific citation that would otherwise be difficult to find.

Creating a List of Citations

Select **Report > List of ... > Citations** from the **Main Menu** bar to open the **List of Citations** Report Definition Screen *(see Figure 10-1)*.

Click [Print & Save] if you plan to run an existing report configuration without modification, or

Select [Options] to open the Report Options screen. This screen has nine tabs; General, Page Options, Fonts, Publication Tools, Sort By, Names, Places, HTML and Miscellaneous. The options on each of these tabs are described in this chapter in the section titled *The Report Definition Process*. Please refer to that section for the details.

Examples

1. *How do I find all citations for a specific source?*

    To run the report, select **Report > List of ... > Citations** from the **Main Menu** bar.

    To identify the subject(s) of the report, first select **Filtered group** and then click the [Add] button.

    Use the following filter and then click [OK].

Field	Operator	Value	Connect
Source Number	= Equals	[?]	End

    Click [Options] to further customize the report.

    Click [OK] when done.

    Click [Print & Save] to print the report. Enter a Value for the Source Number and click [OK].

2. *How do I find a citation in my project that contains a specific character string?*

    Use the following filter:

Field	Operator	Value	Connect
Citation Detail	Contains	[?]	End

    Click [Print & Save] to print the report. Enter a Value, e.g. character string, for the Citation Detail and click [OK].

List of Events

Overview

The **List of Events** is a tabular report that can display up to nine columns of information for each event in the chosen set of records from a given project, including:
- Place information
- Date information
- Memo (Detail) information
- Number of Citations, Exhibits, Incomplete Tasks, Other Witnesses, Tasks or Witnesses
- Name(s), ID#, Flag values, Reference and Surety of Principal(s) (1&2) associated with the tag
- Sentence information
- Tag Type information

In addition, the **List of Events** report can be sorted by up to four of the selected fields.

The default report prints a list of all events in the project. It can also be filtered, by up to eight different fields chosen from the above list, to enable precise selection of a specific group of records *(see Chapter 11, Filtering and Sorting)*.

Creating a List of Events

Select **Report > List of ... > Events** from the **Main Menu** bar to open the **List of Events** Report Definition Screen *(see Figure 10-1)*.

Click [Print & Save] if you plan to run an existing report configuration without modification, or

Select [Options] to open the Report Options screen. This screen has six tabs; General, Page Options, Fonts, Output Columns, HTML and Miscellaneous. The options on each of these tabs are described in this chapter in the section titled *The Report*

Definition Process. Please refer to that section for the details.

Examples

1. *How do I list all events that occurred in a specific place, a city for example?*

   To run the report, select **Report > List of ... > Events** from the **Main Menu** bar.

   To identify the subject(s) of the report, first select **Filtered group** and then click the [Add] button.

   Use the following filter and then click [OK].

Field	Operator	Value	Connect
City	= Equals	[?]	End

   Click [Options] to further customize the report.

   Click the Output Columns tab to select field data that will be included in the report.

   Click [OK] when done.

   Click [Print & Save] to print the report. Enter a Value for the Source Number and click [OK].

2. *How do I create a list of all brides and grooms in my project?*

   To run the report, select **Report > List of ... > Events** from the **Main Menu** bar.

   To identify the subject(s) of the report, first select **Filtered group** and then click [Add].

   Use the following filter and then click [OK].

Field	Operator	Value	Connect
Tag Type Label	= Equals	Marriage	End

   Click [Options] to open the Report Options screen.

   Click the Output Columns tab and make the following entries:

Column	Sort	Contents	Header
1		Prin1 ID#	H_ID#
2	1	Prin1 Last, Given	Husband
3		Prin2 ID#	W_ID#
4		Prin2 Last, Given	Wife
5	2	Date Wide	Date
6		Place	Place

Enter an appropriate field Length for each column.

Select any other desired options and click [OK] to return to the Report Definition Screen.

Click [Print & Save] to print the report.

> *This example report definition assumes that the user has consistently entered males as Prin1 and females as Prin2 for Marriage tags.*

List of Names

Overview

The **List of Names** is a tabular report that can display up to nine columns of information for each subject including:

- Subject's name in different formats
- Subject's ID#
- Flags linked to the subject
- Subject's birth date
- Subject's death date
- Primary Marker
- Linked subject's Reference field
- Tag Type information
- Memo information
- Sentence information

The default version of the report lists the names of every person in the project, including primary and non-primary names. The contents of the report can be filtered by the data contained in the fields listed above, plus citation data from several dozen fields.

The **List of Names** report should be used whenever it is desirable to extract a list of names from your project using the available filters and report output options. It can be used to print a version of the Expanded Picklist in Column Mode (see *the example below*).

Creating a List of Names

Select **Report > List of ... > Names** from the **Main Menu** bar to open the **List of Names** Report Definition Screen *(see Figure 10-1)*.

Click [Print & Save] if you plan to run an existing report configuration without modification, or

Select [Options] to open the Report Options screen. This screen has six tabs; General, Page Options, Fonts, Output Columns, HTML and Miscellaneous. The options on each of these tabs are described in this chapter in the section titled *The Report Definition Process*. Please refer to that section for the details.

Examples

1. *I really like the format of the Expanded Picklist when it is in Column Mode. How can I print a list in that format?*

To run the report, select **Report > List of ... > Names** from the **Main Menu** bar.

Click the [Options] button to open the Report Options screen.

Click the Output Columns tab and make the following entries:

Column	Sort	Contents	Header
1		Primary Marker	P
2	1	Last, Given Names	Name
3		Linked Subj; ID#	ID
4		Linked Subj; Birth* Date –thin	Birth
5		Linked Subj; Death* Date-thin	Death
6		Linked Subj; Reference	Reference

Enter an appropriate field Length for each column.

Select any other desired options and click [OK] to return to the Report Definition Screen.

Click [Print & Save] to print the report.

2. *How can I print a list of married names?*

A prerequisite to creating this report is the existence of a NAME-MARR tag for women who are married. If you imported a data set to your project from an application other than

TMG and did not select the "Assume married name" option, then it is likely that the NAME-MARR tag does not exist. This tag can either be created manually, which potentially is very time consuming, or automatically by using a third party utility developed and supported by John Cardinal *(see Chapter 1, Introduction, Places to find help on the Internet)*.

To run the report, select **Reports > List of... > Names** from the **Main Menu** bar.

Select Filtered Group for the subject(s) of the report *(see Chapter 11, Filtering and Sorting)*.

Use the following filter and then click [OK].

Field	Operator	Value	Connect
Tag Type Label	= Equals	Name-Marr	End

Click [Options] to open the Report Options

Select other desired options and click [OK].

Click [Print & Save] to run the report.

List of People

Overview

The **List of People** (LOP) report is one of TMG's most versatile **List** reports. Like the others, the LOP is a tabular report where each row in the table represents a focus record, in this case a person, and each column an extraction of data related to the focus. In addition, the LOP can be filtered to extract a subset of people from multiple data sets within a project. This can then be used to create a new project, create a new data set in the current project, lock/unlock timelines, or set a flag for those individuals included in the filter.

Creating a List of People

Select **Report > List of ... > People** from the **Main Menu** bar to open the **List of People** Report Definition Screen *(see Figure 10-1)*.

Click [Print & Save] if you plan to run an existing report configuration without modification, or

Select [Options] to open the Report Options screen. This screen has seven tabs: General, Secondary

Output, Page Options, Fonts, Output Columns, HTML and Miscellaneous. The options on each of these tabs are described in this chapter in the section titled *The Report Definition Process*. Please refer to that section for the details.

The **List of People**, Secondary Output tab *(see Figure 10-23)* includes the following options:

- Create new project
  When this option is selected, TMG will identify the subject(s) of the report as defined on the **Report Definition Screen** and copy them to a new project.
- Create new data set in current project
  When this option is selected, TMG will identify the subject(s) of the report as defined on the **Report Definition Screen** and copy them to a new data set in the current project.
- Lock Timelines
- Unlock Timelines
- Change a flag [_____] to [_]
  TMG supports an unlimited number of custom flags that can be defined by the user. A custom flag may be quite simple, for example, containing only two options such as

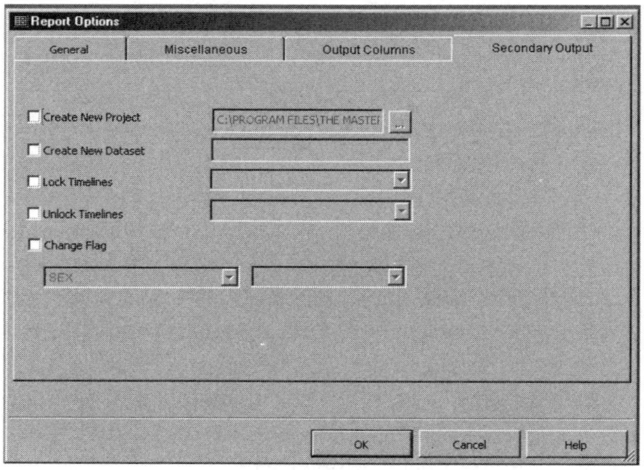

Figure 10-23: Secondary Output Tab

YN (Yes and No). Other flags may be very complex containing several dozen options. In either case, the task of manually setting a flag, especially when done in a large project, can be overwhelming and so time-consuming as to make the task not worthwhile. *The LOP report automates this task for you.*

Select this option to change the value of any flag to a specific value for the subject(s) of the report defined on the **Report Definition Screen**.

- Suppress printing for secondary output – TMG will use the **Print to** option selected on the **Report Definition Screen**, even when **Secondary Output** is selected. It may be desirable, on occasion, to generate the secondary output directly without displaying or printing the regular report. Select this option to disable the **Print to** options for this report configuration.

Example

How do I create an end-of-line (EOL) report?

To run the report, select **Report > List of ... > People** from the **Main Menu** bar.

To identify the subject(s) of the report, first select **Filtered group** and then click the arrow on the **Filtered group** drop-down box.

a. Use the following filter to create an EOL report for all individuals in a project who do not have a father.

Field	Operator	Value	Connect
Father*	Is ID#	0	End

b. Use the following filter to create an EOL report for all individuals in a project who do not have a mother.

Field	Operator	Value	Connect
Mother*	Is ID#	0	End

c. Use the following filter to create an EOL report for all individuals in a project who do not have a father or a mother.

Field	Operator	Value	Connect
Father*	Is ID#	0	And
Mother*	Is ID#	0	End

Click [Options] to further customize the report.

Click [OK] when done.

Click [Print & Save] to print the EOL report.

List of Places

Overview

The **List of Places** is a tabular report that can be used to display up to nine columns of information for each place in the chosen set of records from a given project. Each place, as defined in the **Master Place List**, is printed on a separate line in the report. Output column contents for each place can be selected from any place field, plus all detail level fields and field labels. These fields can also be used to filter, or select a specific set of records for the report. The **List of Places** report can be sorted by up to four of the selected fields.

Creating a List of Places

Select **Report > List of ... > Places** from the **Main Menu** bar to open the **List of Places** Report Definition Screen *(see Figure 10-1)*.

Click [Print & Save] if you plan to run an existing report configuration without modification, or

Select [Options] to open the Report Options screen. This screen has six tabs; General, Page Options, Fonts, Output Columns, HTML and Miscellaneous. The options on each of these tabs are described in this chapter in the section titled *The Report Definition Process*. Please refer to that section for the details.

Example

What place records have "X" as the "Y" where "Y" is a certain field, e.g., state, county or city? For example, what place records include Virginia in the state field?

To run the report, select **Report > List of ... > Places** from the **Main Menu** bar.

To identify the subject(s) of the report, first select **Filtered group** and then click the [Add] button.

Use the following filter and then click [OK].

Field	Operator	Value	Connect
State	= Equals	Virginia	End

Click [Options] to further customize the report.

Click [OK] when done.

Click [Print & Save] to print the report.

List of Repositories

Overview

The **List of Repositories** report contains information about the location of source material used to document your research. It is printed in a table format with two columns. The left column displays the Repository Number. The right column displays either the repository name, or the abbreviation assigned to it, plus the repository memo if selected for printed output.

This report can be used to print the information contained in the **Master Repository List**.

Creating a List of Repositories

Select **Report > List of ... > Repositories** from the **Main Menu** bar to open the **List of Repositories** Report Definition Screen *(see Figure 10-1)*.

Click [Print & Save] if you plan to run an existing report configuration without modification, or

Select [Options] to open the Report Options screen. This screen has seven tabs; General, Page Options, Fonts, Sort By, Places, HTML and Miscellaneous. The options on each of these tabs are described in this chapter in the section titled *The Report Definition Process*. Please refer to that section for the details.

List of Sources

Overview

The **List of Sources** is a tabular report that can include all sources in a project, or a subset of those sources if a filtered group is defined for it. There are three different types of this list:

- Abbreviations
- Titles
- Bibliographic form

The Abbreviations list type includes three columns – the source ID#, the default surety and a user-defined abbreviation of the source.

The Titles list type is similar to the Abbreviation list type, except it includes the full title of the source.

The Bibliographic form list type includes two columns – the source ID# and the source, printed out as if in a bibliography.

Each of the **List of Sources** report types has a number of varied uses. The Abbreviations list type, for example, can be used to validate what will be displayed on the Citations tab of the Tag Entry screen. The Titles list type can be used to validate the source title like it will print in a citation. Both of these reports can be used to validate the default surety value for each source. The Bibliographic form can be used to validate the bibliography template in use on the Output Form tab of the Source Definition screen, and thus the actual bibliographic output for any reports that support this feature.

By establishing creative filters, the **List of Sources** report becomes an invaluable tool to further research at any repository that contains genealogical data. You will know what sources you have already used, and by inference, those you have not. It can also be shared with other researchers who may be investigating common, or collateral lines.

Creating a List of Sources

Select **Report > List of ... > Sources** from the **Main Menu** bar to open the **List of Sources** Report Definition Screen *(see Figure 10-1)*.

Select the desired report configuration and print to location (see *The Report Process, Report Definition Screen*).

Select which sources to include in the report.
- All Sources
- Filtered Group *(See Chapter 11, Filtering and Sorting)*

Click [Print & Save] if you plan to run an existing report configuration without modification, or

Click [Options] to open the **Report Options** screen and enable report customization. This screen has 8 tabs; General, Page Options, Fonts, Publication Tools, Sort By, Places, HTML and Miscellaneous. The options on each of these tabs are described in this chapter in the section titled *The Report Definition Process*. Please refer to that section for the details.

Example

How do I list all sources that are associated with a specific repository?

To run the report, select **Report > List of ... > Sources** from the **Main Menu** bar.

To identify the subject(s) of the report, first select **Filtered group** and then click the [Add] button.

Use the following filter and then click [OK].

Field	Sub field	Operator	Value
Repository	Number	= Equals	[?]

Click [Options] to further customize the report.

Click [Print & Save] to print the report.

List of Tag Types

Overview

The **List of Tag Types** is a tabular report that can display up to nine columns of information for each **Tag Type** in the chosen set of records from a given project, including:
- Abbreviation
- Active Flag
- GEDCOM label
- Group
- Is Custom
- Label
- Past Tense
- Sentence
- Sentence Witness
- Use for Witness Flag

These fields can also be used to filter, or select a specific set of records for the report. The **List of Tag Types** report can be sorted by up to four of the selected fields.

The **List of Tag Types** is an effective tool to identify a group of tags and print a list of their associated sentence and/or witness sentence structures.

Creating a List of Tag Types

Select **Report > List of ... > Tag Types** from the **Main Menu** bar to open the **List of Tag Types** Report Definition Screen *(see Figure 10-1)*.

Click [Print & Save] if you plan to run an existing report configuration without modification, or

Select [Options] to open the Report Options screen. This screen has 6 tabs; General, Page Options, Fonts, Output Columns, HTML and Miscellaneous. The options on each of these tabs are described in this chapter in the section titled The Report Definition Process. Please refer to that section for the details.

Examples

1. *Identify custom Tag Types.*

   To run the report, select **Report > List of ... > Tag Types** from the **Main Menu** bar.

   To identify the subject(s) of the report, first select **Filtered group** and then click [Add].

   Use the following filter and then click [OK].

Field	Operator	Value	Connect
Is Custom			End

   Click [Options] to further customize the report.

   Click the Output Columns tab to select field data that will be included in the report.

   Click [OK] when done.

   Click [Print & Save] to print the report.

2. *Print a list of all Tag Type sentences.*

   To run the report, select **Report > List of ... > Tag Types** from the **Main Menu** bar.

   Set the report focus to All Tag Types.

   Click [Options] to further customize the report.

   Click the Output Columns tab and make the following entries:

Column	Sort	Contents	Header
1	1	Label	Label
2		Sentence	Sentence
3		Sentence Witness	Witness

   Click [OK] when done.

   Click [Print & Save] to print the report.

3. *I have to open each and every tag on the Master Tag Type List in order to identify those that are inactive. Is there an easier way?*

   Yes, select **Report > List of ... > Tag Types** from the **Main Menu** bar.
   Select **Filtered group** and then click [Add].

   Use the following filter and then click [OK].

Field	Operator	Value	Connect
Active Flag Is...	N		End

   Click [Options] to further customize the report.

   Click the Output Columns tab to select field data that will be included in the report.
   Click [OK] when done.

   Click [Print & Save] to print the report.

List of Tasks

Overview

The **List of Tasks** report is used to print research action items contained in the **Research Log**, and can include any, or all, of the following pieces of information:

- Task stages
- Keywords
- Expenses
- Memo
- Blanks when missing
- Event Memos

The **List of Tasks** can include all tasks contained in the **Research Log**, or a targeted subset defined by employing up to eight filters selected from a list of over 300 plus filter options, such as:

- Date or associated text when the task was Designed, Planned, Begun, Progress and Completed
- Task Name
- Expenses
- Whether the task is, or is not, linked to an Event, Person, Repository or Source
- Is not a General task
- Keywords
- Several dozen fields associated with a linked Event, linked Person, linked Repository and linked Source

The **List of Tasks** can be sorted by:
- Type/Person Name
- Date Designed, Planned, Begun, Progress or Completed
- Keyword
- Task Name

Creating a List of Tasks

Select **Report > List of ... > Tasks** from the **Main Menu** bar to open the **List of Tasks** Report Definition Screen *(see Figure 10-1)*.

Click [Print & Save] if you plan to run an existing report configuration without modification, or

Select [Options] to open the Report Options screen. This screen has 7 tabs; General, Page Options, Fonts, Sort By, Names, HTML and Miscellaneous. The options on each of these tabs are described in this chapter in the section titled *The Report Definition Process*. Please refer to that section for the details.

Example

How do I list all General tasks, or those associated with a specific Event? Person? Repository? Source?

To run the report, select **Report > List of ... > Tasks** from the **Main Menu** bar.

Select **Filtered group** and then click the [Add] button.

Use one or more of the following filters and then click [OK].

Field	Connect
Is General	End
Is Linked to Event	End
Is Linked to Person	End
Is Linked to Repository	End
Is Linked to Source	End

Click [Options] to further customize the report.

Click [OK] when done.

Click [Print & Save] to print the report.

List of Witnesses

Overview

The **List of Witnesses** is a tabular report that can display up to nine columns of information for each witness in the chosen set of records from a given project, including:
- Place information
- Date information
- Memo (Detail) information
- Number of Citations, Exhibits, Incomplete Tasks, Other Witnesses, Tasks or Witnesses
- Name(s), ID#, Flag values, Reference and Primary Marker of Principal(s) (1&2) and Witnesses associated with the tag
- Sentence information
- Tag Type information

In addition, the **List of Witnesses** report can be sorted by up to four of the selected fields.

Creating a List of Witnesses

Select **Report > List of ... > Witnesses** from the **Main Menu** bar to open the **List of Witnesses** Report Definition Screen *(see Figure 10-1)*.

Click [Print & Save] if you plan to run an existing report configuration without modification, or

Select [Options] to open the Report Options screen. This screen has 6 tabs; General, Page Options, Fonts, Output Columns, HTML and Miscellaneous. The options on each of these tabs are described in this chapter in the section titled *The Report Definition Process*. Please refer to that section for the details.

Examples

1. *How do I list all witnesses associated with a specific Tag Type?*

   To run the report, select **Report > List of ... > Witnesses** from the **Main Menu** bar.

   Select **Filtered group** and then click the [Add] button.

   Use the following filter and then click [OK].

Field	Operator	Value	Connect
Tag Type Label	= Equals	[?]	And
Is Not Principal			End

Click [Options] to further customize the report.

Click the Output Columns tab to select field data that will be included in the report. If you eliminate the second line of the above filter, TMG will include both Principals and Witnesses in the report. *In this case, be sure to include the Output Field 'Is Principal' in order to distinguish Principals from Witnesses.*

Click [OK] when done.

Click [Print & Save] to print the report. Enter a Value for the Tag Type Label and click [OK].

2. *How do I list all events that have an associated witness?*

To run the report, select **Report > List of … > Witnesses** from the **Main Menu** bar.

Select **Filtered group** and then click the [Add] button.

Use the following filter, and then click [OK].

Field	Operator	Value	Connect
Any Witness ID#	= Equals	[?]	End

Click [Options] to further customize the report.

Click the Output Columns tab to select field data that will be included in the report.

Click [OK] when done.

Click [Print & Save] to print the report. Enter a Value for the Witness ID# and click [OK].

Pedigree Chart

Overview

The **Pedigree Chart**, also known as a family tree chart, is perhaps the most recognizable format to display genealogical data. Each page of the chart includes a focus individual and three or more generations of ancestors – the focus individual's parents, grandparents, great-grandparents, etc. branching out in the shape of a tree.

The Master Genealogist™ (TMG) supports two page formats, one that displays 4-generations and another that displays 5-generations per page.

Continuation pages are created for those ancestral lines that extend beyond the number of generations available on any single page. The end-of-line ancestor on one page whose line continues becomes the focus person on a continuation page. A page reference is printed tying these individuals and pages together.

Most commercial genealogy applications typically print birth, marriage, death and burial information for each individual on the chart. TMG's **Pedigree Chart** report definition defaults to these tags. What separates TMG from other applications, however, is its flexibility to print virtually any **Tag Type** information that is selected by the user in a **Pedigree Chart**.

Creating a Pedigree Chart

Select **Report > Pedigree** from the **Main Menu** bar to open the **Pedigree** Report Definition Screen *(see Figure 10-1)*.

Select the desired report configuration, the subject for the report and the print to location (see *The Report Process, Report Definition Screen*).

Click [Print & Save] if you plan to run an existing report configuration without modification, or

Click [Options] to open the **Report Options** screen and enable report customization. This screen has 11 tabs; General, Page Options, Fonts, Indexes, Publication Tools, Tags, Names, Dates, Places, HTML and Miscellaneous. The options on each of these tabs are described in this chapter in the section titled *The Report Definition Process*. Please refer to that section for the details.

The **Pedigree Chart**, General tab *(see Figure 10-2)* includes the following additional options:

Search ___ generations – Type a numeric value for the total number of generations to include in the report.

Spouse _____ – Enter the ID of focus person's spouse to include that person on the first page of the chart.

Chart Type
  o 4 Generations Per Page
  o 5 Generations Per Page

The **Pedigree Chart**, Tags tab *(see Figure 10-11)* includes the following additional options:

4-Generation Pedigree Setup Rows:

Generation 1-4 – Click the [Top] button to define the tags that will print for each male subject. Up to six different **Tag Types** can be selected from the list and positioned on any available line.

Generation 1-4 – Click the [Bottom] button to define the tags that will print for each female subject. Up to four different **Tag Types** can be selected from the list and positioned on any available line.

5-Generation Pedigree Setup Rows:

Generation 1-3 – Click the [Top] button to define the tags that will print for each male subject. Up to six different **Tag Types** can be selected from the list and positioned on any available line.

Generation 1-3 – Click the [Bottom] button to define the tags that will print for each female subject. Up to four different **Tag Types** can be selected from the list and positioned on any available line.

Generation 4 – Click the [Both] button to define the tags that will print for each subject. Two different **Tag Types** can be selected from the list and positioned on any available line.

Generation 5 – Click the [Both] button to define the tags that will print for each subject. One **Tag Type** can be selected from the list.

The **Pedigree Chart**, Miscellaneous tab *(see Figure 10-16)* includes the following additional options:

◘ Abbreviate names – Long names printed on a **Pedigree Chart** may become truncated due to space restrictions. Select this option to long abbreviate names to (perhaps) avoid truncation.

◘ Print boxes – Standard 4- and 5-generation **Pedigree Charts** can be printed with, or without boxes around each ancestor's name and information contained in the selected tag types. Select this option to print boxes.

◘ Pg 1 Ref, Chart of [F] – Use this option to define what will print in the small box on each page of a **Pedigree Chart** located near the top left of the page. The default, "Chart of [F]" will print "Chart of" followed by the name of the person in position number one on each chart.

Pedigree - Compressed

Overview

The **Compressed Pedigree Chart** is similar to the standard **Pedigree Chart**, but it is not limited to 4- or 5-generations per page. In fact, a suitably defined **Compressed Pedigree** could display as many as 20 generations on a single page because 1) tag information, if selected, is printed on the same line as the ancestor's name, with each tag separated by a comma; 2) blank ancestral lines do not take up unnecessary space; and 3) dates can be printed in full, or formatted to print as just the year.

The **Compressed Pedigree** supports a number of features that are not available with the standard **Pedigree Chart** such as the ability to define charts for multiple subjects, the accumulation of a bibliography and endnotes, plus the inclusion of memos, sources and exhibits as footnotes or endnotes.

Creating a Compressed Pedigree Chart

Select **Report > Pedigree - Compressed** from the **Main Menu** bar to open the Compressed Pedigree **Report Definition Screen** *(see Figure 10-1)*.

Select the desired report configuration, the subject(s) for the report and the print to location (see *The Report Process, Report Definition Screen)*.

Click [Print & Save] if you plan to run an existing report configuration without modification, or

Click [Options] to open the **Report Options** screen and enable report customization. This screen has 15 tabs; General, Page Options, Fonts, Sources, Memos, Exhibits, Indexes, Publication Tools, Sort By, Tags, Names, Dates, Places, HTML and Miscellaneous. The options on each of these tabs are described in this chapter in the section titled *The Report Definition Process*. Please refer to that section for the details.

The **Pedigree – Compressed,** Tags tab includes the following features:

Event Groups – Tag information that will be included on the chart can be selected from the Primary Tag(s) of any, or all, of the following Tag Groups:

- Birth
- Marriage
- Death
- Burial

The **Pedigree – Compressed**, Names tab *(see Figure 10-12)* supports the following additional features:

Other Identifiers

- Generation Numbers – When selected, this option prints the generation number for each individual on the chart immediately after their surname.
  - In Italics

The **Pedigree – Compressed**, Dates tab *(see Figure 10-13)* supports the following additional features:

- Year Only – Select this option to format the date so that only the year is displayed.
- Full – Select this option to include the full date.
  - Months spelled out

The **Compressed Pedigree Chart**, Miscellaneous tab *(see Figure 10-16)* supports the following additional features:

- Unknown Parents – When selected, this option will indicate unknown parents on the chart.
- Truncate to Printer – Select this option to limit the output for each person to one line.

Project Information

Overview

The **Project Information** report is the method used to print the Project Summary information shown after accessing **File > Project Summary** from the **Main Menu** bar. It is a statistical report that reflects several data types, the number of records in each data type, the average number of records of each type per person, the size of the file in bytes and the date and time the file was last updated.

Project Information data types include:

People	Repository links
Names	Repositories
Witnesses	Exhibits
Events	Research Tasks
Places	Timeline Locks
Relationships	Tag Types
Citations	Source Elements
Sources	

Creating a Project Information Report

Select **Report > Project Information** from the **Main Menu** bar to open the **Project Information** Report Definition Screen.

The **Project Information** report can be filtered by a specific data set, by all data sets, or by all unlocked data sets.

Select the desired report configuration, the data set(s) for the report and the print to location.

Click [Print & Save] if you plan to run an existing report configuration without modification, or
Click [Options] to open the **Report Options** screen and enable report customization. This screen has four tabs; General, Page Options, Fonts and HTML. The options on each of these tabs are described in this chapter in the section titled *The Report Definition Process*. Please refer to that section for the details.

Example

My master project contains three data sets. Can I extract statistics related to just one of them?

Yes, the **Project Information** report can be filtered in a number of ways to provide you with just the statistics required.

Select **Reports > Project Information** from the **Main Menu** bar.

On the **Report Definition Screen**, click the arrow on the 'Filter by dataset' drop-down box and highlight the name of the data set from which you want to extract statistics.

Click the [Options] button to open the **Report Options** screen.

Select any desired options and click [OK] to return to the Report Definition Screen.

Click [Print & Save] to print the report.

Relationship Chart

Overview

The **Relationship Chart** plots the relationship of any two direct relations in a data set. Based on your selections on the Focus tab, the **Relationship Chart** produces a drop-down box chart starting with the ancestor, progressing through each generation of descendants until the two focus individuals and all direct relatives in between are printed. Each box contains the names of the direct relative and spouse, plus birth, marriage and death date and place information for each. When selected, the relationship between the focus individuals is computed and displayed at the end of the report.

The **Relationship Chart** provides a convenient way to print the direct-line relatives between two individuals in a data set regardless of how many generations separate them. Since it is printed in graphical form, the **Relationship Chart** conveys a simple, intuitive snapshot of the line(s) of descent.

Creating a Relationship Chart

Select **Report > Relationship Chart** from the **Main Menu** bar to open the **Relationship Chart** Report Definition Screen *(see Figure 10-24).*

The **Relationship Chart** is concerned with the relationship between two people in your data set. The **Report Definition Screen** is used to select the two target people.

Select the desired report configuration, the subjects for the report and the print to location.

Click [Print & Save] if you plan to run an existing report configuration without modification, or

Click [Options] to open the **Report Options** screen and enable report customization. This screen has nine tabs; General, Page Options, Fonts, Indexes, Publication Tools, Names, Places, HTML and Miscellaneous. The options on each of these tabs are described in this chapter in the section titled *The Report Definition Process.* Please refer to that section for the details.

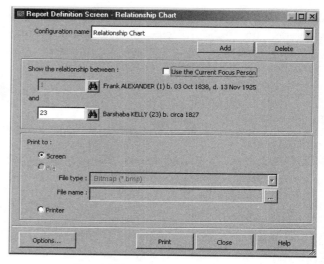

Figure 10-24: Relationship Chart Report Definition Screen

The **Relationship Chart,** Miscellaneous tab has these additional options:

- Closest relationship only – Individuals may be related more than once if they are descended from cousins who married. Only the closest relationship is reported if this option is selected.
- Show relationships – When selected, this option reports the relationship between the two subjects.
- Show "direct drop" if possible.

Statistical Report

Overview

The **Statistical Report** computes the total number of selected people and presents a summary of data including:

Age at first marriage	History Group Tags
Age at first child	Burial Group Tags
Age at last child	Address Tags
Age at death	Other Tags
Age Today	Witnessed Tags
Name Tags	Father Tags
Birth Group Tags	Mother Tags
Death Group Tags	Child Tags
Marriage Group Tags	Sons
Divorce Group Tags	Daughters

For each information type above, the report computes the total population, the average age and number of tags, the standard deviation, the minimum age and maximum age, plus the minimum and maximum ID numbers used to compute the statistics.

Researchers can use the **Statistical Report** to analyze, or interpret, trends and completeness of project information in order to prioritize research tasks.

Creating a Statistical Report

Select **Report > Statistical Report** from the **Main Menu** bar to open the **Statistical** Report **Report Definition Screen**.

Select the desired report configuration, the subject(s) for the report and the print to location (see *The Report Process, Report Definition Screen)*.

Click [Print & Save] if you plan to run an existing report configuration without modification, or

Click [Options] to open the **Report Options** screen and enable report customization. This screen has four tabs; General, Page Options, Fonts, Tags and HTML. The options on each of these tabs are described in this chapter in the section titled *The Report Definition Process*. Please refer to that section for the details.

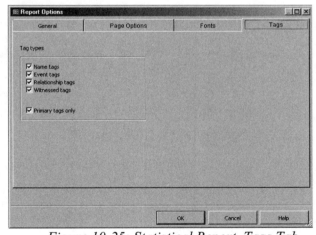

Figure 10-25: Statistical Report, Tags Tab

The **Statistical Report** General tab also includes the following option:
- **Subtotals by Sex** – Select this option to produce two additional sections to the **Statistical Report** that break out the summary of data by gender.

The **Statistical Report**, Tags tab *(see Figure 10-25)* is a variation of the standard tab and includes the following options:

Tag types
- Name tags
- Event tags
- Relationship tags
- Witnessed tags
- Primary tags only

Examples

1. *I am planning a research trip to another county. How can I use the Statistical Report to prioritize my areas of research?*

A properly defined **Statistical Report** will compute the total number of people in the project from your county of interest. It will also compute statistics for birth group, death group and marriage group tags, plus father tags and mother tags among others. From your data, what tag group has the highest average, or the lowest? In other words, from which tag group do you have the most data, or the least data? Use the information gleaned from the **Statistical Report** to focus on finding those few remaining death records or those many birth records. To create this report:

Open the **Statistical Report**. Click the [Add] button located to the right of the Filtered Group option to create a filtered group for everybody in your project who has an event located in your county of interest *(see Chapter 11, Filtering and Sorting)*. If you already have such a filtered group defined, click the down arrow on the Filtered group drop-down box to display a list of available filters. Select [Options] to further customize the report, if desired. Close the **Print Options** screen and print the report.

2. *The default Statistical Report computes totals for everybody in my multi-data set project. How do I create a version that reports on data from only one of the data sets?*

Open a custom Layout that includes the **Project Explorer** before running the report. Set a filter for the **Project Explorer** where Data Set ID equals the ID number of the data set from which you want to generate statistics *(see Chapter 11, Filtering and Sorting)*. Open the **Statistical Report**. Select the **Report Definition Screen** option 'Selected people on the Project Explorer.' Select [Options] to further customize the report, if desired. Close the **Print Options** screen and print the report.

Chapter 11 – Filtering and Sorting

By Allen Mellen

One of the most powerful features of The Master Genealogist is the capability it gives you to filter your previously entered data – that is, to select a portion of the data for special attention. Reasons for filtering can include setting a flag in order to accent people either on screen or in charts, producing a report for a selected portion of your data, making a list to assist in further research, and many other purposes. A filter lets you look at just a portion of your data – for example, all persons named Alexander, all marriages in Tennessee, all births in Australia between 1850 and 1900, all places containing the word Paris, and just about anything else you can think of, singly or in combination.

Most of the filters discussed in this chapter will be those used for the Picklist, the Project Explorer, and several reports including the List of People. These "people filters" are the ones you will probably use most often, and they can be saved in filter files with the file extension[16] "FLP." Other types of filters are discussed at the end of the chapter.

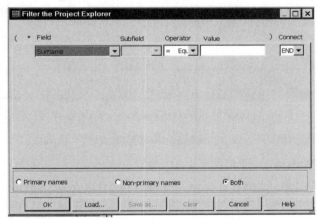

Figure 11-1: Filter the Project Explorer screen

Designing a Filter

Filters can be simple or complex. When you design a filter you need to decide on the target group – the people you wish the filter to include, and on the output – the form in which you wish the results to be presented. Let us first consider a simple filter to identify people in your project born in a specific place, Australia for example. The output could be presented in a filtered Picklist or Project Explorer, a List of People, another report, or perhaps a flag. In this case, we will be filtering the Project Explorer.

Once you have defined the target group and the output, the next step is to express the definition as one or more conditions.

Filter conditions in TMG are generally in the form:
Field   Operator   Value   Connector.[17]

The condition for the group of persons born in Australia can be expressed as "Place of birth is Australia." Here, the Field is "Place of birth;" the Operator is "Is;" the Value is "Australia;" and the Connector is the period or full stop, expressed in TMG filters as "END."

Since we are filtering the Project Explorer in this example, we need to bring up the "Filter the Project Explorer" screen. There are two ways to do this:
1. Choose **Edit > Filter the Project Explorer**, or
2. Click on the [Filter] button in the Project Explorer window.

The screen shows a form with the heading
(* Field Subfield Operator Value) Connect

The first time the screen appears, the form shows one entry consisting of a Field, an inactive Subfield, an Operator, a blank Value, and a Connector (*see Figure 11-1*).

Except for Value, you make entries by choosing from a drop-down list or clicking on a check box.

Field

The drop-down list for Field contains the 9 name fields, all of the flags in the project, a set of entries beginning with the number symbol #, and an

---

[16] Filter files are saved in the same folder as your project. See Windows Help for information on file extensions.

[17] In this simplified version of the form, the Field includes any Primary Marker and Subfield. The Connector includes any Parentheses.

alphabetical list that includes the tag groups and all tags in the project, Witnessed tag groups and tags, as well as other conditions. Entries that are followed by suspension points (that is, three dots or …) have associated Subfields.

For our example filter, scroll to the Birth entries in the drop down list under Field (*see Figure 11-2*).

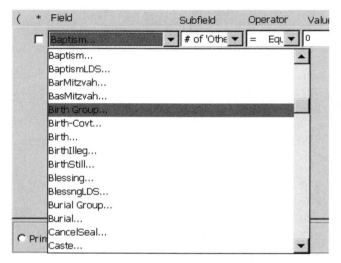

Figure 11-2: Field Drop-down list

For this example, select Birth Group…[18]. The suspension points (…) signify that there will be a Subfield selection available.

Primary Indicator

Since the selected field (Birth Group…) designates a Tag type or Tag Group, you can check a box in the column headed with an asterisk (*****) to indicate that the condition refers to primary tags. If the box is not checked, both primary and non-primary tags will be included in the filter. For this example, check the box under the asterisk (*****) to signify primary birth group tags only.

Subfield

The Subfield drop-down list is activated for Fields that designate tags or tag groups. The Subfields for event tags include items like # of Citations, as well as the Place, Date, and Memo fields of the tag (*seeFigure 11-3*).

---

[18] While in this case, we could probably get the same results by choosing Birth…, in general it is good practice to filter for a Tag Group instead of a single Tag Type so that the filter will be more generally applicable.

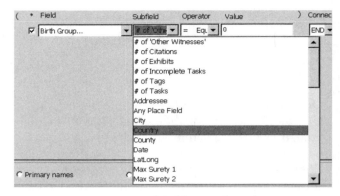

Figure 11-3: Subfield Drop-down list

For this example, select Country.

Operator

The Operator drop-down list varies according to the characteristics of the Field and Subfield. The Subfield in this case is Country, so the available operators apply to a word (*see Figure 11-4*).

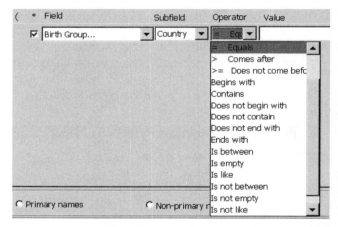

Figure 11-4: Operator Drop-down list

For this example, choose the Operator "= Equals."

Value

When, as in this case, the operator requires a value, enter it. For this example, enter "Australia" as the value. Notice that however you type them the letters are converted to uppercase. Values are not case sensitive.

Now you can choose a Connector.

Connectors

The possible connectors are AND, OR, and END. For filters that require more than one line, choose either AND or OR at the end of each line (*see Figure 11-5*).

Figure 11-5: Connector Drop - down list

In this case, since there is only one condition, select END as the Connector.

The filter conditions define the target group of people (or in some case, the names) you want to appear on your list or report. They are applied to each person in the project[19] one at a time.

The current example has one condition. When this filter is applied to each primary Birth Group tag in the project, the country is compared to Australia. If the country in the tag is Australia, the person with that tag **satisfies the condition**.

Other Considerations

Primary and Non-Primary Names

Both the Project Explorer and the Picklist are lists of names. For both lists, radio buttons at the bottom of the filter screens allow you to select Primary names, Non-primary names, or Both (*see Figure 11-1*). If you select Primary names, the number of names that appears in the header of the list will be the number of people who satisfy the filter condition, since there will be exactly one entry per person.

Filtering Dates with Modifiers

In TMG filters, there is a difference between the treatment of the Subfield **Date** and the Subfield **Year**. The difference is apparent only in connection with dates that have modifiers. The value of a **Date** is always compared to the date in a tag according to the sort sequence as set out in Help topic "Chronological Sort." A value of **Year** is compared according to whether it falls within the period specified by the date in the tag. The date modifiers "after" and "before" are treated as "any time after" and "any time before." Therefore, a condition such as "Year Is greater than 1850" will turn up dates such as "after 1570." In contrast, the condition "Date Comes after 1850" will not turn up dates of

the form "after YYYY" when YYYY is 1849 or earlier.

Relative's Name Group

Conditions using the fields Mother's Name Group... or Father's Name Group... will turn up the **children** of persons with the specified name and not the parents themselves. Similarly, conditions using the fields Child's Name Group..., Daughter's Name Group..., or Son's Name Group... will turn up the **parents** of children with the specified name.

Witnessed tags

Conditions using the Witnessed tag fields will turn up persons in Other Witness roles only.

Combining Filter Conditions

Many filters are constructed using more than one condition, joined by one of the connectors AND and OR. Sometimes, it is a bit tricky to determine which connector to use. AND is used when both conditions must be satisfied. OR is used when it is sufficient that one condition is satisfied. A possible source of confusion exists because in some instances where the word AND is used to define the target group of the filter, OR is used in the filter itself.

*If you want to find persons born in Australia **AND** persons born in New Zealand, the filter must be Birthplace is Australia **OR** birthplace is New Zealand.*

If you have three or more filter conditions and have both of the connectors AND and OR, you can group the conditions using parentheses. TMG follows the standard rule that AND is applied before OR. However, it is a good idea to use parentheses to make certain the conditions are applied correctly. An example is a filter for all persons with a certain surname except those born in the last half of the nineteenth century. The filter must be:

	Surname	Equals	NAME	AND
(	*Birth Date	Comes Before	1850	OR
	*Birth Date	Comes After	1899	) END[20]

Without the parentheses the filter would find people with the Surname NAME who were born before

---

[19] Filters are applied only to persons in **enabled** data sets.

[20] The asterisk * in the example appears as a check mark on the screen.

1850 and **all** people born after 1899 regardless of surname.

Up to eight conditions can be entered on the Filter definition screen.

Report Filters

The Report Filter screen, accessed from the Report Definition screen, has the same conditions as the Picklist and Project Explorer filters (*see Figure 11-6*).

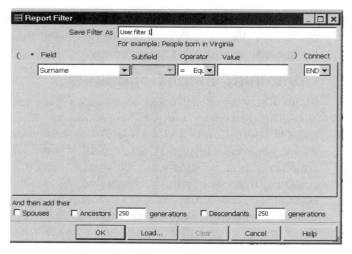

Figure 11-6: Report Filter screen

The eight possible filter conditions in the main section define a "core group." A line at the bottom of the screen offers options to add the spouses, ancestors, and descendants of the core group. Note that if you check both add spouses and add ancestors, you will not get the ancestors of the spouses – rather you will get the spouses and the ancestors of the core group.

The "People" (FLP) filters are used in the following reports:

> Ahnentafel
> Audit
> Descendant Indented Chart
> Descendant Indented Narrative
> Distribution of People
> Family Group Sheet
> Individual Narrative
> Journal
> List of Names
> List of People
> Pedigree - Compressed
> Statistical Report

List of People Secondary Output

The List of People report has a special feature to perform certain secondary actions (Figure 11-7; see also *Chapter 10, Customizing Reports*):

- Create a new project
- Create a new dataset
- Lock and unlock timelines
- Set the value of a flag[21]

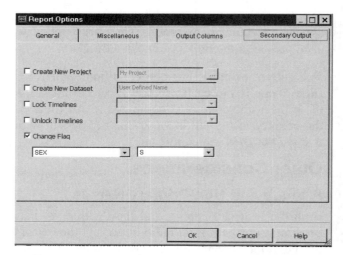

Figure 11-7: List of People Report Options screen, Secondary Output

The ability to set a flag greatly extends the capabilities of the filters. You can run the List of People to set a flag, and then test that flag in another run of the List of People. Using that technique, there is no limit to the number of conditions you can use. See Example 3, "Census Candidates" below.

It is not possible to use nested parentheses in a filter. In rare instances, it might be necessary instead to use a flag and an additional run of the List of People to test that flag so that a complex filter is evaluated correctly.

Examples

Following are a group of filter examples – most have arisen from real life needs.

---

[21] This is called "Change Flag" on the Secondary Output tab of Report Options.

Example 1. Preparing for a trip to a specific place

In preparation for a trip, you may want to have a list of people associated with a specific place. You may wish to set a flag or simply to print a list of the desired people. In either case, you will use a List of People report.

The idea of the filter is

     Event Place   =   Target

The details of your specific filter will depend on your data. Several events in the Sample project take place in Russell County, Virginia. A filter to find the Principals with events in Russell County would be:

    Any Event… County Contains RUSSELL END

If you expect to use a similar filter for more than one county, you can use a question mark enclosed in brackets [?] for the value. Give the Report Configuration a name you can remember and select Print & Save. The Fill in the blank screen appears (*see Figure 11-8*):

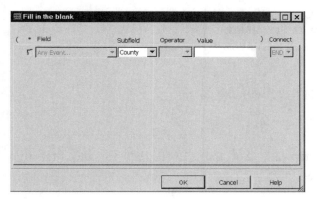

Figure 11-8: Fill in the blank screen

Enter the desired value in the Value column and click [OK].

Example 2. Setting a "Mayflower" flag

The aim is to identify the descendants of a particular progenitor -- Mayflower descendants, for example. This example uses a flag.

The hardest part is identifying the progenitor – in this example, the Mayflower ancestor. Filters will not help you here. Once you have the progenitor identified, the filter itself is easy.

Step 1 – Add the Flag:
In the Flag Manager add the flag
    Mayflower
with the values:
    N = No[22]
    Y = Yes

Step 2 – Set the Flag:
 Run a List of People with
    Secondary Output:
       Change Flag Mayflower#1[23] to Y
for the filter:
    Is a Descendant of ID# NN END

The same filter can be used in the Picklist or Project Explorer without setting a flag. A similar condition can be used for accenting.

Example 3. Census Candidates

The aim is to identify people who might be listed in a particular census, in order to provide a basis for a census search.

Analysis

The solution is to identify people who were alive at the time of the census. You may also wish to include people who might possibly have been alive at the time of the census. There are a number of approaches. These examples use 1925 as the year of the census.

If you are looking only for people whom your data indicates were alive at the time of the census, the simplest solution is to look for people who have at least one event before the census and one event after the census. In that case you can use the filter:

Any Event…	Date[24]	<=	1925	AND
Any Event…	Date	>=	1925	END

If your data set includes many people with posthumous events, such as LDS events, then you need to look for people who have at least one event before the census, one event after the census, and do not have a date of death before the census.

---

[22] The first value in a flag definition is the default and is initially assigned to everyone in the data set
[23] In filter conditions and Secondary Output, the Data set ID is included with the name of the flag.
[24] It is important to use the Subfield Date rather than the Subfield Year if your data includes dates with the modifiers "after" or "before." See "Filtering Dates with Modifiers" in this chapter

The condition *does not have a date of death before the census* can be restated as *has a date of death after the census or lacks a date of death.*

The desired filter would then be:
Any Event Year is not after 1925 AND Any Event Year is not before 1925 AND (Date of Death is before 1925 OR Date of Death is Empty OR Death tag does not exist.)

The precise filter is:

Any Event...	Date	<=	1925	AND
Any Event...	Date	>=	1925	AND
(*Death Group...	Date	>	1925	OR
*Death Group...	Date Is Empty			OR
*Death Group...	# of Tags =		0[25])	END

Persons who may have been alive at the time of the census

There may be people in your data for whom you have incomplete information – people who may have been in the census, although your evidence is not conclusive. This would include people who were born before the census for whom you have no record of date of death. Similarly, there may be people who were active after the census for whom you have no record of date of birth. The filter for the first group would be
Date of Birth is after 1820 AND (Date of Death is Empty OR Death Tag does not exist.)

The filter for the second group would be
Date of Death is after 1925 AND (Date of Birth is Empty OR Birth Tag does not exist.)

The precise filter for these conditions would be:

*Birth Group...	Date	>=	1820	AND
(*Death Group...	Date Is Empty			OR
*Death Group...	# of Tags =		0)	OR
*Death Group...	Date	>	1925	AND
(*Birth Group...	Date Is Empty			OR
*Birth Group...	# of Tags =		0)	END

For clarity, you might wish it were possible to have an additional pair of parentheses around the first three conditions and another around the last three. However, in this case the filter will evaluate correctly because the Connector between the first

three conditions and the second three conditions is OR.

Since only 8 filter clauses are available, it is necessary to use a flag to express all 11 conditions.

The desired filter is:

(Any Event...	Date	<=	1925	AND
Any Event...	Date	>=	1925	AND
(*Death Group...	Date	>	1925	OR
*Death Group...	Date Is Empty		1925	OR
*Death Group...	Tag Does Not Exist		))	OR
(*Birth Group...	Date	>=	1820	AND
(*Death Group...	Date Is Empty			OR
*Death Group...	Tag Does Not Exist		)	OR
*Death Group...	Date	>	1925	AND
(*Birth Group...	Date Is Empty			OR
*Birth Group...	Tag Does Not Exist		))	END

The extra parentheses around the first five conditions and around the last six conditions are not needed except for clarity. To implement this filter:

Step 1: Add the Census and TEMP flags.
In the Flag Manger, add the flag
 Census 1925 Candidate
with the values:
     ? = Unknown
     N = No
     Y = Yes
TEMP[26] with the values
     N = No
     Y = Yes

Step 2 – Set the TEMP flag for the first five conditions.
Run a List of People with
   Secondary Output:
     Change Flag TEMP#1 to Y
for the filter:

Any Event...	Date	<=	1925	AND
Any Event...	Date	>=	1925	AND
(*Death Group...	Date	>	1925	OR
*Death Group...	Date Is Empty			OR
*Death Group...	# of Tags =		0)	END

Step 3 – Add the six remaining conditions and set the Census flag.

---

[25] The expression "# of Tags = 0" is used in TMG 5 to test for the condition "Tag Does Not Exist."

[26] In versions of TMG earlier than 5.0x it was not possible to name a flag TEMP or TEMPORARY. This restriction no longer applies.

Run a List of People again with the same
 Secondary Output:
  Change Flag Census 1925 Candidate#1 to Y
for the new filter:

TEMP#1		=	Y[27]	OR
*Birth Group...	Date	>=	1820	AND
(*Death Group...	Date	Is Empty		OR
*Death Group...	# of Tags	=	0	OR
*Death Group...	Date	>	1925)	AND
(*Birth Group...	Date	Is Empty		OR
*Birth Group...	# of Tags	=	0)	END

The Census 1925 Candidates flag as described in
the preceding paragraphs is only one of the many
ways a flag could be used in census research.
Another way might be to have different values of
the flag such as "A = Alive" for persons known to
be alive at the time of the census and "M = Maybe"
for persons for whom evidence is lacking as to
whether they were alive at the time of the census.

Cleanup

The TEMP flag is no longer needed. You can delete
it in the Flag Manager, or you can reset it to N so it
can be used in other filters.

Resetting a flag

Here is a method of resetting the TEMP flag to N.

Run the List of People with
 Secondary Output:
  Change Flag TEMP to N
for the Subject:
  All people in the project.

Example 4. Descendants and Spouses.

The aim is to assign three values to a flag so the
flag can be used in accenting charts. The three
values are D for direct descendants of the focus
person, S for spouses of the descendants and O for
all other persons.

Designing the filter
A filter defines a subset of the people in your data
and implicitly divides your data into two groups –
those who pass the filter and everybody else. In this
example, three groups are required.

Group 1 is *descendants of the Focus Person*. The
filter condition for this group is straightforward:
  Is a descendant of ID# XX

Group 2 is *the spouses of persons in Group 1*. This
is not quite as obvious.

You can choose "And then add their spouses" in
connection with any core group, but to identify only
the spouses requires three steps.
  1. Identify the core group and set a flag.

  2. Select the core group; add their spouses; and
  set a different flag.

  3. Isolate the spouses, based on the values of
  the two flags.

Group 3 is everyone who is not in either Group 1 or
Group 2.

The solution
Step 1 – Add the Accent flag:
In the Flag Manager add the flag:
  Accent with the values
   O = Other
   D = Descendant
   S = Spouse
  Step 2 – Set the Accent flag for Descendants:
Run the List of People with
 Secondary Output:
  Change Flag Accent to D
for the filter:
  Is a Descendant of ID# XX END

Step 3 – Set the Temp flag
Run the List of People again with
 Secondary Output:
  Change Flag TEMP to Y
for the filter:

Accent	=	D	END

  And then add their Spouses

Step 4 – Identify the Spouses
Run the List of People yet again with
 Secondary Output:
  Change Flag Accent to S
for the filter:

Accent	=	O	AND
TEMP	=	Y	END

---

[27] Strictly speaking, use of the TEMP flag is not really
required in this example. Because the conditions in Step
2 and 3 are joined by OR, an alternative approach would
be simply to set the Census 1925 Candidate flag to Y in
both steps.

Since the default value of Accent was O, the value for everyone else, the flag is now correct for everyone.

Example 5. Persons named NAME and their mothers.

The aim is to assign three values to a flag so that it may be used in accenting charts. The values are N for persons with the surname NAME, M for mothers of persons with the surname NAME, and O for everyone else.

Analysis and design

In order to find persons with a particular **primary** surname, it is necessary to use the Name Group field with the Surname subfield, since the Surname field at the beginning of the drop down list will apply to all name tags. Finding their mothers is similar to example 4. The mothers can be found by the technique of adding ancestors for 1 generation and then picking only females.

The solution

Step 1-- Make sure TEMP flag is reset (or add it) and add a new flag.
In the flag manager add the flag:
    ACCENT2 with the values
        O = Other
        N = surname NAME
        M = Mothers

Step 2 --Set the flag for the persons named NAME.
Run the List of People with
    Secondary Output:
        Change Flag Accent2 to N
for the filter:
    * Name Group... Surname   = NAME   END

Step 3—Set the TEMP flag
Run the List of People   a second time with
    Secondary Output:
        Change Flag TEMP to Y
 for the filter:
    ACCENT2   =   N   END
        And then add their Ancestors for 1 generation.

Step 4 -- Identify the mothers.
Run the List of People a third time with
    Secondary Output:
        Change Flag ACCENT2 to M

for the filter:

ACCENT2	=	O	AND
SEX	=	F	AND
TEMP	=	Y	END

Everyone now has the correct value of the flag ACCENT2.

Example 6. Spin off a branch of a tree.

The aim is to isolate a branch of a tree, that is, the descendants of person NN, their spouses, and any ancestors of the spouses. The isolated branch might then be the focus of a report, or exported to a new data set or GEDCOM file.

Analysis

It seems simplest to set a flag for the desired branch. The desired group has three components:
    The descendants of person NN
    The spouses of the descendants
    The ancestors of the spouses

In the general situation, person NN and the ancestors of person NN are also in the data set but not in the desired group.

We need to identify the spouses, as in Example 4.

Step 1: Add a flag.
In the Flag Manager, add the flag
 Isolate with the values:
    N = No
    Y = Yes
Either reset the TEMP flag or create it with values:
    N = No
    Y = Yes

Step 2: Find the descendants
Run a List of People with
    Secondary Output:
        Change Flag Isolate flag to Y
for the filter:
        Is a Descendant of   ID#   NN   END

Step 3: Set the TEMP flag
Run the List of People again with
    Secondary Output:
        Change Flag TEMP to Y
for the filter:
    Isolate   =   Y   END
        And then add their Spouses

Step 4 – Identify, the spouses
Run the List of People a third time with
  Secondary Output:
    Change Flag Temp to N
for the filter:

Isolate	=	Y	AND
TEMP	=	Y	END

This leaves the TEMP flag equal to Y for the spouses, but not for the descendants.

Step 5-- Add the spouses and their ancestors
Run the List of People a fourth time with
  Secondary Output:
    Change Flag Isolate to Y
for the filter:

TEMP	=	Y	END

  And then add their ancestors for 250 (or fewer) generations

This changes the Isolate flag to Y for both the spouses and their ancestors.

Example 7. Add the ancestors of the target person to the isolated branch.

If the desired group in Example 6 is to include person NN and the ancestors of person NN, then it is easiest to identify person NN and his/her spouse by ID number and add an additional step:

Step 6: Add person NN and NN's ancestors
Run the list of People a fifth time with
  Secondary Output:
    Change Flag Isolate to Y
for the filter

ID Number	=	NN	OR
ID Number	=	Nspouse[28]	OR
Is an Ancestor of ID#		NN	OR
Is an Ancestor of ID#		Nspouse	END

Example 8. Find the Treetops

In this example, we will set a flag for all people both of whose parents are unknown. This flag can be used for accenting and can also be used in filters for creating reports and charts.

Step 1 – Add a flag
In the Flag Manager add the flag TWIG with the values:

N = No
Y = Yes

Step 2 – Set the flag
Run a List of People with
Secondary Output:
  Change Flag TWIG to Y
for the filter:

Father*	Is Not Known[29]		AND
Mother*	Is Not Known		END.

Example 9. Find Cousin Marriages and their descendants.

The aim is to identify cousins who marry and set a flag for them and their descendants in order to accent them on charts.

Analysis.
This can only be done separately for each line of descent. The first step is to identify the descendants of a particular progenitor. Then take the male descendants and identify their spouses, using the technique from example 3. Any spouse who is also a descendant of the progenitor has married her cousin.

Step 1 – Add two flags
In the Flag Manager add both a Cousin flag and a Descendant? flag, each with values:
    N = No
    Y = Yes
Reset or add the Temp flag.

Step 2 – Identify the descendants
Run a List of People with
  Secondary Output:
    Change Flag Descendant? to Y
for the filter:

Is a Descendant of	ID#	N	END

Step 3 – Set the TEMP flag.
Run a List of People a second time with
  Secondary Output:
    Change Flag Temp#1 to Y
for the filter:

Descendant?#1	=	Y	AND
SEX	=	M	END

  And then add their Spouses

---

[28] Nspouse signifies the ID number of the spouse of the target person.

[29] The technique of using ID Number = 0 which was required in earlier versions of TMG will still work.

Step 4 -- Find the female cousins among the spouses
Run the List of People a third time with
  Secondary Output:
    Change Flag Cousin to Y
for the filter:

Temp#1	=	Y	AND
SEX	=	F	AND
Descendant?#1	=	Y	END

Step 5 -- Reset the TEMP flag (see Example 3). Then, repeat Step 3, but for SEX = F.

Step 6 -- Repeat Step 4, but for SEX = M.

At this point, both partners of each cousin marriage have the Cousin flag set to Y.

Step 7 -- Add the descendants of the cousin marriages.
Run the List of People again (this is the sixth time) with
 Secondary Output:
  Change Flag Cousin#1 to Y
for the filter:
  Cousin = Y END
   And then add their Descendants for 250 generations

All descendants of persons in cousin marriages will have the cousin flag set to Y at this point. If there are descendants of other marriages of the cousins, their Cousin flag can be reset to N by the following steps.

Step 8 -- Reset the TEMP flag.

Step 9 -- Find the spouses.
Filter the Project Explorer with the filter:

Cousin	=	Y	AND
# of Spouses >		1	END

Step 10 -- Accent the Cousins
In the Accent Definition screen, select the Accent condition:
       Cousin   =   Y
Choose any convenient color scheme.

Step 11 -- Identify the other spouses.
Using the Project Explorer, find the non-accented spouses of the cousins, and in the Flag Manager change the TEMP flag to Y for these spouses.

Step 12 -- Change the descendants' Cousin flag.
Run the List of People with
  Secondary Output:

Change Flag Cousin to N
for the filter:
    TEMP   =   Y   END
  And then add their descendants for 250 generations.

It should be noted that Steps 8 to 12 do not correctly handle the case where a descendant identified in step 12 has married a cousin. This situation could be detected by inspection of the Project Explorer, if the Accent in Step 10 were applied before Step 7.

Example 10. Create a report for Matrilineal Descent

The aim is to produce a descendant report showing descent of females through their mothers from a female ancestor (the progenitor.)

Analysis
In order to produce a report that shows only some of the descendants of a particular progenitor, it is necessary to make a new data set that contains the desired descendants and omits the rest. Using the new data set, the desired group will be included in any of the following reports with the progenitor as Subject:

- Descendant Box Chart
- Indented Chart
- Indented Narrative
- Journal Report

In this example, we will include not only the female descendants but also their spouses and the parents of the spouses.

Solution
Step 1 -- Add a flag.
In the Flag Manager add a new flag
  Selected
with values
  N = No
  Y = Yes
  S = Spouses
Reset or add the TEMP flag.

Step 2 -- Set the Selected flag
Run a List of People with
  Secondary Output
    Change Flag Selected to Y

for the filter:

	ID Number		N	OR
(	Is a Descendant of	ID#	N	AND
	SEX	Equals	F)	END

Note that this filter will select all of the Female descendants of the progenitor N, including those are descended through their fathers

Step 3 -- Add the Spouses
Run a List of People with
   Secondary Output:
      Change Flag TEMP to Y
for the filter:
   Selected   Equals Y   END
     And then add their Spouses

Step 4 – Identify the Spouses and add their Parents
Run the List of People with
   Secondary Output:
      Change Flag Selected to Y
for the filter

Selected	Does Not Equal	Y	AND
TEMP	Equals	Y	END

    And then add their Ancestors for 1 Generation.

Note that the Core group consists of the spouses only. The Selected flag is changed for both the Core group and their parents.

Step 5 – Make the new Data Set.
Run the List of People with
   Secondary Output:
      Make new Data Set
for the filter
       Selected   Equals   Y   END

It is sufficient to make the new Data Set in the same Project.

Note that the new Data Set will include all of the female descendants of the progenitor N, as well as their spouses and the parents of their spouses.

Step 6 – Generate the desired report
Choose any of the formats for a Descendants report. When you select the Subject of the report, choose the progenitor N in the new data set. Even though the new Data Set includes extra people, they will not be included because they are not linked to the progenitor.

Example 11. Produce a Journal Report for multiple progenitors.

The aim is to produce a Journal report that covers all of the ancestral lines in your data (see the example under "Journal" in *Chapter 10, Customizing Reports*).

The Subjects of the report are the end-of-line male ancestors. The filter in Example 8 sets a TWIG flag to Y for all end-of-line ancestors.

A possible order for the report is the order in which the lines appear in a Pedigree or on the Tree View. To achieve this order, you can assign appropriate Reference numbers and select the Reference field on the Sort By tab. To assign the Reference field, it is necessary first to determine the desired order by examining the Tree view.

The Reference Field is a character field so that it sorts from left to right. If for example, you have 32 different lines, you can assign the progenitors the Reference values 01, 02, 03, …, 30, 31, 32. The leading zeroes are necessary to get the sorting correct. If you later find a person who should come between 03 and 04, for example, you can assign that person the Reference value 035, which will sort between 03 and 04.

The Subject(s) for the report can be either a Filtered group or a Focus Group. In either case, the filter is:
      TWIG   Equals   Y   AND
      SEX   Equals   M   END

In the rare circumstance that the earliest known person in one of your lines is a woman, it is probably easiest to use this filter to generate a Focus Group and then add the ancestor in question to the Focus Group. Then the Subject of the report would be the Focus Group.

Example 12. Assign values to a Related by flag.

The Help topic "Add New Flag" describes possible values for a Related By flag. There is an article at *www.tmgtips.com* that describes a way to set this flag using List of People Secondary output. The technique is a repeated application of the method described in Example 4 for identifying spouses:

First, set a flag for a Core group.

Second, set a temporary flag for the Core group and added spouses, ancestors or descendants.

Third, use the values of the two flags to identify the people added in the second step.

Example 13. Assign values to a Generation flag.

If you desire, you can apply the technique in Example 12 one generation at a time and assign a generation value to a flag or a set of flags. Because flag values are single characters, if you have more than 9 generations you have to use either letters or multiple flags. One system would to assign the numerals 1-9 for the first nine generations and the letters A-Z for generations 10 through 36. An alternative method would be to use two flags - one for the tens digit and one for the units digit.

Filter Conditions using NOT

In TMG 5 filters, the Boolean operator NOT is usually available either in the Operator or directly in the Field. Most conditions, even compound conditions, requiring NOT can be coded directly. For example, the compound condition

NOT born in Australia after 1900

can be expanded to

NOT *(Born in Australia*   ***AND***
        Born after 1900)   *END.*

This in turn can be restated as

        *Birthplace is **not** Australia **OR***
                *Birth date is **not** after 1900 END*

In the same way,

NOT *(Born in Australia*   ***OR***
        Born after 1900)   *END.*
can be restated as

        *Birthplace is **not** Australia **AND***
        *Birth date is **not** after 1900 END[30]*

Other Filter types

Each of the List reports has an associated filter type that can be saved in a filter file with a distinct extension.

        FLP = People and Names

FLC = Citations
FLE = Events
FLL = Places
FLR = Repositories
FLS = Sources
FLY = Tag Types
FLK = Tasks
FLW = Witnesses

All of these filter types work the same way. The filter conditions of course vary depending on the groups being filtered – events, places, tasks, and the rest.

Further aids

Constructing filters is a skill that improves with practice. Don't be afraid to try various filters and see what happens.

There is additional information on the subject of filters, including links to sample filters, available at *www.tmgtips.com*. Help in constructing particular filters can also be obtained from the members of the Rootsweb mailing list, TMG-L.

---

[30] These restatements were formulated by the 19th century English logician and mathematician Augustus De Morgan and are known as De Morgan's laws.

Chapter 12 - Multimedia and Exhibits
By Richard Brogger

This chapter will address three features of The Master Genealogist™: **Exhibit Log**, **Slideshow Manager**, and **Slideshow Viewer**. In addition, I have included some opinions and information that pertains to images, file storage, and so on in: Image Information. If you are not familiar with the basics of digital image files, you may want to read that information first. Hopefully, it will help you understand other topics.

Topic headings that begin with a noun and end with a question mark like "Exhibit Log?" can be read as, "What is the Exhibit Log?" Topic headings that begin with a verb and end with a question mark such as "Attach an Exhibit?" can be read as; "How do I attach an Exhibit?"

The term "Frame" is used in **Slideshow Manager** and in **Visual Chartform™** (VCF). To avoid confusion I will use the term "slide" instead of "frame" when referring to the objects that represent exhibits in the Image Lists.

When instructions are given, they will be based on the SAMPLE Project included with TMG.

Alternative methods are lettered, i.e.: "A", "B", "C", etc.

Numbered steps have a close parenthesis after the number, i.e.: "1)", "2)", "3)", etc.

Multimedia

Multimedia in The Master Genealogist™ can be almost anything that can be seen or heard on your computer. This includes images, audio, video (movie), text or any object produced by an OLE (Object Linking or Embedding) compliant application

Exhibit Log

The **Exhibit Log** is the feature used to add exhibits to The Master Genealogist™ and to access those exhibits. An Exhibit is any media object that is attached to: a person, an event, a Source, a Repository, or attached as a general topic.

Types Of Media Used With The Exhibit Log

Almost any kind of media may be used, such as: image, audio, video, text, and OLE objects. If the item you would like to exhibit is not one of the first four types, it will then fall into the OLE object category. If you have an OLE compliant application on your computer, anything that can be shown using that application can be linked to The Master Genealogist. Keep in mind that an OLE exhibit sent to **Slideshow Manager** and included in an exported slideshow cannot be viewed unless the recipient of the show has the file and the application to open that file.

Open Exhibit Log?

There are three ways to open the **Exhibit Log**:
A. Press <Ctrl>+<F12>.
B. Click on the **Exhibit Log** button (the one showing a camera [📷] on the Toolbar.
C. Click on the **Tools > Exhibit (multimedia) Log** menu item.

Attach An Image, Text, Audio, Or Video File?

You first determine what the object will be attached to: Person, Event, Source, Repository, or General. Then follow the steps below.

Add An Exhibit For A Person?

1) Go to Person View for the correct person.
2) Click the [📷] (**Exhibit Log**) button.
3) Right-click on a blank area of the **Image list** of **Exhibit Log**. (The area where thumbnails are displayed is called the **Image list**.) From the menu select the proper media type and a directory box will appear. Go to the proper folder and select the desired file. Click **[OK]** and the media file will be added to **Exhibit Log**.

Add An Exhibit For An Event?

1) Go to Person View for the correct person.
2) Double-click on the event so that the Tag Entry window opens.

3) Click on the [📷] (Exhibit Log) button in the Tag Entry screen.

4) Right-click on a blank area of the Image list of **Exhibit Log**. From the menu select the proper media type and a directory box will appear. Go to the proper folder and select the desired file. Click **[OK]** and the media file will be added to the event in the **Exhibit Log**.

Add An Exhibit For A Source?

Let's say you have scanned a copy of the obituary for Frank Alexander in the SAMPLE project as shown in the Midland Methodist journal.

1) Open the Master Source List, make sure that the **[More>>]**/**[Less<<]** is set so it shows **[More>>]** and the list is sorted by Source #, then double-click on Source # 15, "Alexander, Frank - obituary".

2) Click the [📷] (Exhibit Log) button on the Source Definition window.

3) Right-click on a blank area of the Image list of **Exhibit Log**. From the menu select the proper media type and a directory box will appear. Go to the proper folder and select the desired file. Click **[OK]** and the media file will be added to the Source in the **Exhibit Log**.

Add An Exhibit For A Repository?

Let's say you have a database or spreadsheet listing every item in the Soergel Collection and you want to attach that database to the Repository.

1) Open the Master Repository List and double-click on repository # 1, "Soergel Collection".

2) Click the [📷] (Exhibit Log) button on the Repository Definition window.

3) Right-click on a blank spot on the Image list of **Exhibit Log**. From the menu select the proper media type and a directory box will appear. Go to the proper folder and select the desired file. Click **[OK]** and the media file will be added to **Exhibit Log**. Keep in mind that such a list is subject to change. If the list is linked using OLE, updates to the list will be reflected in **Exhibit Log**. (Also see: Add an OLE Object).

Add An Exhibit That Is Not For Any Of The Above?

This will be a **General Exhibit**.
1) Open the **Exhibit Log**.
2) From the Focus drop down list, select **General topics Exhibits**.

3) Right-click on a blank spot on the Image list of **Exhibit Log**. From the menu, select the proper media type and a directory box will appear. Go to the proper folder and select the desired file. Click **[OK]** and the media file will be added to **Exhibit Log**.

Name An Exhibit?

1) Open the **Exhibit Log**.
2) Right-click on the Exhibit you want to name.
3) From the menu select **Properties**.
4) Select the **General** tab.
5) Enter the name (up to 30 characters) in the **Topic**: field.
   Note: The topic entry will appear on the slide in the **Exhibit Log**. More important is that the topic may be used to filter exhibits so choose your topic name entry carefully. (Also see: Describe an Exhibit). Slides in the image list will sort by: **None** (The order in which they were added) or by **Exhibit Name**. Names like:
       1909 – First birthday
       1914 – First day of school
       1926 – Graduation
   will sort in chronological order but lack a name for use in a filter. You might use "1909 – Frank Alexander" as the **Topic** and "First birthday" in the **Description.**

Associate An Exhibit With A Paper Copy?

1) Open the **Exhibit Log**.
2) Right-click on the Exhibit you want to name.
3) From the menu select **Properties**.
4) Select the **General** tab.
5) Enter a reference number in the **Reference** field. Let's say you assign all documents a number as they are obtained. You might use a format like: **yyyymmdd.nnn**, where yyyy = year, mmm = month, dd = day and nnn is a number. In the reference field you might enter something like "20001225.019". (Also see: Describe an Exhibit). If an Exhibit is first attached to a Source, a Source Repository can be used.

Describe An Exhibit?

Your topic might be too brief to tell you what the Exhibit is. Your reference number tells you where but not what. This is where the description can help.
1) Open the **Exhibit Log**.

2) Right-click on the Exhibit you want to identify.
3) From the menu select **Properties**.
4) Select the **Description** tab.
5) Enter as much text as you need to fully define the Exhibit. The text entered will also be displayed in the box just below the Image List of the **Exhibit Log** window when the Exhibit is highlighted.

Display Certain Exhibits In The Exhibits Log?

What is displayed at any time is a determined by:

1. **Filter.** This is where a properly selected topic will help. If you have named all the exhibits for a person using his given and surname, you can filter using either or both.

2. **Focus** – You can change what slides are shown by selecting the right focus. You may select **All Exhibits**, **General topics Exhibits**, **A Person**, **An Event**, **A Source**, or **A Repository**. The Person, Event, Source, and Repository options open the **ID** field so that you can enter a specific **ID** number.

3. **Type.** You may choose to limit the displayed Exhibits to say, text Exhibits attached to an event or events for Frank Alexander, or to other specific criteria. The options that you may choose are: **All Types**, **Image**, **Audio**, **Video**, **Text**, or **OLE Objects**.

Display More Exhibits In The Image List?

Revise the number of slides displayed by increasing or decreasing the Row and Column settings. If needed, the window can also be resized.

Find Exhibits For A Person?

A. Go to the person's **Person View** and open the **Exhibit Log**.

B. Click on the [📷] (**Exhibit Log**) button and click on the [🔍] button in the upper right and select the person from the **Picklist**.

Find Where Exhibits are Stored?

1) Open the **Exhibit Log**.
2) Right-click on the Exhibit you want to identify.
3) From the menu select **Properties**.
4) Select the **Info** tab. Here you will find the Type of Exhibit, whether it is internal or external, the full path/name of the file, the size, date, and format.

What Are The Two Boxes Below The Image List?

The Description box on the left will contain the text that you entered in the Exhibit's **Properties** window in the **Description** tab.

The Subject box on the right shows two lines of information. Let's assume that the top line contains the entry: **4, (2-8) / 9** and is explained in Table 12-1.

Entry	Description
4,	Slide number **4** has been selected, i.e., is the focus slide.
(2-8)	Slides **2** through **8** are visible on the Image list area.
/9	Number of slides that meet the selection criteria.

Table 12-1: Slide Tracking

The second line shows information for the slide that is the focus, e.g., is highlighted. First the type of slide is shown, such as **Person, Event, Source or Repository**. Then the ID number for that Person is shown, i.e. **1:1**. If it is an **Event**, **Source**, or **Repository**, the **ID** number for that item will be shown.

Fix A Frowning Face Slide?

The presence of a slide with a yellow "frowny" face indicates that the link assigned to that Exhibit has been lost. This may occur during Import, when the path is not correct. It might also occur if you have moved or renamed a file. You can correct this by right clicking on the slide and selecting **Properties**. On the **General** tab, click **[Load]** and select the correct file.

Attach An OLE Object?

1) Right-click on the Image list and select **Insert new OLE** to display the **ole.ole_object** window.
2) In the TMG File Menu, Click **Edit > Insert Object** from the top menu.
3) Select the ⊙ **Create from File** option.
4) Check ☑ **Link**.
5) Enter the path and name of the file or use the **[Browse]** button to find and select the file.
6) Check ☑ **Display As Icon**.
7) Click on the **[OK]** button. The icon will appear in the window from step 1.

8) Double-click on the icon. If your file type is properly associated with the correct application, that application and file will open.

9) Close the window. A slide showing the **OLE** icon will be added to **Exhibit Log**. If step 8 does not work, open Explorer and double-click on the file used in step 5. If the proper application and file do not open, the file extension is not associated with the application within Windows™.

Buttons On The Exhibit Log

Figure 12-1: Exhibit Log Control Buttons

If you have more Exhibits than can be shown on one page of the Image list, these buttons will let you maneuver to the right page. The [◄] (Previous) and [►] (Next) buttons allow you to step forward and backward one slide at a time. The [◄◄] (Page Up) and [►►] (Page Down) buttons shift the displayed slides one "page" at a time. The [|◄] (Top) button moves the focus of the page to the first slide while the [►|] (Bottom) button moves the focus of the page to the last slide.

If you have slides 7 - 21 of 40 slides shown and click [►], you will have slides 8 - 22 shown. If you the then click the [►►], you will have 23 - 37 shown. In other words, Pages are not fixed as to which slides are shown. What you see depends on the selected slide at which you begin. If the Image List displays 15 slides, [◄◄] or [►►] will move to the previous or next 15 slides depending on the number of slides and the current focus.

Delete An Exhibit?

Right-click on the slide for the exhibit you want to delete and click **[Delete]**. If the Exhibit is an External Exhibit, it will not be deleted from your hard drive – only from the **Exhibit Log**.

Copy An Exhibit To Slideshow Manager?

Right-click on the slide for the Exhibit you want to copy and click **Copy to Slideshow Manager**. The

Exhibit will appear in a new or current slideshow in **Slideshow Manager** and a copy of the Exhibit file will be placed in the **SlideShow** folder.

Copy An Exhibit To A Specific Slideshow In Slideshow Manager?

Click **[Load]** to open the desired Slideshow in which you want to add the Exhibit. Return to the **Exhibit Log** and

A. Right-click on the Exhibit you want to copy, select **Copy to Slideshow Manager**. Be sure that you save the changes to the slideshow before closing **Slideshow Manager**.

B. Make sure that both the **Slideshow Manager** window and the **Exhibit Log** window are visible. Click on the Exhibit and drag a copy to the **Slideshow Manger**.

Be sure that you save the changes to the slideshow before closing **Slideshow Manager**.

View A Text Exhibit?

A. Right-click on the slide for the Exhibit you want to see and click **View**. The text will appear in a window.

B. Double-click on the icon shown on the slide.

View An Ole Exhibit?

A. Right-click on the slide for the exhibit you want to view and click View.

B. Double-click on the icon shown on the slide.

Using either method, a window with an Icon will appear, double-click on the Icon. Your OLE Object and the application will open.

View A Video Exhibit?

A. Right-click on the slide for the Exhibit you want to view and click View.

B. Double-click on the icon shown on the slide. Either way a window will display like *Figure 12-2*.

Figure 12-2: Video Player

Video Player Controls *(see Figure 12-2)*

[Load] You may use this to find and load a specific video file. This button is not functional while viewing a Video.

[Play] Starts the Video playing or resumes playing after the **[Stop/Pause]** button is pressed.

[Stop/Pause] This will stop the Video from playing but will not close the Video window.

[Resume] This will continue playing the Video after the **[Stop/Pause]** button is pressed.

[Play Fullscreen] Instead of playing in a window, the Video will fill the screen. To return to the Viewer and the controls, use the <Esc> key on your keyboard.

[◄] Backward one second of play time.

[►] Forward one second of play time.

[Fit] A Video will normally open so that it fits the viewing area of the Video Player.

[100%] Not all Videos will have sufficient resolution to be played as large as the viewing area, so use this to adjust to the maximum size for this Video.

Click on **[Fit]** and **[100%]** to see their effect.

In *Figure 12-2* the options boxes have been unchecked. When those boxes are checked, the appropriate items shown in *Figure 12-3* will appear in the bottom of the video viewing area.

Figure 12-3:Video Player Controls

☑ **Controls.** This is the master option to display or not display the controls selected.

☑ **Audio.** This causes the Audio Controls to display if the Controls option is selected.

☑ **Statusbar.** This indicates Playing, Paused or Stopped at the left side. At the right side, the Elapsed Time/Total Time or Elapsed Frames/Total Frames is displayed.

☑ **Tracker.** This is a progress bar showing the relative part that is being played. As the video plays the little square block moves to the right.

The block may be dragged left or right to go to another portion of the video.

⊙   **Time.** If selected the Elapsed Time/Total Time is shown on the **Statusbar**.

⊙   **Frames.** If selected Elapsed Frames/Total Frames is shown on the **Statusbar**.

◼   **Movie speed.** Dragging the slider left will slow the video and right will speed it up.

[▶]   **Play.** This will cause the Video to start or continue (after a pause) playing.

[❚❚]   **Pause.** This will pause the video.

[◼]   **Stop.** This will cause the Video to stop playing and reset to the start position.

Image Viewer

To view an image:

    A. In **Exhibit Log** double-click on the image.

    B. In **Exhibit Log** right-click on the image and select View.

The **Image Viewer** contains the control panel shown in *Figure 12-4*. The controls are:

[Load File] If you have another file that you would prefer to use and the Exhibit Name and Description for the current Exhibit are okay, this is an easy means to make the change.

Figure 12-4: Image Viewer Control Panel

[In] Zoom in.

[Out] Zoom out.

[100%] The display size of an image may be too large for the resolution. This button will size the image to match the resolution.

[Zoom Area] After clicking this button, the cursor will change to crosshairs. Drag a box around an area within the image and that selection will fill the viewing area.

[Fit] After using the [100%], [Stretch] or [Zoom Area] buttons, this button will restore the normal view.

[Stretch] This will enlarge the image to fit the full width of the viewing area.

[Flip] Turns the image top to bottom.

[Reverse] Turns the image left to right.

[Resize] *Note: This can create a change in your file.* The dimensions of the image are given in pixels (picture elements). Frank Alexander's Picture is 326x351. Doubling the settings to 652x702 will cause Frank's picture to be shown larger. However, the original file had only so many pixels. Those pixels are now spread apart and the picture quality is reduced. Making the image smaller will usually be fine. It is always best to make a new, properly sized copy from your original file, especially if you use the JPEG format for Exhibits.

[Rotate] *Note: This can create a change in your file.* This can be used to straighten an image that is at an angle. It can also be used to create a different effect. If you rotate an image 45 right, then 90 left, the image must be reduced. Once reduced it will remain the new size.

[90] Same as rotate but with the amount fixed at 90°.

[180] Same as rotate but with the amount fixed at 180°.

[270] Same as rotate but with the amount fixed at 270°.

[OK] Closes the View and retains any changes.

[Close] Closes the View and does not retain any changes.

[Help] Opens the Help file to the correct topic.

Scroll bars

When an image is too large for the Image Viewer window, scroll bars appear. When very large images are viewed, the scrolling action can be very erratic. The cause is known but is outside of TMG control. If the scroll bar does not work well a user can left click on the image and hold down the left mouse button. Moving the mouse will move the image.

Audio View

To View the Audio controls:

    A. In **Exhibit Log** double-click on the audio exhibit.

    B. In **Exhibit Log** right-click on the audio exhibit and select View.

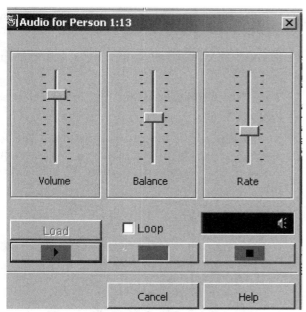

Figure 12-5: Audio Player Controls

The Audio control window appears as is shown in *Figure 12-5*. The various controls are:

Volume. The level at which an audio file plays is determined by three things: (1) the original recording level, (2) the volume control for the computer and (3) this volume control. Until an audio file has been played there is no way to know how loud it will be. Set your computer to a normal volume, slide the Volume slider down, and press [▶] (Play). Now slide the Volume slider up until you get the desired level of sound. Settings are 0 – 100.

Balance. Balances the sound level for left and right speakers. Settings are from 5 (top – left speaker) to –5 (bottom – right speaker).

Rate. Sets the Rate at which a file will be played. Settings are 2.0 (top) – 0.5 (bottom). If you have a recording made on a portable recorder with weak batteries the playback rate will be too fast making the sound higher pitched. Reducing the rate will correct for that effect.

[Load] Can be used to change to a different Audio file.

☑ **Loop** When checked the file will play to the end and then begin again. It will continue to play until another Audio file is played or until you press [Stop].

Time display Shows the Elapsed Time and Total Time for the audio file.

[Close] Changes made will be discarded and the window closed.

[Help] Opens the Help file to the proper topic.

Exhibit Properties.

Right-click on the image and select Properties to access the Properties for an exhibit. If the property is not available for an exhibit type, that type will be dimmed or not display in the window.

General Tab

- **Topic** Enter a name for the exhibit. (Also see: Naming an Exhibit) Audio, Video, Text, Image, OLE.

- **Reference** If you have a numbering system for exhibits, enter the number here. (Also see: Associate an Exhibit) Audio, Video, Text, Image, OLE.

- **Location** This box will show "**External Image File**" if your file is external to **TMG** or "**Internal Image**" if the image is stored within TMG.

- By using the drop down button, [▼] you can change whether the exhibit is internal or external. If an internal exhibit is changed to an external exhibit, the "Save to External Image" dialog box will appear. This will allow you to enter or select a path where the image file is stored. It will allow you to choose that path as your Exhibit folder. It will allow you to name the image file.

  ☑ **Primary** Check Primary if you want the image to be the one used in charts and reports. When Primary has been checked, the Topic will be preceded by an asterisk as in "* 2 Frank Alexander". (2 is the slide number). *Only exhibits for people may be Primary.*

- [Load] If you have a different Image file that you would prefer, you can Load that file. Keep in mind that the Topic and Description will remain the same. For example, maybe you have two files for Frank Alexander: Photo0.bmp and Falexand.jpg. You might have started with Photo0.bmp, but prefer Falexand.jpg. By opening the existing image for Frank Alexander, you can load Falexand.jpg.

- After a new image is loaded, you must click [OK] to save the change. This will also close the Properties window. If you return to Properties for the new image, the [Save as …] button will be active. This will open the "Save to External Image" dialog box mentioned above under Location.

- [Acquire].   You may use this to obtain a new image from a Twain device such as a scanner. Once the file has been acquired, two options become available.

When either of these last two buttons is selected, the file name and path will appear in the field below these buttons.

The preview area displays the Image that will be displayed in **Exhibit Log**.

Description Tab

Text area. Used to describe the Exhibit. Text entered here will also appear in the box on the **Exhibit Log** just below the Image list. What is entered in the Topic field may not be what you would like for a caption when the image is used in a report. If you prefer a different caption, enter the word "Caption" followed by a colon, the caption text and a semicolon. The following text will provide a three-line caption.

Caption: Letter to his children[:CR:]Written by Frank Alexander[:CR]circa 1915;

Any text entered after the semicolon will not be included in the caption. Thus any amount of detail can be entered whether the Caption feature is used or not.

Audio Tab

If there is no audio file loaded, all buttons will be dimmed except for [Load].

[Load]. This tab button applies to audio files only. If you do not like the one loaded, you can load another one.

After an audio file is loaded, the remaining buttons and the status bar will appear. The loaded filename will appear below the buttons

[Delete]. This will delete the audio file.

[Play]. This button will cause the audio file to play as a preview of it.

[Stop]. This will stop the audio file during playback.

Type File. Indicates if the file is an External File or an Internal File.

Status Bar. This indicates if the audio file is playing or stopped and displays the current position and length of playtime of the audio file.

Info Tab
Audio

If audio has been added to an Exhibit the **Info** tab will show data something like:
```
AUDIO
***********************
144,902 bytes, 12/07/1999 4:00:00
C:\TMG\PICS\LONGHAIR.WAV
```
The first line is the size of the file, and the date and time that it was created. The second part is the path and name of the file.

Image

If an image file is loaded, the information for it will be shown. In the case of the image for Frank Alexander and with an audio file attached to that image, the **Info** tab will show something like the following:
```
IMAGE
***********************
External image file
Full name: C:\TMG5\PICS\FALEXAND.JPG
77,211 bytes, 09/01/1996 1:00:00
Format 326x351x8
JPEG File Interchange Format with YUV
4:4:4 color space and Loss less.
AUDIO
***********************
2,088,013 bytes, 08/23/2001 23:34:44
C:\TMG\PICS\LONGHAIR.WAV
```
As you can see you are shown:
- If it is an internal or external file.
- The full path and file name for the image and the audio files.
- The File size, date, and time of the files.
- Format width in pixels x height in pixels x number of bits per pixel.
- Other information about the image file.

Change the icon for an exhibit?

The following files are used as icons for text, audio, video and OLE Exhibits. They are displayed on the appropriate slide to indicate to you what type Exhibit is attached to that slide.

Text.bmp   Sound.bmp   Ole0.bmp   Video.bmp

You may not like to have one or any of these icons and would prefer to display something else. That can be done easily by replacing the file or files found in the Graphics folder in your TMG folder. Whatever image format you have can be used if it is a supported image format. Let's say that you have a file named Speech.jpg and you would like to use it in place of Sound.bmp. Change the name of Sound.Bmp or delete it from the TMG Graphics folder. Rename Speech.jpg as Sound.bmp and place it in the TMG Graphics folder. The next time that the **Exhibit Log** is opened, the new image will be displayed.

Save Image Thumbnails

The **Save image thumbnails** option can be found in **Preferences** > **Current Project Options** > **Advanced.** When this option is **not** selected the image thumbnails must be created before **Exhibit Log** can open each time that the user opens **Exhibit Log.** The more exhibit files that are opened and the larger those exhibit files are, the longer it takes to open the **Exhibit Log.**

If **Save image thumbnails** is selected (the default) your existing image files, whether internal or external, will not be changed. Your image files will be copied, resampled, converted to JPEG format and saved in a new database file.

Since the option is turned on by default, then thumbnails were automatically created when you opened a pre-v5.05 project for the first time. However, some external images may not have been accessible (on a CD, etc.). They will not have been added (*see Refresh Thumbnails below*).

When you view an exhibit, or the properties of an exhibit, it will be your original file that is viewed. It will not be the thumbnail.

Use the thumbnail for the Image window

If you use a layout with a large **Image Window,** it could partly defeat the purpose of thumbnails if the thumbnails are made large. It may be best to turn this option off and let your original be displayed in the **Image Window.**

Thumbnail Size

Just below the **Save image thumbnails** option is **Thumbnail size.** Users can select image widths from 50 to 2000, in increments of 50 pixels. The smaller the setting is, the smaller the thumbnail image and file will be. In addition to the slides in **Exhibit Log,** these thumbnails will be viewed in the **Image Window.** The size of the **Image Window,** if it is used with thumbnails, in your layout will be an important factor in setting **Thumbnail size.**

The dimensions of the thumbnail will determine the image quality when viewed in the **Image Window.** If the thumbnail is too small for the **Image Window** dimensions, image quality will be lessened. If your use of the **Image Window** is only to remind you of the person's general appearance, image quality may not be important.

The dimensions of the thumbnail will also determine the size of the file. Since these thumbnail image files are also included in the backup, you may want to keep the dimensions small or exclude thumbnails from your backup.

Refresh Thumbnails

When you right click on a slide in Exhibit Log, three new options are provided:
- **Refresh this thumbnail**
- **Refresh all thumbnails**
- **Refresh missing thumbnails**

The later two options are also available in the right click menu for the **Image List.**

Slideshow Manager (SSM)

You might wonder why you need the **Slideshow Manager** when the **Exhibit Log** is available. In the **Exhibit Log** you would want to have a picture of a person to appear in the Image Window (*see chapter 4, Customizing the Program*) or to be included in charts (See *Chapter 11, Generating Charts For Use in Visual Chartform™*) and reports (*see Chapter 10, Customizing Reports*). You would want images of documents used for evidence, maps, or a recorded interview. However, we often have dozens of pictures of one person. This is where the **Slideshow Manager** is appropriate.

A slide show produced with **Slideshow Manager** is far different than the slide shows of thirty years ago. Back then it was possible to buy a tape recorder and a slide projector that would function together. A narrative and/or background music could be recorded on the tape recorder on one track and signals for the projector on the other track. Once everything was put together and connected correctly, the sound track and slide were synchronized. Audio and images together required expensive equipment.

Now, using the features in SSM, you can produce even better slideshows and at far less cost. Not only can you include audio but you may also include video or text in the same show. Instead of images

Counter number	What the numbers represent
8,	The slide that currently is selected (has the focus).
(1-8)	Range of slide numbers currently in the Image list.
/18	Total number of slides in the slideshow.

Table 12-2: Slideshow Manager Counters

just popping on screen, you can add transition effects. When your slideshow is finished it can be played on your computer monitor. It can also be exported along with **Slideshow Viewer**, placed on CD or other media and sent to family members to view and enjoy again and again.

Slideshow Manager Image List

Figure 12-6, on the next page, is an example of the **Slideshow Manager Image List**. The Name of show: "SSM Window" tells which slideshow is loaded. The default settings for the number of Rows and Columns are 3 and 5 respectively but may be from 1 to 10 rows or columns. The space where the slides appear is referred to as the Image List. Just below the Image List is the description window and to the right of the description window is the counter.

The buttons shown below control which slides are visible in the Image List. The number of slides on a

If you place the cursor over an empty portion of the Image list and right-click, a menu will appear giving the following options.	
Insert new image	Used to insert a new image slide
Insert new audio	Used to insert a new audio slide
Insert new movie	Used to insert a new video slide
Insert new text	Used to insert a new text slide
Create a new slideshow	Used to create a new slideshow
Save	Functions the same as the **[Save]** button
Export	Functions the same as the **[Export]** button
Play	Functions the same as the **[Play]** button

Table 12-3:Image List Right Click Menu

page will depend on the Rows and Column settings. Using the default settings, the Image list would hold 15 slides. If slides 3 –17 are showing, Page Right, [▶ ▶] will display slides 18 – 32. Previous, [◀] will move one slide so that 17 – 31 are shown. If Next, [▶] was pressed, slides 18 – 32 would be viewed. In the Image List area, you may right-click for different menus.

If you place the cursor over a slide in the Image list and right-click, a menu will appear giving the following options	
Load	Functions the same as the **[Load]** button
Duplicate frame	Make a duplicate of the current slide
Remove frame	Delete the current slide from this slideshow
Remove all frames	Delete all slides from the current slideshow
Preview Full-screen	Shows the current slide full screen
Preview this frame	Shows the current slide in a window
Properties	Where you set the properties for each slide

Table 12-4: Slide Right Click Menu

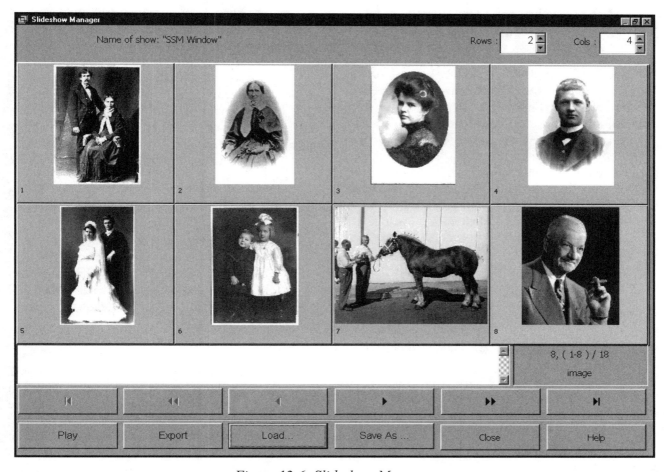

Figure 12-6: Slideshow Manager

Adding Slides to Slideshow Manager

There are four ways to build a **Slideshow Manager** (SSM) slideshow.

1. Load the slides from the **Exhibit Log**. If an existing data set that includes slides is opened, those slides will be in the **Exhibit Log**. When **Exhibit Log** is opened, you can select slides by selecting the right Focus. The focus can be All Exhibits, A Person, An Event, A Source or A Repository. You can also determine what type of object such as: Image, Audio, Video, Text or OLE objects. When you have the right slides available, right-click on the one you want in SSM and select "Copy to **Slideshow Manager**". Repeat the process for all slides you wish to have in a slideshow.

You may also drag and drop a slide from the **Exhibit Log** image list to the slideshow image list.

2. Load from within the **Slideshow Manager**. Open the SSM and load an existing slide show or create a new one. You will see an empty Image list in the SSM window. Right-click anywhere on that area and, from the menu that opens, select the correct option. Once the object type is selected, the Insert new frame to Slideshow window will appear. This will allow you to go to the location where the object file is stored. Select the proper file for the object you want and click **[OK]** or just double-click on the file name. That object will appear in the **Slideshow Manager** Image List.

When adding new slides to an existing slideshow, you may not have an open area of the Image list. Just press [▶] (Next), [▶ ▶] (Page Right) or [▶ ▌] (Last) button until you have an open area on which to right-click.

3. Drag and drop from Windows™ Explorer. Open **Slideshow Manager** and open Windows™ Explorer. In Windows™ Explorer, go to the folder where your slides are filed and select the ones you want to add to SSM. Using standard Windows™ procedures you can hold down <Ctrl> while you click on certain files. You can also select consecutive files by selecting the first one, hold down <Shift> and click on the last one. Once a group has been selected, hold down the left mouse button and drag and drop the entire group onto the **Slideshow Manager** window. Once the button has been released, the slides will be copied into **Slideshow Manager**.

4. Drag and drop from an image organizer program such as, FotoAlbum™ by FotoTime, Inc. You may be using an image organizer or manager program to organize your collection of images. You can also use standard Windows™ drag and drop procedures for many of these.

Sorting slides.

You may change the order of the slides in the Image list by dragging. For example, if you want to move slide 17 so it is right after slide 9, click on slide 17 and hold the button down. A dotted rectangle and plus sign will appear. Drag the cursor so it is positioned over slide 10 and let the button up. Slide 17 will become slide 10 and all the other slides will move to the right.

Setting Slide Properties.

Once the slide is in **Slideshow Manager**, right-click on the thumbnail in the SSM window. From the menu that opens, select "**Properties**". There are four tabs in the Properties window. The features of most of the tabs are the same for all types of slides. Differences are mentioned.

General Tab

[ ] Include in show

This is checked by default. If you do not want to delete the slide from the slideshow but do not want it to play, remove the checkmark by clicking on it. Click again to include.

Duration

Designates how long the image will remain on the screen when a Self-running slideshow is played. For an image with audio this setting will determine the duration of the image. The audio portion will be determined by settings under the Audio tab. For video the duration will be determined by the Video tab settings.

Topic

This is the name that will appear on the thumbnail's frame in the Slideshow Manager Image List.

Fit image to window

This option is selected by default. This will allow the image to fill the window regardless of window size or the entire screen when Full screen is used. Not applicable to video slides.

Limit scaling factor to

This will limit how large the image will be. For example, when an image is saved it may be intended for viewing as a 326 x 351 image. If that limited size is shown full screen on a large monitor, the image will not have enough resolution and look bad. Scaling factor will limit how large the image will be inside a larger window. The factors are 1 to 10. If the file was designed to display as a 326 x 351 image, a factor of 1 will limit it to the intended size. If this results in an image that is too small, you can try increasing the scaling factor. If the image appearance is not acceptable, you may need a higher resolution copy. Not applicable to video slides.

Transition effect

In addition to "No effect" there are 15 other types of effects.

Mode

For each of the transition effects there are different modes that allow you to choose how the effect will appear. When the number of transition effects and the number of modes are combined, there are over 9,000 different effects. To describe each effect and each mode is far beyond the scope of this chapter. I find that most mode names are self-explanatory but it may help to understand a name like, "Wipe4 bottom top left right".

"Wipe" is the type of transition action. "4" indicates the image is divided into four quadrants.

This is not applicable to video slides.

Wipe toward **bottom** from top	Wipe toward **top** from center
Wipe toward **left** from center	Wipe toward **right** from center

Table 12-5: Transition Modes

Delay

This setting will determine how long the transition effect will last. The digits are not seconds. There is no way to predetermine how long a transition will take for a particular setting. File size, window size and type of effect plus the Delay setting will determine how long the transition effect lasts. Not applicable to video slides.

Preview effect

This button will apply the transition effect on the image shown. Keep in mind that the image shown in Properties is small and the effect will be much faster than when shown in a window. If it is too fast to judge the effect, you can set the delay to a large number while deciding. It will require some experimenting to determine the right delay setting. Not applicable to video slides.

Load

Should you decide that the image is not the right file type or for any other reason you want to change, the Load button will allow you to get a different image file. Not applicable to video slides.

Selection Box

To the right of the [Load] button you will see:

    ○ Zoom to selection
    ◉ Show selection   □ Blink

These will be grayed out (dimmed). Move your cursor into the preview window just above. The cursor will change to crosshairs. Hold down the mouse button and drag so that you make a rectangle surrounding the desired portion of the image. The above selections will now be active.

By drawing a box around part of the picture and selecting **Zoom to selection**, that portion of the image will be what appears in your slideshow.

You may draw a box around one person in a group picture to frame and highlight them. Select **Show selection**, the frame will appear when the slide is played. If you select **Blink** the frame will blink. A blinking frame is a good way to call attention to one person in a group or some detail that might not be noticed. In many group pictures the subjects are so close together that the frame would be across another person's face. To avoid this you can make a tiny box just above the subject's head or on their chest.

When you want to name and describe several people in the same picture, duplicate the slide as many times as you have subjects. Then for each slide, use the blinking frame to show to whom the name and description belong, or use **Zoom to selection** to show one person at a time. The same image file is used for all of the duplicates so duplicating a slide does not duplicate the file and bloat your slideshow file.

To remove the rectangle, click anywhere on the image. This is not applicable to video slides.

Description tab

When the slide is shown, you will want to describe what or who is being shown. Here you can enter a fairly long description. Font type, size, bold, italics and color are all available to make it right. In addition, you can set the background color. Any color that your computer can display can be used. This color will fill the area outside the image to the edges of the window or screen. Those who are clever with colors can set the mood by choosing the right colors. When the slide is played, the description will appear below the image. For a video slide, the description will not appear when the video is played.

Audio or Video tab

This may become one of your favorite features. If the transition effect and color are not sufficient to set the mood, add the right audio. Audio can be played for just one slide or can play for the entire slideshow. You may start the slide with the clash of cymbals or a baby's first words, Beethoven or Aunt Betsy's recording. Slides with narration telling the audience the story of the images is hard to beat. This is not applicable to video slides.

[Load]

This button will open the Load audio window where you may select your audio file. Read the Audio controls information before pressing the [Play] button.

[Delete]

This allows you to delete the currently loaded file in order to load a different one.

Audio/Video Controls

In the upper left corner of the audio or video tab are six buttons with a volume control slider just below. These controls are used to select the part of the audio or video file to be used in the slide show. The slider will determine the volume for individual audio files.

Make sure that your computer volume control is set at a normal level. On the audio or video tab use the slider to set the Volume lower then press [Play]. Increase the volume, using the audio or video tab slider, until the loudness is at a desired level. Few audio or video files play at the same level of loudness. Your computer and speaker volume controls will affect the level for the entire slideshow but this control will allow you to preset the volume for each audio or video file.

When you press [Play] you will see the Fragment tracker move. Look just above the Fragment label, you will probably not see anything. Press [Stop], [Reset], [Set Start], [Play]. Now, look just above the Fragment label. You should see **Begin:**, **End:**, and **Duration**: displaying the time in seconds.

Setting the Begin/End time

You may not want to play an entire audio or video file. You may want to begin part way into the audio or video file. You may want to stop before the end is reached. As the file plays watch the End numbers. When the right place is reached for the beginning, record the numbers.

Press the [Reset] and [Play] buttons to start the audio or video file. You will not see the Begin, End and Duration numbers, but you can watch the Elapsed time counter. When the right point in the file is reached, press [Set Start]. Press [Stop] and then [Play] again and watch the End seconds. When the right ending point is reached, record the time. Press play again and when the right ending point is reached press [Set Finish].

The Fragment tracker can also be used to select a segment of an audio or video file. Place your cursor on the slide and press the mouse button. You will see the time pop-up. Drag the slider to the left or right and the time will change. This is where recording the start and end time can be beneficial. Once you have the time desired for the beginning, press [Set Start]. Do the same for the end but press [Set Finish]. If you need to start over, press [Reset].

[ ] Include Audio

You may have an audio file loaded but for some purposes you do not want it to play. Just click on the box to mark or unmark the choice. This is not applicable to video slides.

Allow play into later frames

Let's say you have ten slides for a wedding and an audio file of wedding music. This option will allow the sound to start with this frame but continue into the next nine images. If frame 11 has a different audio file, that will start with frame 11 if that is what you have set. You might also have a narration that covers the entire slideshow. This setting will allow it to play to the end. This is not applicable to video slides.

Play for this frame only

The audio will play only as long as this slide is shown. Not applicable to video.

[ ] Loop audio

If you have 3 minutes of background music and a ten minute slideshow, this setting will allow the audio to repeat as many times as needed to play for the entire slideshow. This is not applicable to video slides.

Status Bar

When an audio or video file is being played, the word "Playing" will appear at the left end of this bar. When a file is stopped the bar will display "Stopped". When an audio or video file is being played or is stopped, at the right end of the Status Bar will be something like 05:10/06:17. This is the Elapsed Time/Total Time.

Info tab

The information shown here is similar to that shown in the Info tab of the **Exhibit Log** Properties window.

Saving a slideshow

As with any computer work you may do, it is good to save your work periodically. To save click **[Save As...]** and the Save Slideshow window will appear. In the window you have radio buttons for two selections.

⊙ **Save Changes to** "Slideshow Name" (default). If you do not want to change the name of the slideshow, press **[OK]**.

○ **Save as new Slideshow**. If you want to save the slideshow using a new name select Save as new Slideshow and enter the new name in the field to the right and press **[OK]**.

Playing a slideshow

If you have loaded just one file into a slideshow, that slideshow will not play. It takes at least two slides to make **[Play]** available. However, it may be one slide duplicated.

When you press **[Play]** a window with the following options will open.

☑ Loop   ☑ Full-screen
☑ Self-running   ☑ Effects

Loop. With this option checked, the slideshow will play through to the end and then begin again.

Full screen. The slideshow will fill the monitor screen when this option is checked. If it is not checked the slideshow will be in a window. You may change the size of the window by dragging an edge.

Effects. Transition effects will be used if this box is checked.

Self-running. With this option the slides will advance automatically according to the delay you have set for each slide. If you want to advance the slides manually, uncheck this option and use the <←> key on your keyboard to return to the previous slide. Use <→> to advance to the next slide.

Control during Slide Show Play Time

When a slideshow is playing, pressing <U> will bring up a menu with the controls shown in Table 12-6.

Loading a Slide Show

If you have a large collection of pictures, you may make several slideshows. Your only limit is the amount of space available in the storage media. Each slideshow that you make will create copies of each image in the Slideshow folder. Each Export will add another copy. If you intend to put 650 MB on a CD and save each export until all are finished, you will need about 2 GB of free space on your hard drive(s). When [Load] is pressed, the Load Slideshow window will appear listing the currently saved slideshows. Move the cursor to highlight the desired slideshow and click on **[Select]** to load that one. You may also rename or delete a slide show in the same way using the appropriate buttons in this window.

Exporting a Slideshow

Before you actually export your slideshow, consider where it should go. It is possible to send it to directly to your CD-ROM but I prefer to put it on my hard drive first. That way I can view the slideshow to make sure that it is just the way I want it to be. I have folders just for slideshow exports.

Click on **[Export]**. The Export Slideshow window will open. Near the top of the window is:

☑ **Include Slideshow Viewer.**

One copy of the viewer is all that is needed for all the slideshows you intend to put on one CD-ROM or other media.

Just below this option is a place to enter the path for your slideshow folder. If you prefer, you can click on the button to the right and browse the directory to get the right path. Once the path is entered or selected, press the **[Export]** button on the Export Slideshow window.

General suggestions

It is suggested that you will want to make your slideshows so they follow family lines. Grand Uncle Charlie's descendants will want to watch the slideshow of close kin more often than slideshows showing distant kin – so make separate slideshows for each family or line.

Images of our ancestors tend to get spread out among a lot of descendants. The large collection of pictures our grandfather had may now be dispersed in the homes of a hundred of his descendants. Genealogists spend a lot of time, money and effort gathering information about families. Often that includes borrowing Granddad's pictures from cousins and making digitized copies of those pictures. Often those pictures that our grandparents treasured never had the names of the subjects recorded.

If we include the known and unknown pictures in a slideshow and distribute copies of the slideshow, it is possible that another relative has a duplicate of your unknown picture. On the back of their copy it may say

"My very lovely grand aunt". Another relative has the same picture but it says "To my godson Jakob, b. 1882, from his aunt Cecile". Bingo! Jakob was your grandfather, Cecile was his mother's sister, and there is now one less unknown in your slideshow. This actually happened to me except there were four copies of the same picture. Two of the four had no information. As a result of sharing my digital copies, all four are now identified. Another benefit of sharing is that relatives I have never met have volunteered to send me pictures to add to the collection.

You may also want to make small charts in VCF to show relationships. Export them in BMP or EMF format and add them to your slideshow (*See Chapter 11, Generating Charts For Use in Visual Chartform*™).

Optimize and Self-optimize

When images are loaded into **Slideshow Manager** they are stored in the Slideshow folder. Files deleted from a slideshow will remain in the Slideshow folder until you choose to Optimize from within TMG. Then any unused files are automatically deleted from the Slideshow folder. If you intend to store files in the Slideshow folder, those files must be in a sideshow. This slideshow may not be intended for sharing but rather for organizing and describing file contents. If you have selected Self-optimize under Preferences > Program Options > Slideshow, the result will be that all image files not used in a slideshow will be deleted when you close **SlideShow Manager**.

The **Slideshow Viewer** topic has been placed on a single page so that it can be copied and included when you send a slideshow to someone.

Slideshow Viewer (SSV)

When you receive an exported slideshow and wish to play it, find and double-click on the filename of the received slideshow. (The default filename will be tmgss.exe although you or the person who created the exported slideshow may have changed the name – especially if more than one slide show has been created.) The Slideshow Viewer will open.

Loop.

With this option checked, the slideshow will play through to the end and then begin again.

Full screen.

The slideshow will fill the monitor screen when this option is checked. If it is not checked the slideshow will be in a window. Change the window's size by dragging an edge.

Effects.

Transition effects will be used if this box is checked.

Self-running.

This option causes the slides to advance automatically according to the delay you have set for each slide. If you want to advance the slides manually, uncheck this option and use the <□> key on your keyboard to return to the previous slide. Use <□> to advance to the next slide.

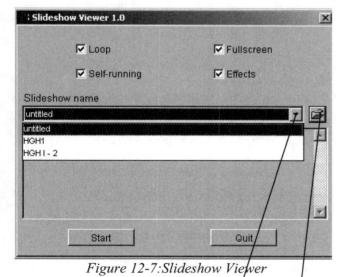

Figure 12-7:Slideshow Viewer

- Drop down list of Slideshows.
- Directory button to open other folders.

If you have several slideshows that have been placed in separate folders, the directory button may be used to go to the right folder. If there is more than one slideshow shown, select the one to play from the drop down list and click [Start].

Controls. When a slideshow is playing, pressing <U> will bring up a menu with the controls shown below.

<R> - Restart	Restarts the slideshow from the beginning
<G> - Continue (Go)	Continues automatic advance after a stop
<L> - Loop On	Turns on Looping.
<Ctrl>+<L> - Loop Off	Turns off Looping.
<I> - Info On	Hides the information such as 5/21 5.00 sec. that appears just below the image. In this example 5/21 is slide 5 of 21 slides in this slideshow and has a 5 second duration.
<Ctrl>+<I> - Info Off	Information is shown
<E> - Effect On	Transition Effects are used.
<Ctrl>+<E> - Effect Off	Transition Effects are not used.
<F> - Fullscreen On	Slideshow is played Fullscreen
<Ctrl>+<F> - Fullscreen Off	Slideshow is played in a window.
<Shift>+< ← > - Reverse	Slideshow will play in reverse and stop on slide number 1 if Loop is off. If Loop is on, the slideshow will return to slide 1 and then Loop to the last slide and continue in reverse until it is stopped.
<Space bar>	Stops the slideshow at the present slide.
Additional SlideshowControls	
<S>	Skip a slide
< ← >	Go back one slide and stop the show
< → >	Go forward one slide and stop the show
<Q> Quick info	Information for that frame
<Shift>+< → >	Same as <G>

Table 12-6: Slideshow Viewer Controls

NOTE: This page may be reproduced to accompany your Slideshow.

IMAGE INFORMATION

Images

Images may be obtained from scanners, digital cameras, or downloaded from the Internet - just to name a few sources. The images may be used in **Visual Chartform™** (VCF), **Slideshow Manager** (SSM), **Slideshow Viewer** (SSV), or in **Exhibit Log** (EL). Images included in **Exhibit Log** can be used in: the **Image** window, **Visual Chartform™** (VCF), various reports, **Slideshow Manager,** and **Slideshow Viewer.**

Whether from a scanner or a digital camera, all digital image files are handled the same and I will not make a distinction.

Black and White is very commonly used to refer to photographs but I will use grayscale for objects that contain shades of gray. Black and White will refer to black on white such as black text on white paper (Line art).

The pages of this book are printed in B&W but figures appear to have gray. What appears to be gray is actually done by using halftones. Halftones are created by using a grid of black dots on white to fool the eye. When more dots or larger dots of black are used in the grid, the result appears to be darker gray while fewer or smaller dots of black will appear to be lighter gray.

Dots per inch (dpi) does not mean the same thing for printers as samples per inch does for scanners. A 300 pixel per inch (ppi) scan can be just right for a 1200 dpi printer.

Printer resolution is referring to individual ink dots, not to picture elements (pixels). One picture element might contain four dots of ink. Just as shades of gray are simulated by halftones, colors are simulated by dots of color. A 600 dpi black and white printer might simulate 101 shades of gray but only print 60 pixels per inch. That is because a 10 x 10 grid of dots is needed to produce one gray pixel. If fewer shades of gray are used, resolution can increase. A 6x6 grid will only produce 37 shades of gray but the resolution can be 100 ppi. If no gray is needed, only black and white, then the printer can print 600 ppi and only then does it match the dpi rating of the printer.

Should Exhibits Be Internal Or External?

Concern	Internal	External
Backing up exhibits	Automatic when data is backed up	Must be done by user.*
	Increases size of each backup	Saves media space
	Each backup takes longer	Only done as needed
Shared copies	Automatically included	Must be added separately
Changing storage location	Part of each project and will go with the project.	Every link will have to be updated to reflect the new location. **
Quantity of exhibits	Limited by storage space	Limited by storage space but removable media, such as CDs, can be used.
Changes	Must be done for each exhibit	Automatic when change is saved to file.
Multiple use	Must be added multiple times	One file can be linked any number of times, even from different projects.
	Can't be used by other programs.	Other programs can use the same file.

* Select "Backup External Exhibits" when making a backup of a Project.
** How hard it will be to change the storage location of external exhibits will depend on how and where they are stored. The task can be as simple as changing the path for "Exhibit folder" in preferences.

Table 12-7: Exhibit Options

What Media Formats Will Work?

This is a very long list and is subject to change so please look for **"Supported Image Formats "** in the TMG Help file. Most file types are supported except for those that use LZW compression such as GIF and some TIFF formats. If a user has a lot of images in a format that is not supported, those images can still be linked using OLE.

Object

All forms of exhibits will be lumped together as being objects. Usually, one object is stored as one file. The object could be one image, many pages of text, or an Excel Workbook.

Digital Image Basics

A film image is continuous tone; but a digital image is composed of pixels much like tiny tiles. If you open a small image, such as an icon, in an image enhancement program like PhotoShop® or Paint Shop, and zoom in enough, you will see square dots. These dots are individual pixels (picture elements).

Imagine a wall 50 feet high and 67 feet long. On this wall is a picture made with one-inch square tiles. From a long distance our eyes will not see individual tiles they will see a picture.

The wall above is 800 tiles long and 600 tiles high. One of the settings for the screen area for monitors is 800 x 600 pixels. Viewed from the right distances, the monitor screen and the wall could show the same image and the resolution would be the same, 800 x 600.

When a color photograph is scanned at 100 ppi, the scanner records the image data for each square that is 1/100th of an inch on each side. If the photograph is 6 x 4 inches, software will create a table with 600 columns and 400 rows. In each space in the table it will record the RGB value. R G B stands for Red, Green, and Blue. These three colors are used to create all of the colors that we see on a monitor.

Each color has a numeric value from 0 to 255 (i.e. 256 shades). By combining the right value for each color 16.7 million colors are possible. In the binary system, an 8-bit byte can contain one of 256 values. To record the value for all three colors requires 24 bits or 3 bytes.

Image Dimensions

When viewed on a monitor, image dimensions are expressed as numbers such as: 800 x 600. This refers to the pixel width and height that make up the image. If you have your "Screen area" in Windows™ Display Properties set at 800 x 600; in this case, an 800 x 600 image will fill the screen. If you have a 1600 x 1200 screen area, the 800 x 600

image will then fill one quarter of the screen, half the height and half the width of the screen.

You may be wondering how large an image will be on your monitor. Sorry, I can't answer that. I could say that all monitors are 72 pixels per inch (ppi) but 72 ppi is a nominal figure. However, you can figure out an approximate number. Unless you have a wide screen monitor with a 19:9 aspect ratio, your monitor has a 4:3 ratio. Any triangle that has two legs that are 3 and 4 units will also have a hypotenuse (diagonal measurement) that is 5 units.

Let's apply this 3-4-5 rule to a 15-inch (381 mm) monitor. Since monitors are measured diagonally we know the hypotenuse is 15 inches or 3 times 5. Multiply the two legs by three (3 times 4) x (3 times 3) and we see that we have a screen 12 inches (305 mm) wide and nine inches (229 mm) high.

Now divide the number of pixels by the inches. 1024/12 = 85.3 ppi. If we then apply that to an image 800 pixels wide, we will get an image about 9.3 inches (236 mm) wide or just over two-thirds of the screen width.

So, the correct value is 85.3 ppi for monitors, right? Not necessarily. This is only correct **if** the monitor has a true 15-inch diagonal viewing area and **if** the screen area is 1024 pixels wide. The ppi for monitors will vary from about 60 to 120. For this reason it is best to forget ppi for monitor images. It is just an approximation.

I am sure you have seen 72 ppi used for a figure. It comes from the early days of Apple computers. It may have been related to character mapping verses bit mapping. Since characters are sized in points and 72 points equals one inch, using 72 ppi on a character mapped screen seems plausible but I am guessing.

On paper, the image dimensions will be expressed in centimeters or inches. Now we can use another factor, image resolution.

Image Resolution

Resolution can be expressed in dots per inch (dpi), pixels per inch (ppi), captures per inch (cpi) or samples per inch (spi). The later two terms apply to scanners or digital cameras while the first applies to printers. Pixels per inch is a term that is outdated for monitors. It originally applied to monitors but when monitors dropped the inches portion, the term lost meaning. I will use dpi to express resolution for printers and ppi for scanners, monitors and most other uses. Keep two things in mind; monitors are no longer rated in inches, and printers are not rated in pixels (one dot of color does not always equal one pixel).

Whether printing or scanning, dpi or ppi is an important factor. The ppi of a scan will affect the dimensions when the image is viewed on a monitor. It will also determine the quality of a printed image. It will also affect file size and the speed at which a computer can handle the file.

Image Color

Line art pixels are represented by just one bit with values of 1 or 0, black or white. At the upper end are high color (16-bit), full color (24-bit) and true color (32-bit) and higher. There is also grayscale (8-bit). Gray has equal values of RGB such as (e.g. 60, 60, 60). Since all three colors have the same value, 8 bits can store 256 shades of gray.

256 times 256 times 256=16.7 million colors and requires 24 bits per pixel. If your image is a color photograph that might be what you want. If the image is just four colors, such as a map, there is no need to use 24-bit color. Images in GIF format have only 256 colors (8-bit) and have been used on the Internet for years. Although you can't use the GIF format in TMG, you can use 8-bit color. For your working copy, always use the fewest possible number of colors.

30-bit color can contain four times as many shades as 24-bit color and 36-bit color can contain 16 times the number of shades of 24-bit. This would seem to indicate that scanning at 48-bits is far better than scanning at 24-bits and it is **if** there is no weak link in the chain (such as low cost electronics that introduce loss and distortion).

Low cost analog to digital converters have made high bit scanners available. If: the object being scanned, the light source, the elements (CCD) that capture the data, and the electronics are all very high quality they will be expensive, and yield a much greater dynamic range.

In scanners that cost thousands of dollars and are used for scanning quality film, high bit color is important. As best I can tell, the average home scanner does not offer much gain from high bit scans. There are too many weak links in the chain (such as lower quality electronics that introduce loss and distortion). 40-bit color may sound good but keep in mind that it may be more sales hype than fact.

Every component must be of equal quality or something will be lost. You might photograph the most beautiful sunset ever seen using the best camera and lens ever made. If you forget that the camera is loaded with the wrong film, that film can be the weak link. When we use scanners to capture an image, we add many links into the chain. Every link between the photo and your eye must be capable of maintaining the image's quality. Whether it is dust on the glass plate or noisy electronics that degrade the quality of the scan makes little difference. The quality is still lost. An inexpensive and a very expensive scanner could have the same resolution and number of bits, but that does not make them equal. Don't be fooled by numbers. Results are what matter and the results from an inexpensive scanner might be sufficient. It does not make sense to try for perfection when it is not required. Conversely, just because you like the results does not mean others will agree.

Image Size

The term 'size' will refer to how large a file is for an object. This will most often be expressed in bytes, kilobytes (KB) or megabytes (MB).

File size for a digital image will be determined by three factors.
- The physical dimensions of the image.
- The resolution.
- The amount of color.

Start with a 6 by 4 image and scan at 100 ppi. The result will be a 600 by 400 pixel image or 240,000 pixels. The third factor, color, will determine how many bits are needed for each pixel. 240,000 pixels at 24 bits per pixel = 5,760,000 bits. 5,760,000 bits times 8 bits per byte = 720 KB.

The dimensions of the scanned photograph are fixed and cannot be changed. We can change the resolution of the scan thus the dimensions, but not the original photo. However, is the entire photograph needed? Very often the portion of the picture that we need is but a fraction of the photograph. A portion of the photograph can be scanned or it can be cropped after the scan. Using either method, we might have a 2 by 3 inch image (200 by 300 pixels or 180 KB) yet retain the important part of the photograph while saving 540 KB.

If 24-bit color is not needed because the image is a "black and white" photo, then using Grayscale (which is 8-bit) will reduce the file to 1/3 the size. If the image is a line art that can be displayed in true Black and White, then we can use 1 bit per pixel. By doing so our file will be just 1/24th the size. To limit file size, use the least number of bits that will give you an acceptable image. (I have converted some color images to grayscale and preferred the results. Try it; you might like it.)

The third factor is resolution, as expressed in pixels per inch. Here again we want to use the lowest number possible. In the example above I used 100 ppi to make a point. It makes the math easy. Would you ever really use a 100 ppi image? If the image is to be viewed on a monitor, 100 ppi is a good number. If the image is to be printed on paper, you might get by with 100 ppi. (Remember that a printer might need a 300 or 600 dpi rating to print 150 ppi) In any case you can't print a higher resolution than that for which your printer is designed. So, if your printer can print at a true 300 ppi and you scan at 600 ppi, you will get no more resolution on the printer than if you had scanned at 300 ppi.

It is very important that image size and image dimensions be considered, as the type of image and the intended use will govern them.

Scanning

Photographs can be a study in itself and so can scanning. There is not enough space to allow a thorough coverage of the topic of scanning. Instead I will suggest buying **A Few Scanning Tips** by Wayne Fulton. You will find a lot of information about scanning at *www.scantips.com*.

The resolution used for scanning is very important. If the resolution is too low, quality will suffer. If the resolution is too high, file size will be much larger then necessary and loading and processing can become very slow. If you are scanning color prints, 300 ppi will capture all the detail. If you are scanning 35 mm negatives or slides, 4,000 ppi will capture most, if not all, of the detail available.

Grayscale prints can have better resolution than color prints and knowledge of the print is important. I have a 1906 photograph and at 2400 ppi I am seeing more detail than at 600 ppi. Above 600 ppi, I should be beyond the limits of the emulsion on the paper, yet, I believe what I see. A way to test is to scan at 300 ppi and zoom in on the image. If you see more detail, try 600 ppi and look again. Don't let your eyes trick you. When an image is larger; fine detail is easier to see. That does not mean the detail was missing at the lower resolution.

Usually it is rare that anything above 600 ppi is needed for a print. Scanning negatives is another matter. Film has much higher resolution than paper. It is doubtful that you will capture all available detail from a very large negative using a flatbed scanner. As the size of the negative gets smaller, there is no way to capture all of the detail using a flatbed scanner. However, is it necessary to capture all of the detail? The subject of the image and what you want will determine that. The negative image might allow you to enlarge to the point you can see the pores in someone's face but do you really want to do that? On the other hand, the subject may have been too far from the camera and you will need all the detail you can get to enlarge the subject.

An Image System

First of all, do not think I am some kind of image guru. I am not. What I do and say is based on what I have learned from others and from experience. My system is just **a** system. It is not **the** system but it is the one I use. I offer some points but consider them as just one of many possibilities. Use what pleases you.

Before I scan an object, I consider the amount of detail in the image and the origin of the image. If the digitized image is to be archived, has fine detail, and is grayscale, I will scan in color at 600 ppi. However, for detailed color prints, I scan at 300 ppi. If my first scan shows something interesting, I may double those figures and scan again. I may not need that high a resolution but if I do, I have it. The resulting file is saved in TIFF format and archived on Compact Disk. I will next open the original TIFF file in an image enhancement program and, if needed, adjust the color. The original print may have had brilliant color but over the years the colors have faded. Often a color shift toward red will occur. Many times a lot can be done to improve the colors.

If the photograph has been mishandled, it may have specks, a fold or even be torn in pieces. With time, patience and the right software, amazing results can be achieved. Once I am satisfied with the enhancement or repair, I save it to a new file in TIFF format on CD.

Let's say that the original print was an 8" x 10" grayscale portrait from the waist up and scanned at 600 ppi with 24-bit color.
(8 times 600) times (10 times 600) times 3 = 86.4MB. This is okay on an archive CD but not for most working copies.

The next step is to crop the image as needed and determine the color and resolution needed for a particular purpose. Some possible purposes for an image are: viewing full screen in a slideshow, printing in a report, viewing in the **Image** window, or including in a chart.

Most pictures contain more than the desired image. I cropped my original print to 5" x 4" and converted to grayscale. Cropping simply means that I selected just part of the picture and discarded what was extraneous.

If the original object was B&W, I will change the working copy to B&W. If it was grayscale, that is what I convert to. Many old pictures have a brownish tone. If it is truly brown tones, it may be a sepia print. More likely, the print is grayscale and the color you see is from dust and smoke. These effects are a form of damage and can often be fixed using a histogram. I will not go into detail about using histograms but **A Few Scanning Tips** does.
My image is now 5" x 4" and that is too large. One use will be in a report and I want the image 3 inches wide. To change the printed dimensions I will scale the image. Scaling means that I will compress the image to fit the space. Scaling is different than re-sampling, (scaling does not lose data). It means we

are putting the same data into a larger or smaller space.

Re-sampling (down sampling) means that I am changing the file size by discarding some of the data. For my cropped image I want 300 ppi for the printer. I will scale the image to 3 inches and re-sample the image to 300 ppi. The result is a 1,028 KB TIFF file or 229 KB JPEG file. It will be a larger file but I will leave it in TIFF. See Lossy Formats, page 22.

Now that I have a file suitable for printing, I need to consider other uses. I will use this picture in **Slideshow Manager** and view it full screen in a 1024 x 768 area. However, 614 x 768 pixels will be full height on screen so I re-sample again and save.
I also want to use this picture in a chart where it will be 1 inch square. When the chart is printed, the printer will use 300 ppi so I want a 300 x 300 image. Since the image is not square, I will use 240 x 300 pixels.

I also want this image to appear in the Image window and 240 x 300 pixels will work fine there. Others may like a larger Image window. If so, another copy may be needed. I have not mentioned another use – images on a web site.
If you have been counting, I now have two image files for archive and three for TMG. An important fact is that all images loaded into **Slideshow Manager** are stored in the Slideshow folder. That leaves me with two more copies. I will load the 300 x 300 image into **Exhibit Log** and make it Primary if it is attached to a person.

The last image, the one I will use just for printouts, will go on a CD. The path on the CD will be exactly like the path for the copy in **Exhibit Log** except for the drive letter. If you use the default folder, it will be:
C:\Program Files\The Master Genealogist\Pics.
If your CD drive is drive D, then the path for the CD is:
D:\Program Files\The Master Genealogist\Pics.

Using Windows™ Explorer, go to the Pics folder and rename it something like "2Pics" so that **Exhibit Log** cannot find **C:\…\Pics**. In TMG, go to **Preferences > Current Project Options > Advanced > Exhibit folder** and enter **D:\Program Files\The Master Genealogist\Pics**. When you open **Exhibit Log** you will see a similar image but it will not be the same file. **Exhibit Log** will have used the file from **D:\…\Pics** because **C:\…\Pics** no longer exists, after being renamed. Print your reports, or whatever it is you are doing, and you will have the proper image file for the task.

I have referred to CDs; but Zip disks, or other removable media, will work. So will a second hard drive, or a second folder on the same hard drive. You can't have two folders with the same path/name on one drive but you can change folder names to, in effect, toggle between folders. Let's say that you have these folders:

  C:\My Pictures\Large
  C:\My Pictures\Medium
  C:\My Pictures\Small

You placed your full sized image files into the Large folder. You placed smaller copies, using the same file name, in the Medium folder and even smaller copies in the Small folder. Using the files in Small, you loaded the exhibits into **Exhibit Log**.

Note: Use of small image files will allow **Exhibit Log** to open faster. If you want to make a report using the files in the **Medium** folder, then using Windows™ Explorer, temporarily change your directory to:

  C:\My Pictures\Large
  C:\My Pictures\Small
  C:\My Pictures\2Small

If **Exhibit Log** expects to find an exhibit file at **C:\My Pictures\Small\Jones44.jpg** and **Jones44.jpg** is found, that will be loaded, even if the file is larger or smaller.

It is important to note that what matters is that the path matches what is entered in Preferences and the file name is the same. The file could be for an image of something else. **Exhibit Log** will not care. How might that fact be used? In SAMPLE, you have Frank's image named "FALEXAND.JPG" and it is primary. For the task at hand you want to have a file named **TN_MAP.TIF** in place of Frank's image. You can change **FALEXAND.JPG** to **F_ALEXAND.JPG**, rename **TN_MAP.TIF** to **FALEXAND.JPG** and place it in the folder with Frank's image. When you print your report, you will see the map instead of Frank's image. The fact that you used a TIFF or other format in place of a

JPEG or other format does not matter in Exhibit Log.

As you have been reading, you may have been wishing you had a CD recorder, Zip drive or even a second hard drive. If storage space is at premium for you, you can't waste it on multiple copies of the same image. In that case, I would use **Slideshow Manager** to store all of my exhibit files. That will place a copy in the Slideshow folder and the temporary copy can be deleted. Also, change the path in **Exhibit folder** in **Preferences** to the path for the **Slideshow** folder.

If the Slideshow folder is used as your primary storage location, one image file can serve many uses. The same file can be used in multiple slideshows and multiple times in **Exhibit Log**. By making multiple slideshows, images can be grouped together by family lines or by image type. You can add a description of each image and you can drag them into the sequence you prefer.

Slideshow Manager was designed for viewing, not maintaining a collection, but it will work. Since one image file can be utilized in several slideshows, you might have a picture of Tom Jones' tombstone in your 'Tombstone' slideshow and use the same picture in your 'Tom Jones Family' slideshow. You might also have it in **Exhibit Log** attached to Tom Jones' Burial tag and to a source. All this and more with just one file.

If you have just one hard disk drive and if you intend to add a lot of objects, I strongly recommend that you consider a large second hard drive and a CD recorder. Image files can be very large, and they will quickly fill a small hard drive.
Hopefully I have given you enough information so that you can develop a system for handling your object files and the objects themselves.

Lossy Formats

JPEG – Joint Photographic Experts Group is the best format for digital images that must be in a small file since it will often compress to $1/10^{th}$ the size. While the small file size is always a benefit, it comes with a price. JPG is lossy. This means that each time the file is opened in an image editor and saved it is compressed again. Each time it is compressed, more quality is lost. Greater compression settings also yield greater loss. You can open and close a JPEG image as many times as you want and no loss will occur but each time that you use "Save" or "Save as" to save that file, loss will occur. For this reason, archive copies should not be stored using the JPEG format. If the only copy you have is *.jpg, open it in your image editor and save it in another format like TIFF. Or ensure that you never make and save changes to the original JPEG. This will not fix what has been lost but it will prevent additional loss.

Photo Shop® is a registered trademark of Adobe Systems Incorporated.

FotoAlbum™ is a trademarks of FotoTime, Inc.

Chapter 13 - Generating Charts for Use in Visual Chartform™
By Robin Lamacraft

Should I use a chart or a report?

The charts produced by **Visual Chartform™** (VCF) are graphical outputs that can extend over many pieces of paper or cover a *very large* piece of paper. The Standard Reports that produce page-oriented text or word-processor documents are described in *Chapter 10, Customizing Reports*.

VCF is a separate but tightly coupled chart-drawing application, which is used by TMG to construct its charts. This separation of functionality provides exceptional power and flexibility found in no other genealogical chart construction software to date. This chapter describes the settings that you can make within TMG to get the desired chart constructed. The later part of this chapter gives guidelines on how to make those charts more effective.

How do you make a chart?

Making a chart in The Master Genealogist™ (TMG) is a simple process.

Here is an *overview* of that sequence:

1. Select *one of* the following alternatives from the **Main Menu**:
   - **Reports > Ancestor Box Chart**
   - **Reports > Descendant Box Chart**
   - **Reports > Hourglass Box Chart**
   - **Reports > Fan Chart**

2. Select a **Chart configuration** on the **Report Definition screen**.

3. (Optional) Click [Options] to adjust any settings in this configuration.

4. Click [Make Chart].

The above steps are described in this chapter.

The editing, saving and printing of a chart within VCF are described in *Chapter 14, Working with Charts in Visual Chartform™*.

What is a Box Chart?

In a box chart, the details about a person are placed within a rectangular area which traditionally has an outline drawn around it, hence the name box. If the box chart flows from one generation to the next vertically on the page, these boxes are arranged in rows. Columns of boxes are used in charts that flow horizontally across the page from one generation to the next. Connecting lines are always drawn from the child to the parent. Where siblings are shown, the boxes are drawn in their birth date sequence.

Charts may be drawn in one of 4 orientations (or flows) *left to right*, *right to left*, *top to bottom* or *bottom to top*.

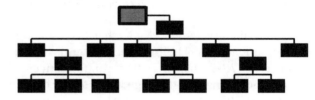

Figure 13-1: A Top to Bottom Descendant Box Chart

A **Descendant Box Chart** starts at a focus person and progresses forward in time displaying the details of successive descendant generations. *Figure 13-1* shows a gray filled rectangle representing the details of the focus person and a number of black filled rectangles each representing another person's details. Descendant Box Charts are also known as **drop-charts**.

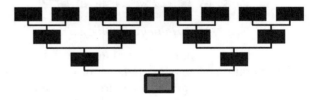

Figure 13-2: A Bottom to Top Ancestor Box Chart

An **Ancestor Box Chart** starts at the focus person and progresses backwards in time displaying the details of successive ancestral generations. In *Figure 13-2* the gray filled rectangle represents the details of the focus person and each black filled rectangle represents another person's details. Ancestor Box Charts are also known as **pedigree charts**.

The **Hourglass Box Chart** is a combination of an ancestor box chart joined to a descendant box chart where both charts start from the same focus person,

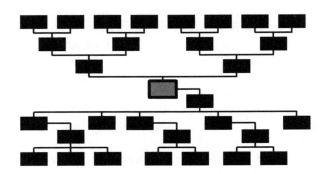

Figure 13-3: An Ancestors at top Hourglass Box Chart

the gray filled rectangle; each chart is drawn in opposite orientation. The traditional hourglass chart *(see Figure 13-3)* has a bottom to top **ancestor chart** at the top half of the page and a top to bottom **descendant chart** drawn below it using a common box for the focus person.

What is a Fan Chart?

Figure 13-4: A Half-circle Fan Chart

A fan chart is a curved version of an ancestor chart. Each generation of persons is bent into an arc and successive ancestral generations are placed on arcs of larger and larger radius. Because of the restricted space on the perimeter of an ancestral fan chart there are limited options available for the user to vary the way that these charts are constructed. These charts can be constructed from a full circle, half-circle *(see Figure 13-4),* down to any wedge shape and may be drawn in any orientation. Fan charts are also known as **circular charts**.

COMMENT - An ancestral fan chart does not display clearly when there are a large number of generations (over about 10) as the outer ring can become very crowded. It is a rare data set that has researched almost all 1023 ancestors of the 10 generations of the focus person. As the number of generations is increased the chart needs to be made very much bigger. It then needs to be printed on a large-sized piece of paper or many smaller sheets.

Selecting the type of chart

Each of the chart types has a purpose. You should consider both the reason for creating the chart (*What is it to show?*) and how much detail should the chart show (*Who is the audience?*). Do you want to show the ancestors of a particular person or the descendants of that particular person or **both** the ancestors and the descendants of one person? How much detail should you include for each person? How will the chart be viewed? Do you need to build a combination of charts to show the information required?

Once you have selected a chart type from the **Reports** menu the **Report Definition screen** will open.

The Reports Definition Screen

The **Configuration name** pull-down on the **Report Definition Screen** (*see Figure 13-5*), can be used to show and select a configuration for this chart. TMG comes with one standard definition for each chart type. Before you start to change any settings it is recommended that you click [Add] and create a personal copy of this definition under a new meaningful name. This will let you select your version for later charts with your personal adjustments.

The settings in the selected **Configuration name** are used to construct the chart when you click [Make Chart]. You may make adjustments by clicking [Options] first.

WARNING - Any changes that you make while within the **Chart Options screen** may overwrite the previous settings in the selected **Configuration name**.

Next you select the *focus person.*

When you select the **Destination** of the chart generation process, you have two choices:

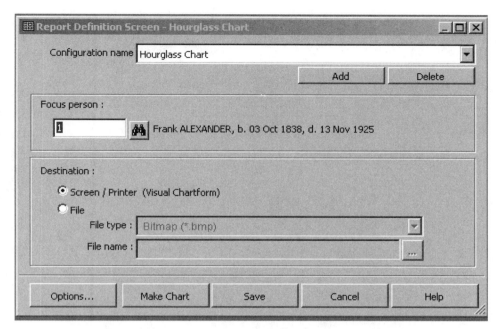

Figure 13-5: The Report Definition Screen

- **Screen** - this will cause VCF to open where you can view and edit the chart.

- **File** – this will save the chart as a graphical format file. You can select the name of the file, the folder where it is to be saved and the graphical format for the file, (for example BMP, JPG or VC2).

Click [Make Chart]. This may take some time to complete. If you selected the **Screen Destination**, VCF will open to display a chart generated using the default settings of that charting configuration.

NOTE - All Chart Options have sensible defaults so you don't have look at the Chart Options unless you find something that you would like to change.

TIP - To see the current values of the chart settings or make adjustments before making the chart click [Options] and the **Chart Options** screen will open.

Select a **Configuration name** and then click [Delete] to delete it. Note that you are unable to delete the Standard definition.

If you make changes in Chart Options that you wish to save without creating a chart then click [Save].

Each **Configuration name** that is saved creates a file with the .RPT extension by that name in the folder where Reports are saved. This folder is by default the Reports folder of the TMG5 installation

folder. However, you may change this in **File > Preferences; Project Settings > Advanced**. Unfortunately, VCF chart form does not also use this setting so chart files will by default be saved in the Reports folder of the TMG5 installation folder. You need to navigate to an alternative folder if it is your wish not to store user files within the Application file folders.

In the following description, we will look at the **Chart Options** screen tab by tab.

NOTE - In the following sections describing the tabs of the Chart Options screen, the screen captures for Hourglass Box Charts are used. These contain all the settings for both Ancestor Box Charts and Descendant Box Charts. The corresponding screens for the Chart Options for Fan Charts are similar but not identical

The Chart Options screen

The **Chart Options Screen** (*see Figure 13-6*) allows you to change (customize) the way in which a chart is constructed and displayed.

For **Box Charts** (Ancestor, Descendant and Hourglass) the tabs are labeled:

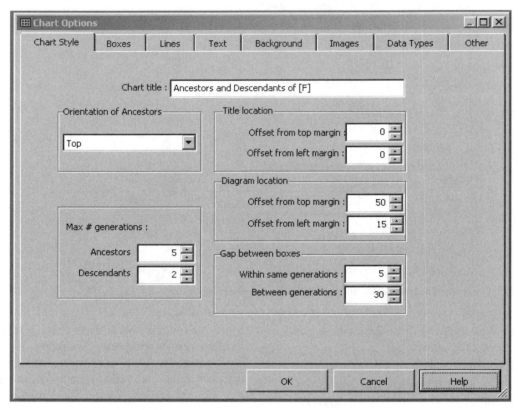

Figure 13-6: Chart Options Screen, Chart Style Tab

- **Chart Style** - title, orientation, generations and spacing
- **Boxes** - size, fill, border, accents and frames
- **Lines** - styles, widths, color
- **Text** - fonts, size, color
- **Background** - solid or image
- **Images** - images in each box
- **Data Types** - designing the contents of a box
- **Other** - settings about names, places, etc

For **Fan Charts** the tabs are labeled:
- **Chart Style** - title, orientation, generations and spacing

- **Researcher Box** - size, fill, border, accents and frames
- **Lines** - styles, widths, color
- **Text** - fonts, size, color
- **Background** - solid or image
- **Other** - settings about names, places, etc.

Box Chart Notation

Figure 13-7 below illustrates terms that are used in the following descriptions. The single letters in small rectangles are referred to in the text of those items

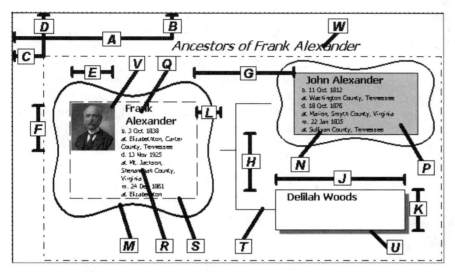

Figure 13-7: Some Components of a Box Chart

Chart Options: Chart Style tab

The settings available in the **Chart Style** tab are:

- **Chart title** (*see Figure 13-7*, W) - a text string that may include the symbol **[F]**, which will be replaced by the primary name of the *focus person*, for example "Ancestors of [F]" (without the quotes) will become "Ancestors of Frank Alexander" on the chart when Frank Alexander is the focus person.

  TIP - This feature means that you can configure a chart once and not have to edit the title if you choose a different focus person.

- **Title location** (*see Figure 13-7*, A and B) – Specify in pixels the distance from the top-left of the canvas where the title will be placed. This position can be edited after the chart has been constructed if your choice happens to overlap with the chart details.

- **Chart size** - Set the maximum number of generations. In the case of Hourglass Box Charts, there are settings for the maximum number of generations for both Ancestors and Descendants.

  TIP - Initially set the maximum number of generations to a low value while you run some test charts to validate the layout and other settings for your chart. This will speed up your

refinement cycle, as it will reduce the size of the test charts to be constructed.

- **Diagram location** (*see Figure 13-7*, C and D) - Specify in pixels the distance from the top left of the canvas where the rectangle bounding the chart will be placed. This position can be edited after the chart has been constructed if your choice has too much or too little border space.

- **Gap between boxes** (*see Figure 13-7*, G and H) (BOX CHARTS ONLY) - Specify in pixels the gap between the boxes from one generation to the next and secondly, the gap between boxes in the same generation.

COMMENT - Both these gap settings are critical for a well-presented chart. They cannot be changed globally after the chart has been generated. It is not possible in a single command in VCF to increase the spacing between all boxes. However you can drag boxes to adjust each gap on a gap-by-gap basis. It is therefore much easier to set this before you generate a chart rather than retro-editing the spacing. If box **frames** (see section on Accents below) are included, both gaps between boxes should be made larger; this compensates for the space taken up by the frames.

- **Orientation** (BOX CHARTS ONLY) - this is a critical setting determining the final shape of the finished chart and whether the chart will satisfy the purpose for which it is intended. For an Ancestor Chart or a Descendant Chart, there are four options, *left to right*, *right to left*, *top to bottom* and *bottom to top*.

Figures 13-8 through 13-11 illustrate the orientation options using a descendant box chart as an example. In an Hourglass Chart, again there are four options *left*, *right*, *top* and *bottom*.

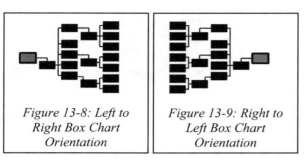

Figure 13-8: Left to Right Box Chart Orientation   *Figure 13-9: Right to Left Box Chart Orientation*

Charts that are oriented from **top** or **bottom** will be shorter in height and potentially very wide compared with the same chart with a **left** or **right** orientation.

Figure 13-10: Bottom to Top Box Chart

TIP - Chart orientation is a very important factor in building more complex charts or when building sub-charts that you can later paste together on a single canvas within VCF.

CHART ORIENTATION AND CHART SIZE: Charts with generations displayed horizontally, e.g., using either *top to bottom* or *bottom to top* orientations, are wider and shallower in height than the *right to left* and *left to right* orientations. This is because the width of the *top to bottom* or *bottom to top* charts is the sum of the widths of the boxes in the generation with the most persons. The height of the chart is related to the height of boxes in each generation multiplied by the number of generations displayed. In charts with generations displayed vertically, e.g., *right to left* and *left to right* orientations, the height of the chart is the sum of the heights of the boxes in the generation with the most people. The width of these charts is related to the box width multiplied by the number of generations displayed.

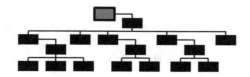

Figure 13-11: Top to Bottom Box Chart Orientation

- **Fan Dimensions** (<u>FAN CHARTS ONLY</u>) - Set the **starting angle** in degrees and the **total arc angle** in degrees. The starting angle has its zero at 9 on a clock face and increases in a clockwise direction with 12 on the clock face being 90 degrees, 3 on the clock face being 180 degrees and 6 on the clock face being 270 degrees as starting angles. A full circle is 360 degrees of total arc angle while a half circle is 180 degrees. There are some examples in the VCF on-line Help file.

- **Arc Radius** (<u>FAN CHARTS ONLY</u>) - Set the minimum number of non-curved text generations. In the center of a fan chart there is more space to place the person details. In the curved text generations the person details are output as if they were part of the rim of the wheel of that radius. The number of non-curved text generations is the number of generations for which the person details are needed to be output like the spokes of a wheel (that is, along a radius) for them to fit in the available space.

TIP (<u>FAN CHARTS ONLY</u>) - Do not make the number of generations too large (the effective maximum is about ten), as there is little space to output the details of persons at the perimeter. The number of generations of curved text probably should not exceed four. Fan charts that are 240 degrees or 180 degrees total arc angle are often easier to read.

Chart Options: Researcher Box tab (**FAN CHARTS ONLY**)

The **Researcher Information** tab controls the box that contains the researcher's name, address and the date on which the chart was prepared:

- **Box Size** - - The box **Width** sets the width of the Researcher Information box placed on the chart. The height of all boxes cannot be less then the **Minimal height**. If there is more content in a box its height will increase automatically. You may choose to make the box wider or narrower when editing the chart and the height will change to compensate for the change in width.

- **Box Fill** - Set the type of fill color and pattern for the researcher box.

- **Frame** (outside box) - The researcher box can either have a gray shadow or not.

NOTE: The settings on this tab do not become active until the **Researcher Information** setting on the **Other** tab is set to one of *Top left*, *Top right*, *Bottom left* or *Bottom right*.

Chart Options: Boxes tab
(BOX CHARTS ONLY)
The **Boxes** tab (*see Figure 13-12*) has a series of settings:

- **Box size** (<u>BOX CHARTS ONLY</u>) - The box **Width** (*see Figure 13-7*, J) (in Pixels) sets the width of all boxes constructed in the chart. The height of all boxes cannot be less then the **Minimal height** (*see Figure 13-7*, K). If there is more content in a box its height will increase automatically. You may choose to make an individual box wider or narrower when editing the chart and the height will change to compensate for the change in width. <u>If you</u>

<u>want to make all boxes equal in height then</u> increase the **Minimal Height** to be higher than the tallest box.

- **Box Border** (*see Figure 13-7*, N) (<u>BOX CHARTS ONLY</u>) - The outline of the box can have a number of styles, colors and line widths or the outline may be *Transparent* (no outline drawn (*see Figure 13-7*, S)). Select a color by clicking […].

NOTE - If the line width is greater than one pixel then the broken line styles are not available. Consider the line width and color according to the guidelines given later in this chapter.

<u>Box fill</u> (*see Figure 13-7*, P) (<u>BOX CHARTS ONLY</u>) - If you want the background image to be behind the contents of the

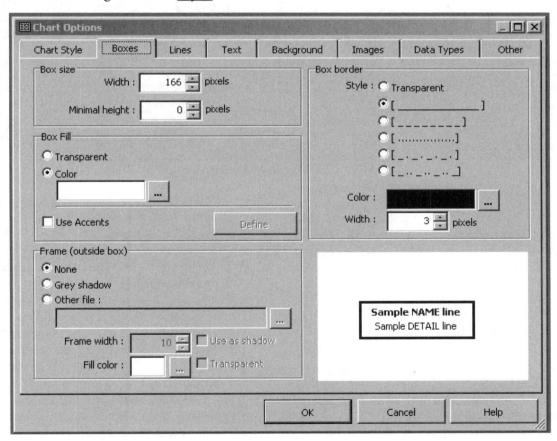

Figure 13-12: Chart Options Screen, Boxes Tab

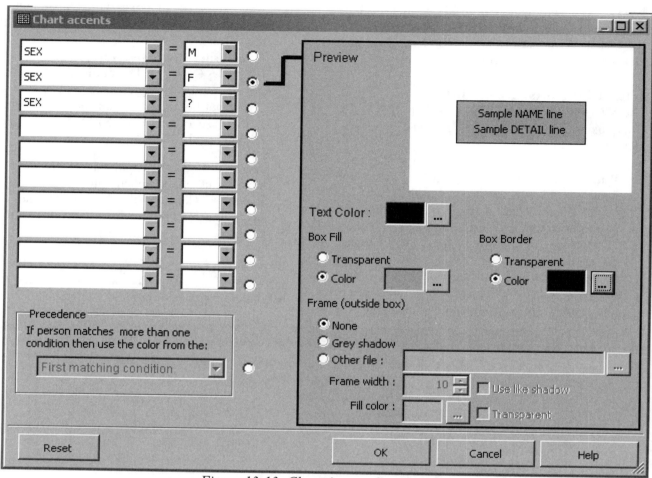

Figure 13-13: Chart Accents Screen

box or you have <u>no</u> colored background then choose **Transparent**. If you want all box fill colors to be the same select a color by clicking [...]. To use accents to differentiate between boxes according to flags attached to each person check the **Use Accents** box. The **Chart accent** screen will open (see the **Chart Accents** section below).

- **Frame (outside box)** (*see Figure 13-7*, M) (<u>BOX CHARTS ONLY</u>) Frames come in many designs. The **Box Border** is usually set to **Transparent** when using Frames.

- Select **Other File** and click [...] then the **Select Frame** screen will open (see the **Chart Frames** section below).

COMMENT - A more traditional style of chart would have the **Frame** set to *None* or *Gray Shadow* (*see Figure 13-7*, U).

Chart accents (<u>BOX CHARTS ONLY</u>)

The **chart accenting** (*see Figure 13-13*) feature can control the Box fill color, Box border color, Box text color and Box frame of each box on a chart. The values of the flags associated with each person in the data set (*see Chapter 5, Customizing the Data*) are used to provide this control. There are ten accenting conditions that may be specified. Each accenting condition tests for equality of one flag to one of its defined values. If more than one accenting condition apply to a person, then a rule is provided to control the outcome. The chart boxes of persons whose flag values do not satisfy any accenting condition are drawn using the settings on the Boxes tab. The [Reset] button will set the chart accents to the first 10 screen accents that defined using flags settings. Screen accents that do not use flags in their conditions or there are 10 accents already in use are discarded.

NOTE - The color settings for **Names** and **Data lines** chosen on the **Text** tab are overridden, and *black* is used while accents are turned on.

To apply an accent, select one of the ten flag equality conditions. Then use the left pull-down to reveal a list of the flags used in the current data set from which to select the required one. Now select the pull-down to the right of the equals sign and select the value that you want that flag to equal for this accenting. Note that the radio button for that accent has a dot in it. This enables the use of the controls in the box marked Preview. Here you can control a number of effects and preview the results:

- **Text color** - The same actions as the text color buttons on the **Text** tab.
- **Box fill** - The same actions as the **Box fill** on the **Boxes** tab.
- **Box border** - The same actions as the **Box border** on the **Boxes** tab.
- **Frame (outside box)** - The same actions as the **Frame (outside box)** on the **Boxes** tab.

If the flag values of a person match more than one accenting condition, then on the **Precedence** pull-down you have the following choices *First matching condition* or *Conflict color*. With this later case the user can define another set of box attributes.

TIP - Use accents to color-code your chart in the following ways:
- Sex of descendant and marriage partners
- Place or country of birth, death or marriage
- Trait, like red hair, or medical condition

Box Frames (BOX CHARTS ONLY)

A **frame** (*see Figure 13-14*) is a way of decorating a **chart** with a scalable graphic (seen in the Select Frame screen below) that surrounds chart boxes. TMG comes with a library of frames that is divided

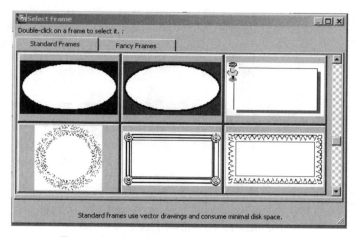

Figure 13-14: The Select Frame Screen

into 2 categories **Standard Frames** and **Fancy Frames**. In *Chapter 14, Working with Charts in Visual Chartform™*, there are instructions of how to design and save your own frames.

- **Standard Frames** are efficient. They are vector drawings and consume minimal disk space.
- **Fancy frames** that offer more intricate patterns are based on bitmapped graphics and use *much* more hard disk space for a saved chart.

TIP - Each frame has a **Border thickness** (*see Figure 13-7*, L) that needs to be considered when setting the **Gap between boxes** (s*ee Figure 13-7*, G and H) on the **Chart Style** tab. When you use frames in a chart-accenting scheme it is advisable to choose frames that have similar border thickness.

Chart Options: Lines tab

The Lines tab (*see Figure 13-15*) has the following settings:

- **Connector lines** (*see Figure 13-7*, T) - Set the line style, line width and line color for the lines from **parent to child** and **between spouses**.
- **Sibling lines** (ANCESTOR BOX and HOURGLASS BOX CHARTS ONLY) - Set the line style, line width and line color for the lines that **join the siblings** of ancestors (when the **Include Siblings of Ancestors** option on the **Other** tab is checked.

NOTE - Broken line styles are not available if you select a line width greater than one pixel.

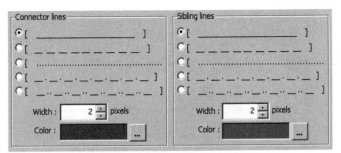

Figure 13-15: Part of Chart Options Screen: Lines Tab

Figure 13-16:Part of Chart Options Screen: Text Tab

TIP - Line widths of one pixel are too narrow for use on charts to be viewed at a distance. On some printers they are not printed clearly. Experiment with widths of two or three pixels, especially if you are printing a chart on a colored background. You may find that some gray colors do not print well on some printers. To avoid confusion, you are advised not make the two line style settings the same (color or style) unless you make then significantly different in width.

Chart Options: Text tab

The **Text** tab (*see Figure 13-16*) has a series of settings (each of the same form) for four different parts of a chart. Each setting has two buttons:

- Clicking [F] (abbreviation of Font) opens a font selector screen. Here you can select the font, font style, and size.

   TIP - When selecting a font, remember that it is better to have not more than three fonts in use on a chart. If you intend to have your chart printed on another computer (that is, not by the computer on which that the chart was constructed), then that other computer will also need your selected font installed.

- Clicking [C] (abbreviation of Color) opens a color selector screen. When choosing a color please re-read the section above on Text Color Selection.

The four different text settings that can be set independently are:

- **Title** (*see Figure 13-7*, W) - The size and color of the chart title can be controlled to distinguish it from the rest of the content of the chart.

- **Names** (*see Figure 13-7*, Q) - The top line of text in each box contains the Primary Name of that person.

- **Data lines** (*see Figure 13-7*, R) (<u>BOX CHARTS ONLY</u>)- The subsequent information lines in a box, Birth, Death, Marriage, etc.

   TIP - It is better if the Name is in larger font size than the rest of the information in the box (the **Data Lines**). It is often useful to distinguish the Name from the other information by making it a different color or different font. The choice of font size is dependent on the use of the chart and the desire to produce a chart on a small number of pages.

- **Researcher info** (<u>FAN CHARTS ONLY</u>) - The font settings for text lines of the Researcher's Box.

- **Manual entry (default)** - The default font settings used when editing this chart in VCF.

Chart Options: Background tab

The **Background** tab (*see Figure 13-17*) allows the following styles of background:

- **Solid** - Select a color to be placed as a background of your chart. Choose white if you don't want any background. See the section above on color selection to achieve a better output.

- **Image** - Click [...] to select an image as a background for your chart. Be aware that the image will get stretched to fit the chart canvas and may become distorted.

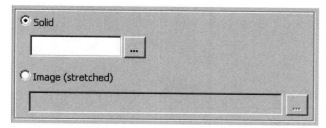

*Figure 13-17: Part of Chart Options Screen:
Background Tab*

TIP - Covering all the paper with ink by including a solid background or using an image as a background takes time to print and increases the cost. Using an image may not give you the effect that you expect because of the way the image is stretched. A large high-resolution image will greatly increase the size of the chart file.

TIP - You will have control over a background image if you wait to insert it using tools in VCF.

Chart Options: Images tab (BOX CHARTS ONLY)

You can choose whether you wish boxes to contain the primary image of a person (*see Figure 13-7*, V). By using the Exhibit Log, a primary image for each person may be defined *(see Chapter 12, Multimedia)*. Use the **Images** tab to define the placement of the image.

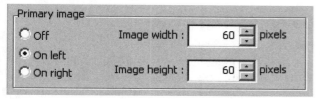

Figure 13-18: Part of Chart Options Screen: Images Tab

The setting '*Off*' means no box on the chart has an image displayed within it.

If there is a primary image associated with the person of a box, then the setting of *On Left* or *On Right* will place that image within the box at its top left or top right respectively. The other text information in the box (name, birth, death, etc) will be placed around the image. When there is no primary image for this person, then no space is left in the box for an image.

COMMENT - The **Image width** needs to be considered when setting the **Box Width** on the **Boxes** tab.

The output **Image Width** (*see Figure 13-7*, E) and **Image Height** (*see Figure 13-7*, F) in pixels may be set here. The choice of output image size is related to the size (in pixels) of the primary image. Condensing a high-resolution picture into a small number of pixels in the output is extremely wasteful of computing power and will make the construction of the chart and any editing operation much slower. These large image files also significantly increase the size of the chart file. The opposite is also true. Expanding a very low-resolution picture to fill a larger number of output pixels will create a poor quality display in which the underlying pixel structure is evident.

TIP – High-resolution Primary images used within person boxes on charts should be reduced to a lower resolution in an image manipulation package before they are used in the Exhibit Log *(see Chapter 12, Multimedia)*.

Chart Options: Data Types tab

(BOX CHARTS ONLY)
The **Data Types** tab (*see Figure 13-19*) has a series of settings:

- **Box type** (BOX CHARTS ONLY) - Depending on the chart type this will list descriptions of the types of related persons whose **Box contents** can be separately customized on this tab. When you select one of the entries in this box entry the list of 9 items under **Box contents** will show the default items for that type of box.

  TIP - Review each entry in this list to ensure that the boxes for all the persons on the chart have the content that you expect. The abbreviation **Abbr** that is output on some Data Type lines is set on the Tag Type definition.

- **Box contents** (BOX CHARTS ONLY) - Clicking on one of the [1] to [9] buttons will open the **Selected tag types** screen (*see Figure 13-21 in the next section*).

- **Place preposition** (BOX CHARTS ONLY) - Allows a selection of 3 alternatives (*At, In* or *(blank)*) for the preposition that may be inserted before any place information on the chart. NB - This choice is dependent on the way that the place information has been entered in the data set and which Places options have been selected on the **Other** tab.

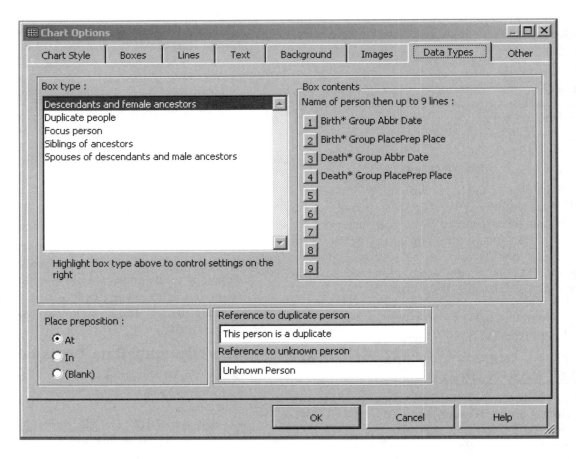

Figure 13-19: The Chart Options Screen: Data Type Tab

- **Reference to duplicate person**
  (BOX CHARTS ONLY) - You may enter a phrase to be output within a duplicated person's box. The default phrase is *"This person is a duplicate"*. When, in the contents of a Duplicated person Box type, the **Reference to a duplicate person** item has been selected, this duplicate person phrase will be output within subsequent boxes of persons that have already been displayed on the chart.

- **Reference to unknown person**
  (BOX CHARTS ONLY) - You may enter a phrase to be output within an unknown person's box. The default phrase is *"Unknown person"*.

Selected Tag Types
(BOX CHARTS ONLY)

As this list (*see Figure 13-20*) contains all Tag Types available in TMG you may find this list overpowering. It has over 1500 items on it that may be selected for output. Remember that this list is listed alphabetically and so even within one general area there may be many items that look similar. Select an item very carefully.

TIP - If you modify the selections here away from the standard, it is suggested that you create some small charts (by limiting the number of generations) and focused around persons that have this different kind of data to check that the output is what you expect.

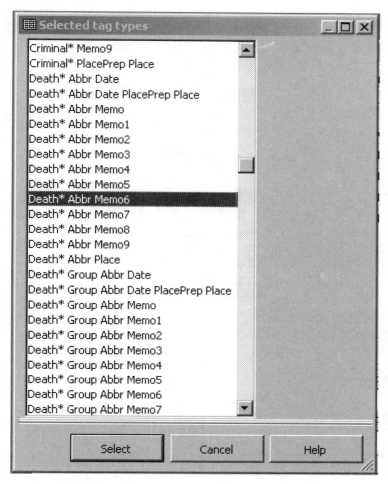

Figure 13-20: Selected Tag Types Screen

Chart Options: Other tab

The **Other** tab (*see Figure 13-21*) has a series of settings:

- **Identifiers** - These four choices allow the person **ID number** or the **Reference field** or **Both** or **None** to be appended to each person's name on the chart.
- **Surety** - The surety threshold acts as a filter determining which persons are shown in the chart (see *Chapter 7, Sources* for an explanation of Surety levels). Primary relationships with a surety less then the threshold will not be displayed.
- **Exclusion** - Checking these boxes **Show excluded data** and **Show sensitive data** (excluded data and sensitive data are described in *Chapter 5, Customizing the Data*) allows

suitably annotated tag information to be output that would normally not be shown.

- **Places** (BOX CHARTS ONLY) - Checking these boxes select the Place elements that will be output wherever a place has been entered in TMG. *Use Place Styles* is an alternative method of controlling the place output on a chart. When this option is checked, the Output Template of each place's Place Style is used to control the output of the place information.
- **Names** – This gives three choices, all for the capitalization of names, with **No Caps** meaning display the name as it is in the data set, while **Surname caps** makes all letters in a surname capitals and **All Caps** capitalizes both given names and surnames.
- **Miscellaneous** - A collection of check boxes to turn on or off certain chart construction details.

Include siblings of ancestors (ANCESTOR and HOURGLASS BOX CHARTS ONLY) - Output the siblings of each ancestor thus showing all the children of the ancestor's parents.

Blanks for missing data - Outputs a line for data that is missing in the data set.

Remove blank lines (BOX CHARTS ONLY) - Does not output the blank lines caused by items that are not set for that person.

Suppress details for living people - Replaces all details with the text "is living" NOTE - This option affects those persons whose LIVING flag equals "Y" to suppress their details. Persons with values of LIVING equals "?" and "N" are not suppressed.

Visible connection ports (BOX CHARTS ONLY) - Makes the connection points on the chart visible (these may be turned off in VCF).

Month spelled out (BOX CHARTS ONLY) - Output the full month name instead of the usual three-letter abbreviation.

Center curved text (FAN CHARTS ONLY) – Centers text versus left justifying each line of text in the box.

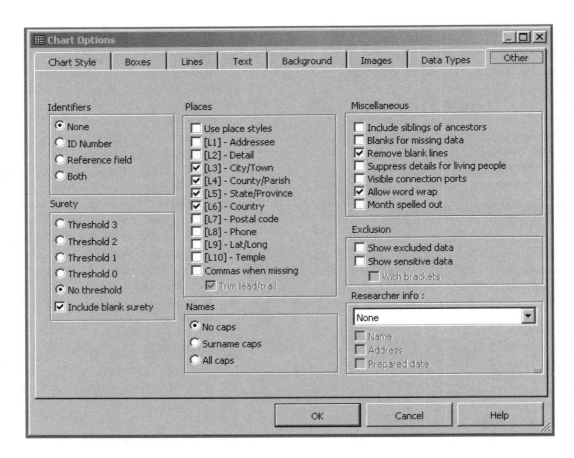

Figure 13-21: Chart Options Screen, Other Tab

Arrows on lines (<u>FAN CHARTS ONLY</u>) - Places arrows on the lines between the parents that point to their child.

Life span dates (<u>FAN CHARTS ONLY</u>) - Outputs life span as (***Birth date - death date***) or (***Birth year - death year***).

Researcher Info - If the Researcher box is requested it is placed at one corner (***Top left***, ***Top right***, ***Bottom left*** or ***Bottom right***) of the chart to identify its author. Optionally the researcher's ***Name***, ***Address*** or ***Prepared Date*** can be included.

GUIDELINES FOR CHARTING

The scope of a box chart

Each chart is constructed by VCF starting at a focus person. The chart is extended away from the focus person by adding appropriately related persons to the list of persons in the chart. This process continues until either there are no further persons in

that branch in the data set or the generation limit has been reached.

The focus person is specified on the **Report Definition screen**. The maximum number of generations is specified on the **Chart Style** tab.

TIP - This process does not always produce a chart that only includes the persons that you want to show. In the descendant box chart in *Figure 13-22*, the top gray box is the focus person. If the number of generations had been set to 4 then the chart would finish where the dashed line cuts off lower generations. Sometimes you want a chart that only displays those persons represented by the solid black boxes, while not showing the person boxes with white diagonal crosses.

To make a chart that cannot be specified using the maximum number of generations means that either you need to prune the tree of relationships before generating a chart or you must delete the unwanted persons from the chart after it has been generated. (Both approaches can involve a lot of editing time.)

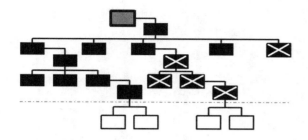

Figure 13-22: Pruning the Scope of a Descendant Chart

- Within TMG, you could create a temporary new data set that matches the requirements and then create the chart using this temporary data set (*see Chapter 11, **Filters and Sorting**). Alternatively, you could modify the existing data set by altering the particular parent/child relationships to become non-primary before the chart is created. This removes a primary relationship to the next generation. In this case the primary status of these relationships would need to be restored after the chart had been constructed. However, using this method ensures the chart is constructed in an already compacted format.

- In the second method you generate the full chart then manually delete the branches that should not be displayed. Remember deleting branches can create large areas of white space. Further moving of parts of the chart is then necessary to eliminate these white holes.

Guidelines for color selection

You can select custom colors for lines, text, fill, and shadows *(see Figure 13-23)*. Here are some guidelines based on my personal experience to assist you make color selections.

The choice of a color is dependent on three considerations:

1. Is the color to be used as a foreground text or line to be contrasted against a background?
2. Is the color a background that covers a region of the chart? (E.g. a box fill, box shadow, or a solid background)
3. How is the chart to be finally produced? Is the chart to be printed on white paper and viewed at a distance of four feet (1.2m) or stored on a CD and displayed on a computer screen? Is it likely that those who view the chart may have poorer eyesight and therefore need higher contrast?

In general, the Basic 48 colors provided by the color selector are only suitable as intense foreground colors. It is stressed that all these colors are too intense to be used as fill colors for inkjet printing if another member of that same set is to be used as the foreground color. The colors seen on a computer screen often appear much paler than when finally printed by inkjet printers. You are advised to select custom colors for fill colors if you are printing on paper. You may use as many Custom Colors as you like but you can only save sixteen of them for easy later use.

There are two common methods of specifying colors used in computing – in general RGB (Red, Green, Blue) is used for computer monitors, while CMYK (Cyan, Magenta, Yellow, Black) is used in most inkjet printers. In TMG and VCF you specify colors in RGB but they have to be converted into CMYK for printing. The conversion between these two forms and the final rendering of colors is very process dependent. The choice of paper (e.g., coated, matte, gloss etc), the type and the resolution of the equipment together with the settings used in the printing process can lead to different qualities of finished product. Color printing should always be done on coated paper as this minimizes the bleeding of the ink droplets and also saves on ink. Hi-gloss or photo paper can greatly increase the cost over matte surfaced paper and is unnecessary unless the chart has high quality images within it.

Some inkjet printers and lower resolution laser printers cannot print clearly shades of gray text especially when the font size is also small (8pt and smaller). Small text is best printed in one of the 16 basic colors formed by the printer using simple combinations of the Cyan, Magenta, Yellow and Black ink colors. Larger text can be printed in other colors where the effect of individual dots of ink is masked. In small text the individual colored dots tend to give a broken edge to the typeface with some salt and pepper textures.

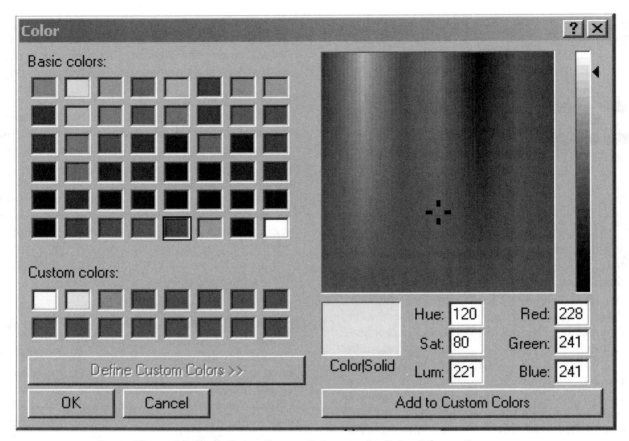

Figure 13-23: Defining Custom Colors on the Color Selector Screen

Guidelines for selecting background and fill colors for inkjet printing

These colors will print with a low intensity that will maintain a good contrast against black or darker colors.

1. Select a new Custom color box (you may also want to replace an existing one).
2. Click [Define Custom Colors >>].
3. Move the vertical slider at the right until the **Lum:** (luminance) value is between 210 (pale) and 230 (very pale). Using less than 210 will cause some colors (not all) to become too intense on some printers. At greater than 230, the color becomes almost the same as white.
4. Now select the cross in the rainbow colored space and drag it to the color of your preference.
5. If you want to save this color for a later use, click [Add to Custom Colors] then click [OK], otherwise click [OK].

Guidelines for selecting foreground text and line colors for printing

These colors will print with an intensity that will contrast against the background colors selected by the method above.

1. Select a new Custom color box (you may also want to replace an existing one).
2. Click [Define Custom Colors >>].
3. Move the vertical slider at the right until the **Lum:** (luminance) value is between 40 (very dark) and 120 (mid). Using greater than 120 will cause some colors (not all) give too little contrast. Below a luminance of 40, the colors are almost the same as black.
4. Now select the cross in the rainbow colored space and drag it to the color of your preference.
6. If you want to save this color for a later use, click [Add to Custom Colors] then click [OK], otherwise click [OK].

Guidelines for using images in charts

You should be aware that not all files that are labeled as images or have an image format specific extension are validly formatted image files. Some propriety software does not write files exactly to the common standard. Other software is tolerant of some of these shortcomings. Test every file to ensure that it will be previewed correctly in the Exhibit Log. If you find a supposedly graphic file that will not display within a VCF chart try reading them into another image manipulating program and save the image as a supported file type with a new name. Otherwise, you may have to re-capture the image (if you can).

Secondly, pictures that appear clearly on a computer monitor may not print on your or a commercial printer's equipment the way that you expect. Some colors will be darker than on the computer screen, some dark areas (like shadows) will lose detail. You may need to adjust these images to get the best result. Further study of this subject will aid in producing good results. It would be advisable to get some tests printed first by your printer before you commit to a larger more costly chart-printing job.

Images can be used in three ways within a chart:

1. **As a background for the whole chart.**
   BMP, JPEG, PCX, TIF, TIFF, TGA or EMF image format files can be used as a background. Consider the following.
   - The image will be 'stretched' to ensure that it matches the aspect ratio of the canvas on which the chart is drawn. (This can lead to gross distortions of the background. Any background image should have pale shades if dark colored connecting lines are used to maintain the contrast between these lines and the background.)
   - Using a background image increases the size of the chart file.
   - Using a background image often considerably increases the time taken to print a chart, the amount of ink used and (if it is done commercially) the cost to print it.

2. **As a primary image of a person placed within a box.** (BOX CHARTS ONLY)
   As before BMP, JPEG, PCX, TIF, TIFF, TGA or EMF image file formats can also be used for the primary image to be placed within a box. Be mindful of five issues.
   - Using internal images will considerably inflate the data set backup file size.
   - External images should not be moved once they have been associated with persons in a TMG data set.
   - The images used as primary pictures in boxes should not be original images. Rather these images should be cropped, re-sampled and resaved as smaller images with lower resolution than the pictures that you want to archive. For these passport-like shots that will be printed to fit within typically a 1.5 inch by 1.5 inches (40mm by 40mm) space in a box on a chart images that are 400 by 600 pixels seem quite adequate. Do not worry about the dpi (dots per inch) at which an image is saved. The important characteristic is to have sufficient pixels (but not an excessive number) in both directions. For inserting into chart boxes the images should not exceed 900 by 900 pixels in size.
     WARNING - Some people try to use too high a resolution with several thousand pixels in both directions for primary images in the Exhibit Log. This quickly inflates the size of chart files. Over 100 high-resolution images can lead to VC2 chart files that are more than 180Mb. If they are printed commercially they may cost much more to print because some commercial printers charge by time.
   - If you convert a color picture to a grayscale you may need to increase the contrast. Some image processing packages do not do a good job at this conversion and when the nominally B&W images are then printed on color equipment there is a bleeding of colors at some high contrast edges.

3. **As an annotation added to a chart** *(See Chapter 14, Working with Charts in Visual Chartform™).*
   Adjust the width in pixels and the height in pixels of each image used as an annotation to match the requirement of a maximum of 600 dots per inch (dpi) at their final printed size. These images can require very large amounts of storage for minimal visual gain. Please refer to

the comments about primary images attached to a person described in the previous section.

Charts can get very large

WARNING - Charts can become very large, sometimes over fifty feet (fifteen meters) in one direction. The settings that you choose can radically affect this size. Chart file sizes may be very large if the chart has a background image, has a lot of images on it, or a lot of frames on it.

WARNING - Users of the Windows 95™, Windows 98™ and Windows ME™ operating systems should be aware that there is a size limitation in the underlying Microsoft product that manifests itself at about twenty-eight feet (8.6 meters). The problem is due to an error in the scaling of large drawings leading to lines that disappear and come in from the opposite edge to where they were heading. (This problem does not occur with Windows NT™, Windows 2000™ or Windows XP™).

Relationships between persons within a chart

The charts constructed by VCF are **genealogical charts**; that is, the lines drawn from generation to generation should represent natural biological relationships of child to parent. There are several social and family history issues that lead to the question *"On a chart why do some persons show and others do not show?"* There is the alternative of adding individuals by manually editing the chart in VCF the chart after it has been constructed *(see Chapter 14, Working with Charts in Visual Chartform™).*

Step, adopted and foster parents – If you want to include a non-biological relationship, like stepfather, in a chart as it is being constructed you will need to designate that father person as the primary father of that child. This means that the biological father and the stepfather cannot be linked to the same child *'as a father'* in the same chart. On a chart a person can have only one male and female parent. It is important to realize that by changing a stepfather to become a primary parent of that child will lead to false inferences about that child's ancestry (and the child's descendant's ancestry) in any ancestral chart created after that change using that modified data. After the chart has been

generated you can manually select and change these lines to dashed to make them distinct. Unfortunately, this has three disadvantages; there is no standard way of representing these relationships, manually editing them means that you may omit to edit some of them and finally, it is not possible to create dashed lines that are visible at a distance of four feet (1.2m) as dashed lines can only be one pixel line width.

Mixed sibling families - The **genealogical family** within a chart is not the same as the **social family**. In a descendant chart, the biological children of one parent who has had a number of partners can be shown with respect to their designated primary parents (for example, one descendant father and his consecutive partners). In this case, all children with a common father will be shown in separate family groups linked to their respective mothers. However, such a chart will not show children of those mothers by other male partners unless a primary father association with the first mentioned father has replaced those children's primary biological father.

Half-siblings of ancestors - In an ancestral box chart, TMG has an option to show the siblings of each ancestor. Half siblings of these ancestors cannot be shown without (unwisely) changing the Primary parent relationship of those half-siblings.

Descendants of ancestors - In an ancestral box chart, TMG cannot show the descendants of the ancestral siblings.

Duplicated persons *(Because of inter-marriage between related persons)* - This can become a difficult problem to represent. The simplest way is to accept the duplication. If however, you need or want to remove the duplicated trees of descendants (or ancestors) then within VCF edit the chart, annotate it and draw extra lines to make it all linked up again. It would be unreasonable to expect VCF to do this automatically. There are a lot of personal preferences in making a choice about the way this will be done. Whatever is done will require connecting lines to cross over lines and possibly to weave a path across the chart, particularly if there is a difference in the generations between the ancestries.

Concepts are given in *Chapter 14, **Working with Charts in Visual Chartform™*** that can overcome some of these limitations.

What you can't edit later

Once a chart has been created there are some properties that the user cannot change except by reconstructing the chart.

You cannot change the following elements after a chart has been generated:

- Replace or delete the background image.
- Increase the number of generations in a chart and get extra boxes within automatically added to the chart.
- Change the selection of fields as box contents in all the boxes.
- Any use of frames in a chart.
- The orientation of a chart.

You cannot operate over the whole chart in one action to do the following, but you can change individual properties on an object–by-object basis:

- The width of boxes (and get the spacing of the boxes to be maintained).
- The spacing between boxes within a generation.
- The spacing of boxes between generations.
- The definition of the content of the boxes (with more or less lines of information).
- All uses of an accenting color
- The use of frames.
- Fonts selected by where they are used.
- Line styles selected by where they are used.

It is desirable that you get these settings correct before you click [Make Chart]. It is a considerable saving in editing effort to get it the way you want it using the chart generation process ***before you start editing a chart***.

Getting a VCF chart printed?

The Chartform Delivery™ printing service accessed via **Reports > Charting Printing** is operated by Wholly Genes Software. See *www.chartform.com*. It is a good value for North American customers, but the costs of delivery, customs fees, delivery delays, etc. need to be considered by users in the rest of the world before using this service.

To find a list of VCF chart printing services in other parts of the world visit the **Resources** section of the Wholly Genes web site at: *www.whollygenes.com*.

Improving your charts

Consider the intended use and audience for your chart. It is very easy to produce a large wasteful chart that does not convey the right messages to the viewing audience. Some charts are suitable as research aids while others can be beautiful wall hangings.

Some questions that you should ask:

1. **Is this chart a research tool?** To help you understand the pattern of relationships and where you need to do further research, output as much detail as you have space, use smaller type for text, leave blanks for unknown data and use accents to assist that analysis.

2. **Is this chart intended to encourage access to more evidence?** Output blank spaces for data elements that are missing, leave plenty of white space on the chart, use a larger type size that can be read by elderly relatives. Adding images in the person box often encourages others to find more images.

3. **Is this chart for display at a family reunion?** Make sure that the names used are ones that the audience recognizes so put nicknames in brackets to help the recognition process. It is often better to have an overall (umbrella) descendant chart for the first 2 or 3 generations and then a series of detailed descendant or hourglass charts one for each significant sub-tree of descendants. This reduces the number of persons crowding around a single display. It is also a technical difficulty to support a very long chart without it tearing.

4. **Is this chart for use with a published work?** Cross-reference the chart to the page number where that person's main information is in the published work. You can manually edit the boxes of your chart to do this. Better still, create a custom tag whose Memo has the page reference information to where that person's main information is in the published work and output the Tag Memo as an extra line in each box.

5. **What is the size of the chart?** Use **Tools > Diagram > Diagram Measurements** in VCF to discover the size of the chart canvas. Often a chart can become too large to display or its shape becomes unwieldy and it may be better to either change the orientation of the chart or to consider producing several charts of sub-sections of the original chart. Occasionally it is possible to use some placement tricks or to use smaller type sizes or box widths to reduce these problems.

6. **What can be added to the chart to give it more appeal?** Add maps, annotated old photographs of houses, ships, medals, cars, family gatherings, places of interest, coats of arms, descriptive text and anecdotes.

7. **Do the abbreviations on data type lines of the chart agree with the cultural expectation of the audience?** In Europe, for example, different abbreviations and symbols for birth, death and marriage are used.

8. **Are areas of white space used to advantage to separate areas of the chart?** It is sometimes important to manually separate groups of ancestors or groups of descendants to reduce the entanglement of different families that can occur in some charts as VCF tries to minimize the total canvas size. It may be more effective to drag apart some groups of boxes creating white space to make these separate groups more obvious.

9. **Is the type size of text large enough to be read at the viewing distance?** As a chart gets bigger and if it is to be used for a wall display at a reunion then it is sensible to slightly increase the font sizes to make the text readable from a distance of four feet (1.2m). 14pt for names and 12pt for the data lines would be more appropriate starting values but this is also dependent on the choice of font for each type of output.

10. **Is the choice of font appropriate to be read at the viewing distance?** Fonts of the same size can be very different in their readability at a distance. Script, handwriting and black-letter (Old English) font faces are very poor. All upper case, extra bold and very condensed styles can also be poor. It is good practice not to use more than three font faces in any chart.

Choose the common fonts (like Arial) if you want to impart information. Only use decorative fonts if you are trying to produce a visually appealing end product that you wish to frame.

11. **Are the lines thick enough to be seen at the viewing distance?** The default width of lines is often too narrow for good compression of a large chart at a viewing distance of four feet (1.2m). Try four pixel width lines as a first try for larger charts. The choice of line width and color depends on whether there is a background color or image.

12. **Does the line color offer sufficient contrast to be seen at the viewing distance?** Make sure that the colors of all connecting lines have sufficient contrast against their respective background colors.

13. **Is the contrast between foreground and background colors adequate?** Make sure that the colors of any text have sufficient contrast against their respective background or fill colors.

14. **Is there a legend for any color-coding of the chart?** If you are using any color **accenting** or using **frames** that are controlled by **flag values** then you should manually add an appropriate legend box to your chart.

15. **Would the chart be better presented as a series of linked separate charts?** If the chart has become too large or very elongated or it is difficult to follow some long lines then there may be advantages in splitting such a chart into series of separately constructed charts. This group of charts can be linked by suitable annotations.

16. **Are some connection lines too long to follow from one part of a chart to another?** This is the classic reason to split the chart into a series of charts. One chart (the umbrella chart) is constructed by limiting the number of generations to the important few generations. This umbrella chart displays the persons that would normally be spread out over extensive distances when displayed on a large overall chart in a much more compact way. A series of smaller charts can be generated, each sub-tree attaches to the compact umbrella chart. This concept will not be a solution to all charting

problems. Because of inter-marriage between related persons there are duplicated persons that you may want to link.

17. **Would the chart be better presented with more or less information per person?** Depending on the purpose for constructing the chart, it may be better to have more information per person (in the case of a chart to aid your research) or less information per person so that you can get more generations on the same sized piece of paper. The choice of information and the way that this information is presented will depend on the audience for the chart or on physical limits of the printing facilities available to you.

18. **Are the boxes too close together?** Often we cram a large number of persons (or generations) onto a chart of a certain size. However, this can be false economy if then the chart is discarded as being too difficult to read. There are settings to space the chart out and then repaginate the chart so that boxes do not cross page breaks. Use of white space can help the viewer to interpret the chart.

19. **Is the background appropriate or confusing?** If you want a background behind your chart choose one that is muted and has similar color tones over its whole area. Either a background texture or an image of a sepia (old-style brown) photograph, which has been modified not to have large dark areas.

20. **Can color be used to help the audience understand or filter the chart in their mind?** Should you use **accent colors** and **flag controlled** selection of box frames to emphasize patterns within your chart. For example, in a data set where emigration is a feature use color to code the place of birth of each person (you could do the same for their place of death).

21. **Is it sensible to get this chart printed on a single piece of paper rather than sticking many smaller pages together?** It depends on the cost, the expected lifetime of the chart, how the chart is to be displayed and whether you have the patience to stick a large number of Letter or A4 pages together.

Chapter 14 - Working with Charts in Visual Chartform™
By Robin Lamacraft

Overview of Visual Chartform™

Visual Chartform™ (VCF) is a drawing package that constructs a genealogical chart according to the instructions specified and supplied to it after the user clicks [Make Chart] in TMG. The chart that is produced from the 'standard' or 'default' settings may satisfy many users. A chart file may be saved at any time (with the file extension .VC2). A chart file may be printed from VCF.

The first sections in this chapter address –
"What can the VCF tools do?"

The latter sections relate to –
"How can I do this in VCF?"

If you wish to vary the chart shape, chart layout, to delete some information or want to annotate a chart with maps, text, lines and images then VCF has a comprehensive range of the tools available. Most other genealogical charting packages do not offer such comprehensive facilities.

TIP - Before embarking on editing a chart, ensure that the data on the chart are correct and all the desired chart settings have been used. It is far quicker to go back to TMG, change the settings, and then make another chart. Editing a chart can be quite quick for small charts but for larger charts it can take many hours of (artistic) effort. Remember that if you reconstruct the chart again, all of your editing in VCF will need to be done again.

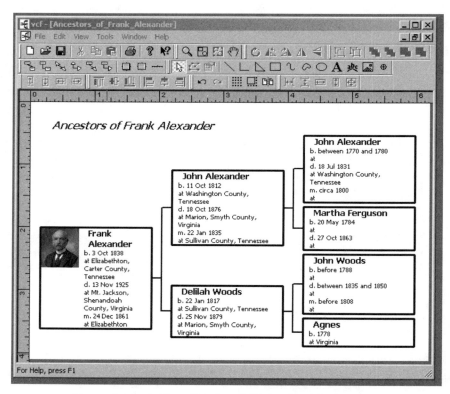

Figure 14-1: A Chart Displayed Within Visual Chartform

Using VCF from TMG

When you click [Make Chart] within TMG a new VCF window is opened. The constructed chart is displayed using the whole window space *(see Figure 14-1)*. This gives the best use of screen space at that time but it hides the multi-view and multi-chart power of VCF from most users.

If you click ⊞ **Restore Window** (on the right end of the **Main Menu** just below the window title bar) your chart will become a document frame in the VCF window. When VCF is opened from TMG, the VCF application adds a separate entry to your Windows task bar and you can switch between VCF and TMG in the normal way.

Using VCF from the Start Menu

When you start VCF directly from the Windows Start Menu, VCF is just like any other application. Use **File > Open** to select and open a file so that you can view and edit it. These files have a .VC2 extension and are often saved in the TMG **Reports** folder (as set in TMG using **File > Preferences**; **Project – Advanced** section and which defaults to the Reports sub-folder within your TMG installation folder). Each file will open into a new window within VCF. By using **Window > New Window** you can open another view of the currently active document that may then be manipulated independently of the other windows. The *currently active chart document* is the whole chart that is associated with the window that is currently active. This gives you the opportunity to make these windows at different levels of zoom so that you can see the detail in one and the context in the other at the same time. An action in one view window is reflected in the other.

Opening a VC2 File from Windows

In Windows Explorer, you can double-click the icon adjacent to the .VC2 file name and VCF will open and display that chart.

The VCF Main Menu

The **Main Menu** has 6 entries:
- **File** - file operations, exporting and printing
- **Edit** - general editing and selecting components
- **View** - toolbars, view grid and zoom
- **Tools** - align, nudge, order, group, separation and diagram management
- **Window** - window arrangement and window list
- **Help** - on-line help and version details

NOTE - The description of the **Main Menu** items is integrated with that of the corresponding toolbar buttons. This is because many of the **toolbar buttons** access the same functions as the **Main Menu** entries.

All Those VCF Toolbar Buttons!

There are 10 **toolbars** (groups of buttons with related actions). When you first open VCF, the toolbars are docked at the top of the Main window in three rows. All toolbars have a raised vertical bar at their left-hand end that you can click to drag that toolbar out to float over your chart (or anywhere on your screen(s)). If you slowly drag a toolbar over another edge of the main window it will dock there.

The toolbars may be grouped for convenience by function (i.e. those buttons having related operations) and are described together in the following sections:
- File, printing and help
- Managing your view of a chart
- Selecting, copying, grouping chart objects
- Adjusting layout and rotating chart objects
- Grouping and Ordering Chart Objects
- Editing chart objects
- Creating new chart objects
- Customizing VCF

Figure 14-0-1: The Visual Chartform Toolbar Buttons

File, Printing and Help

	Menu Selection	Hot-Key	Description
	File > New	<Ctrl>+N	**Create new chart document.** This creates a blank canvas.
	File > Open...	<Ctrl>+O	**Open an existing chart document.** Allows you to select and open a VCF file (With the .VC2 extension).
	File > Close		**Close the active chart document.**
	File > Save	<Ctrl>+S	**Save the active chart document.** Allow you save the active document as a new VCF file either with a new name or with the same name as an existing file with a warning of overwriting it.
	File > Save As...		**Save the active chart document with a new file name.** (With the VC2 extension.)
	File > Export...		**Export the active chart document into another file format.** (Supports JPG, BMP and EMF formats.)
	File > Run Command File...		**Runs a VCF command file.** *(Reserved for problem solving by Technical Support.)*
	File > Page Setup...		**Select a printer and its page properties.** Select page size, page orientation and width of page margins.
	File > Print Cut Marks		**Prints markings on the pages to show where to cut and paste the sheets together to form one large sheet.**
	File > Print	<Ctrl>+P	**Print the active chart document.**
	File > Print Preview		**Preview the active chart document.** This uses your Page Setup settings to display a view for each printed page using the selected printer's own software (the printer driver) to compose these views.
	File > Properties		**Displays the properties of the active chart document.**
	Help > About		**Display program information, version number and copyright.**
	(none)		**Display help for clicked on buttons, menus and windows.**

Table 14-1: File, Printing and Help

TIP - Always use **File > Print Preview** to check your output before printing. Alignment problems and overlap problems seen here will also appear on the printed output.

The recently used Chart Configurations will be listed on the bottom of the Reports menu and they can be selected directly from there.

Managing Your View of a Chart

	Menu Selection	Hot-Key	Description
🔍	(none)		**Zoom.** Once this feature has been selected, the place on the chart that is left-clicked in the active window becomes the new center of the window and the image is magnified one step (zoom in). This can be done many times; each time the image is zoomed in further. A right-click zooms out the image one step. To turn off **Zoom**, select 🔖 on the Drawing toolbar
	View > Zoom to Fit		**Zoom to fit.** Changes the scale of the current active window to make the whole chart visible (within the scaling limits).
	(none)		**Zoom to fit selection.** Zooms in or out the current active window to a scale to make the current selection fit the visible window.
✋	(none)		**Pan.** Once this has been selected, click and drag on the active window and the chart image will move with the cursor. To turn off **Pan**, select 🔖 on the Drawing toolbar.
	View > Zoom Normal		**Zoom normal.** Show the chart at 100% scaling (may make a large part of the chart be off screen).
	View > Zoom Percent		**Zoom Percent.** Show the current active window at a scale selected from the alternatives (50%, 75%, 100%, 200%).
	View > Zoom Custom...		**Zoom Custom.** Show the current active window at user entered scale between 10% and 1000%.
	Window > New Window		**New Window.** This creates a new window view of the current active chart document. Each window that is an alternative view on the same chart has **:1, :2,** etc appended to its title bar. The results of actions in one window are reflected in the display in the other. The zoom and pan states of each window are independent. You can have at least 10 views of a document. TIP - When you save a chart you are saving the whole document and not just the currently active view of that document.
	Window > Cascade		**Cascade.** Arranges opened windows successively to the right and down the screen so that their title bars can be read.
	Window > Tile		**Tile.** Arranges all the currently open windows to occupy non-overlapping nearly equal areas of the screen.
	View > Grid		Turn grid on or off (toggle) **show grid.**
▯▯	**View > Page Bounds**		Turn grid on or off (toggle) **show page boundaries.**
	View >Ports	\<Ctrl>+M	Turn grid on or off (toggle) **show connection ports.**
	View >Rulers	\<Ctrl>+R	Turn grid on or off (toggle) **show rulers** on each chart window.
	View > Grid Properties...		**Set spacing of grid.** This can be in the range 0.0625 to 6 inches (1.5875 to 152.4 mm).
	View > Full Screen	\<F11>	**Expands VCF to fill the whole screen.**

Table 14-2: Managing Your View of a Chart

Sizing a Chart

	Menu Selection Hot-Key	Description
	<u>T</u>ools > <u>D</u>iagram > Size to <u>C</u>omponents	**Resizes the canvas** (to just contain the objects with clear space to the right and at the bottom). This is useful if you have moved some objects creating some blank space to the right or at the bottom.
	<u>T</u>ools > <u>D</u>iagram > Size to Components Exact	**Resizes the canvas** (to just contain the objects without clear space to the right and at the bottom). This is useful if you have moved some objects creating some blank space to the right or at the bottom and wish to close the last page boundary at the right or at the bottom. It is also used when making your own frames.
	<u>T</u>ools > <u>D</u>iagram > <u>D</u>iagram Measurements	**The diagram measurements.** The units of distance measurement and the size of the canvas. You may select other units and create more space on the canvas in which to place new objects.
	<u>T</u>ools > <u>D</u>iagram > <u>R</u>esize Drawing	**Resize drawing.** To shrink or enlarge a chart before printing by setting the horizontal or vertical size for the new chart. WARNING - *This process can't be undone.*
	<u>T</u>ools > <u>D</u>iagram > Repaginate Drawing	**Repaginate.** To move boxes around to avoid the page boundaries. WARNING - *This process can't be undone.* TIP: This process uses the current Page Properties of the selected printer so make sure that the desired paper size and orientation is selected on the right printer before you use this feature - use <u>F</u>ile > **Page Set<u>u</u>p...** first.

Table 14-3: Sizing a chart

Selecting, Copying and Deleting Chart Objects

Drawings are made up of numerous elements named **objects**. Each object can be manipulated independently.

	Menu Selection or Mouse Action Hot-Key	Description
	Left-click on <u>object</u>	**Select object.** Make this object the sole selection.
	<Ctrl>+left-click on <u>box</u>	**Add to or Remove box from selection.** If the object is not selected then select it, if it is selected, then make it unselected.
	<Ctrl>+left-click on <u>line</u>	**Add a point to a previously selected line.**
	<Shift>+left-click on <u>object</u>	**Add to or Remove object from selection.** If the object is not selected then select it, if it is selected, then make it unselected.
	Left click on <u>object</u>, then **drag** when cursor is four arrowheads	**Move object.** The object is moved. (Hint: Once you are moving the object press the <Shift> and the object will only move in one axis.)

	Menu Selection or Mouse Action	Hot-Key	Description
	Left-click on <u>background</u>, then **drag** dotted outline		**Select objects in rectangular outline.** Marks all objects within the rectangle as selected.
	<Ctrl>+left-click on <u>object</u>, then **drag**		**Copy object.**
	Edit > Select All	<Ctrl>+A	**Select all objects on the canvas.**
✄	**Edit > Cut**	<Ctrl>+X	**Cut the selection and put it on the clipboard.**
▤	**Edit > Copy**	<Ctrl>+C	**Copy the selection to the clipboard.**
▤	**Edit > Paste**	<Ctrl>+V	**Insert the clipboard contents at the insertion point.**

Table 14-4: Selecting, copying and deleting chart objects

RIGHT-CLICK on a Box Object:
This opens a pop-up or shortcut menu whose items depend on the type of object. Two special cases are available for **right-click** of a person box.

Right-click > Select Generation	In the chart, select all other person boxes at the same generation as the selected box.
Right-click > Select Siblings and Spouse(s)	In the chart, select all other person boxes that represent siblings and spouse(s) of the person of the selected box.

Table 14-5: Right click menu selection of objects on a chart

Drawings are made up of numerous elements named **objects**. Each object can be manipulated independently.

Grouping and Ordering Chart Objects

	Menu Selection	Hot-Key	Description
⊞	**Tools > Structure > Group**		**Group selected objects.**
⊞	**Tools > Structure > Ungroup**		**Ungroup selected objects.**
⊞	**Tools > Structure > Bring to front**		**Bring selected objects to the front of a stack of objects.**
⊞	**Tools > Structure > Send to back**		**Send the selected objects to the back of a stack of objects.**
⊞	**Tools > Structure > Bring forward**		**Bring selected objects forward one position.**
⊞	**Tools > Structure > Send backward**		**Send selected objects backward one position.**

Table 14-6: Grouping and ordering objects on the chart

HINT: The **Tools > Structure** toolbar buttons may be easier to use with small selected objects rather than accessing the equivalent right-click menu item. This is because the selection focus of a small object can quickly shift to another nearby object. This is especially true when you want to bring an isolated connection point object to front so that you can then drag it easily.

Rotating Chart Objects

	Menu Selection	Hot-Key	Description
↻	(none)		**Rotate each selected object about its own center.** Place the cursor over one of the selected objects, click and drag the clicked point. The collection of objects will be rotated to follow the radius from the first clicked point as the cursor is moved.
	(none)		**Rotate the selected objects 90° clockwise about their own centers.**
	(none)		**Counter clockwise Rotation by 90°.**
	(none)		**Flip the selected objects about their own vertical centers.**
	(none)		**Flip the selected objects about their own horizontal centers.**

Table 14-7: Rotating objects on a chart

	Menu Selection	Hot-Key	Description
	Tools > Nudge > Nudge Up	*or* **UP arrow**	**Nudge selected objects up one increment.**
	Tools > Nudge > Nudge Down *or* **DOWN arrow**		**Nudge selected objects down one increment.**
	Tools > Nudge > Nudge Left *or* **LEFT arrow**		**Nudge selected objects left one increment.**
	Tools > Nudge > Nudge Right *or* **RIGHT arrow**		**Nudge selected objects right one increment.**
	Tools > Align > Align Top		**Align the tops of selected objects.**
	Tools > Align > Align Middle		**Align the middles of selected objects.**
	Tools > Align > Align Bottom		**Align the bottoms of selected objects.**
	Tools > Align > Align Left		**Align left sides of selected objects.**
	Tools > Align > Align Center		**Align centers of selected objects.**
	Tools > Align > Align Right		**Align right sides of selected objects.**
	Tools > Distribution > Space Across		**Equally space selected objects horizontally.**
	Tools > Distribution > Space Down		**Equally space selected objects vertically.**
	Tools > Distribution > Same Width		**Make width of selected objects the same.**
	Tools > Distribution > Same Height		**Make height of selected objects the same.**
	Tools > Distribution > Same Size		**Make width and height of selected objects the same.**

Table 14-8: Adjusting the layout of objects on a chart

HINT: It is not always obvious how the **Tools** > **Align** toolbar actions determine the alignment point. Make sure that you only select one row or column of objects of the same type when you use **Tools** > **Distribution** toolbar actions otherwise you may get unexpected outcomes.

Editing Chart Objects

	Menu Selection	Hot-Key	Description
⬡	*(none)*		**Select mode.** Once this is active, you can select objects.
⬡	*(none)*		**Edit individual vertices of lines and polycurves.**
⬡	**Edit > Properties**		**Edit object properties.**
⬡	**Edit > Undo**	<Ctrl>+Z	**Undo the last operation.**
⬡	**Edit > Redo**	<Ctrl>+Y	**Redo the last undone operation.**
⬡	**View > Snap to Grid**		**When an object is moved the top left of it is locked to align with the grid.**

Table 14-9: Editing the properties of objects on a chart

HINT: As you edit a chart, a history of the actions is kept so that the **Edit** > **Undo** and **Edit** > **Redo** toolbar actions can operate. After a while keeping the history can slow down further editing actions. Selecting the **File** > **Save** toolbar action to save the chart changes, closing VCF, and then re-opening the saved chart file in VCF will clear this history. Many operations will then act more quickly again.

Basic Objects in a Chart

Basic objects are elements that can be placed on a canvas. They can be grouped into new more useful objects. To simplify the description of editing of basic objects, they have been divided into groups of increasing complexity:

- **Image objects** (no properties available to edit).
- **Line-based objects**: (straight line, polyline, polycurve and port connecting lines).
  Line properties: line width, line color, line style.
- **Region enclosing objects**: (rectangle, ellipse, polygon, and polyshape).
  Line properties: line width, line color, and line style for the perimeter line.
  Fill properties: fill foreground color, fill background color and fill hatch pattern for the region fill.
- **Text objects:** (text and curved text)
  Line properties: line width, line color, and line style for the perimeter line.

Fill properties: fill foreground color, fill background color and fill hatch pattern for the text object.
Text properties: font, font size, font style and font color for the text.

Compound Objects in a Chart

- **Box objects:** (chart box, shadowed chart box)
  Line properties: line width, line color, and line style for box border component.
  Fill properties: fill foreground color, fill background color and fill hatch pattern for box rectangle component.
  Text properties: font, font size, font style and text color for each text component of the box contents.

Editing the Properties of an Object

Once an object has been selected, a right-click will reveal a menu like the one shown in *Figure 14-3* (the focus person box of the chart in *Figure 14-1*). Selecting the **Detail Properties** menu item opens the **Components** window.

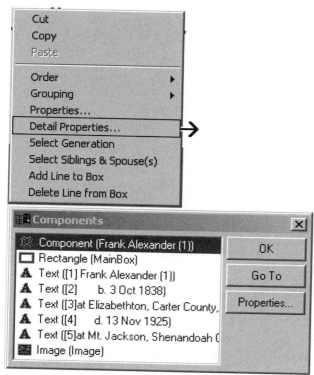

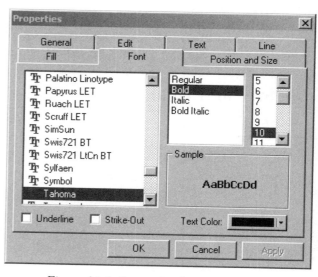

Figure 14-4: Properties Screen, Font Tab

Figure 14-3: Right Click Menu and Detail Properties

Selecting one of these numbered Text components and clicking [Properties...] opens the following **Properties** dialogue (small window). There are 7 tabs that appear in the **Properties** window of many simpler objects. This explanation and screen shot also applies to objects with fewer properties.

The **Font** and **Text** tabs are examined first. Later the **Line** and **Fill** tabs will be discussed. Finally the **Edit** tab will be discussed. The **General** and **Position and Size** tabs are for information only.

The **Font** tab is a common method of font selection from which you can select any of your installed True Type fonts.

The **Text** tab has a field labeled **Text** where you can enter or view the text that will be printed. The remainder of the tab has settings that control the way that the text field is aligned and how longer text entries will be handled when they exceed the extent of a single line.

TIP - If you check **Multiple lines** then it is advisable to also check the **Word Break**. Then when you create narrow boxes in a chart the Surname of long names can wrap onto a second line. Sometimes when there has been a change to longer line, you may have to select the box after completing the edit to make the box be redrawn.

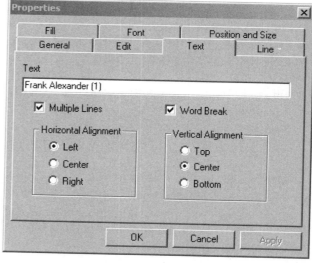

Figure 14-5: Properties Screen, Text Tab

The **Line** tab (with the Main Rectangle of person box selected) looks like *Figure 14-6* showing the selections for **line color**, **line style** and **line width**.

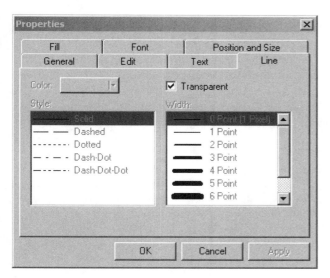

Figure 14-6: Properties Screen, Line Tab

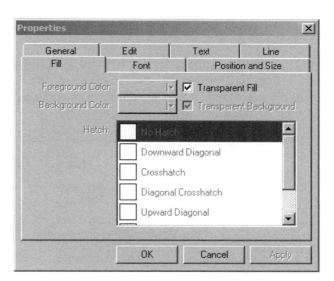

Figure 14-7: The Hatch Tab of the Properties Screen

TIP - You **must** use *solid* line style to be able to have thicker line widths.

TIP - You **must** use width 0 (1 Pixel) if you wish to use any other line style than *solid*.

The **Fill** tab (with the Main Rectangle of person box selected) looks like *Figure 14-7* showing the selections for the **Hatch, Foreground Color**, **Background Color**, the **Transparent Fill** and the **Transparent Background.** The definition of foreground and background are confusing to some users. When the **Hatch** is solid only the **Foreground Color** is seen. The **Background Color** is what is seen in the gaps of the hatching pattern. When the **Transparent Fill** is checked, no other setting applies. When the **Transparent Background** is checked the **Background Color** is not used.

Editing the Properties of a Collection of Objects in One Action

Select all the objects within a rectangular region using a marquee. This marquee method is done by moving the mouse to one corner of the region to be selected, left-click and then while holding the left button down drag the mouse to the diagonally opposite corner of the rectangular selection region. A dashed rectangle will be drawn on the screen while this dragging is being done. When you have reached the other corner release the mouse button.

All objects totally enclosed by the selection rectangle will now become selected. Or you can select them individually using **<Shift> +left-click** to build up a collection of selected objects. In each case it is possible to make certain changes to all the objects' properties in one editing action. When the cursor has the four arrow-headed form, right-click and select **Properties** from the pop-up or shortcut menu. This **Properties** screen that opens looks like the one which has been described in figures 14-4 to 14-7, but there are some limitations on what you can and can't sensibly edit this way.

If you select another **Font**, then this will be applied to all **Text** objects within the selection set. You may not want to change all the font sizes to a new common size as this would make names and data lines have the same font size. Similarly, if you change the *Line Color* and *Line Width,* this will apply to the border of boxes and to the connection lines within the selections set.

TIP - This is a powerful facility but make sure you have your selection set right first. Luckily the **Undo** <Ctrl>+Z works on these operations if you get it wrong.

Editing Multi-point Lines and Shapes

For polylines and polycurves - select the object and the segment joining points (or shape control points for polycurves) will become visible. Each point may be dragged to a new location and clicking on the background will terminate editing.

When a polygon or polyshape is selected the resizing handles shown are based on a rectangle that contains the shape. These handles can be dragged around to stretch the shape horizontally or vertically. Click the ⬚ **Edit Individual Vertices** button to edit the shape of a selected polygon or polyshape to change the display to show the vertex and shape control points. These extra points that become visible can be dragged around to change the shape of the curve. Clicking on the background terminates this editing mode.

Editing Connection Lines Between Person Boxes

One of the most difficult editing tasks to the new user is keeping the connecting lines tidy as you move the person boxes around. As you move a box the connecting lines appear to jump around. Finally when you have dragged the person boxes to the desired places you now want to tidy up the connecting lines. ***This can be hard to control.***

First we need to define a **port** or **connection point**. A port is a point on the canvas where an end of a connection line is anchored. When you move the other end of a connection line, the line acts like an

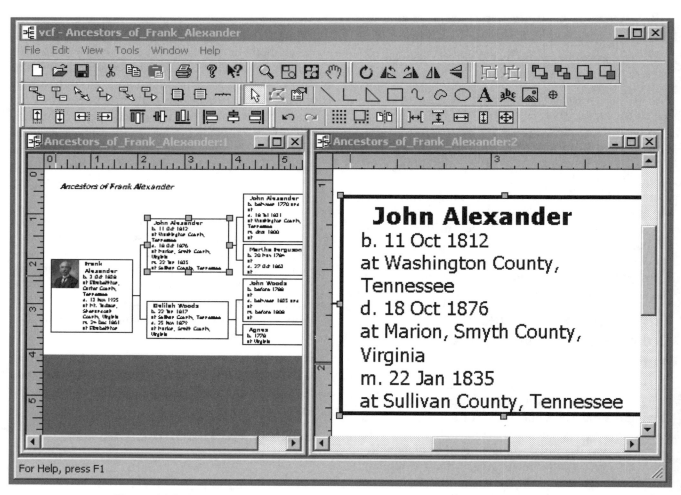

Figure 14-8: Using Two Windows at Different Zoom Levels to View The Same Chart

elastic band and it stretches to maintain its anchorage at the port. Ports can be at the edges of objects and they can be isolated points placed on the canvas.

Now it helps to understand how these links are constructed. The connecting lines are drawn orthogonally, that is, they use a series of connected straight lines that are always vertical or horizontal to get from the start point (a port) to the end point (another port) of a line.

When a descendant box chart is drawn in VCF, each person box has three ports on each of its four sides. The connection lines always join a person box at one of its ports. But the lines do not go from one port on one box to a port on another box — **each line only goes part way**.

In other words the line from the spouse is drawn to an isolated point (the common point) between the generations and then a separate line is drawn from this common point (port) to a port on each of the children boxes. This common point acts like a collector of all the children links allowing only one line back to that parent. Sometimes when you move a box the connector line can become disconnected from the port. So how do you go about getting this repair done? The best way is to avoid getting into many of the problems in the first place. First, you should make your view of the chart as complete as possible to make the job easier. Set **View > Rulers, View > Grid, View > Ports** and **View > Page bounds** all on. If possible, use VCF in full screen mode. Use **Window > New Window** to open a second window as another view of the same chart. Use **Window > Tile** to tile the windows on the screen. Select a region of interest for this window using **Left-click then drag** and click the ⊞ (**Zoom to Selection**) to set the zoom level on the first window far enough out so that you can see an overview of your actions. Now repeat this operation for the second window so it is highly magnified. Pan that window until it is focused where you want to make the adjustments *(see Figure 14-8)*.

It is easy to make a mistake and not select all the important objects in a region before you try a move. If you follow these instructions you will have less hassles in making changes.

Use the marquee method (as described above in the section entitled Editing the Properties of a Collection of Objects in One Action) to select all objects in a rectangular region, especially those attached to all the orthogonal lines of interest. Don't worry if you appear to get too many objects, as that is much easier to correct than possibly missing some small but important connection objects that you may not have seen. You can deselect those unwanted objects from your selection. Place the mouse over an object until the four-arrowhead cursor appears and then use <**Shift**>+**left-click** to deselect that object. Do this as many times as you need until you reach your desired selected set. Now use the ⊞ **Group** button to group the selected objects (the Grouping operation may take a while on older computers with little memory). Now select the grouped object and drag it to where you want it. The connection lines that attach to objects outside of the grouped object will remain connected and the lines should stretch and contract as required.

When you have completed a change in one area and need to make a change in an adjacent area you may need to ⊞ **Ungroup** the previous collection so that you can include only some of these objects in the next group.

To make these orthogonal lines move to where you want them can be difficult. First select the isolated connection point and use **right-click > Order > Bring to Front**. With this connection point selected use the **Nudge** button or the arrow keys to move it around and the orthogonal lines will change shape in a controlled manner stretching to the connection points new position.

Changing the route that orthogonal lines take can be frustrating. While redrawing, VCF tries to minimize the length of the line, the number of bends in the lines, and tries to keep a minimum distance from other boxes. While doing all this it does not take into account whether another line is also using the same track (or very nearly) leading to cluttered and confusing charts after they have been redrawn. Often the best solution is to delete the existing confusing line, create an intermediate connection point and then make the line as two segments where the user has control over the position of the intermediate connection point. Most editing errors can be avoided if you realize that the intergenerational line is not continuous but two orthogonal lines that join to a connection point. You will need to select or to move that connection point.

The Edit tab on the Component Properties screen

The **Edit** tab *(see Figure 14-9)* has a collection of check boxes that control the editing characteristics of each object. Most of the time you do not have to worry about them.

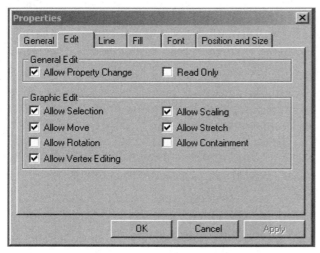

Figure 14-9: Creating New Line-based Objects

TIP - If you draw a rectangle around the whole chart or a group of boxes in the chart, then you may need to visit this tab. Under normal settings in the **Edit** tab, once you have drawn the enclosing rectangle, you will not be able to use the mouse to select a group of objects in a single action. You need to select the enclosing rectangle and check the ***Read Only*** box and uncheck the ***Allow Selection*** box on its Edit tab. Now you will be able to select other objects within a rectangular region of the chart within the enclosing rectangle.

Creating New Simple Chart Objects

(These buttons have no keyboard equivalents.)

The buttons visible in the Drawing toolbar act differently than most other toolbar buttons. Click a button to select the type of object you wish to create and when the mouse cursor is on the drawing area it will change to show that the drawing tool is active.

Unless there are specific instructions within the table below for that object, move the mouse to where you want the top left of the object to be drawn. **Left-click and drag** to the bottom right point of the desired sized object and then release the mouse button.

╲	**Draw a straight line.**
∟	**Draw a multi-segmented line or polyline.** Left click to start and then click at each point where you want the line to bend and double-click on the last point.
⌇	**Draw a polycurve.** Left click to start and then click in successive groups of 3 points. The first 2 points in each triplet will act as control points and two points will appear away from the curve while the line will pass through the third point. Double-click on the last point. Adjust the shape of the curve by dragging any point.
⊕	**Insert a connection point or port.**

Table 14-10: Creating new line-based objects

▭	**Draw a rectangle.**
◺	**Draw a polygon.** Left click to start and then left-click at each point where you want the line to bend and double-click on the last point.
⌒	**Draw a polyshape.** Left click to start and then left-click in successive groups of 3 points. The first 2 points in each triplet will act as control points and two points will appear away from curve while the line will pass through the third point. Double-click on the last point. Adjust the shape of the curve by dragging any point.
◯	**Draw an ellipse.**
A	**Insert text characters enclosed in a rectangle.**
abc	**Insert curved text characters enclosed in a circle.**
🖼	**Insert a graphic image.** Supports the following image file formats (BMP, JPG, PCX, TIF, TIFF, TGA and EMF)

Table 14-11: Creating new enclosed area objects

Creating Special Charting Objects

(None of these have keyboard equivalents.)

All the buttons in the Symbols toolbar act differently than most other toolbar buttons. Click a button to select the type of object you wish to create and when you have the mouse over the canvas the cursor will change to indicate that the drawing tool is active. Move the mouse to where you want the top left of the object to be drawn (or the starting point of connecting line). Click and drag out the object to the required size. The sequence of drawing these objects can have an effect on the outcome.

Line drawing method	Number of arrowheads on connection line		
	none	1	2
Straight			
Orthogonal			

Table 14-12: Connecting line objects

These line drawing tools create lines that join one connection point to another connection port. The lines formed by these tools line will stretch and contract in length as the objects containing the connection point at either end are moved. As the mouse approaches a connection point its form changes to be a plus sign surrounded by a circle. When you release the mouse with the cursor in this state, the line will attach to the connection point. Double clicking the line of any of the above will add a text box formed initially at the midpoint between the ends of the line.

The symbol has an additional connection point at its mid point.

TIP - To draw an orthogonal line in the shape that you want takes some practice. The route for each orthogonal line will be re-evaluated each time the screen is redrawn. To ensure that an orthogonal line takes the desired path, create it as a series of lines that are connected to extra connection points that you have added to the canvas.

Connection box without shadow

Connection box with shadow

These buttons will add boxes to a chart that are like empty person boxes that you can fill manually. They are limited to 5 lines of text and have no provision to add an image. They have the same connection point structure as a person box.

Customizing VCF

There are many ways of customizing the view and actions of VCF. The options on the **View** menu like **View > Toolbars** can turn on or off the presence of any of the 10 toolbars. Also on the **View** menu are items like **Page Bounds**, **Ports**, **Rulers**, **Grid**, **Snap to Grid**, **Angle Snap** and **Grid Properties** all of which will change the view or actions of VCF. The options **Tools > Diagram > Diagram Measurements** and **File > Page Setup...** are settings that effect actions of VCF. Finally, there is the **Edit > Default Properties** item where you can modify some of the properties used to create new objects.

TIP - If you do a lot of chart editing by creating new objects then it is well worth adjusting these values to match your most common usage. It will save you a lot of individual property editing later.

Printing Charts and Printer Properties

In **File > Page Setup**, the *Printer*, its *Paper Size* and *Page Orientation* are selected. The choice of printer determines the range of page sizes that can be selected. For each page size, the selected printer's support software (known as its driver) defines the maximum printable region of that page that the printer can print. Many printers cannot print right to the edge of the paper. The Page Setup choices are used to calculate the page bounds (**View > Page Bounds**) that can be seen on the chart canvas when that option is turned on.

Fortunately, if you save the chart as a .VC2 file by using **File > Save As**, this file can be opened on another computer running the same or a later version of VCF and all of the page sizes for its printer can be used for page boundary calculation. This is the way some chart printing services work. For your set up you may choose to print on Letter (or A4) paper size to get the layout of the chart. The printing service can adjust the Custom Paper Size of its wide format roll-fed printer to match the total size of your chart. In most cases these services can print your whole chart on a single piece of paper.

The quality of the printing process and the longevity of the product are determined by many factors: the choice of paper (coated, gloss, matte, archival, etc), the choice of ink (dye or pigment), the resolution of the printer and the proposed intended storage and display of the chart. The costs can vary a lot according to the choice of materials, the area of paper and the time to print the job (related to the area of paper that is covered by ink).

TIP - It is not recommended to laminate a chart as a method of prolonging the life of its printed image. It is impossible to restore a laminated object. Some conservators say that the adhesive used in the laminating process is detrimental to the ink. To keep a chart for a long time, choose the best methods of production and when not in use store it rolled up in a tube (well sealed against very small insects) and placed in a low fire risk and low flood risk, warm, dry location. A small amount of camphor in the tube will help in that process. Most black inks have longer lives than colored inks. Archival paper and ink are available from some printing services to increase the life of the output by at least ten times.

Repagination of a Chart

A chart can be repaginated in two ways. Just changing the paper orientation, width of margins, or selected paper size in the selected printer in **File > Page Setup** can cause the page bound lines on the chart to be recalculated.

However, when a chart is laid out, the program takes no consideration of the selected page properties (as they could change before printing). A consequence of this is that some boxes are likely to cross the page bounds. If that chart were printed, parts of these boxes would be printed on up to four pages. This can make getting a good result from pasting pages together very difficult. To overcome this, the feature **Tools > Diagram > Repaginate** is designed to automatically insert extra space before page breaks so that every box is within one page.

Changing the Shape of a Chart

Genealogical box charts that are produced automatically by charting programs tend to be elongated in either height or width. This makes them wasteful of materials or difficult to print on most equipment. It also makes them unmanageable to display. This section will describe a technique that can be used to reduce both these problems causing very little loss in clarity of the charts.

The trick is to identify where the larger sub-trees of information are placed and to selectively move them out of alignment. During this process you should be careful to maintain the link to their original attachment point. The amount of movement required needs to be far enough to clear the display of the adjacent sub-trees. Once this has been done the space that they occupied can be collapsed out. This is easier to see by comparing before and after diagrams than it is to explain in words. This method can be adapted to ancestral and descendant box charts in all orientations.

Figures 14-10 and 14-11 on the next page show before and after reshaping the chart - the unfilled boxes have been moved out of alignment.

The example is rather simple but it shows the concept. If the chart has the right structure it is possible to collapse the longer side of the chart to about 60% of its original longer side by approximately doubling the dimension in the other direction. For example, reshaping a fourteen-foot by one-foot chart (4.2m by 300mm) into an eight-foot by two-foot (2.4m by 600mm) chart is often considered advantageous. This method maintains the birth order sequencing of children and keeps larger family groups together.

WARNING - Generations will no longer be on the same horizontal line.

TIP - You could change the color of the fill of the boxes of successive generations to make that difference more obvious to the viewer. This is illustrated in the diagram of *Figure 14-11*.

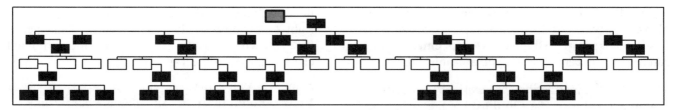

Figure 14-10: A Top to Bottom Descendancy Chart as Generated

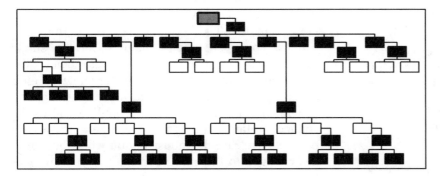

Figure 14-11: A Top to Bottom Descendancy Chart After Reshaping

This process is quite simple although it might take some time to achieve with a large chart. The following description is based on a top to bottom orientation chart, in which you start at the left of the chart and work to the right. For left to right charts, you would start at the top and work down. Identify the first suitable sub-tree of boxes of sufficient size to move. Use the marquee method (described earlier) to select that sub-tree and remove the unwanted objects from the selection as described earlier. Now group this selection and drag the grouped object to the required place. Later it may be required to ungroup it to allow for further internal edits. Use the same technique to group the remainder of the chart to the right of the sub-tree that was moved and drag this grouped object to the left until the gap is sensibly closed and then ungroup that last group. Repeat this sequence across the chart.

Use Your Imagination!

Visual Chartform™ provides a unique capability. Create several charts (by using different specifications) within TMG and save each chart file (with a VC2 extension). Then cut and paste them together to form one big chart. This way you can get the layout and content of the chart that you want. It also gives you the opportunity to be creative.

The "bow tie descendant" box chart *(see Figure 14-12)* is created from three separate charting requests to TMG.

1. A right to left Ancestor Box Chart of the father.

2. A left to right Ancestor Box Chart of the mother.

3. A top to bottom Descendant Box chart of the father.

Each chart is created normally in VCF, then the menu item **File > Save As…** is used to save each chart as a distinctly named file.

Use **Tools > Diagram > Diagram Measurements.** Note down the width and height of each chart. In the target big chart we want to put the first and second chart side by side across the top. We want to place the third chart across the bottom below the first two charts. Hence an approximate width of the final chart is the larger of the sum of the widths of the two ancestor box charts or the width of the descendant box chart. The approximate height of the final chart will be the larger of the ancestor box heights plus the height of the descendant box chart.

Combining Charts

Create a blank canvas just a bit larger than the calculated area that you have worked from the noted sizes of your smaller charts and your design of the final chart. Use **File > New** to create the blank canvas and then set its size by **Tools > Diagram > Diagram Measurements**. You can re-size the canvas when you are finished.

The following instructions are explicit to the above example, combined chart to illustrate the technique. Now open the first chart file above, and in its window use <Ctrl>+A (**Select All**), then the ▢ (**Group**) button and when the selection has finished (it might take a while) then choose ▣ or <Ctrl>+C (**Copy**) to put the whole chart on the clipboard. Now click near the top left of your large blank canvas and click ▣ or <Ctrl>+V (**Paste**). After a short while, dependant on the size of the chart you are copying, the copied chart will appear.

COMMENT - You Copy *from* one previously constructed chart window and Paste *into* the combined chart window.

Now open the second chart file above and repeat the same sequence except that you should click in the new window (the pasting point) to the top and right of the previously pasted chart. (This means that you will probably have to scroll the combined chart window to the right so that you can see this point.). You may want to use ▣ or **View > Zoom to Fit** to show you your results so far. Finally, open the third file above and repeat the sequence, pasting this chart to the left and below both of the previously pasted charts.

Now with the three separate charts on the same canvas, you need to edit them to form a single linked chart. To do this you must delete the redundant person boxes and reconnect their attachment lines to the corresponding remaining box for that person. Select the dangling end of the connection line and drag it to the edge of the person box. Only release the mouse button when the cursor has changed to the small circle when you are near the connection point of that box that you wish the line in your chart to use. To improve the aesthetics you may choose to move some items around to create a final chart.x

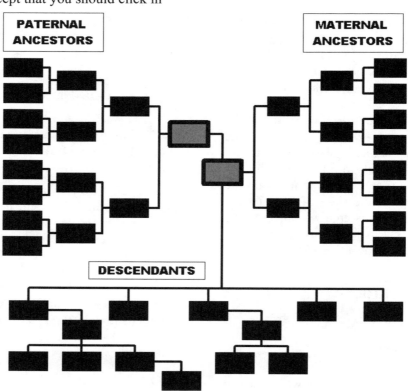

Figure 14-12: A Combined Chart - A "Bow-tie Descendant" Chart

At any time in this process you can save your chart by using **File > Save As...** to save intermediate copies of your editing (e.g. mychart_n.vc2, etc.) in case you have difficult recovery problems. Because you can save a chart file and then at a later time you can open that file, it is possible to build complex charts over many days without worrying about power failures causing you to loose your hard work.

Adding Decoration to Your Chart - Lines, Text and Images

VCF gives you the tools *but not the imagination!* A number of enhancements to charts are possible e.g. - to add images of groups of people and draw lines from the chart to each person in the image, add images of places where people lived, show old documents, emigration ships, maps of previous places of living, coats of arms, etc. These can be in color or black and white. You can print text using more fancy typefaces, print on special textured paper. You can add decoration using frames or other publishing graphics. It really depends on the purpose of the chart. You can increase the life of your chart by using archival pigment-based UV tolerant inks on archival paper.

Creating and using Your Own Frames

Open VCF from the Start menu and on a blank canvas draw a frame for a box about the normal size of a box as its inside dimensions say 2.5in wide by one inch high (38mm by 25mm). The example *(see Figure 14-13)* here is composed of a larger gray rectangle with a white rectangle superimposed with a black triangle at each corner. Group the whole drawing and then drag it to the top left of the canvas.

Figure 14-13: A Simple Frame

Tools > Diagram > Size to Components Exact will move your diagram up to the top left and then reduce the canvas to fit this new layout. Then use **File > Export...** to export it to an EMF file into the **Frames** folder under your TMG5 installation. The form of the file name should be *anyname(nnS)*.emf in which the *nn* is the width (in pixels) of the frame border (e.g. PhotoAlbum(30S).emf). The 'S' indicates that it is a Standard frame drawn using vector graphics. Other forms of frame can be made that use bitmapped graphics and these have an 'F' for Fancy in their name.

Now this frame is available for use within the **Box** tab settings on the **Chart Options** in TMG. Above is an example chart *(see Figure 14-14)* using this frame with the SAMPLE data set.

Exporting a Chart to Become an Exhibit or Into a Word Processor Document

Charts can be exported to JPG, BMP or EMF image file formats using **File > Export...**. The choice of format depends how the file is to be used. JPG is probably best for inclusion in a Slide Show or as an Exhibit *(see Chapter 12- Multi-Media)*.

Figure 14-14: A Descendant Box Chart Using the Simple Frame

WARNING - **Charts can be *VERY LARGE.*** Examine the size of what you choose what to export to match your required use of that image file.

Exporting a chart as an EMF has special advantages if you want to:

- Insert the file in a word processor document.
- Edit it before you use it.

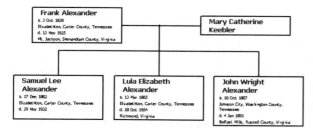

Figure 14-15: An Edited Version of a Descendant Chart

The chart in *Figure 14-15* is an edited version of some of the children of Frank Alexander from the SAMPLE data set. This chart has been laid out using the British convention for representation of marriages with a line between the partners and the children tied to mid point of this line. The British convention is to use a double line for the link between the parents but the VCF line styles do not include this style.

This chart file was exported as an EMF file and inserted into a Microsoft Word document using **Insert > Picture > From File....** Once inserted into the document, double-clicking the image opened the drawing in a new window within the Microsoft

Word Picture Editor. Now each element in the VCF drawing is available for editing.

The ***extreme example*** shown in *Figure 14-16* illustrates this flexibility. The editing made here illustrates some of the issues listed in the guidelines for improving charts at the end of the previous chapter.
- Readability of some fonts
- Number of fonts on a page
- Use of gray text
- Use of transparent box fill
- Use of a background

The chart has been edited in the following ways:
- Double line style replaced a single line style in one line – this can be achieved in Microsoft Word as it has additional line styles not supported by VCF.
- A box shape has been substituted for another shape
- Fonts have been changed in size and face
- Some boxes have been resized
- Some text lines have been moved
- A background has been inserted

WARNING - When editing an exported EMF file in this way, the linkages between the elements are no longer active and it is easy to produce an erroneous result. But you have the power to do your own thing.

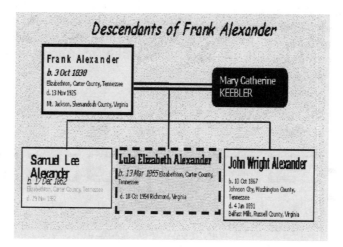

Figure 14-16: The Chart of Figure 14-15 After Further Editing

Chapter 15 - Exporting Data

By Jim Byram

TMG5 can export to two general types of data files (**File > Export**). In the first case, data are exported to one of five types of GEDCOM files (GEDCOM 4.0, Personal Ancestral File™, Ancestral File™, Temple Ready™ and GEDCOM 5.5). In the second case, which we'll call 'Data File' export, the contents of the TMG data files are exported to a set of text/data exchange/spreadsheet files. For all data exports, an **Export Wizard** is used.

Data exchange and GEDCOM

GEDCOM files are the *terralingua* of genealogy programs – in other words, the only common language allowing communication between the different programs. More precisely, GEDCOM files are the standard medium of computerized data exchange between users of genealogy software programs (see GEDCOM Overview below).

When you exchange data with other users whether directly or indirectly (for example, via the Internet), you need to make decisions about what data you plan to share and how to share that data. Are you planning to publish the result of your many years of research effort? Maybe you want to limit what you share until your book or CD-ROM is published. How do you respect the privacy of living persons included in your data? Who is that person who has asked you to share your data? Is your data going to appear on a web page without your concurrence? These are non-trivial decisions that require careful thought.

If you plan to exchange data by way of GEDCOM files, you need to understand what data is exported and in what form. You need to understand what data is *not* exported and why. GEDCOM is a loose standard subject to interpretation and misinterpretation by programmers. This results in variations in the GEDCOM files exported by different programs. GEDCOM files work fine when exporting most simple data (birth, marriage, death and burial events with sources) as well as most individual and family events and attributes.

More complex programs such as TMG can record data in forms never anticipated by the current GEDCOM 5.5 standard (see the Export Considerations section below). You need to understand the limitations of GEDCOM files and make decisions very early in your use of TMG about how important GEDCOM export is to your work and whether you need to record your data in TMG so as to maximize what data can be exported. The **Export Considerations** section looks at whether tags have one or two principals, whether you record witnesses in TMG tags, how you record census data, and other issues.

To pull this together, you need to decide how important GEDCOM export is to you very early in your use of TMG. What data is critical to export? How do you enter your data? Do you need to limit what advanced TMG features are used in order to maximize GEDCOM export?

GEDCOM Export

GEDCOM Overview

GEDCOM is an acronym for Genealogical Data COMmunication and the GEDCOM standard was developed by the Family and Church History Department of The Church of Jesus Christ of Latter-day Saints (LDS Church). The current version 5.5 standard was released in final form in January 1996 and this version is supported by all genealogy programs in common use today.

A GEDCOM file is a structured text file divided into several sections.

- **Header** – data detailing the origin, version and character set of the GEDCOM.

- **Individual records** – individuals and their names, events, attributes, and relationships.

- **Family records** – families and their events and attributes.

- **Sources** – where the individual and family data were obtained (books, census records, etc.).

- **Repositories** – where the sources were located (libraries, historical societies, etc.)

- **Trailer** – a marker allowing the importing program to recognize the end of the GEDCOM file.

The GEDCOM files exported by TMG will include the above records and follow this sequence. If the GEDCOM export 'Source' option (see below) is not selected, the Sources and Repository records will not be included.

GEDCOM files are *lineage-linked* meaning that the individuals in the file are tied to other individuals by their relationships... either parent-parent relationships or parent-child relationships.

A GEDCOM file is composed of a series of lines arranged in a hierarchical order. Each line has a *level* number, a *tag*, and an optional value (or text) following the tag. By convention, tags will be in upper case. The data in a GEDCOM file is organized into *records* and each record begins at level 0. TMG tags are exported to GEDCOM tags. An individual's primary name is exported as a GEDCOM NAME tag. A Birth event is exported as a GEDCOM BIRT tag and most other TMG tags are exported to various types of GEDCOM tags. Here is an example of a typical GEDCOM individual event tag.

```
1 BIRT
2 DATE 01 JAN 1900
2 PLAC Worcester, Worcester Co., Massachusetts
2 SOUR @S7@
3 PAGE J. A. Smith gravestone
```

The lines of this example represent:

the GEDCOM birth tag
the birth date
the birth place
a source citation for the birth
the citation detail

Since a GEDCOM file is a text file, you can review and edit the GEDCOM files that you export as long as you are careful to save the file as a text file (not as a word-processing file). Notepad and Microsoft Word both make suitable GEDCOM file editors. Some genealogy programs will require that the GEDCOM file be saved using the MS-DOS 8+3 naming convention (FILENAME.GED) and the names must include a file type of .GED for genealogy programs to recognize them.

The **Export Wizard** gives you some control over the GEDCOM export process. To learn more about GEDCOM files, use your browser and go to the GEDCOM FAQ on the FamilySearch™ web site (*http://www.familysearch.org/Eng/Home/FAQ/frameset_faq.asp?FAQ=faq_gedcom.asp*). From this web page, you can download a copy of the GEDCOM 5.5 Standard in the self-viewing Novell Envoy document format. The Envoy format lets you add your own notes and commentary to the document.

The Export Wizard

To export a GEDCOM file:

Select **File > Export**, from the menu bar.

The **Export Wizard** will appear.

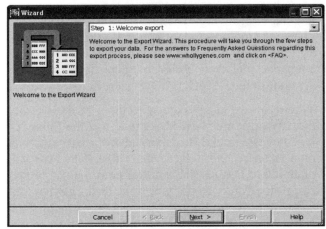

Figure 15-1: Export Wizard, Welcome export

Step 1: Welcome export *(see Figure 15-1)*

Click [Next].

Step 2: Export to *(see Figure 15-2)*

Select the Export file type by highlighting 'Gedcom (*.ged)'.

Specify the GEDCOM filename and path by:

Entering name in the 'Export file name' field,

Entering the destination folder path into the 'Put in folder' field, or

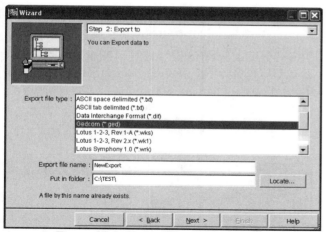

Figure 15-2: Export Wizard, Export to

Click [Locate] and browse to the folder.

The default GEDCOM export filename is NewExport. The file type will always be .GED.

The default destination folder comes from the entry in **File > Preferences > Options > Current Project Options > GEDCOM** field.

If you change the filename and path in the Wizard, your entries will be saved and used the next time that you run the Wizard.

Click [Next] to select an export configuration file.

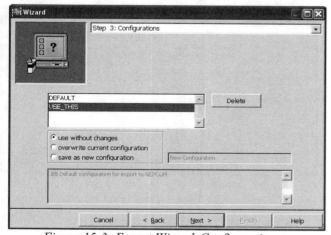

Figure 15-3: Export Wizard, Configurations

Step 3: Configurations *(see Figure 15-3)*

The Export Wizard uses configuration files that are saved in the ..\Reports folder located in the TMG5 program folder. There is a 'DEFAULT' configuration and you can create and save custom

configurations such as the custom configuration named 'USE_THIS' shown in the illustration above. The DEFAULT configuration cannot be modified. On the Configurations screen, you have several options.

Select an existing configuration and select 'use without changes'. This means that you will start with a pre-defined configuration and when you finish the Wizard, the configuration file *will not be overwritten*; however, as you step through the Wizard, you can make whatever changes to the various options that you wish and the changes will be used for the current export.

Select an existing configuration and select 'overwrite the current configuration'. This means that you will start with a pre-defined configuration and plan to make various changes as you step through the Wizard. When you finish the Wizard, the current configuration file will be overwritten.

Select 'save as new configuration' and enter a configuration name in the field to the right. You can enter comments about the configuration in the larger field at the bottom of the Wizard. You will begin with the settings for the configuration selected when you opened the Step 3: Configurations screen (in other words, the saved settings of the configuration last run). When you finish the Wizard, your settings will be saved under the new configuration name.

Existing configurations can be removed with the [Delete] button.

Click [Next] to specify what people to export.

Step 4: Export what people *(see Figure 15-4)*

You now select whom to export.

To export only one person, select 'Current Focus Person' to export the person who was the focus in the Details window when you started the Export Wizard, or, alternatively, click the

![binoculars icon] button and select any other individual from the Picklist.

To export a group of people, select the radio button to the left of the list box to use the current data set. You can select an alternate data

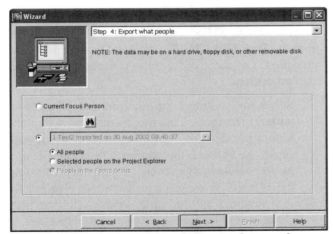

Figure 15-4: Export Wizard, Export what people

set using the list box. You then have three choices.

> Select 'All people' to export all individuals in the data set.

> Select 'Selected people on the Project Explorer' to export those individuals selected on the Project Explorer before you started the Export Wizard, or

> Select 'People in the Focus Group' to export those individuals added to the Focus Group before you started the Export Wizard.

Keep in mind, if you choose the latter two group options, 'Selected People on the Project Explorer' or 'People in the Focus Group', you will need to have defined the group *before* running the Export Wizard. Using the Project Explorer or Focus Group to specify a group of people is discussed further in the 'Export What People' section below.

Click [Next] to begin selecting options.

Step 5: Option Screen 1

(see Figures 15-5 and 15-6)
The Destination determines the GEDCOM version and character set.

> The version can be GEDCOM 4.0, GEDCOM 5.5, Personal Ancestral File ™, Ancestral File ™ or Temple Ready ™. You would typically want to select GEDCOM 5.5 since this is the current standard. Users exporting to one of the other GEDCOM

formats will presumably understand why they would use an alternative format.

The character set can be ANSI, ANSEL or IBMPC. The GEDCOM 5.5 standard specifies ANSEL as the preferred character set and says that characters above 128 (high-bit characters) will only be recognized correctly when ANSEL is used.

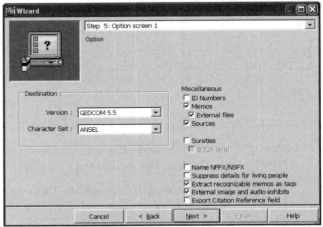

Figure 15-5: Export Wizard, Option screen 1- GEDCOM version 5.5 selected

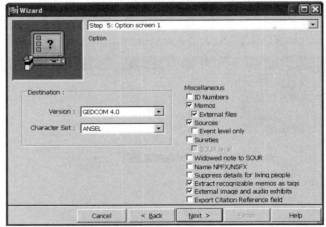

Figure 15-6: Export Wizard, Option screen 1- GEDCOM version 4.0 selected

Miscellaneous options include:

> ID Numbers. The TMG ID# will be exported as a REFN tag if this option is selected. There are two reasons not to select this option.

>> First, the TMG ID# is used as the INDI number for each individual exported to

GEDCOM so the ID#s are preserved already.

Second, ID#s exported as REFN tags will conflict if the Reference fields are exported as REFN tags.

<u>Memos.</u> Memos will be exported as NOTE tags subordinate to event tags if this option is selected. Note that if a memo contains multiple elements (M1, M2, etc.) the entire memo (all elements) is exported.

This does not affect the export of TMG Note tags or memos that are exported as a value for a GEDCOM tag such as OCCU or SSN. These data will be exported even if this option is not selected.

<u>External Files.</u> This option is only active if the Memo option is selected. A TMG memo, rather than containing text, can reference an external text file. If this option is selected, the contents of the text file will be exported as a NOTE tag subordinate to each event tag. If the memo references multiple external text files, only the contents of the first external text file will be exported.

For example, if a Birth event had a memo field with a link to an external text file and both the Memo option and the External Files option are selected, the contents of the text file will be exported as a NOTE tag subordinate to the GEDCOM BIRT tag.

<u>Sources.</u> This setting determines whether source citations and the referenced sources are exported. If the citation detail has multiple CD elements, only CD1 is exported.

<u>Event level only.</u> This option modifies the Sources option and is only present when the GEDCOM output version is not GEDCOM 5.5. For example, when GEDCOM 4.0 output is selected, the source citation data is formatted differently when this option is selected.

GEDCOM 4.0 output ('Event level only' not selected):

```
1 BIRT
2 DATE 1 JAN 1900
3 SOUR @C125@
2 PLAC Anycity, Anycounty, Anystate
3 SOUR @C125@
...
0 @C125@ SOUR
1 TITL @S1@
1 TEXT page 22
```

GEDCOM 4.0 output ('Event level only' selected):

```
1 BIRT
2 DATE 1 JAN 1900
2 PLAC Anycity, Anycounty, Anystate
2 SOUR @C125@
...
0 @C125@ SOUR
1 TITL @S1@
1 TEXT page 22
```

In the 'unselected' example, the source citation is subordinate to the DATE and PLAC tags. In the 'selected' example, the source citation is subordinate to the BIRT tag.

<u>Sureties.</u> This option only affects export if the Sources option is selected. If selected, a QUAY tag is exported with the surety value assigned to the Principal 1 (P1) for a given citation. For example, if a Birth tag had a source citation with a surety value of 3 for the P1, a QUAY tag would be created in the GEDCOM subordinate to the SOUR (source citation) tag with a value of 3.

```
1 BIRT
2 SOUR @S1@
3 QUAY 3
```

With only the Sureties option selected, if there are multiple source citations, a QUAY tag is exported for each citation.

```
1 BIRT
2 SOUR @S1@
3QUAY 3
2 SOUR @S3@
3QUAY 1
2 SOUR @S2@
3QUAY 2
```

No QUAY tags will be exported for source citations having a negative ('-') surety for the P1.

SOUR level. This option modifies the results of the Sureties option and is only active when the Sureties option is selected. If this option is selected, the exported QUAY tag will be exported at the same GEDCOM level as the SOUR (source citation) tag.

```
1 BIRT
2 SOUR @S1@
2 QUAY 3
```

With both the Sureties and SOUR level options selected, if there are multiple source citations, only one QUAY tag will be created and it will have the highest value used among the citations. Using the multiple-citation example above, the exported QUAY tag will have a value of 3, the highest surety used.

```
1 BIRT
2 SOUR @S1@
2 SOUR @S2@
2 SOUR @S3@
2 QUAY 3
```

Widowed note to SOUR. This option is only present when the GEDCOM output version is not GEDCOM 5.5. Some programs export text notes or event details ("of malaria") using a SOUR (source citation) tag. This is probably not the output form intended by the researcher. For example:

```
1 DEAT
1 SOUR @C156@
...
0 @C156@ SOUR of malaria
```

This SOUR data was probably intended to be subordinate to the DEAT (Death) tag as the cause of death (2 NOTE of malaria). The SOUR tag was exported at the same level as the DEAT tag.

When used like this, the SOUR tag is 'widowed' in the GEDCOM file and unassociated with an event as well as unattached to an actual source record.

The Advanced Wizard for GEDCOM import has an option to 'Convert widowed SOURce tags'. If such a structure is recognized, the import places the widowed text into the memo of a TMG Note tag. When this data is exported to a GEDCOM 4.0 file with the 'Widowed note to SOUR' option selected, the data is exported using the same structure as the original GEDCOM.

Name NPFX/NSFX. Names will be exported in the following form:

```
1 TITL Title
1 NAME Prefix GivenName /PreSurname
   Surname/ Suffix
2 NPFX Prefix
2 GIVN GivenName
2 SPFX PreSurname
2 SURN Surname
2 NSFX Suffix
```

This form is necessary for some genealogy programs to import name components to the correct fields.

Suppress details for living people. When this option is selected, only the primary name, sex and relationships are exported for individuals with their living flag set to '?' or 'Y'. Data for those individuals with their living flag set to 'N' are exported as specified by the GEDCOM export settings.

The point of this setting is to allow you to post your research data in a public setting such as on the Internet while, at the same time, respecting the privacy rights of living persons.

Extract recognizable memos as tags. If you export a tag that corresponds to a GEDCOM attribute (for example, a Reference tag that is exported as a GEDCOM REFN tag) and TMG recognizes the first word of the memo as a legal GEDCOM tag followed by a colon, then TMG will export using that GEDCOM tag.

Examples:

Your data include a TMG Reference tag and the memo contains:

AFN: 8LSC-W5

In the Export Wizard, by default, 'Extract recognizable memos as tags' is selected. The data would be exported to GEDCOM as follows:

1 AFN 8LSC-W5

If you unselect 'Extract recognizable memos as tags', the data would be exported as:

1 REFN AFN: 8LSC-W5

Note that this option does not modify data exported from the Reference *field*.

External image and audio exhibits. Links to external image and audio files attached to individuals will be exported as OBJE tags. Most importing programs will use this information to add the links to their multimedia libraries. If you send a GEDCOM to a correspondent without any accompanying image and sound files, you will want to unselect this option.

Export Citation Reference field. If this option is selected, an entry in the Reference field from the Citation screen will be exported in a PAGE tag subordinate to the appropriate SOUR (source citation) tag. If data exists in the Citation Detail field, the reference value will be appended to the citation detail in the PAGE tag following a semicolon ';' separator.

2 SOUR @S15@
3 PAGE page 12; XYZ123

Click [Next] for more options.

Step 6: Option Screen 2 *(see Figure 15-7)*

Tag Types. You can select None, All or Selected.

When you choose Selected tag types, a field shows with all tag types from the current data set. By default, all tag types are selected as indicated by check marks. Note

that you might have saved a mix of marked and unmarked tags in a custom GEDCOM export configuration.

You can [Unmark All] tags and, when one or more tags are unmarked, [Mark All] tags.

You can [Mark] or [Unmark] any single tag using the buttons or by double-clicking the tag name.

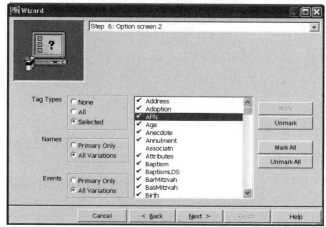

Figure 15-7: Export Wizard, Option screen 2

Names. You can select Primary Only or All Variations.

Events. You can select Primary Only or All Variations.

Click [Next] for more options.

Step 7: Option Screen 3 *(see Figure 15-8)*

Reference field. You can select to export the Reference field (located in the Other Info box on Person view of the Details screen) as Ancestral File # (AFN), Reference (REFN) or Social Security # (SSN).

Exclusion. You can choose whether to export excluded data (Show Excluded Data) or sensitive data (Show Sensitive Data) and, if so, whether to mark that data by enclosing the text in brackets (With Brackets).

Remember that excluded data has been marked with a single exclusion marker ('-') and sensitive data has been marked with braces ('{}'). Data that you have marked with the double exclusion marker ('--') will not be exported irrespective of the Exclusion option settings.

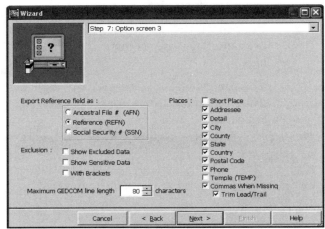

Figure 15-8: Export Wizard, Option screen 3

Maximum GEDCOM line length. You can set the maximum length of a line in the GEDCOM file to a value from 20 to 234 characters.

Text lines that cause the GEDCOM line length to exceed this setting will be broken up with each continuing part preceded by a GEDCOM CONT tag.

Adjustment to the GEDCOM line length may be necessary to facilitate the import of your data by some genealogy programs or online services. In most cases, a setting of 80 should suffice.

Places. You can select what place levels to export to the GEDCOM file.

Short Place. Short place is an alternative to using the data from the place levels (Addressee through Temple). When you select this option, only the short place data will be exported irrespective of whether any following place options are selected. The place used in the GEDCOM output will be the short place data that you entered for a given place in the Master Place List (Tools > Master Place List).

If for a given place, you did not enter short place data, the output will follow the short place template entered in Preferences (**File > Preferences > Options > Current Project Options > Other > Short place template** field. The default short place

template is <[CITY], ><[COUNTY], ><[STATE]>. This template might also appear as <L3,> <L4,> <L5> depending on how your project was originally created.

If Short Place is not selected, you can select to export the Addressee, Detail, City, County, State, Country, Postal Code, Phone and Temple (TEMP) place levels as appropriate to the data recorded for any given tag.

Temple (TEMP). This option serves two purposes. When the Temple (TEMP) option is selected:

The data from the Temple field from TMG LDS tags (BaptismLDS, ConfirmLDS, Endowment, SealChild, SealSpouse) will be exported to a GEDCOM TEMP tag subordinate to the event.

1 BAPL
2 DATE 1 JAN 1950
2 TEMP SLAKE

Latitude/longitude data from TMG non-LDS tags will be added to the data exported to a GEDCOM PLAC tag subordinate to the event.

1 BIRT
2 DATE 1 JAN 1950
2 PLAC 2 PLAC Attalaville, Attala Co., MS,,,, 330035N0894720W

Commas When Missing. You can choose to have 'place holder' commas inserted for any missing place levels. This would facilitate the import of your data into any program that uses structured place levels.

If you select 'Commas When Missing', you can additionally select to trim unnecessary leading and trailing commas (Trim Lead/Trail).

Click [Next] to finish.

Step 8: Finish *(see Figure 15-9)*

When you click [Finish], your GEDCOM export will proceed. The output file will be located using the file name and path that you specified in Step 2 of the Export Wizard.

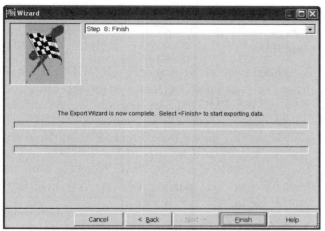

Figure 15-9: Export Wizard, Finish

If you chose to modify an existing GEDCOM export configuration file or to create a new configuration file in Step 3, that new configuration will be saved to the ..\Reports folder located in your TMG5 program folder or in an alternate folder if you specified one in Preferences (**File > Preferences > Options >Current project Options > Advanced > Reports** field. You might, for example, have a different reports folder for each of your projects.

Custom GEDCOM export configuration files

The default settings are read-only in the sense that you can't save an altered Default export configuration file. You'll notice in *Figure 15-03* that I used a custom export configuration file named USE_THIS. For the most part, the default export configuration should be satisfactory for GEDCOM exports; however, there are usually a few settings that you would like to change.

My USE_THIS configuration has the following changes: Changed 'Export what people' from Current Focus Person to All people; and Added Addressee, County, Postal Code and Phone to the Place selections.

You might want to save several special purpose export configuration files... for example, configurations fine-tuned for export to certain genealogy programs or to make a GEDCOM for download from your web site.

'Export What People'

If you are exporting a selected group of people, you have two choices – 'Selected People on the Project Explorer' or 'People in the Focus Group'. The choice is a matter of your intent and work habits.

In both cases, you can save your choice either by saving a filter for the Project Explorer or by saving a Focus Group. The Project Explorer has the advantage if the group will be dynamic – in other words, the composition of the group will change over time. The Focus Group works fine if the group will be static – in other words, once you select the group members and save the Focus Group, the members will not change in the future.

Some things to remember –

- If you filter the Project Explorer to build your group, you need to select the individuals before running the Export Wizard. For example, filter the Project Explorer (PE) for a given flag setting. Restrict the result to Primary names. Click on the first name in the PE and SHIFT Click on the last name in the PE to select all names. Run the Export Wizard and, when you get to the 'Export what people' screen, select 'Selected People on the Project Explorer'.

- If you have saved a Focus Group, open the Focus Group window and [Load...] the saved focus group. Run the Export Wizard and, when you get to the 'Export what people' screen, select 'People in the Focus Group'.

GEDCOM Export Considerations

There is an inevitable conflict between the limitations of the GEDCOM standard and the capabilities of recording data in TMG. At some point, you might need to strike a balance between using all of TMG's features and limiting your data recording options to facilitate GEDCOM export. This section discusses some of the issues that you need to consider. Experiment with various ways to enter your data in TMG. Be familiar with the GEDCOM export choice in tag type definitions. Test the various GEDCOM export options and see what effects the options have. Learn to read a GEDCOM file and understand the limits of this medium. And, last, don't be afraid to edit GEDCOM files.

Appendix G – TMG and GEDCOM File Export Comparison summarizes all of the default GEDCOM export settings and behavior for the default TMG5 tags. Each standard TMG tag is listed showing the GEDCOM export tag selection and whether the TMG tag is exported to an individual record (I), a family record (F) or to either an individual or family record (I/F) depending on whether the TMG tag has one or two principals. These I and F settings are shown for each of the five types of GEDCOM file types that TMG5 supports. Footnotes to the table cover exceptions and variations.

Exactly what data is exported to a GEDCOM file? Individuals and (within the bounds of the operable GEDCOM standard (for example, see the GEDCOM 5.5 section below) and as determined by your GEDCOM export options) all data linked to those individuals are exported. Unlinked data such as unlinked sources and repositories are not exported.

GEDCOM version 5.5 is the current and universally supported GEDCOM format and the remainder of this section will discuss export to GEDCOM 5.5 files. From the Appendix, you will notice that some GEDCOM tags are not supported by the GEDCOM 5.5 standard and you might want to consider exporting to a GEDCOM 4.0 file if necessary to resolve some GEDCOM export issues.

GEDCOM 5.5

The GEDCOM 5.5 specifications have some limitations of which you should be aware. TMG adheres closely to the standards.

ADDR tags are not supported in individual and family records. Address tags with the default 'GEDCOM export as:' setting of ADDR will not export to a GEDCOM 5.5 file. Similarly, PHON tags are not supported in individual and family records. Telephone tags with the default 'GEDCOM export as:' setting of PHON will not export.

Dates and places are not supported for NOTE tags. Note tags with only a Principal 1 (P1) are exported as individual events. Note tags with P1 & P2 who are married are exported as family events. Date and place data will not be exported in either case. Note tags with P1 & P2 who are not married are not exported.

You need to be aware that some GEDCOM tags can be either individual or family tags depending on whether the TMG tag has one or two principals. These tags include CENS (census), NOTE and EVEN (event) tags. For example, a TMG Note tag with only a P1 will be exported as a NOTE tag to the individual's record. A TMG Note tag with P1 and P2 who are married will be exported as a NOTE tag to their family record.

Witnesses. GEDCOM does not support other individuals (TMG witnesses) linked to either individual or family records. If you have witnesses linked to any TMG tag and export that tag to a GEDCOM file, the witness links and any witness individual not otherwise selected for export will not be exported.

Workarounds

The following workarounds will result in non-standard GEDCOM 5.5 files. The data may or may not be imported into other genealogy programs. For example, ADDR tags added to a GEDCOM 5.5 file will almost always be imported.

Address and Telephone Tags. Export address tags under an unused acceptable GEDCOM 5.5 tag name (for example, BARM) and use global search & replace to change them to ADDR in the GEDCOM file. You will also need to delete the DATE line for these tags in the GEDCOM file. If you want the Addressee, Postal Code and Phone place fields exported with the other address information, be sure to select those place choices on the Export Wizard Step 7: Option screen 3 screen. Telephone tags can be exported in a like manner. Alternatively, you can leave the GEDCOM field in the tag type definitions blank and export the TMG Address and Telephone tags as GEDCOM EVEN tags. Other programs may or may not import the ADDR and PHON tags.

> Microsoft Word example when using BARM for Address tags. In the replace dialog, select 'Use wildcards'. Search for: 1 BARM*2 PLAC and Replace with: 1 ADDR)

Note tags. You can use the work-around for the Note date/place problem suggested for ADDR tags.

Export note tags under an unused acceptable GEDCOM 5.5 tag name (for example, BASM) and use global search & replace to change them to NOTE in the GEDCOM file. The note tags with P1 and with P1 & P2 who are married will be exported as individual tags with date/place data.

There is a much simpler fix for the NOTE tag date/place issue. Go to the tag type definition screen for TMG note tags and change the 'GEDCOM export as:' setting to 1 EVEN 2 TYPE. Now your TMG note tags will be exported as EVEN (event) tags of type NOTE and will include date/place data. You might also want to apply this fix to any other TMG tags being exported as GEDCOM NOTE tags. Just remember that exporting non-standard data such as this doesn't guarantee that other genealogy programs will import it.

Census Events

Census can be an export problem depending on how you choose to record census data in TMG. There is a diverse and on-going discussion on the TMG Mailing List (TMG-L) about how to record census events in TMG. There are many 'right' answers to this question but you need to be aware of the GEDCOM export consequences of some of the alternatives.

CENS can be either a GEDCOM 5.5 individual event or a family event depending on whether the data has one or two principals. TMG will export all Census tags with Principal 1 (P1) and Principal 2 (P2) who are married into GEDCOM family records. If P1 and P2 are not married, the Census tag won't be exported. Some use a Census recording scheme described by Diana Begeman (*www.halcyon.com/begeman/Census.htm*). A 'census person' is entered as P2. These Census tags don't export to GEDCOM.

To elaborate on using census as a 'family' event… If you record a TMG Census event with two principals and they are married, this data will be exported to the GEDCOM record for this family as a CENS tag. After import into another program, you will usually find the census data as a marriage event (in other words, an event shared by the husband and wife). Any links to witnesses in the TMG Census tag will be lost in the export/import process.

If you enter the Head of Household as the P1 and everyone else as witnesses, the census tags are exported as GEDCOM CENS tags. The tags appear in the GEDCOM under the individual record of the P1. The witness links are not exported so the census data is actually exported only for the HOH.

You might consider having a tag in TMG for each census entry for each individual (i.e., no P2 and no witnesses). This would conform to the NARA citation recommendations for census. I would suggest two tags, one for HOH and one for all others in the household, each tag with its own sentence structure. The TMG 'Copy tag' facility (**Add > Copy Tag**) makes this very easy to do.

Another trick might be to use witnesses but list all witnesses in the memo field so a record of the non-HOH persons is exported.

Anyone interested in the issue of recording Census tags in TMG should search the TMG-L archives and read the discussions.

Name Variants

Some genealogy programs either don't import name variants (multiple NAME tags), import name variants incorrectly or both. In the latter case, the result would be that only one name variant is imported and it's not the primary variant so you have no choice but to limit the GEDCOM to the primary name only. In a GEDCOM export from TMG, the primary name variant will come first. This is correct. However, some programs incorrectly consider the last encountered GEDCOM NAME tag to be primary.

Export of Custom Tags

Custom tags with only a Principal 1 (P1) are best exported by setting the tag type definition option 'GEDCOM export as:' to 1 EVEN 2 TYPE (**Tools > Master Tag Type List > Tag Type List > Tag Type Definition > Other tab > GEDCOM export as:** selection). Witness links will not be exported. The tags will be exported as:

```
1 EVEN
2 TYPE tagname
```

The sentence structure might be copied to the memo so that the essential tag data is exported. If you use the memo field for text, the TMG memo field elements (M1, M2… M9) would allow both memo text and sentence structure text to be entered into the memo field and all memo elements are exported to the GEDCOM file.

Custom tags (non-family) with P1 & P2 need to have an acceptable GEDCOM 5.5 individual attribute or event tag or they won't export (i.e., enter an appropriate tag name into the GEDCOM field on the Tag Type Definition Screen). They will appear under P1 and P2. The custom tag name will be lost. You could edit these entries to 1 EVEN 2 TYPE entries in the GEDCOM. Witness links will not be exported. The sentence structure might be copied to the memo to make these tags make sense.

Custom tags with P1 and P2 using an acceptable family event tag will export as family events. If P1 & P2 are married, custom tags with P1 & P2 and with the tag definition option 'GEDCOM export as:' set to 1 EVEN 2 TYPE will export as family events with the structure:

        1 EVEN
        2 TYPE tagname

P1 & P2 Married	Tag Definition GEDCOM setting	GEDCOM Export Result
Yes	1 EVEN 2 TYPE	Family tag
Yes	Individual event tag	Individual tags
Yes	Family event tag	Family tag
No	1 EVEN 2 TYPE	No tag export
No	Individual event tag	Individual tags
No	Family event tag	No tag export

Table 15-1: Export Summary for Custom Tags

with P1 & P2

Some programs will import these family tags into marriage facts or the marriage note. As with census events discussed above, these custom tags will typically end up as marriage events shared by the husband and wife after import into another program. If you want to have these custom events

imported as individual events by another program, you might need to reconsider how the data is recorded in TMG. Do you add both P1 and P2 to your custom tags? Do you want to record the custom tags under each individual's record using only P1? Remember, again, that witness links will not be exported.

Some Last Thoughts

All data to be exported to GEDCOM 5.5 files must use legal version 5.5 tags or have the tag type definition option 'GEDCOM export as:' to 1 EVEN 2 TYPE. Note that some default TMG tag types have inappropriate GEDCOM tags for version 5.5 export entered on their Tag Type Definition screen and need to be changed if you wish to export those tags to GEDCOM 5.5 files.

GEDCOM export is an area where you need to experiment until you achieve the desired results. With proper preparation of your TMG data and proper selection of the GEDCOM export options, you can export most TMG data into a version 5.5 GEDCOM. Even so, the resulting GEDCOM might require some editing to optimize the data for import to another program.

GEDCOM Export to Selected Destination Programs

The following notes cover issues encountered when GEDCOM files exported from TMG5 are imported into other genealogy programs. These notes don't cover all of the possibilities but give you some idea of what will happen to your data on import to another program.

A .LST file is created by the importing program as a record of issues encountered during the import. The .LST file is typically saved in the same folder as the GEDCOM file being imported. TMG5 saves the .LST file in the project folder of the project into which the GEDCOM file was imported. .LST files vary somewhat between different importing programs but usually describe each encountered issue with:

- the line number in the GEDCOM file where the issue was encountered,

- the type of issue or a warning or error message (that may or may not be helpful),

- specific data or one or more lines of GEDCOM code that triggered the problem, and

- the import action taken (what was done with this GEDCOM data).

Here's a .LST file example from a Family Tree Maker import:

Line 7720: Tag: DATE, invalid date: FROM 1950 TO 1978, line ignored.

This example consists of the GEDCOM line number, the GEDCOM tag and the import issue, the data that resulted in the error, and the action taken during import.

Warnings may simply be telling you to check the imported data to make sure that it was imported correctly.

Evaluating issues after a GEDCOM import requires that you look at:

- the .LST file,

- the GEDCOM file in the area of the line number triggering the .LST file error report or warning, and, perhaps,

- the data that has been imported by the program doing the import.

You might also need to study the appropriate sections of the GEDCOM 5.5 specifications to fully understand the GEDCOM data. This process is less complicated than it sounds and just requires a bit of practice. GEDCOM import errors and warnings tend to be repetitive. In other words, a given type of error or warning might occur many times during the import and will be reported an equal number of times in the .LST file. This type of repetition usually accounts for the bulk of .LST file entries.

Ancestry Family Tree 9.0.3 (AFT)

A .LST file for the import is created and the details can optionally be included in each individual's notes. Only the primary NAME tag is imported and other NAME tags are discarded. The primary name sources are linked to the 'Record.' You need to select the 'Name NPFX/NSFX' option for prefixes/suffixes to be handled properly. NICK tags are not imported by AFT and ADDR tags are imported but subordinate NOTE tags and ADDR

sources are not imported. Addresses will need cleanup. Notes from OCCU tags are added to the event Description field while notes from other event tags such as CENS and RESI are disconnected from the events and put into the general Notes field. NCHI tags are not imported. Sources for NOTE tags are not imported. Links to image files are imported but are not recognized as photos and are not marked default. Once you edit the link to select the item type and mark the image default, it displays properly.

Family Origins® 10 (FOW10)

A .LST file for the import is created. Family origins 10 and earlier versions of FOW incorrectly import the last of multiple name tags as primary and drop the other names. In defining your GEDCOM export, you need to select the 'Name NPFX/NSFX' option for prefixes/suffixes to be handled properly and select the 'Names - Primary only' choice. Sources for NAME tags are not imported. NICK, ADDR, and NCHI tags are not imported. The links to external image files are not imported.

Family Tree Maker® 10 (FTW10)

A .LST file for the import is created. All NAME tags and their sources are imported and the primary name is marked as primary. NICK tags are not imported. FROM… TO dates as well as nonstandard dates are considered to be invalid and are ignored. A FixDates utility is available (*http://home.speedfactory.net/pkmorse/fixdates.html*) to preprocess a GEDCOM before FTW import and to deal with dates that FTW won't import. Notes from OCCU tags are added to the event Comment/Location field while notes from other event tags such as CENS and RESI are disconnected from the events and put into the general Notes field. ADDR tags are imported and will need cleaning up. Address text that exceeds the field length is truncated. DSCR and NCHI tags are not imported. The Source title CONT lines are not added to the Title field but the full title and source abbreviation are added to the Comments field. Source memos go into the Source quality field and may be clipped if too long. Unlike earlier FTW versions, the repository NAME line is no longer imported to Source Location field. Sources for NOTE tags are not imported.

Generations® 8.6.0.0 (Gen8) (also Generations® Plus 8.5a)

A .LST file for the import is not created. This means that you don't have the one tool required to make an overall assessment of the success of the import. Name elements are imported to the correct fields. Multiple imported NAME tags have the given names and surnames concatenated (Parthenia/Partheny Winham/Dalrymple/Gardner). This behavior is not optional and can only be averted by selecting the 'Names - Primary only' GEDCOM export option in TMG. Unrecognized tags are marked as *New [tagname] and the event name can be edited during import or afterwards. Tags not recognized and needing renaming include NICK, DSCR, EDUC, GRAD, NCHI, OCCU and all custom events exported as 1 EVEN 2 TYPE tags. Most of these tags are set to be imported as events. EDUC and GRAD are set to be imported as custom notes but you should change these to be imported as events. GEDCOM tags such as NICK and SSI that have a 'value' can be imported as facts. If a tag has text in a subordinate NOTE tag (such as OCCU) and you import it as a fact, the note text will be lost. BETWEEN… AND dates are considered nonstandard. These and irregular dates can be retained and a sort date saved at the event level. The source ABBR tag is imported as a *New [ABBR] source field and the field name can be corrected globally after import. Although OBJE tags that link to external exhibit files are imported as events, the images and other files are not linked to the individual.

Legacy 4.0.0.129 (Legacy)

An ERROR.LOG for the import is created in the Legacy program folder. I would suggest renaming this file to a .LST file using the GEDCOM name and moving it to a safe place before it is overwritten. NICK tags are unrecognized and the data are added to the General note field. NCHI tags with a non-numeric count of children are added to the General or Marriage note field as appropriate. If a Legacy note field contains multiple GEDCOM 1 NOTE tags, there is no longer a connection between each note and its source although all of the sources will be attached to the Legacy note.

FamilySearch™ Personal Ancestral File 5 (PAF5)

A .LST file for the import is created and the listing file data can optionally be included in each individual's notes. Only the primary name variant is imported although the program has fields for other variants. The primary name sources are marked as being linked to the 'Record.' NICK tags are not imported. Notes from OCCU tags are added to the event Description field while notes from other event tags such as CENS and RESI are disconnected from the events and put into the general Notes field. ADDR tags are imported to a single field and will need cleanup; however, subordinate NOTE tags and ADDR sources are not imported. Sources for 1 NOTE tags are not imported. Links to image files are imported but the default image needs to be marked in order to display.

'Data File' Export.

Most users consider 'export' to be synonymous with 'GEDCOM export' but TMG has another option that allows almost all user-entered data to be exported. For lack of a better term, we'll call this alternative 'Data File' export. An example of data not exported by this option would be internal images.

TMG stores the data for each project in a series of files rather than in a single file. For example, names are stored in one file, events in another and sources in yet another. This collection of files is located in one folder for each project and together the files for each project make up a database. For export to a selected 'Data File' format, there will be one exported data file of the selected export type corresponding to each TMG database file (.DBF) with user data. You initiate 'Data File' export from an open project using the **Export Wizard (File > Export)**.

As we proceed through the Export Wizard for 'Data File' export, we'll refer to the illustrations for GEDCOM export. The screens are identical except for the step numbers used on the third and fourth screens.

When you start the Export Wizard, you are greeted by the **Step 1: Welcome export** screen (*see Figure 15-1*). You click [Next] to proceed to the **Step 2: Export to** screen (*see Figure 15-2*). You select the

'Export file type' and fill in the 'Export file name' and 'Put in folder' fields. Since there is no default output folder setting in Preferences for 'Data File' export, the destination folder must be specified on this screen. The 'Data File' export file name and export path entries are saved for subsequent runs of the Export Wizard.

The export file type can be ASCII (*.txt); ASCII comma delimited (*.txt); ASCII space delimited (*.txt); ASCII tab delimited (*.txt); Data Interchange Format (*.dif); Lotus 1-2-3, Rev 1-A (*.wks); Lotus 1-2-3, Rev 2.x (*.wk1); Lotus Symphony 1.0 (*.wrk); Lotus Symphony 1.10 (*.wr1); Microsoft Excel worksheet (*.xls); Microsoft Excel version 5.0 (*.xls); Microsoft Multiplan version 4.01 (*.mod); Symbolic Link (sylk) or System Data Format (*.sdf). Presumably, any user using 'Data File' export will understand these various export file types and which file type to choose.

After selecting the export file type, click [Next] to go to the **Step 3: Export what people** screen (*see Figure 15-4*). This screen lets you select the people to be exported. The choices are either the current focus person or another selected individual or a group chosen from one selected data set (All people, Selected people in the Project Explorer or People in the Focus Group). These are the only options for 'Data File' export. Click [Next] to go to the **Step 4: Finish** screen (*see Figure 15-9*) and click [Finish] to initiate the export.

If you now use Windows™ Explorer to open the destination folder that you specified in Step 2, you will see 21 files with a part of their name being the file name that you specified in Step 2. The remainder of each file name will reflect the names of the project files from which the data was exported. The files will be formatted according to the export file type that you specified in Step 2. For example, if you export to Microsoft Excel worksheet (*.xls), the destination folder will contain 21 .XLS files.

'Data File' export is clearly not a feature that will be used by the average TMG5 user. To make use of the exported data files, you would need to write a custom database application or to develop a spreadsheet to handle the data directly. Alternatively, you could write a program (called a 'filter') to convert the data to a file format readable by another genealogy program.

Appendix A – Glossary

Administrator
See System Administrator

Automatic "Relation" Tag
A special Tag Type that computes and displays the first relationship found, if any, for everyone in a data set relative to the focus person.

Backup
The process by which data in a project is saved in a file for future use in the event data is lost due to a system crash or for whatever reason.

BMDB
An acronym for Birth, Marriage, Death, and Burial, the usual basic events for which data is gathered about a person.

Canvas
The rectangular (white) space on which the contents of the chart are displayed.

Citation
(1) A record describing the material supporting the data to which the record is attached.
(2) The printed reference to material supporting data.

Citation Detail
The additional information about a source that may be used to describe the material noted in the Source record.

Collate Sequence
The order in which characters and numbers are alphabetized for a particular language.

Computer Administrator
See System Administrator

Configuration
This is a saved list of settings or options. It may be reused for the creation of the same type of report at a later time.

Data set
A collection of ancestor and/or descendant data and related events, sources, repositories, research tasks and exhibits.

Export
A process by which data is manipulated and stored in files for use with another program.

Flag
A one-character field that may be used to codify information about a person or classify individuals into categories.

Focus Group
A group of persons on which various operations may be performed.

Focus Person
The person used as the starting point when navigating the relationships in a data set to find all the persons to be displayed on a chart.

Frame
This is used with Exhibits and in Slideshows and is synonymous with Slide. This is also used in Visual Chartform to mean the decorative scalable graphic that surrounds a chart box.

GEDCOM
An acronym for GEnealogical Data COMmunication, a general protocol used for transferring data from one program to another.

History Tag
A special type of tag that has no principals, only Witnesses.

Image Thumbnail
A small, low resolution, image created by TMG from existing exhibits and used instead of the (possibly) high resolution exhibit(s) to maximize throughput

Import
A process by which the program reads, interprets, and appropriately stores data from external files either from another program or from an earlier version of TMG.

Irregular Date
A value entered in a Date field which is not a valid date.

Layout

The way in which the TMG main screen is designed and includes the Toolbars, windows, their sizes, and positions.

Memo

A text field used to enter miscellaneous data beyond, date and place information

OLE

An abbreviation for Object Linking and Embedding, a protocol by which an object, such as a spreadsheet, graph or word processing document can be inserted, or embedded, in another file.

Picklist

A search tool for finding persons, Sources, and other information in a project or data set.

Pixels

Picture elements - the smallest elements on a screen. Visual Chartform uses pixels as its unit of measure of some distances. As a guide, most computer systems set to the standard Windows screen font size, have about 96 pixels per inch (3.8 pixels per mm) at normal (100%) display.

Primary Name

The actual name that is used for a person on a chart. See *Chapter 5, Customizing the Data* for more information.

Primary Relationship

Only one relationship between a father or mother and child may be primary and this is the one used to link persons for the purpose of drawing a chart.

Principal

One or two persons who as witnesses are most closely associated with an event (see also Witness)

Project

Contains one or more independent data sets that are separated from each other by a "firewall" that protects data in one data set from that of other data sets.

Project Explorer

A window that provides an overview of the data in a project.

Repository

(1) The physical location in which source material may be found.
(2) A record in a data set describing the place in which source material may be found.

Restore

The process by which data in a backup file is placed in the regular project data files.

Sentence Structure

The pattern by which data is printed for narrative reports based on the content of the Tag.

Slide

Used with Exhibits and in Slideshows to mean an image, audio, video, or OLE file for display or playing.

Sort Date

An element of data that is used to position or sequence a Tag within the Person View.

Source

(1) The original material from which you obtained data (a book, a census schedule, a birth certificate).
(2) A record within a data set describing documentary material.

Source Element

The individual fields that comprise a Source Template.

Source Group

A collection of Source Elements. Only one element from a Source Group may be used in any one Source record.

Source Template

The pattern of Source Elements. Text, and punctuation used to develop citations.

SQZ

Pronounced "squeeze," the compressed file format created by running a TMG Backup.

Style

A template by which name or place data is labeled in records or presented in reports.

Surety

A numerical value representing the user's evaluation of a source as to the credibility of the data given.

System Administrator

A person who has administrative privileges on a computer running Windows NT, Windows 2000, Windows XP or later. Installation of TMG or some components of TMG under one of these operating systems may require a person with administrative privileges.

Tag

Used to record information about the events, names, and relationships associated with a person or persons in your data set.

Tag Group

A grouping of Tag Types into major administrative groups.

Tag Type

A record used to enter data of a certain kind to describe a name, an event, a relationship, or other data.

Timeline

A database containing items of historical interest by date.

witness

A person associated with an event either as a Principal or as a Witness.

Witness

A person associated with an event but not as a Principal.

WYSIWYG

An acronym for 'What You See Is What You Get'.

Appendix B - Standard Tag Types & Sentences

The following table shows the standard tags supplied with The Master Genealogist, the Tag Group to which each belongs, and the GEDCOM label used when exporting data to a GEDCOM file. In addition, the standard Tag (Principal) and Witness Sentences for each Tag are shown. Tags that do not have a Tag or a Witness Sentence or a GEDCOM label are noted as "-N/A-" in the appropriate Sentence field.

TAG LABEL	TAG GRP	GEDCOM LABEL
TAG or PRINCIPAL SENTENCE		
WITNESS SENTENCE		
Address	Address	ADDR
<As of [D],> [P] <and [PO]> lived at [L]		
<As of [D],> [W] was living with [P] <and [PO]> at <[L]>		
Adoption	Other	ADOP
[P] <was|and [PO] were> adopted <[D]> <[L]>		
[W] witnessed the adoption of [P] <and [PO]> <[D]> <[L]>		
AFN	Other	AFN
[PP] Ancestral File Number is [M]		
-N/A-		
Age	Other	AGE
[P1] was [A] <as of [D]>.		
-N/A-		
Anecdote	Other	-N/A-
[M]		
[W] was a witness [M]		
Annulment	Other	ANUL
The marriage of [P] and [PO] was annulled <[D]> <[L]>		
[W] witnessed the annulment of [P] <and [PO]> <[D]> <[L]>		
Associatn	Other	ASSO
[P] <was|and [PO] were> associated <[D]> <[L]>		
[W] witnessed the association of [P] <and [PO]> <[D]> <[L]>		
Attributes	Other	ATTR
[P] <was|and [PO] were> [M] <[D]> <[L]>		
-N/A-		
Baptism	Birth	BAPM
[P] was baptized <[D]> <[L]>		
[W] witnessed the baptism of [P] <and [PO]> <[D]> <[L]>		
BaptismLDS	Other	BAPL
[P] <was|and [PO] were> baptized in the LDS church <[D]> <[L]>		
[W] witnessed the baptism in the LDS church of [P] <and [PO]> <[D]> <[L]>		

TAG LABEL	TAG GRP	GEDCOM LABEL
TAG or PRINCIPAL SENTENCE		
WITNESS SENTENCE		
BarMitzvah	Other	BARM
[P] received [PP] bar mitzvah <[D]> <[L]>		
[W] witnessed the bar mitzvah of [P] <and [PO]> <[D]> <[L]>		
BasMitzvah	Other	BASM
[P] received [PP] bas mitzvah <[D]> <[L]>		
[W] witnessed the bas mitzvah of [P] <and [PO]> <[D]> <[L]>		
Birth	Birth	BIRT
[P] was born <[D]> <[L]>		
[W] witnessed the birth of [P] <and [PO]> <[D]> <[L]>		
Birth-Covt	Birth	BIC
[P] was born in the covenent <[D]> <[L]>		
[W] witnessed the birth in the covenent of [P] <and [PO]> <[D]> <[L]>		
BirthIlleg	Birth	ILLE
[P] was born illegitimate <[D]> <[L]>		
[W] witnessed the illegitimate birth of [P] <and [PO]> <[D]> <[L]>		
BirthStill	Birth	STIL
[P] was stillborn <[D]> <[L]>		
[W] witnessed the stillbirth of [P] <and [PO]> <[D]> <[L]>		
Blessing	Other	BLES
[P] <|and [PO]> received a blessing <[D]> <[L]>		
[W] witnessed the blessing of [P] <and [PO]> <[D]> <[L]>		
BlessngLDS	Other	BLSL
[P] <was|and [PO] were> blessed in the LDS church <[D]> <[L]>		
[W] witnessed the blessing in the LDS church of [P] <and [PO]> <[D]> <[L]>		
Burial	Burial	BURI
[P] was buried <[D]> <[L]>		
[W] witnessed the burial of [P] <and [PO]> <[D]> <[L]>		

TAG LABEL	TAG GRP	GEDCOM LABEL
TAG or PRINCIPAL SENTENCE		
WITNESS SENTENCE		

CancelSeal	Other	CANC
The sealing for [P] <and [PO]> was cancelled <[D]> <[L]>		
[W] witnessed the cancelled sealing of [P] <and [PO]> <[D]> <[L]>		

Caste	Other	CAST
[P] <was|and [PO] were> belonged to the [M] caste <[D]> <[L]>		
[W] belonged to the [M] caste <[D]> <[L]>		

Census	Other	CENS
[P] <and [PO]> appeared on the census <of [D]> <[L]>		
[W] appeared on the census <of [D]> in the household of [P] <and [PO]> <[L]		

Christning	Birth	CHR
[P] was christened <[D]> <[L]>		
[W] witnessed the christening of [P] <and [PO]> <[D]> <[L]>		

Codicil	Other	CODI
[P] <|and [PO]> wrote a codicil <[D]> <[L]>		
[W] witnessed the codicil of [P] <and [PO]> <[D]> <[L]>		

Communion1	Other	FCOM
[P] <|and [PO]> received First Holy Communion <[D]> <[L]>		
[W] witnessed the First Holy Communion of [P] <and [PO]> <[D]> <[L]>		

Confirmatn	Other	CONF
[P] <was|and [PO] were> confirmed <[D]> <[L]>		
[W] witnessed the confirmation of [P] <and [PO]> <[D]> <[L]>		

ConfirmLDS	Other	CONL
[P] <was|and [PO] were> confirmed by the LDS church <[D]> <[L]>		
[W] witnessed the confirmation in the LDS church of [P] <and [PO]> <[D]> <[L]>		

Criminal	Other	CRIM
[P] <was|and [PO] were> [M] <[D]> <[L]>		
[W] was a witness that [P] <was|and [PO] were> [M] <[D]> <[L]>		

Death	Death	DEAT
[P] died <[D]> <[L]> <[A]>		
[W] witnessed the death of [P] <and [PO]> <[D]> <[L]>		

Descriptn	Other	DESR
[P] <was|and [PO] were> described <as [M]> <[D]> <[L]>		
[W] witnessed the description of [P] <and [PO]> <as [M]> <[D]> <[L]>		

Divorce	Divorce	DIV
[P] and [PO] were divorced <[D]> <[L]>		
[W] witnessed the divorce of [P] <and [PO]> <[D]> <[L]>		

Divorce Fl	Divorce	DIVF
[P1] filed for divorce from [P2] <[D]> <[L]>		
[W] witnessed the divorce filing of [P] <and [PO]> <[D]> <[L]>		

Education	Other	EDUC
[P] <was|and [PO] were> educated <[D]> <[L]>		
[W] witnessed the education of [P] <and [PO]> <[D]> <[L]>		

Emigration	Other	EMIG
[P] <|and [PO]> emigrated <[D]> <from [L]>		
[W] emigrated with [P] <and [PO]> <[D]> <[L]>		

Employment	Other	EMPL
[P] <was|and [PO] were> employed <by [M]> <[D]> <[L]>		
[W] was employed <by [M]> with [P] <and [PO]> <[D]> <[L]>		

Endowment	Other	ENDL
[P] received [PP] endowment <[D]> <[L]>		
[W] witnessed the endowment of [P] <and [PO]> <[D]> <[L]>		

Engagement	Other	ENGA
[P] <was|and [PO] were> engaged <[D]> <[L]>		
[W] witnessed the engagement of [P] <and [PO]> <[D]> <[L]>		

Event-Misc	Marriage	EVEN
[P] <was|and [PO] were> [M] <[D]> <[L]>		
[W] was a witness when [P] <was|and [PO] were> [M] <[D]> <[L]>		

Excommuntn	Other	EXCO
[P] <was|and [PO] were> excommunicated <[D]> <[L]>		
[W] witnessed the excommunication of [P] <and [PO]> <[D]> <[L]>		

Father-Ado	Other	-N/A-
-N/A-		
-N/A-		

Father-Fst	Relationship	-N/A-
-N/A-		
-N/A-		

Father-God	Relationship	-N/A-
-N/A-		
-N/A-		

TAG LABEL	TAG GRP	GEDCOM LABEL
TAG or PRINCIPAL SENTENCE		
WITNESS SENTENCE		
Father-Nat	Relationship	-N/A-
-N/A-		
-N/A-		
Father-Oth	Relationship	-N/A-
-N/A-		
-N/A-		
Father-Ste	Relationship	-N/A-
-N/A-		
-N/A-		
GEDCOM	Relationship	GEDC
Unrecognized GEDCOM data: [M] <[D]> <[L]>		
-N/A-		
Graduation	Other	GEDC
[P] <was|and [PO] were> graduated <[D]> <[L]>		
[W] witnessed the graduation of [P] <and [PO]> <[D]> <[L]>		
History	History	-N/A-
-N/A-		
[W] witnessed [M] <[D]> <[L]>		
HTML	Other	-N/A-
(see also [M])		
(see also [M])		
Illness	Other	-N/A-
[P] <was|and [PO] were> ill with [M] <[D]> <[L]>		
[W] witnessed the illness of [P] <and [PO]> <[D]> <[L]>		
Immigratn	Other	IMMI
[P] <|and [PO]> immigrated <[D]> <to [L]>		
[W] witnessed the immigration of [P] <and [PO]> <[D]> <[L]>		
Living	Other	-N/A-
[P] <was|and [PO] were> living <[D]> <[L]>		
[W] was a witness to the fact that [P] <was|and [PO] were> living <[D]> <[L]>		
Marr Bann	Marriage	MARB
Marriage banns for [P] <and [PO]> were published <[D]> <[L]>		
[W] witnessed the publication of marriage banns of [P] <and [PO]> <[D]> <[L]>		
Marr Cont	Marriage	MARC
A contract for the marriage of [P] and [PO] was signed <[D]> <[L]>		
[W] witnessed the marriage contract of [P] <and [PO]> <[D]> <[L]>		

TAG LABEL	TAG GRP	GEDCOM LABEL
TAG or PRINCIPAL SENTENCE		
WITNESS SENTENCE		
Marr Lic	Marriage	MARL
[P] and [PO] obtained a marriage license <[D]> <[L]>		
[W] witnessed the marriage license of [P] <and [PO]> <[D]> <[L]>		
Marr Sett	Marriage	MARS
A settlement for the marriage [P] and [PO] was made <[D]> <[L]>		
[W] witnessed the marriage settlement of [P] <and [PO]> <[D]> <[L]>		
Marriage	Marriage	MARR
[P] married [PO] <[PARO]> <[D]> <[L]>		
[W] witnessed the marriage of [P] <and [PO]> <[D]> <[L]>		
Milit-Beg	Other	-N/A-
[P] <|and [PO]> began military service <[D]> <[L]> <[M]>		
[W] witnessed the beginning of military service of [P] <and [PO]> <[D]> <[L]>		
Milit-End	Other	-N/A-
[P] <|and [PO]> ended military service <[D]> <[L]>		
[W] witnessed the end of military service of [P] <and [PO]> <[D]> <[L]>		
Misc	Other	MISC
[P] <was|and [PO] were> [M] <[D]> <[L]>		
[W] was a witness to [M] with [P] <and [PO]> <[D]> <[L]>		
Mother-Ado	Relationship	-N/A-
-N/A-		
-N/A-		
Mother-Fst	Relationship	-N/A-
-N/A-		
-N/A-		
Mother-God	Relationship	-N/A-
-N/A-		
-N/A-		
Mother-Nat	Relationship	-N/A-
-N/A-		
-N/A-		
Mother-Oth	Relationship	-N/A-
-N/A-		
-N/A-		

TAG LABEL	TAG GRP	GEDCOM LABEL
TAG or PRINCIPAL SENTENCE		
WITNESS SENTENCE		
Mother-Ste	Relationship	-N/A-
-N/A-		
-N/A-		
Name-Baptm	Name	-N/A-
[PP] baptism name was [N] <[M]>		
-N/A-		
Name-Chg	Name	-N/A-
<On [D]> [PP] name was legally changed to [N] <[M]>		
-N/A-		
Name-Marr	Name	-N/A-
As of [D],>[PP] married name was [N] <[M]>		
-N/A-		
Name-Nick	Name	-N/A-
<As of [D],> [P] also went by the name of [N] <[M]>		
-N/A-		
Name-Var	Name	-N/A-
<As of [D],> [P] was also known as [N] <[M]>		
-N/A-		
Namesake	Other	NAMS
[P1] was named for [P2]		
-N/A-		
Nationalty	Other	NATI
The nationality of [P] <and [PO]> was [M]		
-N/A-		
Natlzation	Other	NATU
[P] <was|and [PO] were> naturalized <[D]> <[L]>		
[W] witnessed the naturalization of [P] <and [PO]> <[D]> <[L]>		
Note	Other	NOTE
[P] <|and [PO]> [M] <[D]> <[L]>		
[W] was a witness [M] with [P] <and [PO]> <[D]> <[L]>		
NullifyLDS	Other	NULL
[PP] ordinance was nullified by the LDS church <[D]> <[L]>		
[W] witnessed the ordinance nullification of [P] <and [PO]> <[D]> <[L]>		
Num Child	Other	NCHI
[P] <|and [PO]> had [M] children		
-N/A-		

TAG LABEL	TAG GRP	GEDCOM LABEL
TAG or PRINCIPAL SENTENCE		
WITNESS SENTENCE		
Num Marr	Other	NMR
[P] <was|and [PO] were> married [M] times		
-N/A-		
Occupation	Other	OCCU
[P] <was|and [PO] were> [M] <[D]> <[L]>		
[W] was associated with [P] <and [PO]> [M] <[D]> <[L]>		
OrdinacLDS	Other	ORDL
[P] <|and [PO]> participated in an ordinance in the LDS church <[D]> <[L]>		
[W] witnessed the ordinance in the LDS church of [P] <and [PO]> <[D]> <[L]>		
Ordinance	Other	ORDI
[P] <|and [PO]> partipicated in an ordinance <[D]> <[L]>		
[W] witnessed the ordinance of [P] <and [PO]> <[D]> <[L]>		
Ordination	Other	ORDN
[P] <was|and [PO] were> ordained <[D]> <[L]>		
[W] witnessed the ordination of [P] <and [PO]> <[D]> <[L]>		
Parent-Ado	Relationship	-N/A-
-N/A-		
-N/A-		
Parent-Fst	Relationship	-N/A-
-N/A-		
-N/A-		
Parent-God	Relationship	-N/A-
-N/A-		
-N/A-		
Parent-Nat	Relationship	-N/A-
-N/A-		
-N/A-		
Parent-Oth	Relationship	-N/A-
-N/A-		
-N/A-		
Parent-Ste	Relationship	-N/A-
-N/A-		
-N/A-		
Probate	Burial	PROB
[PP] estate was probated <[D]> <[L]>		
[W] witnessed the probate of the estate of [P] <and [PO]> <[D]> <[L]>		

TAG LABEL	TAG GRP	GEDCOM LABEL
TAG or PRINCIPAL SENTENCE		
WITNESS SENTENCE		

TAG LABEL	TAG GRP	GEDCOM LABEL
PrsmCancel	Other	PRES
[PP] ordinance was presumed cancelled <[D]> <[L]>		
[W] witnessed the cancelled ordinance of [P] <and [PO]> <[D]> <[L]>		
Psgr List	Other	PASL
[P] <was|and [PO] were> found on a passenger list <[D]> <[L]>		
[W] was found on a passenger list with [P] <and [PO]> <[D]> <[L]>		
Ratificatn	Other	RATI
[P] <was|and [PO] were> ratified <[D]> <[L]>		
[W] witnessed the ratification of [P] <and [PO]> <[D]> <[L]>		
Rebaptism	Birth	REBA
[P] was rebaptized <[D]> <[L]>		
[W] witnessed the rebaptism of [P] <and [PO]> <[D]> <[L]>		
Reference	Other	REFN
Reference: [M] <[D]> <[L]>		
[W] was a witness to [M] with [P] <and [PO]> <[D]> <[L]>		
Religion	Other	RELI
[P] <was|and [PO] were> [M]		
[W] was [M] with [P] <and [PO]> <[D]> <[L]>		
Reseal	Other	RESE
[P] <was|and [PO] were> resealed <[D]> <[L]>		
[W] witnessed the resealing of [P] <and [PO]> <[D]> <[L]>		
Residence	Other	RESI
[P] <|and [PO]> lived <[D]> <[L]>		
[W] lived with [P] <and [PO]> <[D]> <[L]>		
Restoratn	Other	REST
[P] <was|and [PO] were> restored <[D]> <[L]>		
[W] witnessed the restoration of [P] <and [PO]> <[D]> <[L]>		
Retirement	Other	RETI
[P] <was|and [PO] were> retired <[D]> <[L]>		
[W] witnessed the retirement of [P] <and [PO]> <[D]> <[L]>		

TAG LABEL	TAG GRP	GEDCOM LABEL
SealChild	Other	SLGC
[P] <was sealed as a child|and [PO] were sealed as children> to [PAR] <[D]>		
[W] witnessed the sealing of [P] <|and [PO]> to [PAR] <[D]> <[L]>		
SealParent	Birth	SLGP
[P] was sealed as a parent to [PO] <[D]> <[L]>		
[W] witnessed the sealing of parent to child of [P] <and [PO]> <[D]> <[L]>		
SealSpouse	Marriage	SLGS
[P] was sealed as a spouse of [PO] <[D]> <[L]>		
[W] witnessed the sealing to spouse of [P] <and [PO]> <[D]> <[L]>		
SSN	Other	SSN
[PP] Social Security Number was [M] <[D]> <[L]>		
-N/A-		
Stake	Address	STAL
<As of [D],> [P] <and [PO] > <[L]>		
-N/A-		
Telephone	Other	PHON
[PP] telephone number was [M] <[D]> <[L]>		
-N/A-		
VoidLiving	Other	VOIL
[PP] ordinance by proxy was cancelled <[D]> <[L]>		
[W] witnessed the cancellation of the ordinance by proxy of [P] <and [PO]>		
WAC	Other	WAC
[P] <was|and [PO] were> received [PP] initiatory ordinances <[D]> <[L]>		
[W] witnessed the initiatory ordinances of [P] <and [PO]> <[D]> <[L]>		
Will	Other	WILL
[P] left a will <[D]> <[L]>		
[W] witnessed the will of [P] <and [PO]> <[D]> <[L]>		

Appendix C - Sentence Variables and Embedded Codes

The following is a quick reference list of the variables that may be used in Sentence Structures in TMG Tags. For details, see *Chapter 6, Sentence Structures*.

Variable	Meaning
Name Variables for Principals	
[P] or [P+]	Current Principal's name (note 1)
[PG]	Current Principal, Given name
[PF]	Current Principal, First word of given name
[PGS]	Current Principal, Possessive given
[PFS]	Current Principal, Possessive first word of given name
[PS]	Current Principal, Possessive name
[PO]	Other Principal's name
[POG]	Other Principal, Given name
[POF]	Other Principal, First word of given name
[POGS]	Other Principal, Possessive given
[POFS]	Other Principal, Possessive first word of given name
[POS]	Other Principal, Possessive name
[P1]	First Principal, Full name
[P1G]	First Principal, Given name
[P1F]	First Principal, First word of given name
[P1GS]	First Principal, Possessive given name
[P1FS]	First Principal, Possessive first word of given name
[P1S]	First Principal, Possessive name
[P2]	Second Principal, Full Name
[P2G]	Second Principal, Given name
[P2F]	Second Principal, First word of given name
[P2GS]	Second Principal, Possessive given name
[P2FS]	Second Principal, Possessive first word of given name
[P2S]	Second Principal, Possessive name

Variable	Meaning
Name Variables for Witnesses	
[W] or [W+]	Current Witness (note 1)
[WO]	Other Witnesses
Name Variables for Roles (see note 2)	
[R:*Role*] or [R+:*Role*]	Full name of the person in the role (note 1)
[RG:*Role*]	Given name of the person in the role
[RF:*Role*]	First name of the person in the role
Name Variables for Parents	
[PAR]	Current Principal's Parents
[PARO]	Other Principal's Parents
[PAR1]	First Principal's Parents names
[PAR2]	Second Principal's Parents names
[FATH]	Father of the current principal
[MOTH]	Mother of the current principal
Pronoun Variables	
[PP]	Current Principal, Possessive Pronoun
[OBJ]	Current Principal, Objective Pronoun
[RP:*Role*]	Nominative pronoun for the person in the role
[RS:*Role*]	Possessive pronoun for the person in the role
[RM:*Role*]	Objective pronoun for the person in the role

Notes:
1. May substitute the nominative pronoun (he or she), unless the "+" version is used.

2. The "*Role*" indicates the name of a role is to be entered, as [R:Minister] or [RA:Bride]

Variable	Meaning
Name Tag Variables for Names (see Note)	
[P]	Current Principal's name
[N]	Name of the current principal in the current tag
[PP]	Current Principal, Possessive Pronoun
[OBJ]	Current Principal, Objective Pronoun
Note: These may only be used in the Name Tag Sentences	

Variable	Meaning
Age Variables	
[A]	Age of the current principal in years
[AE]	Exact age (years, months, and days) of current principal
[AO]	Age of the other principal in years
[AOE]	Exact age of the other principal
[A1]	Age of the first principal in years
[A1E]	Exact age of first principal
[A2]	Age of the second principal in years
[A2E]	Exact age of second principal
[RA:*Role*]	Age of the person in the role
[RE:*Role*]	Exact age of the person in the role

Variable	Meaning
Date Variables	
[D]	Date
[DD]	Date including the day of the week

Variable	Meaning
Place Variables	
[L]	Place data (all fields, as specified by Place Style or report options)
[L1] or [LA] or [ADDRESSEE]	Addressee field
[L2] or [LD] or [DETAIL]	Detail field
[L3] or [LCI] or [CITY]	City field
[L4] or [LCN] or [COUNTY]	County field
[L5] or [LS] or [STATE]	State field
[L6] or [LCR] or COUNTRY]	Country field
[L7] or [LZ] or [ZIP]	Postal Code field
[L8] or [LL] or [LATLONG]	Latitude - Longitude field
[L9] or [LP] or [PHONE]	Telephone field
[L10] or [LT] or [TEMPLE]	Temple field

Variable	Meaning
Memo Variables	
[M]	The Memo field
[M1] ... [M9]	Segments of a split Memo
<[M0]>	Forces a Memo field to **not** print

The following Embedded Codes may be used in Sentence Structures, Memo and other data fields, in Source Templates, and in Source Elements. Most are described in more detail in *Chapter 6, Sentence Structures*. Embedded Citations are described in *Chapter 7, Sources*

Code	Meaning
Formatting Text	
[BOLD:]*text*[:BOLD]	Text is bold
[UND:]*text*[:UND]	Text is underlined
[ITAL:]*text*[:ITAL]	Text is italicized
[SUP:]*text*[:SUP]	Text is printed as superscript
[SUB:]*text* [:SUB]	Text is printed as subscript
[CAP:]*text*[:CAP]	Text is in uppercase
[SCAP:]*test*[:SCAP]	Text is in small caps

Code	Meaning
Embedded Citations	
[CIT:]source #:surety; citation detail[:CIT]	Inserts citation to indicated source

Code	Meaning
Special Characters	
[:CR:]	Carriage return (new line)
[:TAB:]	Tab character (or equivalent number of spaces)
[:NB:]	Non-breaking space

Code	Meaning
Report Font Codes – See Note 1.	
[FONTT:]*text*[:FONTT]	Text font style
[FONTS:]*text* [:FONTS]	Surname font style
[FONTG:]*text*[:FONTG]	Given Names font style
[FONTD:]*text*[:FONTD]	Dates font style
[FONTL:]*text*[:FONTL]	Places font style
[FONTM:]*text*[:FONTM]	Memos font style
[FONTE:]*text*[:FONTE]	Exponents font style
[FONTB:]*text*[:FONTB]	Labels font style
[FONTI:]*text*[:FONTI]	Titles font style
[FONTP:]*text*[:FONTP]	Page Numbers font style

Note: 1. These codes would apply the font options as selected on the **Report Definition** screen [Options] button Font tab.

Code	Meaning
Special Format Codes	
[HID:]*text*[:HID]	Text is hidden
[INDEX:]*text* [:INDEX]	Creates Index entry for specified text
[SIZE:]<number>;*text* [:SIZE]	Text is printed in the point size (number) chosen
[EMAIL:]*text*[:EMAIL]	Text is treated as e-mail address
[HTML:]text[:HTML]	Text is treated as HTML codes
[WEB:]*text*[:WEB]	Text is treated as Internet link

Appendix D - Translation of Source Types

TMG features two distinct sets of default **Source Types** modeled after the categories from two style guides; *Cite Your Sources* by Richard S. Lackey and *Evidence! Citation & Analysis for the Family Historian* by Elizabeth Shown Mills. TMG users can easily change from one default category to the other, or to a custom category based on either default *(see Chapter 7, Sources)*. This table shows how source types drawn from one default category are translated to source types drawn

from the other. For example, a TMG Source record based on *Cite Your Sources* using the Periodical source type (left column), would translate to the *Evidence!* Article (Journal) source type (center column). Similarly, a TMG Source record based on *Evidence!* using the Article (Serialized; Annotated Citation) source type (center column) would translate to the *Cite Your Sources* Periodical source type (right column).

How Source Types Drawn From One Style Guide Translate To The Other		
Cite Your Sources ➜	*Evidence!* ➜	*Cite Your Sources*
	Ancestral File(TM)	Unpublished / Miscellaneous
Periodical	Article (Journal)	Periodical
	Article (Serialized; Annotated Citation)	Periodical
Civil Vital Record	Baptismal Record	Civil Vital Record
Family Bible	Bible Record	Family Bible
	Birth Registration (Local Level)	Civil Vital Record
	Birth Registration (State Level)	Civil Vital Record
	Book (Authored by an Agency)	Book, Pamphlet, or Monograph
Book, Pamphlet, or Monograph	Book (Authored)	Book, Pamphlet, or Monograph
	Book (Compiled Records)	Book, Pamphlet, or Monograph
	Book (Edited)	Book, Pamphlet, or Monograph
	Book (Multi-Authored)	Book, Pamphlet, or Monograph
	Book (Multi-Volume)	Book, Pamphlet, or Monograph
	Book (Multi-Volume, Compendium)	Book, Pamphlet, or Monograph
	Book (One of Series)	Book, Pamphlet, or Monograph
	Book (Paginated, with Numbered Entries)	Book, Pamphlet, or Monograph
	Book (Reprint)	Book, Pamphlet, or Monograph
	Book (Revised Edition)	Book, Pamphlet, or Monograph
	Book Chapter	Book, Pamphlet, or Monograph
State/Federal Land Record	Bounty-Land File (Federal, Unfilmed)	State/Federal Land Record
	CD-ROM (Produced from Original Records)	Unpublished / Miscellaneous
	CD-ROM (Produced from Prior Publication)	Unpublished / Miscellaneous
Church/Cemetery Record	Cemetery Marker	Church/Cemetery Record
	Cemetery Marker (Published)	Church/Cemetery Record
Census Record	Census Compendium	Census Record
	Census, Federal (Filmed)	Census Record
	Census, Federal (Local/State Copy)	Census Record
	Census, State	Census Record
	Church Minute	Church/Cemetery Record
	City (or County) Directory	Unpublished / Miscellaneous
	Computer Software	Unpublished / Miscellaneous
	DAR Genealogical Records Committee Report (DAR Library Copy)	Unpublished / Miscellaneous
	DAR Genealogical Records Committee Report (Local/State Copy)	Unpublished / Miscellaneous
	Death Registration (Local Level)	Civil Vital Record
	Death Registration (State Level)	Civil Vital Record
	Deed (State Level)	State/Federal Land Record
	Deed (Town or County Level)	State/Federal Land Record
	Diary or Journal (Manuscript)	Unpublished / Miscellaneous

How Source Types Drawn From One Style Guide Translate To The Other		
Cite Your Sources →	*Evidence!* →	*Cite Your Sources*
	Diary or Journal (Published, Edited)	Unpublished / Miscellaneous
	Dissertation	Unpublished / Miscellaneous
	Dissertation (Microfilmed)	Unpublished / Miscellaneous
	E-Mail Message	Unpublished / Miscellaneous
	Electronic Database (Family File)	Unpublished / Miscellaneous
	Electronic File (Image from Private Files - Annotated)	Unpublished / Miscellaneous
	Electronic File (Image fm.Public Archives)	Unpublished / Miscellaneous
	Electronic File (Listserve Message)	Unpublished / Miscellaneous
	Electronic Web Site	Unpublished / Miscellaneous
	Electronically Published Paper (Previously Published in Hard Copy)	Unpublished / Miscellaneous
	Family Group Sheet (with Annotation)	Unpublished / Miscellaneous
	Government Document (Published)	Book, Pamphlet, or Monograph
	International Genealogical Index™ Entry	Unpublished / Miscellaneous
Oral Communication	Interview	Oral Communication
	Law, Federal	Unpublished / Miscellaneous
	Law, State	Unpublished / Miscellaneous
	Lecture (Taped)	Unpublished / Miscellaneous
	Legal Case (Published Report)	Unpublished / Miscellaneous
	Legal Case (Unpublished)	Unpublished / Miscellaneous
Letter	Letter (Annotated Citation)	Letter
	Lineage Application	Unpublished / Miscellaneous
	Manuscript (Filmed for Distribution)	Book, Pamphlet, or Monograph
	Manuscript (Filmed, Limited Distribution)	Book, Pamphlet, or Monograph
Unpublished / Miscellaneous	Manuscript (Unfilmed)	Unpublished / Miscellaneous
	Map (Historic)	Unpublished / Miscellaneous
	Map (Topographic)	Unpublished / Miscellaneous
	Marriage (Church - Certificate)	Church/Cemetery Record
	Marriage (Church - Copy, Copyist Known)	Church/Cemetery Record
	Marriage (Church - Copy, Copyist Unknown)	Church/Cemetery Record
	Marriage (Church - Original Record)	Church/Cemetery Record
	Marriage (Civil)	Civil Vital Record
Military Record	Military - Service File (Filmed)	Military Record
	Military Record (Manuscript)	Military Record
	National Archives Film/Fiche (Basic Form)	Unpublished / Miscellaneous
	National Archives Manuscript (Basic Form)	Unpublished / Miscellaneous
	National Archives Regional (Unofficial Film Holdings)	Unpublished / Miscellaneous
	Naturalization Record	Unpublished / Miscellaneous
Newspaper	Obituary/Newspaper Item	Newspaper
	Pension File (Filmed)	Unpublished / Miscellaneous
	Periodical (Issued in Multiple Series)	Periodical
	Photo, Portrait, or Illustration (Archival) (With Annotation)	Unpublished / Miscellaneous
	Photograph (Private Possession) (Annotated with Provenance)	Unpublished / Miscellaneous
Courthouse Record	Probate File	Courthouse Record
	Research Report	Unpublished / Miscellaneous
	Series - Book (with Subsets)	Book, Pamphlet, or Monograph
	Ship Passenger List (Filmed)	Unpublished / Miscellaneous
	Social Security Death Index (SSDI)	Unpublished / Miscellaneous
	Syllabus Material	Unpublished / Miscellaneous
Tax List	Tax Roll, Filmed	Tax List
	Tax Roll, Unfilmed	Tax List
	Thesis	Unpublished / Miscellaneous
	Town Record	Civil Vital Record
	Translated Work	Unpublished / Miscellaneous

How Source Types Drawn From One Style Guide Translate To The Other		
Cite Your Sources ➔	Evidence! ➔	Cite Your Sources
	Video	Unpublished / Miscellaneous
	Vital Record (Filmed)	Courthouse Record
	Vital Record (Published)	Civil Vital Record
	Will (Recorded)	Courthouse Record
	Will (Unrecorded, Consulted Off-Site)	Courthouse Record

Appendix E – Standard Source Groups and Source Elements

TMG **Source Templates** are constructed using **Source Elements**, each of which is an alias that represents a **Source Element Group**. Only one Element from the same Element Group can be used in the same Template. Each Element used in a Template becomes a data entry field for a source using that template. When TMG generates a narrative report, the footnotes (or endnotes), short footnotes (or short endnotes) and bibliography entries used in the report are constructed using the templates and data for each source.

Below is a list of the **Source Element Groups** and the [Source Elements] used to represent each Group.

Author
  [Agency]
  [Author]
  [First Party]
  [Informant]
  [Speaker]

Citation Detail
  [CD]
  [CD1]
  [CD2]
  [CD3]
  [CD4]
  [CD5]
  [CD6]
  [CD7]
  [CD8]
  [CD9]

Citation Reference
  [Cref]

Comments
  [Comments]
  [M]
  [M1]
  [M2]
  [M3]
  [M4]
  [M5]
  [M6]
  [M7]
  [M8]
  [M9]
  [Memo]
  [Memo1]
  [Memo2]
  [Memo3]
  [Memo4]

  [Memo5]
  [Memo6]
  [Memo7]
  [Memo8]
  [Memo9]

Compiler
  [Compiler]

Date
  [Compile Date]
  [Date]
  [File Date]
  [Interview Date]
  [Printout Date]
  [Publish Date]
  [YEAR]

Edition
  [Edition]
  [Record Group]
  [Subset Volumes]

Editor
  [Editor]

File Reference
  [File Name]
  [File Reference]

Film Number
  [Film Number]
  [Film]

Location
  [Address]
  [Author Address]
  [Compiler Address]
  [Informant Address]
  [Jurisdiction]
  [Listserve]

  [Location]

Pages
  [Document]
  [Pages]
  [Page]

Publisher
  [Publisher]

Publisher Location
  [Publisher Address]
  [Publisher Location]

Record Number
  [Call Number]
  [File Number]
  [Manuscript Info]
  [Number]
  [Record Info]
  [Record Number]
  [Register]

Record Type
  [Record Type]

Repository
  [Repository]

Repository Info
  [Repository Address]
  [Repository Info]

Repository Reference
  [Repository Reference]

Second Date
  [Original Date]
  [Period]
  [Second Date]
  [DATE VIEWED]

Second Location
[Author E-Mail]
[Recipient Address]
[Second Location]
[URL]
[STATE]

Second Person
[Applied to]
[Interviewer]
[Photographer]
[Present Owner]
[Reader]
[Recipient]
[Second Party]
[Second Person]
[Ship Name]
[Translator]

Series
[Series]
[Subset]
[WEBSITE]

Short subtitle
[Short Article Title]
[Short Chapter Title]
[Short Essay Title]
[Short Record Title]
[Short Register Title]
[Short Subtitle]

Short title
[Short Bible Title]
[Short Book Title]
[Short Compilation Title]
[Short Journal Title]
[Short Newspaper Title]
[Short Title]

Subject
[Family Info]
[Household]
[Name of Person]
[Spouses' Names]
[Subject]
[Testator]

Subtitle
[Article Title]
[Chapter Title]
[Essay Title]
[Record Title]
[Register Title]
[Subtitle]

Title
[Bible Title]
[Book Title]
[Compilation Title]
[Journal Title]
[Newspaper Title]
[Title]

Version
[Roll]   [IMAGE]
[Version]
[STATE ONLINE]

Volumes
[Volumes]
[Volume]

Appendix F - Source Templates

These are the default templates that TMG uses to build full footnotes (**FF**), short footnotes (**SF**), and bibliographic references (**B**), according to source type. The templates were designed according to Wholly Genes' interpretation of two style guides, *Cite Your Sources* by Richard Lackey and *Evidence!* by Elizabeth S. Mills (see below).

Users should note that the source templates were constructed by Wholly Genes, Inc., according to their particular interpretation of the style guides and are not intended to suggest endorsement on the part of their authors, nor does Wholly Genes warrant that they accurately reflect the intentions of those authors. Users are encouraged to consult the style guides in question to ensure proper usage.

Section 1 – Source Categories as drawn from: Lackey, Richard S., *Cite Your Sources: A Manual for Documenting Family Histories and Genealogical Records.* (Jackson, Mississippi: University Press of Mississippi, 1980).

— Book, Pamphlet, or Monograph —
FF: [AUTHOR], [ITAL:][TITLE][:ITAL] in [ITAL:][SERIES][:ITAL]<, [VOLUME]> (<[EDITION]; >[PUBLISHER ADDRESS]: [PUBLISHER], [PUBLISH DATE])<, [PAGE]>< [CD]>.
SF: [AUTHOR], [ITAL:][SHORT TITLE][:ITAL]<, [PAGE]>< [CD]>.
B: [AUTHOR]. [ITAL:][TITLE][:ITAL] in [ITAL:][SERIES][:ITAL]<, [VOLUME]> (<[EDITION]; >[PUBLISHER ADDRESS]: [PUBLISHER], [PUBLISH DATE]).

— Census Record —
FF: [TITLE]<, [PAGE]>< [CD]>< [REPOSITORY]>.
SF: [SHORT TITLE]<, [PAGE]>< [CD]>.
B: [TITLE]<, [REPOSITORY]>.

— Church/Cemetery Record —
FF: [TITLE], [PUBLISH DATE]<, [PAGE]>< [CD]>< [MEMO]>< [REPOSITORY]>.
SF: [SHORT TITLE]<, [PAGE]>< [CD]>.
B: [TITLE], [PUBLISH DATE]<, [MEMO]>< [REPOSITORY]>.

— Civil Vital Record —
FF: [TITLE], [PUBLISH DATE]<, [PAGE]>< [CD]>< [MEMO]>< [REPOSITORY]>.
SF: [SHORT TITLE]<, [PAGE]>< [CD]>.
B: [TITLE], [PUBLISH DATE]<, [MEMO]>< [REPOSITORY]>.

— Courthouse Record —
FF: [TITLE], [PUBLISH DATE]<, [PAGE]>< [CD]>< [MEMO]>< [REPOSITORY]>.
SF: [SHORT TITLE]<, [PAGE]>< [CD]>.
B: [TITLE], [PUBLISH DATE]<, [MEMO]>< [REPOSITORY]>.

— Family Bible —
FF: [ITAL:][TITLE][:ITAL] (<[EDITION]; >[PUBLISHER ADDRESS]: [PUBLISHER], [PUBLISH DATE]<, [CD]>< [REPOSITORY]>.
SF: [ITAL:][SHORT TITLE][:ITAL]<, [CD]>.
B: [ITAL:][TITLE][:ITAL] (<[EDITION]; >[PUBLISHER ADDRESS]: [PUBLISHER], [PUBLISH DATE])<, [REPOSITORY]>.

— Letter —
FF: [TITLE], [PUBLISH DATE]<, [CD]>< [MEMO]>< [REPOSITORY]>.
SF: [SHORT TITLE]<, [CD]>.
B: [TITLE], [PUBLISH DATE]<, [MEMO]>< [REPOSITORY]>.

— Military Record —
FF: [TITLE], [PUBLISH DATE]<, [PAGE]>< [CD]>< [MEMO]>< [REPOSITORY]>.
SF: [SHORT TITLE]<, [PAGE]>< [CD]>.
B: [TITLE], [PUBLISH DATE]<, [MEMO]>< [REPOSITORY]>.

— Newspaper —
FF: [ITAL:][TITLE][:ITAL], ([PUBLISHER ADDRESS]: [PUBLISHER], [PUBLISH DATE])<, [PAGE]>< [CD]><; [REPOSITORY]>.
SF: [ITAL:][SHORT TITLE][:ITAL]<, [PAGE]>< [CD]>.
B: [ITAL:][TITLE][:ITAL], ([PUBLISHER ADDRESS]: [PUBLISHER], [PUBLISH DATE])<, [REPOSITORY]>.

— Oral Communication —
FF: [TITLE], [PUBLISH DATE]<, [PAGE]>< [CD]>< [MEMO]>< [REPOSITORY]>.
SF: [SHORT TITLE]<, [PAGE]>< [CD]>.
B: [TITLE], [PUBLISH DATE]<, [MEMO]>< [REPOSITORY]>.

— **Periodical** —
FF: [AUTHOR], "[TITLE]", [ITAL:][SERIES][:ITAL]<, [VOLUME]><, [PAGE]><, [CD]>.
SF: [AUTHOR], "[SHORT TITLE]"<, [PAGE]><, [CD]>.
B: [AUTHOR], "[TITLE]," [ITAL:][SERIES][:ITAL]<, [VOLUME]>.

— **State/Federal Land Record** —
FF: [TITLE], [PUBLISH DATE]<, [PAGE]><, [CD]><, [MEMO]><, [REPOSITORY]>.
SF: [SHORT TITLE]<, [PAGE]><, [CD]>.
B: [TITLE], [PUBLISH DATE]<, [MEMO]><, [REPOSITORY]>.

— **Tax List** —
FF: [TITLE]<, [PAGE]><, [CD]><, [REPOSITORY]>.
SF: [SHORT TITLE]<, [PAGE]><, [CD]>.
B: [TITLE]<, [REPOSITORY]>.

— **Unpublished / Miscellaneous** —
FF: [TITLE], [PUBLISH DATE]<, [MEMO]><, [PAGE]><, [CD]><, [REPOSITORY]>.
SF: [SHORT TITLE]<, [PAGE]><, [CD]>.
B: [TITLE], [PUBLISH DATE]<, [MEMO]><, [REPOSITORY]>.

Section 2 – *Source Categories as drawn from: Mills, Elizabeth Shown,* Evidence!: Citation & Analysis for the Family Historian *(Baltimore: Genealogical Publishing Company, 1997).*

— **Ancestral File(TM)** —
FF: [COMPILER], compiler, "[TITLE]";< [CD],> [ITAL:]Ancestral File[:ITAL]<, [VERSION]> <([DATE]), >[REPOSITORY], [REPOSITORY ADDRESS]<. Hereinafter cited as "[SHORT TITLE]">.
SF: [COMPILER], "[SHORT TITLE]", [ITAL:]Ancestral File[:ITAL]<, [CD]>.
B: [ITAL:]Ancestral File[:ITAL]<, [VERSION]>. [REPOSITORY], [REPOSITORY ADDRESS]<, [DATE]>.

— **Article (Journal)** —
FF: [AUTHOR], "[ARTICLE TITLE]", [ITAL:][JOURNAL TITLE][:ITAL] <[VOLUME]>< ([DATE])><: [CD]>. Hereinafter cited as "[SHORT ARTICLE TITLE]">.
SF: [AUTHOR], "[SHORT ARTICLE TITLE]"<, [CD]>.
B: [AUTHOR]. "[ARTICLE TITLE]", [ITAL:][JOURNAL TITLE][:ITAL]< [VOLUME]> <([DATE])>.

— **Article (Serialized; Annotated Citation)** **FF:** [AUTHOR], "[TITLE]," [ITAL:][SERIES][:ITAL]<, [DATE]><, [COMMENTS]><, [CD]><. Hereinafter cited as "[SHORT TITLE]">.
SF: [AUTHOR], "[SHORT TITLE]," [ITAL:][SERIES][:ITAL]<, [DATE]><, [CD]>.
B: [AUTHOR], "[TITLE]." [ITAL:][SERIES][:ITAL]<. [DATE]>.

— **Baptismal Record** —
FF: [VOLUME], [TITLE]<: [CD]><, ([DATE])><, [COMMENTS]>, [REPOSITORY], [REPOSITORY ADDRESS]<. Hereinafter cited as [SHORT TITLE]>.
SF: [VOLUME], [SHORT TITLE]<: [CD]><, [DATE]>, [REPOSITORY].
B: [REPOSITORY ADDRESS]. [REPOSITORY]. [TITLE]<, [DATE]>.

— **Bible Record** —
FF: [FAMILY INFO], [ITAL:][BIBLE TITLE][:ITAL]<, [EDITION]> ([PUBLISHER ADDRESS]: [PUBLISHER], [PUBLISH DATE]); [PRESENT OWNER], [LOCATION]<, [CD]><. Hereinafter cited as [SHORT BIBLE TITLE]>.
SF: [SHORT BIBLE TITLE]<, [CD]>.
B: [FAMILY INFO]. [ITAL:][BIBLE TITLE][:ITAL]<, [EDITION]>. [PUBLISHER ADDRESS]: [PUBLISHER], [PUBLISH DATE]. [PRESENT OWNER], [LOCATION].

— **Birth Registration (Local Level)** —
FF: [SUBJECT] entry, [RECORD TYPE]< [NUMBER]><, [CD]>< ([DATE])>, [REPOSITORY], [REPOSITORY ADDRESS].
SF: [SUBJECT] entry, [RECORD TYPE]< [NUMBER]><, [CD]>< ([DATE])>.
B: [REPOSITORY ADDRESS]. [RECORD TYPE]. [SUBJECT] entry.

— **Birth Registration (State Level)** —
FF: [NAME OF PERSON], [RECORD TYPE]< [FILE NUMBER]><, [CD]> ([FILE DATE]), [REPOSITORY], [REPOSITORY ADDRESS].
SF: [NAME OF PERSON], [RECORD TYPE]< [FILE NUMBER]><, [CD]> ([FILE DATE]).
B: [REPOSITORY ADDRESS] [REPOSITORY]. [NAME OF PERSON] [RECORD TYPE].

— **Book (Authored by an Agency)** —
FF: [AGENCY], [ITAL:][TITLE][:ITAL] ([PUBLISHER ADDRESS]: [PUBLISHER]<, [PUBLISH DATE]>)<, [CD]><. Hereinafter cited as [ITAL:][SHORT TITLE][:ITAL]>.
SF: [AGENCY], [ITAL:][SHORT TITLE][:ITAL]<, [CD]>.
B: [AGENCY]. [ITAL:][TITLE][:ITAL]. [PUBLISHER ADDRESS]: [PUBLISHER]<, [PUBLISH DATE]>.

— Book (Authored) —
FF: [AUTHOR], [ITAL:][TITLE][:ITAL] ([PUBLISHER ADDRESS]: [PUBLISHER], [PUBLISH DATE])<, [CD]><. Hereinafter cited as [ITAL:][SHORT TITLE][:ITAL]>.
SF: [AUTHOR], [ITAL:][SHORT TITLE][:ITAL]<, [CD]>.
B: [AUTHOR]. [ITAL:][TITLE][:ITAL]. [PUBLISHER ADDRESS]: [PUBLISHER]<, [PUBLISH DATE]>.

— Book (Compiled Records) —
FF: [COMPILER], compiler, [ITAL:][TITLE][:ITAL] ([PUBLISHER ADDRESS]: [PUBLISHER]<, [PUBLISH DATE]>)<, [CD]><. Hereinafter cited as [ITAL:][SHORT TITLE][:ITAL]>.
SF: [COMPILER], [ITAL:][SHORT TITLE][:ITAL]<, [CD]>.
B: [COMPILER]. [ITAL:][TITLE][:ITAL]. [PUBLISHER ADDRESS]: [PUBLISHER]<, [PUBLISH DATE]>.

— Book (Edited) —
FF: [EDITOR], editor, [ITAL:][TITLE][:ITAL] ([PUBLISHER ADDRESS]: [PUBLISHER]<, [PUBLISH DATE]>)<, [CD]><. Hereinafter cited as [ITAL:][SHORT TITLE][:ITAL]>.
SF: [EDITOR], [ITAL:][SHORT TITLE][:ITAL]<, [CD]>.
B: [EDITOR]. [ITAL:][TITLE][:ITAL]. [PUBLISHER ADDRESS]: [PUBLISHER]<, [PUBLISH DATE]>.

— Book (Multi-Authored) —
FF: [AUTHOR], [ITAL:][TITLE][:ITAL] ([PUBLISHER ADDRESS]: [PUBLISHER]<, [PUBLISH DATE]>)<, [CD]><. Hereinafter cited as [ITAL:][SHORT TITLE][:ITAL]>.
SF: [AUTHOR], [ITAL:][SHORT TITLE][:ITAL]<, [CD]>.
B: [AUTHOR]. [ITAL:][TITLE][:ITAL]. [PUBLISHER ADDRESS]: [PUBLISHER]<, [PUBLISH DATE]>.

— Book (Multi-Volume) —
FF: [AUTHOR] [ITAL:][TITLE][:ITAL]<, [VOLUME]> ([PUBLISHER ADDRESS]: [PUBLISHER]<, [PUBLISH DATE]>)<, [CD]><. Hereinafter cited as [ITAL:][SHORT TITLE][:ITAL]>.
SF: [AUTHOR] [ITAL:][SHORT TITLE][:ITAL]<, [CD]>.
B: [AUTHOR]. [ITAL:][TITLE][:ITAL]<. [VOLUME]>. [PUBLISHER ADDRESS]: [PUBLISHER]<, [PUBLISH DATE]>).

— Book (Multi-Volume, Compendium) —
FF: [AUTHOR], "[ESSAY TITLE]," [ITAL:][BOOK TITLE][:ITAL], ([PUBLISHER ADDRESS]: [PUBLISHER], [DATE])<, [VOLUME]><, [CD]><, [COMMENTS]><. Hereinafter cited as "[ITAL:][SHORT BOOK TITLE][:ITAL]">.
SF: [AUTHOR], "[ESSAY TITLE]," [ITAL:][SHORT BOOK TITLE][:ITAL]<, [VOLUME]><, [CD]><, [COMMENTS]>.
B: [AUTHOR], "[ESSAY TITLE]," [ITAL:][BOOK TITLE][:ITAL]<, [VOLUME]>, ([PUBLISHER ADDRESS]: [PUBLISHER]<, [DATE]>)<. [COMMENTS]>.

— Book (One of Series) —
FF: [AUTHOR], [ITAL:][TITLE][:ITAL], [SERIES] ([PUBLISHER ADDRESS]: [PUBLISHER]<, [PUBLISH DATE]>)<, [CD]><. Hereinafter cited as [ITAL:][SHORT TITLE][:ITAL]>.
SF: [AUTHOR], [ITAL:][SHORT TITLE][:ITAL]<, [CD]>.
B: [AUTHOR]. [ITAL:][TITLE][:ITAL]. [SERIES]. [PUBLISHER ADDRESS]: [PUBLISHER]<, [PUBLISH DATE]>.

— Book (Paginated, with Numbered Entries) —
FF: [COMPILER], compiler, [ITAL:][TITLE][:ITAL] ([PUBLISHER ADDRESS]: [PUBLISHER]<, [PUBLISH DATE]>)<, [CD]><. Hereinafter cited as [ITAL:][SHORT TITLE][:ITAL]>.
SF: [COMPILER], [ITAL:][SHORT TITLE][:ITAL]<, [CD]>.
B: [COMPILER], compiler. [ITAL:][TITLE][:ITAL]. [PUBLISHER ADDRESS]: [PUBLISHER]<, [PUBLISH DATE]>.

— Book (Reprint) —
FF: [AUTHOR], [ITAL:][TITLE][:ITAL] ([ORIGINAL DATE]; reprint [PUBLISHER ADDRESS]: [PUBLISHER]<, [PUBLISH DATE]>)<, [CD]><. Hereinafter cited as [ITAL:][SHORT TITLE][:ITAL]>.
SF: [AUTHOR], [ITAL:][SHORT TITLE][:ITAL]<, [CD]>.
B: [AUTHOR]. [ITAL:][TITLE][:ITAL]. [ORIGINAL DATE]. Reprint [PUBLISHER ADDRESS]: [PUBLISHER]<, [PUBLISH DATE]>.

— Book (Revised Edition) —
FF: [AUTHOR], [ITAL:][TITLE][:ITAL], [EDITION] ([PUBLISHER ADDRESS]: [PUBLISHER]<, [PUBLISH DATE]>)<, [CD]><. Hereinafter cited as [ITAL:][SHORT TITLE][:ITAL]>.
SF: [AUTHOR], [ITAL:][SHORT TITLE][:ITAL]<, [CD]>.
B: [AUTHOR]. [ITAL:][TITLE][:ITAL]<. [EDITION]>. [PUBLISHER ADDRESS]: [PUBLISHER]<, [PUBLISH DATE]>.

— Book Chapter —
FF: [AUTHOR], "[CHAPTER TITLE]," in [ITAL:][BOOK TITLE][:ITAL]<, [EDITOR], editor>. ([PUBLISHER ADDRESS]: [PUBLISHER]<, [PUBLISH DATE]>)<, [CD]><. Hereinafter cited as "[SHORT CHAPTER TITLE]">.
SF: [AUTHOR], "[SHORT CHAPTER TITLE]"<, [CD]>.
B: [AUTHOR]. "[CHAPTER TITLE]." In [ITAL:][BOOK TITLE][:ITAL]<. [EDITOR], editor>. [PUBLISHER ADDRESS]: [PUBLISHER]<, [PUBLISH DATE]>.

— Bounty-Land File (Federal, Unfilmed) —
FF: [NAME OF PERSON] [RECORD TYPE]<; [FILE NUMBER]>< [CD]>; [SERIES]; [RECORD GROUP]; [REPOSITORY], [REPOSITORY ADDRESS].
SF: [NAME OF PERSON] [RECORD TYPE]<; [FILE NUMBER]><, [CD]> [REPOSITORY], [REPOSITORY ADDRESS].
B: [REPOSITORY ADDRESS]. [REPOSITORY]<. [RECORD GROUP]><. [SERIES]>.

— CD-ROM (Produced from Original Records)

FF: [COMPILER], [ITAL:][COMPILATION TITLE][:ITAL]., CD-ROM ([PUBLISHER ADDRESS]: [PUBLISHER]<, [DATE]>)<, [SUBJECT]><, [CD]><. Hereinafter cited as [ITAL:][SHORT COMPILATION TITLE][:ITAL]>.
SF: [SUBJECT], [ITAL:][SHORT COMPILATION TITLE][:ITAL]<, [CD]>.
B: [COMPILER]. [ITAL:][COMPILATION TITLE][:ITAL]. CD-ROM. [PUBLISHER ADDRESS]: [PUBLISHER]<, [DATE]>.

— CD-ROM (Produced from Prior Publication)

FF: [SUBJECT], [COMPILATION TITLE], CD-ROM ([PUBLISHER ADDRESS]: [PUBLISHER]<, [DATE]>)<, [COMMENTS]><, [CD]><. Hereinafter cited as [SHORT COMPILATION TITLE]>.
SF: [SUBJECT], [SHORT COMPILATION TITLE]<, [CD]>.
B: [COMPILATION TITLE], CD-ROM. [PUBLISHER ADDRESS]: [PUBLISHER]<, [DATE]>.

— Cemetery Marker —

FF: [NAME OF PERSON] [RECORD TYPE]< [REPOSITORY REFERENCE]>, [REPOSITORY], [REPOSITORY ADDRESS]; [READER]<, [DATE]><, [CD]>.
SF: [NAME OF PERSON] [RECORD TYPE], [REPOSITORY], [REPOSITORY ADDRESS]<, [CD]>.
B: [REPOSITORY ADDRESS]. [REPOSITORY]. [RECORD TYPE].

— Cemetery Marker (Published) —

FF: [AUTHOR], [ITAL:][TITLE][:ITAL] ([PUBLISHER ADDRESS]: [PUBLISHER]<, [DATE]>)<, [CD]><. Hereinafter cited as [ITAL:][SHORT TITLE][:ITAL]>.
SF: [AUTHOR], [ITAL:][SHORT TITLE][:ITAL]<, [CD]>.
B: [AUTHOR], [ITAL:][TITLE][:ITAL]. [PUBLISHER ADDRESS]: [PUBLISHER]<, [DATE]>.

— Census Compendium —

FF: [COMPILER], [ITAL:][TITLE][:ITAL] ([PUBLISHER ADDRESS]: [PUBLISHER]<, [PUBLISH DATE]>)<, [RECORD INFO]><, [CD]><. Hereinafter cited as [ITAL:][SHORT TITLE][:ITAL]>.
SF: [ITAL:][SHORT TITLE][:ITAL]<, [CD]>.
B: [COMPILER]. [TITLE] ([PUBLISHER ADDRESS]: [PUBLISHER]<, [PUBLISH DATE]>).

— Census, Federal (Filmed) —

FF: [HOUSEHOLD],< [DATE]> [RECORD TYPE], [REPOSITORY ADDRESS]<, [RECORD INFO]>, [REPOSITORY]< [FILM]><, [CD]>.
SF: <[DATE]> [RECORD TYPE], [REPOSITORY ADDRESS]<, [RECORD INFO]><, [CD]>.
B: [REPOSITORY ADDRESS].< [DATE]> [RECORD TYPE]<. [FILM]>. [REPOSITORY].

— Census, Federal (Local/State Copy) —

FF: [HOUSEHOLD],< [DATE]> [RECORD TYPE], [REPOSITORY ADDRESS]<, [RECORD INFO]><, [REPOSITORY REFERENCE]> [REPOSITORY]<, [CD]>.
SF: <[DATE]> [RECORD TYPE], [REPOSITORY ADDRESS]<, [RECORD INFO]><, [CD]>.
B: [REPOSITORY ADDRESS].< [DATE]> [RECORD TYPE].< [REPOSITORY REFERENCE]> [REPOSITORY].

— Census, State —

FF: [HOUSEHOLD],< [DATE]> [RECORD TYPE], [LOCATION], [RECORD INFO], [REPOSITORY] [REPOSITORY ADDRESS]<, [CD]>.
SF: <[DATE]> [RECORD TYPE], [LOCATION], [RECORD INFO]<, [CD]>.
B: [LOCATION].< [DATE]> [RECORD TYPE]. [REPOSITORY] [REPOSITORY ADDRESS].

— Church Minute —

FF: [SUBJECT]<, [VOLUME]><, [CD]>, [TITLE], [PUBLISHER ADDRESS]<; [REPOSITORY REFERENCE]>, [REPOSITORY], [REPOSITORY ADDRESS]<. Hereinafter cited as [SHORT TITLE]>.
SF: [SUBJECT]<, [VOLUME]><, [CD]>, [SHORT TITLE].
B: [PUBLISHER ADDRESS]. [TITLE].< [REPOSITORY REFERENCE],> [REPOSITORY], [REPOSITORY ADDRESS].

— City (or County) Directory —

FF: [ITAL:][TITLE][:ITAL] ([PUBLISHER ADDRESS]: [PUBLISHER]<, [DATE]>)<, [CD]><. Hereinafter cited as [ITAL:][SHORT TITLE][:ITAL]>.
SF: [ITAL:][SHORT TITLE][:ITAL]<, [CD]>.
B: [ITAL:][TITLE][:ITAL]. [PUBLISHER ADDRESS]: [PUBLISHER]<, [DATE]>.

— Computer Software —

FF: [ITAL:][TITLE][:ITAL] Software ([PUBLISHER ADDRESS]: [PUBLISHER]<, [DATE]>)<, [COMMENTS]><, [CD]><. Hereinafter cited as [ITAL:][SHORT TITLE][:ITAL]>.
SF: [ITAL:][SHORT TITLE][:ITAL]<, [COMMENTS]><, [CD]>.
B: [ITAL:][TITLE][:ITAL] Software. [PUBLISHER ADDRESS]: [PUBLISHER]<, [DATE]><, [COMMENTS]>.

— DAR Genealogical Records Committee Report (DAR Library Copy) —

FF: [ITAL:][TITLE][:ITAL], [SERIES]< ([COMMENTS])><, [CD]><. Hereinafter cited as [ITAL:][SHORT TITLE][:ITAL]>.
SF: [ITAL:][SHORT TITLE][ITAL]<, [CD]>.
B: "[TITLE]," [SERIES]; [REPOSITORY], [REPOSITORY ADDRESS].

— DAR Genealogical Records Committee Report (Local/State Copy) —

FF: [AUTHOR], "[TITLE]", [SERIES]< ([COMMENTS])><, [CD]><; [REPOSITORY REFERENCE]>, [REPOSITORY], [REPOSITORY ADDRESS]<. Hereinafter cited as "[SHORT TITLE]">.
SF: [AUTHOR], "[SHORT TITLE]"<, [CD]>.
B: [AUTHOR], "[TITLE],"< [COMMENTS]>. [REPOSITORY REFERENCE], [REPOSITORY], [REPOSITORY ADDRESS].

— Death Registration (Local Level) —

FF: [NAME OF PERSON] entry, [TITLE]<, [VOLUME]><, [CD]>, [REPOSITORY], [REPOSITORY ADDRESS]<. Hereinafter cited as [SHORT TITLE]>.
SF: [SHORT TITLE]<, [VOLUME]><, [CD]>.
B: [REPOSITORY ADDRESS]. [REPOSITORY]. [RECORD TYPE]. [NAME OF PERSON] entry.

— Death Registration (State Level) —

FF: [NAME OF PERSON], [RECORD TYPE] [NUMBER]< ([FILE DATE])>, [REPOSITORY], [REPOSITORY ADDRESS]<, [CD]><. Hereinafter cited as [SHORT TITLE]>.
SF: [NAME OF PERSON], [SHORT TITLE]<, [CD]>.
B: [REPOSITORY ADDRESS]. [REPOSITORY]. [RECORD TYPE]. [NAME OF PERSON] certificate.

— Deed (State Level) —

FF: [TITLE]< [VOLUME]><: [CD]>, [REPOSITORY], [REPOSITORY ADDRESS]<. Hereinafter cited as [SHORT TITLE]>.
SF: [SHORT TITLE]< [VOLUME]><: [CD]>, [REPOSITORY].
B: [REPOSITORY ADDRESS]. [REPOSITORY]. [TITLE]<, [DATE]>.

— Deed (Town or County Level) —

FF: [TITLE]<, [VOLUME]><: [CD]>, [PUBLISHER], [PUBLISHER ADDRESS]<. Hereinafter cited as [SHORT TITLE]>.
SF: [SHORT TITLE]<, [VOLUME]><: [CD]>.
B: [PUBLISHER ADDRESS]. [PUBLISHER]. [TITLE]<, [DATE]>.

— Diary or Journal (Manuscript) —

FF: "[TITLE]," (MS<, [DATE]>; [LOCATION])<, [CD]>; [REPOSITORY REFERENCE], [REPOSITORY]; [REPOSITORY ADDRESS]<. Hereinafter cited as "[SHORT TITLE]">.
SF: "[SHORT TITLE],"<, [CD]>.
B: [AUTHOR], "[TITLE]"<. [DATE];> [LOCATION]. [REPOSITORY REFERENCE], [REPOSITORY]; [REPOSITORY ADDRESS].

— Diary or Journal (Published, Edited) —

FF: [EDITOR], editor, [ITAL:][TITLE][:ITAL] ([PUBLISHER ADDRESS]: [PUBLISHER]<, [DATE]>)<, [CD]><. Hereinafter cited as [ITAL:][SHORT TITLE][:ITAL]>.
SF: [EDITOR], [ITAL:][SHORT TITLE][:ITAL]<, [CD]>.
B: [EDITOR], editor. [ITAL:][TITLE][:ITAL]. [PUBLISHER ADDRESS]: [PUBLISHER]<, [DATE]>.

— Dissertation —

FF: [AUTHOR], "[TITLE]" ([RECORD TYPE], [LOCATION]<, [DATE]>)<, [CD]><. Hereinafter cited as "[SHORT TITLE]">.
SF: [AUTHOR], "[SHORT TITLE]"<, [CD]>.
B: [AUTHOR], "[TITLE]." [RECORD TYPE], [LOCATION]<, [DATE]>.

— Dissertation (Microfilmed) —

FF: [AUTHOR], "[TITLE]" ([RECORD TYPE], [LOCATION], [ORIGINAL DATE])<, [EDITION]> ([PUBLISHER ADDRESS]: [PUBLISHER]<, [PUBLISH DATE]>)<, [CD]><. Hereinafter cited as "[SHORT TITLE]">.
SF: [AUTHOR], "[SHORT TITLE]" <, [CD]>.
B: [AUTHOR], "[TITLE]." [RECORD TYPE], [LOCATION], [ORIGINAL DATE]<. [EDITION]>. [PUBLISHER ADDRESS]: [PUBLISHER]<, [PUBLISH DATE]>.

— E-Mail Message —

FF: [AUTHOR], "[TITLE]," e-mail message from [AUTHOR E-MAIL] ([ADDRESS]) to [RECIPIENT]<, [DATE]><, [CD]><. Hereinafter cited as "[SHORT TITLE]">.
SF: [AUTHOR], "[SHORT TITLE]," e-mail to [RECIPIENT]<, [DATE]><, [CD]>.
B: [AUTHOR] "[TITLE]." E-mail message from [AUTHOR E-MAIL] at [ADDRESS]<. [DATE]>.

— Electronic Database (Family File) —

FF: [COMPILER], online [URL], [AUTHOR] ([LOCATION])<, downloaded [DATE]><, [CD]>.
SF: [COMPILER]<, [DATE]><, [CD]>.
B: [COMPILER]. Online [URL], [AUTHOR]. [LOCATION]<. Text downloaded [DATE]>.

— Electronic File (Image from Private Files - Annotated) —

FF: [AUTHOR], [RECORD TYPE]<, [DATE]>, [LOCATION].< [COMMENTS],>< [CD]>.
SF: [AUTHOR], [RECORD TYPE]<, [COMMENTS]><, [CD]>.
B: [AUTHOR], [RECORD TYPE]<, [COMMENTS]>.

— Electronic File (Image from Public Archives)

FF: [RECORD TYPE]: [SUBJECT], by [PHOTOGRAPHER]; [SERIES]; [REPOSITORY], [REPOSITORY ADDRESS]. Online [URL]; [FILE NAME]<; Printout dated [PRINTOUT DATE]><, [CD]>.

SF: [SUBJECT] [RECORD TYPE], by [PHOTOGRAPHER]<, [CD]>.

B: [SUBJECT]. Photo by [PHOTOGRAPHER]. [SERIES]; [REPOSITORY], [REPOSITORY ADDRESS]. Online [URL]; [FILE NAME]<. Printout dated [PRINTOUT DATE]>.

— Electronic File (Listserve Message) —

FF: [AUTHOR], [SUBJECT] in "[TITLE]", listserve message to [LISTSERVE], [ORIGINAL DATE]<. Printout dated [PRINTOUT DATE]><, [CD]><. Hereinafter cited as [SHORT TITLE]>.

SF: [AUTHOR], [SUBJECT] in "[SHORT TITLE]," listserve message [ORIGINAL DATE]<, [CD]>.

B: [AUTHOR]. [SUBJECT], "[TITLE]." Listserve message to [LISTSERVE]<. [ORIGINAL DATE]>.

— Electronic Web Site —

FF: [TITLE], online [URL]<, [CD]><. Hereinafter cited as [SHORT TITLE]>.

SF: [SHORT TITLE], online [URL]<, [CD]>.

B: [TITLE]. Online [URL].

— Electronically Published Paper (Previously Published in Hard Copy) —

FF: "[ARTICLE TITLE]"<, [VOLUME]>< [COMMENTS]><, [CD]>, [ITAL:][TITLE][:ITAL], online [URL]<, printout dated [PRINTOUT DATE]>. Previously published in hard copy ([PUBLISHER ADDRESS]: [PUBLISHER]<, [ORIGINAL DATE]>)<. Hereinafter cited as "[ITAL:][SHORT TITLE][:ITAL]">.

SF: [ITAL:][SHORT TITLE][:ITAL], online<, [VOLUME]>< [COMMENTS]><, [CD]>.

B: [ITAL:][TITLE][:ITAL]. [PUBLISHER ADDRESS]: [PUBLISHER]<, [ORIGINAL DATE]>. Online [URL]<. Printout dated [PRINTOUT DATE]>.

— Family Group Sheet (with Annotation) —

FF: [AUTHOR], "[TITLE]"<, [COMPILE DATE]> ([COMPILER ADDRESS]). [COMMENTS]<, [CD]><. Hereinafter cited as "[SHORT TITLE]">.

SF: [AUTHOR], "[SHORT TITLE]"<, [COMMENTS]><, [CD]>.

B: [AUTHOR]. "[TITLE]"<. Compiled [COMPILE DATE]>. [COMPILER ADDRESS].

— Government Document (Published) —

FF: [SUBJECT], [ITAL:][TITLE][:ITAL] ([PUBLISHER ADDRESS]: [PUBLISHER]<, [DATE]>)<, [CD]><. [COMMENTS]><. Hereinafter cited as [ITAL:][SHORT TITLE][:ITAL]>.

SF: [ITAL:][SHORT TITLE][:ITAL]<, [CD]>.

B: [AUTHOR]. [ITAL:][TITLE][:ITAL]. [PUBLISHER ADDRESS]: [PUBLISHER]<, [DATE]>.

— International Genealogical Index (TM) (IGI) Entry —

FF: [SUBJECT], [ITAL:]International Genealogical Index (IGI)[:ITAL] ([REPOSITORY ADDRESS]: [REPOSITORY]<, [DATE]>)<, [CD]>.

SF: [ITAL:]International Genealogical Index (IGI)[:ITAL]<, [CD]>.

B: --

— Interview —

FF: Interview with [INFORMANT] ([INFORMANT ADDRESS])<, by [INTERVIEWER]><, [INTERVIEW DATE]>. [REPOSITORY] ([REPOSITORY ADDRESS])<. [COMMENTS]><, [CD]>.

SF: Interview, [INFORMANT]<, [INTERVIEW DATE]><, [CD]>.

B: [INFORMANT], interview.< [INTERVIEW DATE],> [INFORMANT ADDRESS]. [REPOSITORY]; [REPOSITORY ADDRESS].

— Law, Federal —

FF: "[ARTICLE TITLE]"<, [ORIGINAL DATE]><, [JURISDICTION]> in [EDITOR], editor, [ITAL:][TITLE][:ITAL] ([PUBLISHER ADDRESS], [PUBLISHER]<, [DATE]>)<, [CD]><. Hereinafter cited as "[SHORT ARTICLE TITLE]">.

SF: "[SHORT ARTICLE TITLE]"<, [ORIGINAL DATE]><, [JURISDICTION]><, [CD]>.

B: [EDITOR], editor. [ITAL:][TITLE][:ITAL]. [PUBLISHER ADDRESS], [PUBLISHER]<, [DATE]>.

— Law, State —

FF: "[ARTICLE TITLE]"<, [ORIGINAL DATE]><, [COMPILER], compiler>, [ITAL:][TITLE][:ITAL] ([PUBLISHER ADDRESS], [PUBLISHER]<, [DATE]>)<, [CD]><. Hereinafter cited as "[SHORT ARTICLE TITLE]">.

SF: "[SHORT ARTICLE TITLE]"<, [ORIGINAL DATE]>, in < [COMPILER],> [ITAL:][SHORT TITLE][:ITAL]<, [CD]>.

B: [COMPILER], compiler. [ITAL:][TITLE][:ITAL]. [PUBLISHER ADDRESS], [PUBLISHER]<, [DATE]>.

— Lecture (Taped) —

FF: [SPEAKER], "[TITLE]" (lecture, [LOCATION], [ORIGINAL DATE]); [RECORD TYPE] available as [FILE NUMBER] ([PUBLISHER ADDRESS]: [PUBLISHER]<, [PUBLISH DATE]>)<, [CD]><. Hereinafter cited as "[SHORT TITLE]">.

SF: [SPEAKER], "[SHORT TITLE]" (lecture, [LOCATION], [ORIGINAL DATE])<, [CD]>.

B: [SPEAKER]. "[TITLE]." Lecture, [LOCATION], [ORIGINAL DATE]. [RECORD TYPE] [FILE NUMBER]. [PUBLISHER ADDRESS]: [PUBLISHER]<, [PUBLISH DATE]>.

— Legal Case (Published Report) —
FF: [AUTHOR], [ITAL:][TITLE][:ITAL], [VOLUME] ([PUBLISHER ADDRESS]: [PUBLISHER]<, [PUBLISH DATE]>)<, [CD]><; [COMMENTS]><. Hereinafter cited as [ITAL:][SHORT TITLE][:ITAL]>.
SF: [ITAL:][SHORT TITLE][:ITAL]<, [COMMENTS]><, [CD]>.
B: [AUTHOR], [ITAL:][TITLE][:ITAL]<, [VOLUME]>. [PUBLISHER ADDRESS]: [PUBLISHER]<, [PUBLISH DATE]>.

— Legal Case (Unpublished) —
FF: [ITAL:][FIRST PARTY][:ITAL] v. [ITAL:][SECOND PARTY][:ITAL], [RECORD INFO]<, [VOLUME]><: [CD], [REPOSITORY], [REPOSITORY ADDRESS].
SF: [ITAL:][FIRST PARTY][:ITAL] v. [ITAL:][SECOND PARTY][:ITAL], [RECORD INFO]<, [VOLUME]><: [CD]>, [REPOSITORY].
B: [REPOSITORY ADDRESS]. [REPOSITORY]<. [RECORD INFO]>.

— Letter (Annotated Citation) —
FF: Letter from [AUTHOR] ([AUTHOR ADDRESS]) to [RECIPIENT]<, [DATE]>;< [REPOSITORY REFERENCE]> [REPOSITORY] ([REPOSITORY ADDRESS])<. [COMMENTS]><, [CD]>.
SF: Letter, [AUTHOR] to [RECIPIENT]<, [DATE]><, [CD]>.
B: [AUTHOR], letter.< [DATE],> from [AUTHOR ADDRESS], to [RECIPIENT].< [REPOSITORY REFERENCE]> [REPOSITORY]; [REPOSITORY ADDRESS].

— Lineage Application —
FF: Lineage application of [SUBJECT]<, [FILE NUMBER]>, [APPLIED TO]<, [VOLUME]><, [COMMENTS]><, [CD]>.
SF: [APPLIED TO], [SUBJECT]<, [FILE NUMBER]><, [VOLUME]><, [COMMENTS]><, [CD]>.
B: [APPLIED TO], Application of [SUBJECT]<, [FILE NUMBER]><, [VOLUME]>.

— Manuscript (Filmed for Distribution) —
FF: [ITAL:][TITLE][:ITAL];< [FILM]> ([PUBLISHER ADDRESS]: [PUBLISHER]<, [PUBLISH DATE]>)<, [ROLL]><, [CD]><. Hereinafter cited as [ITAL:][SHORT TITLE][:ITAL]>.
SF: [ITAL:][SHORT TITLE][:ITAL]<, [ROLL]><, [CD]>.
B: [ITAL:][TITLE][:ITAL]<. [FILM]>. [PUBLISHER ADDRESS]: [PUBLISHER],< [PUBLISH DATE]> [ROLL].

— Manuscript (Filmed, Limited Distribution)
FF: [LOCATION], [TITLE]<: [CD]>; [FILM], [REPOSITORY], [REPOSITORY ADDRESS]<. Hereinafter cited as [SHORT TITLE]>.
SF: [LOCATION], [SHORT TITLE]<: [CD]>; [FILM].
B: [LOCATION], [TITLE]. [FILM], [REPOSITORY], [REPOSITORY ADDRESS].

— Manuscript (Unfilmed) —
FF: [SUBJECT]<, [RECORD TYPE]><, [DATE]><, [FILE NUMBER]>, [REPOSITORY], [REPOSITORY ADDRESS]<, [CD]>.
SF: [SUBJECT]<, [RECORD TYPE]><, [DATE]> [REPOSITORY]<, [CD]>.
B: [SUBJECT] <. [DATE]>.< [FILE NUMBER],> [REPOSITORY], [REPOSITORY ADDRESS].

— Map (Historic) —
FF: [AUTHOR], [ITAL:][TITLE][:ITAL] ([PUBLISHER ADDRESS]: [PUBLISHER], [DATE])<, [COMMENTS]><, [CD]><. Hereinafter cited as [ITAL:][SHORT TITLE][:ITAL]>.
SF: [AUTHOR], [ITAL:][SHORT TITLE][:ITAL]<, [DATE]><, [CD]>.
B: [AUTHOR]. [ITAL:][TITLE][:ITAL]. [PUBLISHER ADDRESS]: [PUBLISHER], [DATE].

— Map (Topographic) —
FF: [AUTHOR], [ITAL:][TITLE][:ITAL]<, [SERIES]><, [FILE NUMBER]><, [DATE]><, [CD]><. Hereinafter cited as [ITAL:][SHORT TITLE][:ITAL]>.
SF: [ITAL:][SHORT TITLE][:ITAL]<, [SERIES]><, [DATE]><, [CD]>.
B: [AUTHOR], [ITAL:][TITLE][:ITAL]<, [SERIES]><. [DATE]>.

— Marriage (Church - Certificate) —
FF: [SPOUSES' NAMES] marriage<, [DATE]>, [REPOSITORY], [REPOSITORY ADDRESS]. [MANUSCRIPT INFO]<, [CD]>.
SF: Certificate, [SPOUSES' NAMES] marriage< of [DATE]><, [CD]>.
B: [SPOUSES' NAMES]. [RECORD TYPE]. [REPOSITORY], [REPOSITORY ADDRESS]. [MANUSCRIPT INFO].

— Marriage (Church - Copy, Copyist Known) —
FF: <[TRANSLATOR], translator, >"[REGISTER TITLE]" (<[REPOSITORY REFERENCE];> [REPOSITORY], [REPOSITORY ADDRESS])<, [CD]><. Hereinafter cited as "[SHORT REGISTER TITLE]">.
SF: [TRANSLATOR], "[SHORT REGISTER TITLE]"<, [CD]>.
B: [TRANSLATOR], "[REGISTER TITLE]"<. [REPOSITORY REFERENCE]>. [REPOSITORY], [REPOSITORY ADDRESS].

— Marriage (Church - Copy, Copyist Unknown) —
FF: [SPOUSES' NAMES] marriage<, [DATE]>, in [REGISTER TITLE]< ([COMMENTS])>: [MANUSCRIPT INFO], [REPOSITORY], [REPOSITORY ADDRESS]<, [CD]><. Hereinafter cited as [SHORT REGISTER TITLE]>.
SF: [SHORT REGISTER TITLE]< ([COMMENTS])>: [MANUSCRIPT INFO], [REPOSITORY]<, [CD]>.
B: [REPOSITORY ADDRESS] [REPOSITORY]. [RECORD TYPE].

— Marriage (Church - Original Record) —

FF: [SPOUSES' NAMES] marriage<, [DATE]>, in [REGISTER TITLE], [MANUSCRIPT INFO], [REPOSITORY], [REPOSITORY ADDRESS]<, [CD]><. Hereinafter cited as [SHORT REGISTER TITLE]>.

SF: [SHORT REGISTER TITLE]: entry for [SPOUSES' NAMES]<, [DATE]> [REPOSITORY], [REPOSITORY ADDRESS]<, [CD]>.

B: [REPOSITORY ADDRESS] [REPOSITORY]. [RECORD TYPE].

— Marriage (Civil) —

FF: [TITLE]<: [CD]>, [REPOSITORY], [REPOSITORY ADDRESS]<. Hereinafter cited as [SHORT TITLE]>.

SF: [SHORT TITLE]<: [CD]>.

B: [REPOSITORY ADDRESS] [REPOSITORY] [RECORD TYPE].

— Military - Service File (Filmed) —

FF: [SUBJECT], [ITAL:][TITLE][:ITAL]<, [FILM]><, [CD]> [PUBLISHER], [PUBLISHER ADDRESS]<. Hereinafter cited as [ITAL:][SHORT TITLE][:ITAL]>.

SF: [SUBJECT], [ITAL:][SHORT TITLE][:ITAL]<, [FILM]><, [CD]>.

B: [ITAL:][TITLE][:ITAL]<. [FILM]>. [PUBLISHER ADDRESS], [PUBLISHER].

— Military Record (Manuscript) —

FF: "[RECORD TITLE]"<, [RECORD INFO]>; [REPOSITORY]; [REPOSITORY ADDRESS]<, [CD]><. Hereinafter cited as "[SHORT RECORD TITLE]">.

SF: "[SHORT RECORD TITLE]"<, [CD]>.

B: [REPOSITORY ADDRESS]. [REPOSITORY]<, [RECORD INFO]>.

— National Archives Film/Fiche (Basic Form) —

FF: [DOCUMENT], [FILE NAME]<; [SERIES]>; [ITAL:][FILM][:ITAL]<; [NUMBER]> ([PUBLISHER ADDRESS]: [PUBLISHER])<, [ROLL]><, [CD]>.

SF: [DOCUMENT]; [FILM]<, [ROLL]><, [CD]>.

B: [FILM]<, [NUMBER]>. [PUBLISHER ADDRESS]: [PUBLISHER]<. [ROLL]>.

— National Archives Manuscript (Basic Form) —

FF: [DOCUMENT], [FILE NUMBER]; [FILE NAME]<, [SERIES]>; [RECORD GROUP], [REPOSITORY], [REPOSITORY ADDRESS]<, [CD]>.

SF: [DOCUMENT], [FILE NUMBER]; [FILE NAME]<, [SERIES]>; [RECORD GROUP], [REPOSITORY]<, [CD]>.

B: [REPOSITORY ADDRESS], [REPOSITORY]. [RECORD GROUP]<. [SERIES]>. [FILE NAME]. [DOCUMENT].

— National Archives Regional (Unofficial Film Holdings) —

FF: [TITLE], [RECORD TYPE], [REPOSITORY ADDRESS]<, [CD]>; [REPOSITORY]<, [FILM]><. Hereinafter cited as [SHORT TITLE]>.

SF: [SHORT TITLE], [RECORD TYPE], [REPOSITORY ADDRESS]<, [FILM]><, [CD]>.

B: [REPOSITORY ADDRESS], [RECORD TYPE]. [REPOSITORY]<, [FILM]>.

— Naturalization Record —

FF: [SUBJECT], [RECORD TYPE], [FILE NUMBER]<, [CD]>< ([DATE])>; [REPOSITORY], [REPOSITORY ADDRESS].

SF: [REPOSITORY] [RECORD TYPE]<, [FILE NUMBER]><, [CD]>< ([DATE])>, [REPOSITORY ADDRESS].

B: [REPOSITORY ADDRESS], [REPOSITORY], [TITLE], [FILE NUMBER]< ([DATE])>.

— Obituary/Newspaper Item —

FF: [ARTICLE TITLE], [ITAL:][NEWSPAPER TITLE][:ITAL], [LOCATION]<, [DATE]><, [PAGE]><, [CD]><. Hereinafter cited as [SHORT NEWSPAPER TITLE]>.

SF: [ITAL:][SHORT NEWSPAPER TITLE][:ITAL]<, [DATE]><, [PAGE]><, [CD]>.

B: [ITAL:][NEWSPAPER TITLE][:ITAL], [LOCATION]<, [DATE]>.

— Pension File (Filmed) —

FF: [NAME OF PERSON] file; [FILE NUMBER]; [ITAL:][SERIES][:ITAL]<; [FILM]> ([PUBLISHER ADDRESS]: [PUBLISHER])<, [COMMENTS]><, [CD]>.

SF: [NAME OF PERSON], [RECORD TYPE], [FILE NUMBER]<, [FILM]><, [COMMENTS]><, [CD]>.

B: [ITAL:][SERIES][:ITAL]<. [FILM]>. [REPOSITORY ADDRESS]: [REPOSITORY].

— Periodical (Issued in Multiple Series) —

([DATE])><: [CD]><. Hereinafter cited as "[SHORT ARTICLE TITLE]">.

SF: "[SHORT ARTICLE TITLE]"<, [CD]>.

B: "[ARTICLE TITLE]," [ITAL:][TITLE][:ITAL]<, [SERIES]><, [VOLUME]>< ([DATE])>.

— Photo, Portrait, or Illustration (Archival) (With Annotation) —

FF: [SUBJECT] [RECORD TYPE]; [REPOSITORY], [REPOSITORY ADDRESS]<. [COMMENTS]><, [CD]>.

SF: [SUBJECT] [RECORD TYPE]; [REPOSITORY]<, [CD]>.

B: [SUBJECT]. [RECORD TYPE]. [REPOSITORY]. [REPOSITORY ADDRESS].

— Photograph (Private Possession) (Annotated with Provenance) —

FF: [SUBJECT] [RECORD TYPE]<, [COMMENTS]>, [REPOSITORY] ([REPOSITORY ADDRESS])<, [CD]>.

SF: [SUBJECT] [RECORD TYPE]<, [DATE]>, [REPOSITORY]<, [CD]>.

B: [SUBJECT]. [RECORD TYPE]. [DATE], [REPOSITORY], [REPOSITORY ADDRESS].

— Probate File —

FF: [NAME OF PERSON], [TITLE] [FILE NUMBER]< ([SERIES])>, [REPOSITORY], [REPOSITORY ADDRESS]<, [CD]><. Hereinafter cited as [SHORT TITLE]>.

SF: [SHORT TITLE] [FILE NUMBER]< ([SERIES])><, [CD]>.

B: [REPOSITORY ADDRESS], [REPOSITORY]. [FILE NUMBER]< ([SERIES])>><, [DATE]>, [NAME OF PERSON].

— Research Report —

FF: "[TITLE]"<, [DATE]>, [AUTHOR] ([AUTHOR ADDRESS]), to [RECIPIENT] ([RECIPIENT ADDRESS])<, [CD]>; [REPOSITORY], [REPOSITORY ADDRESS]. Hereinafter cited as "[SHORT TITLE]">.

SF: [AUTHOR], "[SHORT TITLE]"<, [CD]>.

B: [AUTHOR]. "[TITLE]" to [RECIPIENT]; [RECIPIENT ADDRESS]<. [DATE]>. [REPOSITORY], [REPOSITORY ADDRESS].

— Series - Book (with Subsets) —

FF: <[AUTHOR], >[ITAL:][TITLE][:ITAL]<, [VOLUME]> ([PUBLISHER ADDRESS]: [PUBLISHER]<, [PUBLISH DATE]>), [ITAL:][SUBSET][:ITAL]<, [SUBSET VOLUMES]><, [CD]><. Hereinafter cited as [ITAL:][SHORT TITLE][:ITAL]>.

SF: <[AUTHOR], >[ITAL:][SHORT TITLE][:ITAL]<, [SUBSET VOLUMES]><: [CD]>.

B: [AUTHOR]. [ITAL:][TITLE][:ITAL]<, [VOLUME]>. [PUBLISHER ADDRESS]: [PUBLISHER]<, [PUBLISH DATE]>. [ITAL:][SUBSET][:ITAL]<, [SUBSET VOLUMES]>.

— Ship Passenger List (Filmed) —

FF: [NAME OF PERSON] entry; [ITAL:][SHIP NAME][:ITAL] [RECORD TYPE]<, [DATE]><, [CD]>; in [ITAL:][SERIES][:ITAL]<; [FILM]> ([PUBLISHER ADDRESS]: [PUBLISHER])<, [ROLL]>.

SF: [NAME OF PERSON], [ITAL:][SHIP NAME][:ITAL] [RECORD TYPE]<, [DATE]><; [FILM]><, [CD]><, [ROLL]>.

B: [ITAL:][SERIES][:ITAL]<. [FILM]><, [ROLL]>. [PUBLISHER ADDRESS]: [PUBLISHER].

— Social Security Death Index (SSDI) —

FF: [SUBJECT], [FILE NUMBER], [TITLE], [ITAL:][SERIES][:ITAL] ([PUBLISHER ADDRESS]: [PUBLISHER]<, [DATE]>)<. [COMMENTS]><, [CD]><. Hereinafter cited as [SHORT TITLE]>.

SF: [SUBJECT], [FILE NUMBER], [SHORT TITLE], [ITAL:][SERIES][:ITAL]<, [CD]>.

B: [TITLE], [ITAL:][SERIES][:ITAL]. [PUBLISHER ADDRESS]: [PUBLISHER]<, [DATE]>.

— Syllabus Material —

FF: [AUTHOR], "[ARTICLE TITLE]," [ITAL:][TITLE][:ITAL], [RECORD TYPE] ([PUBLISHER ADDRESS]: [PUBLISHER]<, [DATE]>)<, [CD]><. Hereinafter cited as "[SHORT ARTICLE TITLE]">.

SF: [AUTHOR], "[SHORT ARTICLE TITLE],"<, [CD]>.

B: [AUTHOR]. "[ARTICLE TITLE]," [ITAL:][TITLE][:ITAL]. [RECORD TYPE] ([PUBLISHER ADDRESS]: [PUBLISHER]<, [DATE]>).

— Tax Roll, Filmed —

FF: [NAME OF PERSON] entry<, [DATE]> [TITLE]<, [CD]>, [LOCATION]<; [FILM]>; [REPOSITORY], [REPOSITORY ADDRESS]<. Hereinafter cited as [SHORT TITLE]>.

SF: [REPOSITORY ADDRESS]< [DATE]> [SHORT TITLE]<, [CD]>.

B: [LOCATION] [TITLE]<, [DATE]>. [REPOSITORY], [REPOSITORY ADDRESS].

— Tax Roll, Unfilmed —

FF: [NAME OF PERSON] entry, [TITLE], [LOCATION]<, [CD]>; [REPOSITORY], [REPOSITORY ADDRESS]<. Hereinafter cited as [SHORT TITLE]>.

SF: [SHORT TITLE], [LOCATION]<, [CD]>.

B: [LOCATION]. [TITLE]. [REPOSITORY], [REPOSITORY ADDRESS].

— Thesis —

FF: [AUTHOR], "[TITLE]" ([RECORD TYPE], [LOCATION]<, [DATE]>)<, [CD]><. Hereinafter cited as "[SHORT TITLE]">.

SF: [AUTHOR], "[SHORT TITLE]"<, [CD]>.

B: [AUTHOR], "[TITLE]." [RECORD TYPE], [LOCATION]<, [DATE]>.

— Town Record —

FF: [TITLE]<, [VOLUME]><: [CD]>, [REPOSITORY], [REPOSITORY ADDRESS]<. Hereinafter cited as [SHORT TITLE]>.

SF: [SHORT TITLE]<, [VOLUME]><: [CD]>.

B: [REPOSITORY ADDRESS], [RECORD TYPE], [REPOSITORY].

— Translated Work —

FF: [AUTHOR], [ITAL:][TITLE][:ITAL]<, [VOLUME]>, [TRANSLATOR], translator ([PUBLISHER ADDRESS], [PUBLISHER]<, [DATE]>)<, [CD]><. Hereinafter cited as [ITAL:][SHORT TITLE][:ITAL]>.

SF: [AUTHOR], [ITAL:][SHORT TITLE][:ITAL], ([TRANSLATOR], translator)<, [VOLUME]><: [CD]>.

B: [AUTHOR], [ITAL:][TITLE][:ITAL]<, [VOLUME]>, [TRANSLATOR], translator. [PUBLISHER ADDRESS]: [PUBLISHER]<, [DATE]>.

— Video —

FF: [AUTHOR], [ITAL:][TITLE][:ITAL], [RECORD TYPE] ([PUBLISHER ADDRESS]: [PUBLISHER]<, [DATE]>)<, [CD]><. Hereinafter cited as [ITAL:][SHORT TITLE][:ITAL]>.
SF: [AUTHOR], [ITAL:][SHORT TITLE][:ITAL], [RECORD TYPE]<, [CD]>.
B: [AUTHOR], [ITAL:][TITLE][:ITAL]. [RECORD TYPE]. [PUBLISHER ADDRESS]: [PUBLISHER]<, [DATE]>.

— Vital Record (Filmed) —

FF: [COMPILER ADDRESS], [TITLE]<, [VOLUME]>, [REPOSITORY], [REPOSITORY ADDRESS]<, [CD]><. Hereinafter cited as [SHORT TITLE]>.
SF: [COMPILER ADDRESS], [SHORT TITLE]<, [VOLUME]><: [CD]>.
B: [COMPILER ADDRESS]. [TITLE]. [REPOSITORY REFERENCE]. [REPOSITORY], [REPOSITORY ADDRESS].

— Vital Record (Published) —

FF: [COMPILER], [ITAL:][TITLE][:ITAL] ([PUBLISHER ADDRESS]: [PUBLISHER]<, [PUBLISH DATE]>)<, [VOLUME]><, [COMMENTS]><, [CD]><. Hereinafter cited as [ITAL:][SHORT TITLE][:ITAL]>.
SF: [ITAL:][SHORT TITLE][:ITAL] (published)<, [CD]>.
B: [COMPILER]. [ITAL:][TITLE][:ITAL]. [PUBLISHER ADDRESS]: [PUBLISHER]<, [PUBLISH DATE]>.

— Will (Recorded) —

FF: [TESTATOR] will ([DATE]), [TITLE]< [VOLUME]><: [CD]>, [REPOSITORY], [REPOSITORY ADDRESS]<. Hereinafter cited as [SHORT TITLE]>.
SF: [SHORT TITLE]< [VOLUME]><: [CD]>.
B: [REPOSITORY ADDRESS]. [REPOSITORY], [TITLE]<, [DATE]>.

— Will (Unrecorded, Consulted Off-Site) —

FF: [TESTATOR] will< ([DATE])>, [TITLE] [FILE NUMBER], [REPOSITORY], [REPOSITORY ADDRESS]<, [CD]><. Hereinafter cited as [SHORT TITLE]>.
SF: [TESTATOR] will, [SHORT TITLE], [REPOSITORY]<, [CD]>.
B: [REPOSITORY ADDRESS]. [TITLE]<, [DATE]>. [TESTATOR]. [REPOSITORY].

Appendix G - TMG and GEDCOM File Export Comparison
Default Export Settings and GEDCOM Tag Properties

TMG5 Tag Type	TMG5 Export GEDCOM tag	Destination GEDCOM Version[1]					LDS Tags[3]	Comment
		GEDCOM 4.0 (I or F)[2]	GEDCOM (PAF) (I or F)	GEDCOM (AF) (I or F)	GEDCOM (TR) (I or F)	GEDCOM 5.5 (I or F)		
Address[4]	ADDR	I	I					
Adoption	ADOP	I	I	I	I	I		
AFN	AFN	I	I	I	I	I		
Age	AGE	I	I					
Anecdote[5]		I	I	I	I	I		
Annulment	ANUL	F	F	F	F	F		
Associatn[6]	ASSO							not exported
Attributes	ATTR	I	I					
Baptism	BAPM	I	I	I	I	I		
BaptismLDS	BAPL	I	I	I	I	I	LDS	
BarMitzvah	BARM	I	I	I	I	I		
BasMitzvah	BASM	I	I	I	I	I		
Birth	BIRT	I	I	I	I	I		
Birth-Covt	BIC	I	I				LDS	
BirthIlleg	ILLE	I	I					
BirthStill	STIL	I	I					
Blessing	BLES	I	I	I	I	I		
BlessngLDS	BLSL	I	I				LDS	
Burial	BURI	I	I	I	I	I		
CancelSeal	CANC	F	F				LDS	
Caste	CAST	I	I	I	I	I		
Census	CENS	I/F	I/F	I/F	I/F	I/F		
Christning	CHR	I	I	I	I	I		
Codicil	CODI	I	I					
Communion1	FCOM	I	I	I	I	I		
Confirmatn	CONF	I	I	I	I	I		
ConfirmLDS	CONL	I	I	I	I	I	LDS	
Criminal	CRIM	I	I					
Death	DEAT	I	I	I	I	I		
Descriptn	DSCR	I	I	I	I	I		
Divorce	DIV	F	F	F	F	F		
Divorce Fl	DIVF	F	F	F	F	F		
Education	EDUC	I	I	I	I	I		
Emigration	EMIG	I	I	I	I	I		
Employment	EMPL	I	I					
Endowment	ENDL	I	I	I	I	I	LDS	
Engagement	ENGA	F	F	F	F	F		
Event-Misc	EVEN	I/F	I/F	I/F	I/F	I/F		
Excommuntn	EXCO	I	I					
GEDCOM	GEDC	I/F	I/F					
Graduation	GRAD	I	I	I	I	I		

TMG5 Tag Type	TMG5 Export GEDCOM tag	Destination GEDCOM Version[1]					LDS Tags[3]	Comment
		GEDCOM 4.0 (I or F)[2]	GEDCOM (PAF) (I or F)	GEDCOM (AF) (I or F)	GEDCOM (TR) (I or F)	GEDCOM 5.5 (I or F)		
History[6]								not exported
HTML		I/F	I/F	I/F	I/F	I/F		
Illness		I	I	I	I	I		
Immigratn	IMMI	I	I	I	I	I		
Living		I	I	I	I	I		
Marr Bann	MARB	F	F	F	F	F		
Marr Cont	MARC	F	F	F	F	F		
Marr Lic	MARL	F	F	F	F	F		
Marr Sett	MARS	F	F	F	F	F		
Marriage	MARR	F	F	F	F	F		
Milit-Beg		I	I	I	I	I		
Milit-End		I	I	I	I	I		
Misc	MISC	I	I					
Name-Baptm[7]		ALIA	ALIA	NAME	NAME	NAME		
Name-Chg[7]		ALIA	ALIA	NAME	NAME	NAME		
Name-Marr[7]		ALIA	ALIA	NAME	NAME	NAME		
Name-Nick[7]	NICK	ALIA	ALIA	NICK	NICK	NICK		
Name-Var[7]		ALIA	ALIA	NAME	NAME	NAME		
Namesake[6]	NAMS							not exported
Nationalty	NATI	I	I	I	I	I		
Natlzation	NATU	I	I	I	I	I		
Note[8]	NOTE	I/F	I/F	I/F	I/F	I/F		
NullifyLDS	NULL	I	I				LDS	
Num Child	NCHI	I/F	I/F	I/F	I/F	I/F		
Num Marr	NMR	I	I	I	I	I		
Occupation	OCCU	I	I	I	I	I		
OrdinacLDS	ORDL	I	I				LDS	
Ordinance	ORDI	I	I				LDS	
Ordination	ORDN	I	I	I	I	I		
Probate	PROB	I	I	I	I	I		
PrsmCancel	PRES	I	I				LDS	
Psgr List	PASL	I	I					
Ratificatn	RATI	I	I				LDS	
Rebaptism	REBA	I	I					
Reference	REFN	I/F	I/F	I/F	I/F	I/F		
Religion	RELI	I	I	I	I	I		
Reseal	RESE	I	I				LDS	
Residence	RESI	I	I	I	I	I		
Restoratn	REST	I	I					
Retirement	RETI	I	I	I	I	I		
SealChild	SLGC	I	I	I	I	I	LDS	
SealParent	SLGP	I	I				LDS	
SealSpouse	SLGS	F	F	F	F	F	LDS	
SSN	SSN	I	I	I	I	I		
Stake	STAL	I	I				LDS	
Telephone[4]	PHON	I	I					

TMG5 Tag Type	TMG5 Export GEDCOM tag	Destination GEDCOM Version[1]					LDS Tags[3]	Comment
		GEDCOM 4.0 (I or F)[2]	GEDCOM (PAF) (I or F)	GEDCOM (AF) (I or F)	GEDCOM (TR) (I or F)	GEDCOM 5.5 (I or F)		
VoidLiving	VOIL	I	I				LDS	
WAC	WAC	I	I				LDS	
Will	WILL	I	I	I	I	I		

[1] TMG5 exports GEDCOM files in five destination formats: GEDCOM 4.0, Personal Ancestral File™, Ancestral File™, Temple Ready™ and GEDCOM 5.5.

[2] For each export destination format, the table notes whether the TMG tag is exported as an individual tag (I) or as a family tag (F). A tag marked (I/F) can be exported either as an individual tag or a family tag. A blank field indicates that the tag is not exported.

[3] LDS – GEDCOM tags of interest to members of The Church of Jesus Christ of Latter-Day Saints.

[4] TMG Address and Telephone tags are not exported to the Ancestral File™, Temple Ready™ and GEDCOM 5.5 formats. The GEDCOM 5.5 specifications do not allow **1 ADDR** and **1 PHON** tags subordinate to **INDI** tags.

[5] Tags without a specified GEDCOM export tag are exported as **1 EVEN 2 TYPE** GEDCOM tags. For example, the TMG5 Anecdote tag would be exported to GEDCOM as **1 EVEN 2 TYPE Anecdote**.

[6] TMG Associatn and Namesake tags require two principals and don't fit normal export patterns as either individual or family tags. The TMG History tag has no principals and, thus, can't be exported.

[7] All name tags will export as GEDCOM **NAME** tags if primary. Non-primary name tags export to the GEDCOM 4.0 and Personal Ancestral File™ formats as GEDCOM **ALIA** tags. Non-primary Name-Nick tags export to Ancestral File™, Temple Ready™ and GEDCOM 5.5 as GEDCOM **NICK** tags and all other non-primary name tags export as GEDCOM **NAME** tags.

[8] Dates for TMG Note tags are not exported to the Ancestral File™, Temple Ready™ and GEDCOM 5.5 formats.

List of Contributors

Richard Brogger began entering genealogy data into a computer in 1988. He used database programs including Microsoft Access. In 1996 he began using Family Tree Maker along with Access. In January 2000 he purchased the Master Genealogist and soon after, stopped using both Family Tree Maker and Access.

Richard resides in a heavily wooded area east of Jamestown, Tennessee where he spends most of his time doing genealogy related computer work.

Jim Byram lives in Framingham, MA, is a reformed academic and is a long time user of microcomputers. Jim started using computers to support his genealogy research with Family Tree Maker in the '80s and moved to TMG shortly after it was first commercially released in 1993. Jim co-directs the Eastern Massachusetts TMG Users Group and is a TMG beta tester. In his spare time, Jim writes articles about genealogy software and related subjects for Family Chronicle magazine and uses computer graphics to visually display the data that elucidates differing site conditions in underground construction projects.

John Cardinal is a co-founder and the Chief Technical Officer of EXIT41 www.exit41.com and Elm Square, Inc. www.elmsquare.com. John has 23 years of experience developing technical solutions for customer information systems and applications. At EXIT41, his technical focus has been on designing Restaurant Management Systems for the Quick Serve Restaurant industry, as well as designing Internet-enabled applications for EXIT41's subsidiary Elm Square. Prior to the founding of EXIT41, he was the Vice President of Systems Development for Epsilon, a leading supplier of marketing software and services.

John has been a user of The Master Genealogist (TMG) since 1999. He is the author of four companion programs for TMG. *John Cardinal's TMG Utility* provides three-dozen database modification features. Many are aimed at correcting common data consistency problems. Others are designed to help convert data to take advantage of the power of TMG. *On This Day (OTD)* will send a list of B-M-D-B anniversaries to the screen, to HTML, or to Microsoft Outlook as appointment events. With one click, OTD will create a year's worth of monthly calendars, complete with an index. *Mocakebi* (pronounced "moe-kah-kee-bee") is a read-only browser for TMG databases. The newest companion program, *Second Site,* creates a web site from a TMG database.

Jeffry L. Clenard was born and raised in Southern California. He attended California State University Northridge where he earned a bachelor's degree in History and a master's degree in Business Administration (MBA). He has worked in various sales and marketing roles in the computer industry since 1979 for companies such as Unisys, Digital Equipment Corporation, Hitachi and Oracle Corporation where his interest in technology and computer science emerged. He is currently engaged as an independent computer consultant.

Jeff has been interested in history and historical research since his childhood. But it was his wife, the former Colleen Marie Hicks, who first piqued his interest in genealogy during a trip to Salt Lake City in 1985 for researching an unpublished book on her family history. He bypassed a round of golf to visit the LDS Family History Library with her, and while there made a simple discovery, the name and address of his great-grandfather listed in a 19th century Los Angeles city directory. That simple discovery acted as a catharsis for him, and coalesced his major personal interests in family, history, travel and technology.

Jeff investigated and used several genealogy applications during his early research which grew to include trips to libraries, cemeteries and government offices plus travels to other parts of the United States, England, Ireland, France and Germany for first-hand research. While he continues to investigate most personal computer-based genealogy programs, he has relied upon The Master Genealogist as his primary "workhorse" application since its first release as a Microsoft Windows program.

In addition to his genealogical endeavors, Jeff enjoys several outdoor activities such as golfing, camping, hiking and gardening. He is an avid reader of history, science fiction, and science articles on physics, astronomy and cosmology, and enjoys watching films of the same genres. Jeff currently resides in Northern California with his wife Colleen and daughter, Caitlin.

Lee H. Hoffman was in the U. S. Navy for over 20 years where he was in aviation electronics, maintenance and data analysis. After Navy retirement, he was with McDonnell-Douglas Corporation on the F-18 Hornet aircraft project until 1979 when he moved back to his home state of Kentucky where he was a Data Processing Manager. In 1989, he became an independent computer consultant retiring in 1997 to devote most of his time to genealogy.

Interested in genealogy since his youth, Lee did not do much active research until his return to Kentucky in 1979 when he acquired a powerful genealogy program that he used until The Master Genealogist became available in 1993. When many questions about TMG were repeatedly being asked online, he created the TMG Tips web site www.tmgtips.com where he posted articles, tutorials, tips, hints, and helps written by himself and by other users. Also about this time, he began writing the TMG Tips column in each issue of *Everton's Genealogical Helper Magazine* (now re-named *Everton's Family History Magazine*).

Lee is married to the former Sue Ellen Wilson who also retired in 1997 after teaching school. They live in Central Kentucky in their new home that Lee built last year. They enjoy going to genealogical conferences where they usually gather with other users at the Wholly Genes exhibit booth and talk with other TMG users there.

Robin Lamacraft is an Australian genealogist who has been a committed and innovative user of TMG since 1995. He has been a frequent correspondent on the TMG-L message list and has been a beta tester of TMG since version 3.5. In 1978, Robin commenced his worldwide Lamacraft one-name family history project that has been dominated by

sources of evidence originating in the British Isles. Since 1997, he has coordinated the largest TMG User Group in Australia. The Adelaide user group has met monthly at his house. Robin is married to Melissa Gibbs and they have two children, Scott and Freya.

While an electronics technician, Robin commenced programming for a defense establishment in 1961. He then graduated in statistics and computer science. Early in his professional career he was a statistical consultant in the fields of the social sciences, agriculture and the environment. In 2000, Robin retired early from a long career as a research scientist in which he focused on the computer-based visualization of complex data systems such as the manufacturing and assembly of aircraft at Boeing and automobiles at General Motors.

Encouraging *culturally sensitive* advances in genealogical software is one of Robin's continuing interests. *Culturally sensitive* genealogical software correctly represents and displays evidence with respect to the cultural origin of that evidence. Some of the new features within TMG5 are a result of discussions that he initiated on TMG-L. His other genealogical interests are in creating better tools and better methods of visualizing family history data for use in one-name and community studies.

Robin is the principal of a consultancy specializing in the use of information technology in social history. He also operates a chart printing service for genealogists in Australia and New Zealand.

Allen Mellen began working with computers in 1968, when he was responsible for testing a large pension actuarial program. In 1981, after 20 years in the pension field, he began teaching mathematics and computer science in a public high school in New York City's Chinatown.

Having come into a cache of family documents in the early 1980's, Allen was inspired by the example of his mother-in-law, an accomplished genealogist, and began his own research. At the outset, he kept his data in word processing documents on Commodore computers. In 1991 he used macros in his Commodore 128 word processor to convert his data to a GEDCOM file so he could transfer it to a genealogy program on the IBM PC. He switched to TMG when version 3.0 was released in May 1997, and soon he was answering questions on TMG-L about filters and other TMG matters. He also has a web page devoted to TMG.

Allen has an M.A. in English literature, is interested in English church history and liturgy, and is a serious lover of opera and of operetta, especially Gilbert and Sullivan. Allen and his wife Liz (Elizabeth Glencairn Hanson) live in New York City, where they are involved in church and community affairs on the upper west side of Manhattan. Their daughter, Jane Dudley, lives in Vermont. Allen and Liz have a summer cottage in Susquehanna County, Pennsylvania, where one branch of Allen's family settled over the thirty years from 1795 to 1825.

Allen is a member of the National Genealogical Society, the New England Historic and Genealogical Society, the New York Genealogical and Biographical Society, the Susquehanna County Historical Society, and the local historical societies of Brooklyn and Harford townships in Susquehanna County.

Terry Reigel was born in Chico, in northern California. He was raised on a farm there, and graduated from Chico State College. His career started with Pacific Telephone, in California, before moving to its parent firm, AT&T. After eighteen years working in New Jersey and New York City, he and his wife, Nancy, both retired from AT&T and moved to Boone, in the mountains of western North Carolina, overlooking Tennessee. He has two grown sons, one of whom is married and has two children.

Computers have interested Terry since college, when to the dismay of his mechanical engineering advisor, he insisted on taking electives in computer logic. He continued to use computers as tools at work and at home, starting with early time-share systems then moving to desktop computers when they became available. His obsession with genealogy is relatively recent, sparked by receipt of extensive work by one of Nancy's cousins on her mother's ancestry, and the essence of a lifetime of research by another cousin on his mother's side. He has since worked to document his and Nancy's paternal lines as well as fleshing out the two lines he inherited.

Terry's passion for documentation led him to The Master Genealogist in 1999. He is an active participant on the TMG-List, and has published articles on the use of TMG on his web site at www.reigelridge.com/tmg, as well as articles in TMG user group publications.

Dorothy Turner lives in Marriottsville, Maryland. She holds a BS degree in Information Systems Management, which helped her in getting a job with Wholly Genes, Inc. where she discovered the wonders of genealogy. She has been with them since April 1998 and is one of their leading tech support people. Prior to work with Wholly Genes, she held various positions with the National Security Agency both in the United States and Germany. While in Germany, she traveled extensively throughout Europe, which lead to her enjoyment of traveling within the States and Europe.

INDEX